Assessing Pragmatic Competence in the Japanese EFL Context

Assessing Pragmatic Competence
in the Japanese EFL Context:
Towards the Learning of Listener Responses

By

Pino Cutrone

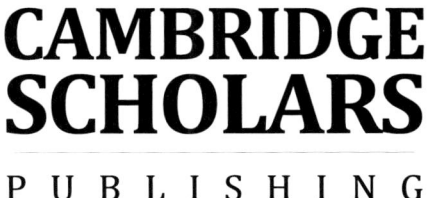

Assessing Pragmatic Competence in the Japanese EFL Context:
Towards the Learning of Listener Responses,
by Pino Cutrone

This book first published 2013

Cambridge Scholars Publishing

12 Back Chapman Street, Newcastle upon Tyne, NE6 2XX, UK

British Library Cataloguing in Publication Data
A catalogue record for this book is available from the British Library

Copyright © 2013 by Pino Cutrone

All rights for this book reserved. No part of this book may be reproduced, stored in a retrieval system, or transmitted, in any form or by any means, electronic, mechanical, photocopying, recording or otherwise, without the prior permission of the copyright owner.

ISBN (10): 1-4438-4606-6, ISBN (13): 978-1-4438-4606-6

TABLE OF CONTENTS

List of Figures, Tables and Appendices xi

Key to Acronyms and Abbreviations xiv

Key to Abbreviations in Results' Tables xvi

Preface xvii

Chapter One 1
The Background of the Study
   1.1   Introduction
   1.2   The Japanese EFL Context
      1.2.1   A brief history of English education in Japan
      1.2.2   EFL in Japan compared to other Asian settings
   1.3   A Brief Description of JEFL Speakers
   1.4   Language Transfer in the JEFL Context
   1.5   Individual Differences: A Focus on Affective Variables
      1.5.1   Foreign language anxiety
      1.5.2   The development of the WTC model
      1.5.3   WTC in Japanese contexts
   1.6   Examining the Term *Culture* as Used in this Study
   1.7   Important Values Pertaining to Japanese Culture
      1.7.1   Group harmony
      1.7.2   The public self vs. the private self
      1.7.3   Differing concepts of politeness
   1.8   Communication across Cultures
      1.8.1   What is intercultural communication (IC)?
      1.8.2   Intercultural communicative competence (ICC)
   1.9   Using a Gricean Framework for Intercultural Analysis
      1.9.1   Maxim of quantity
      1.9.2   Maxim of manner
      1.9.3   Maxim of quality
      1.9.4   Maxim of relevance
   1.10   Conclusion

Chapter Two 34
Review of the Literature
- 2.1 Introduction
- 2.2 Identification of Listener Backchannel Expressions
- 2.3 Differentiating a Backchannel from a Turn
- 2.4 Types of Backchannels
- 2.5 Functions of Backchannels
  - 2.5.1 Continuer
  - 2.5.2 Display of understanding content
  - 2.5.3 Agreement
  - 2.5.4 Support and empathy toward the speaker's judgement
  - 2.5.5 Strong emotional response
  - 2.5.6 Minor addition
  - 2.5.7 Clarification
  - 2.5.8 Non-understanding
  - 2.5.9 Disagreement or dissatisfaction
- 2.6 Backchannels across Cultures
  - 2.6.1 Frequency
  - 2.6.2 Variability
  - 2.6.3 Discourse contexts favouring backchannels
  - 2.6.4 Simultaneous speech
- 2.7 The Development of Backchannel Behaviour
  - 2.7.1 The acquisition of backchannels
  - 2.7.2 L1-L2 transfer of backchannel behaviour
- 2.8 Issues Involving Japanese EFL/ESL Speakers' Listenership
  - 2.8.1 Miscommunication and negative perceptions in IC
  - 2.8.2 Understanding Japanese backchannel behaviour
  - 2.8.3 *Aizuchi* in Japanese relative to English backchannels
- 2.9 Instructional Approaches Relative to this Study
  - 2.9.1 Explicit and implicit learning
  - 2.9.2 The effects of instruction on pragmatic development
  - 2.9.3 Practical reasons for this study
  - 2.9.4 Assessing backchannel behaviour
- 2.10 Research Questions and Hypotheses
- 2.11 Conclusion

Chapter Three 90
Methodology
   3.1   Introduction
   3.2   Participants
      3.2.1   Japanese EFL learners
      3.2.2   Native English speakers
   3.3   Procedures
   3.4   Methods of Collecting Data
      3.4.1   Observations
      3.4.2   Questionnaires
      3.4.3   Interviews
   3.5   Methods Used to Transcribe
   3.6   Overview of Data Analysis Procedures
      3.6.1   Observed backchannel behaviour
      3.6.2   WTC
      3.6.3   Conversational micro-skills
      3.6.4   ICC
      3.6.5   Analysis of levels and gains
      3.6.6   Cross-sectional vis-à-vis longitudinal analysis
      3.6.7   Statistical analysis
   3.7   Conclusion

Chapter Four 129
Cross-sectional Results and Discussion

Part One: The Cross-sectional Results
   4.1   Introduction
   4.2   Frequency
      4.2.1   Involvement in the conversation
   4.3   Variability of Use
      4.3.1   Non-word vocalisations, content words and phrases
   4.4   Discourse Contexts Favouring Backchannels
      4.4.1   Simultaneous speech backchannels
   4.5   Questionnaires: Participants' Conversational Satisfaction
   4.6   Interviews
      4.6.1   Factors affecting backchannel behaviour
      4.6.2   Functions of backchannels across cultures
      4.6.3   Perceptions of backchannels across cultures

Part Two: Discussion of Cross-sectional Results
    4.7   Frequency
    4.8   Involvement in the Conversation
    4.9   Variability
    4.10   Discourse Contexts
    4.11   Simultaneous Speech Backchannels
    4.12   Examining Participants' Conversational Satisfaction
        4.12.1   Analysing positive results
        4.12.2   Analysing negative results
        4.12.3   Key issues, inconsistencies and other influences
        4.12.4   Cultural influences and their impact on instruction
    4.13   Micro-level Analysis of Students' Levels
        4.13.1   Backchannel behaviour
        4.13.2   Conversational repair strategies
        4.13.3   Involvement in the conversations
        4.13.4   ICC
    4.14   Conclusion

Chapter Five 172
Longitudinal Results and Discussion

Part One: The Longitudinal Results
    5.1   Introduction
    5.2   Frequency
        5.2.1   Group A (Explicit)
        5.2.2   Group B (Implicit)
        5.2.3   Group Z (Control)
        5.2.4   Differences in BC frequency across groups over time
    5.3   Involvement in the Conversations
        5.3.1   Group A (Explicit)
        5.3.2   Group B (Implicit)
        5.3.3   Group Z (Control)
        5.3.4   Conversational involvement across groups over time
    5.4   Variability of Use
        5.4.1   Group A (Explicit)
        5.4.2   Group B (Implicit)
        5.4.3   Group Z (Control)
        5.4.4   Differences in variability of backchannel use over time

5.5   Discourse Contexts Favouring Backchannels
    5.5.1   Group A (Explicit)
    5.5.2   Group B (Implicit)
    5.5.3   Group Z (Control)
    5.5.4   Comparing discourse contexts favouring backchannels
5.6   Simultaneous Speech Backchannels
    5.6.1   Group A (Explicit)
    5.6.2   Group B (Implicit)
    5.6.3   Group Z (Control)
    5.6.4   Differences in SSBs over time
5.7   NES Observers' Perceptions
    5.7.1   Group A (Explicit)
    5.7.2   Group B (Implicit)
    5.7.3   Group Z (Control)
    5.7.4   Longitudinal differences in NES observers' perceptions
5.8   Interviews
    5.8.1   Dealing with situations of non-understanding
    5.8.2   Perceived development from the Pre-test to Post-test 1
    5.8.3   Perceived development from Post-test 1 to Post-test 2
5.9   Profiling Performances
    5.9.1   Listening behaviour
    5.9.2   Proficiency

Part Two: Discussion of Longitudinal Results
   5.10   Improvements in Listening Behaviour
       5.10.1   Approximating the backchannel norms of NESs
       5.10.2   Involvement in conversation
       5.10.3   Conversational repair strategies
       5.10.4   ICC
   5.11   Analysis
       5.11.1   Analysis relative to previous research
       5.11.2   Analysis relative to the noticing hypothesis
       5.11.3   Micro-level analysis of students' gains
   5.12   Conclusion

Chapter Six 239
Conclusion
   6.1 Introduction
   6.2 Overview of this Study
      6.2.1 Limitations
      6.2.2 Summary of findings
      6.2.3 This study's contribution to knowledge
   6.3 Implications of this Study
      6.3.1 Methodological implications
      6.3.2 Theoretical implications
      6.3.3 Practical implications
   6.4 Recommendations for future research

Appendices 252

Bibliography 310

Index 343

LIST OF FIGURES, TABLES AND APPENDICES

Figures

Figure 5-1 Comparing BC frequencies of the three groups over time 175
Figure 5-2 Comparing WTC scores of the three groups over time 179
Figure 5-3 Comparing word output of the three groups over time 180
Figure 5-4 Comparing the number of questions of the three groups 180
Figure 5-5 Comparing the proportions of minimal backchannels over time 196
Figure 5-6 Comparing the proportions of extended backchannels over time 196
Figure 5-7 Comparing the proportions of final CBs attracting BCs 203
Figure 5-8 Proportions of BCs constituted by BCs at final CBs.......................... 203
Figure 5-9 Non-laughter SSBs of the three groups over time.............................. 207
Figure 5-10 NESs' perceptions between three groups: Group 1 items 214
Figure 5-11 NESs' perceptions between three groups: Group 2 items 215
Figure 5-12 Comparing NONUs eliciting unconventional BCs 218
Figure 5-13 Comparing NONUs eliciting lengthier CRSs 219

Tables

Table 2-1 English backchannels and Japanese *aizuchi* in general use 60
Table 3-1 Characteristics pertaining to members of Group A............................... 96
Table 3-2 Characteristics pertaining to members of Group B............................... 96
Table 3-3 Characteristics pertaining to members of Group Z................................ 97
Table 3-4 Summary of data, and types and purposes of analyses 123
Table 4-1 Differences in frequency of backchannels across cultures 131
Table 4-2 Number of questions across cultures 131
Table 4-3 Types of verbal backchannels across cultures 132
Table 4-4 Types of nonverbal backchannels across cultures................................ 133
Table 4-5 Minimal responses versus extended responses across cultures........... 134
Table 4-6 Variability in non-word vocalisations 135
Table 4-7 Variability in isolated content words 135
Table 4-8 Variability in multi-word backchannel phrases and expressions 135
Table 4-9 Use of repetitions as backchannels across cultures............................... 136
Table 4-10 Discourse contexts of backchannels across cultures 137
Table 4-11 SSBs across cultures.. 138
Table 4-12 Participants' conversational satisfaction... 139
Table 5-1 Differences in frequency of BCs over time for Group A 173
Table 5-2 Differences in frequency of BCs over time for Group B 174
Table 5-3 Differences in frequency of BCs over time for Group Z 174

Table 5-4 Group A's involvement in the conversation over time 177
Table 5-5 Group B's involvement in the conversation over time 177
Table 5-6 Group Z's involvement in the conversation over time 178
Table 5-7 Variability of Group A's verbal backchannels over time 182
Table 5-8 Variability of Group A's nonverbal BCs over time 183
Table 5-9 Group A's use of minimal versus extended BCs over time 184
Table 5-10 Variability of Group A's non-word vocalisations over time 185
Table 5-11 Variability of Group A's isolated content words over time 185
Table 5-12 Variability of Group A's multi-word BC phrases over time 185
Table 5-13 Group A's use of repetitions as backchannels over time 186
Table 5-14 Variability of Group B's verbal backchannels over time 187
Table 5-15 Variability of Group B's nonverbal BCs over time 188
Table 5-16 Group B's use of minimal versus extended BCs over time 189
Table 5-17 Variability of Group B's non-word vocalisations over time 189
Table 5-18 Variability of Group B's isolated content words over time 190
Table 5-19 Variability of Group B's multi-word BC phrases over time 190
Table 5-20 Group B's use of repetitions as backchannels over time 190
Table 5-21 Variability of Group Z's verbal backchannels over time 191
Table 5-22 Variability of Group Z's nonverbal BCs over time 192
Table 5-23 Group Z's use of minimal versus extended BCs over time 193
Table 5-24 Variability of Group Z's non-word vocalisations over time 193
Table 5-25 Variability of Group Z's isolated content words over time 194
Table 5-26 Variability of Group Z's multi-word BC phrases over time 194
Table 5-27 Group Z's use of repetitions as backchannels over time 194
Table 5-28 Discourse contexts of Group A's backchannels over time 199
Table 5-29 Discourse contexts of Group B's backchannels over time 200
Table 5-30 Discourse contexts of Group Z's backchannels over time 201
Table 5-31 SSBs of Group A over time 204
Table 5-32 SSBs of Group B over time 205
Table 5-33 SSBs of Group Z over time 206
Table 5-34 NESs' conversational satisfaction ratings of Group A 209
Table 5-35 NESs' conversational satisfaction ratings of Group B 210
Table 5-36 NESs' conversational satisfaction ratings of Group Z 212
Table 5-37 Reactions at points of non-understanding for Group A 216
Table 5-38 Reactions at points of non-understanding for Group B 217
Table 5-39 Reactions at points of non-understanding for Group Z 217

Appendices

Appendix A: Heuristic model of variables influencing WTC 252
Appendix B: Participation consent forms for NESs (A) and JEFLs (B) 253
Appendix C: Information sheets for participants 255
Appendix D: Ten item personality inventory (TIPI) and scores 262
Appendix E: Lesson details for each group 264
Appendix F: Willingness to communicate scale and scores 276
Appendix G: Inventory of conversational satisfaction for NES interlocutors 279

Appendix H: Inventory of conversational satisfaction for JEFLs 280
Appendix I: Inventory of conversational satisfaction for NES observers 281
Appendix J: List of potential BC functions used in playback interviews 283
Appendix K: Data record sheet pinpointing instances of miscommunication 284
Appendix L: Sample transcription 285
Appendix M: Individual backchannel frequencies of cross-sectional data 293
Appendix N: Spearman rho correlation analyses of cross-sectional data 295
Appendix O: Correlation analyses involving JEFL scores and performance 301
Appendix P: Development of successful/non-successful JEFLs 303
Appendix Q: Development of higher/lower proficiency JEFLs 305
Appendix R: NES interlocutors' mean ratings of JEFLs 306
Appendix S: The six research questions (RQs) of this study 309

KEY TO ACRONYMS AND ABBREVIATIONS

ACT	Adaptive Control of Thought
ACTFL	American Council for the Teaching of Foreign Languages
CA	Conversation Analysis
CALL	Computer Assisted Language Learning
CANCODE	Cambridge and Nottingham Corpus of Discourse in English
CP	Grice's Cooperative Principle
DCT	Discourse Completion Test
EFL	English as a Foreign Language
EIL	English as an International Language
ELF	English as a Lingua Franca
ELT	English Language Teaching
ESL	English as a Second Language
ETS	English Testing Service
FFI	Form-Focused Instruction
FLA	Foreign Language Anxiety
FLCAS	Foreign Language Classroom Anxiety Scale
FTA	Face-Threatening Act
IC	Intercultural Communication
ICC	Intercultural Communicative Competence
ID	Individual Learner Difference
IMT	Information Manipulation Theory
JEFL	Japanese Student of English as a Foreign Language
JESL	Japanese Student of English as a Second Language
JFL	Japanese as a Foreign Language
L1	First Language
L2	Second Language

LCIE	Limerick Corpus of Irish English
MEXT	Japanese Ministry of Education, Culture, Sports, Science and Technology
NES	Native English Speaker
NEO-PI-R	NEO Personality Inventory, Revised
NMMC	Nottingham Multi-Modal Corpus
NS	Native Speaker
NNS	Non-Native Speaker
OC3	Oral Communication III Class
OPI	Oral Proficiency Interview
PPMCC	Pearson Product-Moment Correlation Coefficient
Spearman rho	Spearman Rank Correlation Coefficient
SLA	Second Language Acquisition
SS	Simultaneous Speech
SSB	Simultaneous Speech Backchannel
STEP	Standard Test of English Proficiency
TCU	Turn-Constructional Unit
TIPI	Ten Item Personality Inventory
TOEFL	Test of English as a Foreign Language
TOEIC	Test of English for International Communication
TRP	Transition-Relevance Place
UoN	University of Nagasaki
VOICE	Vienna-Oxford International Corpus of English
WTC	Willingness to Communicate

KEY TO ABBREVIATIONS IN RESULTS' TABLES

BC	Backchannel
CB	Clausal boundary
CLAR	Clarification backchannel
CRS	Conversational repair strategy
DC	Discourse context eliciting backchannels
NONU	Situation of non-understanding in which JEFL spoke
NONCLAR	Non-clarification backchannel
NV	Nonverbal
Opps	Opportunities
REPs	Backchannels constituted by repetitions of primary speaker's speech

Preface

"The moment one starts to think of language as discourse, the entire landscape changes, usually, forever." (McCarthy & Carter 1994: 201)

When I first read the above-mentioned quotation in my early days of graduate school, I did not attach too much importance to it. I suppose, at the time, I rather naively believed that I understood it (at least vaguely) and left it at that. Over the years however, I was quite surprised at how my interpretation of that quote would evolve and actually come to define my experience as a linguist. I realize now that only someone who has dedicated years to the unusual and meticulous task of transcribing conversations in attempts to decipher patterns and give meaning to such features of communication (i.e., discourse) as the length of pauses between syllables, and the precise instances where headnods and clausal boundaries coincide, could possibly understand what McCarthy and Carter meant. Undoubtedly, my years of closely analysing the finer points of conversations in this way have influenced my perspective of everyday communication. While my passion and heightened awareness of such things have served me well academically, I sometimes have to remind myself that most non-linguists are (quite justifiably) not really interested in trying to understand everyday communication in any great depth. Thus, in addition to the heartfelt gratitude I would like to express to my friends and loved ones for their kind and unwavering support over the years, I also feel I should acknowledge how patient and understanding they were of me when I may have behaved somewhat unorthodoxly in my quest to dig deeper into the underpinnings of communication. Tomomi, my better half, thank you for being such a loving and supportive wife and creating the type of happy home where dreams truly do come true. Maya and Sophia, my beautiful little girls, you continue to inspire me every day, and I feel so very blessed and proud that you are my daughters. Thank you mom, dad, Nic, Owen, Teresa, Brian, Victoria, Maria, Chris, Zackery and Isabella for your unconditional love and support. Also, special thanks to the very best friends anyone can ever hope to have, the Thomson and Ortega families, who always believed in me even when I doubted myself.

Since this book is based on the study I conducted to complete my PhD thesis, I would be remiss not to mention the many wonderful people who helped me in a professional capacity to make it to the other side of my doctoral journey. To start with, I would like to thank the members of Faculty and Staff in the University of Reading's Applied Linguistics Program, who were always willing to lend a helping hand when I needed it. In particular, I would like to thank the three academic advisors I was fortunate to have at various points of my study. First, many thanks to Dr Kristyan Spelman-Miller, who supervised me through the crucial first two years in which I carried out my experiment. Second, I would also like to thank Dr Lisa McEntee-Atalianis, who guided me through the third year of my study and helped shape my writing style in the early stages. Third, I wish to express my sincere thanks and appreciation to my final supervisor, Dr Alan Tonkyn, who graciously took me on at a time when he had a multitude of other responsibilities in his many departmental roles. Dr Tonkyn was instrumental in the mentoring of my research, reviewing draft after draft of my work, providing valuable critiques and insights, and ultimately helping to bring my thesis documentation to fruition.

I would also like to extend my deep gratitude to the contributions of the following people: my PhD examiners, Dr Jacqueline Laws and Dr Anne O'Keeffe, for the extensive discussion and feedback that made my oral defence such a pleasurable experience, Dr Fred Anderson, who guided me informally in Japan in the stages leading up to and shortly after my admission into the course, Gavin Marinelli for his assistance with the reliability check of the transcribed conversations, Dr Richard Hodson, David Robinson and Joel Hensley for taking the time to proofread various aspects of my work, Dr Chris Bradley for assisting me in developing some of the videotaped materials used in the instructional phase of this study, Dr Brian Spitzberg, Dr Nigel Ward, Dr Terese Thonus, Dr Sam Gosling and Barbara Brozyna for taking the time to discuss various issues related to my research, Dr Atsushi Oshio, Dr Hiroshi Moryasu and Paul Chatfield for the patience they exhibited in assisting me with the statistical procedures used in this study, all the kind and willing participants of my study who made this research project possible, and to my current and former colleagues at Nagasaki University and Nagasaki Prefectural University respectively, who helped to provide the optimum conditions for carrying out this project.

Moreover, I would like to acknowledge how fortunate I have been to be researching a subject area which I have always found fascinating at a time when it is sorely needed. Though I certainly had no inkling of it at the time, I suppose my curiosity of intercultural pragmatics can be traced back to my childhood, which involved being raised by my Italian-immigrant parents in a native-English speaking community in Winnipeg, Canada. I still remember when my Canadian friends would come over to our house and become quite alarmed when they heard what they believed to be my parents shouting, when, in fact, my parents were simply having lively discussions about food, soccer and other topics they were passionate about. Interestingly, I remember visiting Italy with some friends when I was older and hearing some of my Italian relatives ask my parents why I, and some of my friends, appeared so calm and subdued. Paradoxically, in a similar scenario in Japan several years later, some Japanese students at the university I worked at commented to our staff on how I and the other non-Japanese teachers were especially lively and enthusiastic people. There clearly is a cultural element that influences how human beings perceive the things and behaviours around them, and the differing perspectives that shape our worldly views have always fascinated me.

Thus, when I moved to Japan fifteen years ago, I already had a deep appreciation of how conversational styles and perceptions could potentially differ across cultures. Hence, due to its complexities and multifaceted nature where communication is concerned, Japan provided the perfect platform for one such as myself to develop, but never really satisfy, their curiosity. In my first days in Japan, I noticed and experienced firsthand how listening styles seemed to differ across cultures (both in the L1 and L2), and how these differences sometimes contributed to miscommunication and/or negative perceptions across cultures. Initially, my observations were limited to everyday interactions with shop clerks and the like, in which the communication stakes were low and miscommunication was most often dismissed as fun and humorous. However, once I had started teaching EFL in Japan, the stakes in communicating with my students and the office staff at our school were raised beyond what I had experienced previously. I now had important goals to achieve and time restraints to contend with. Thus, it was here in the professional domain that I first began to understand what a real-world problem this was. For instance, it was extremely difficult to ever know if my students were following what I was saying because many of them would simply continue nodding and saying *uhuh* regardless of whether they understood or not. Throughout the course of a semester – or even a lesson – it would become apparent that a great many students that seemed to be indicating understanding were actually faking it. As a thinking person, I became even more curious about this topic, and I began to consider such questions as: What does this behaviour stem from? Is it an interpersonal communication issue per se, or does it have more to do with the context and a different culture of learning? Are listener responses (called backchannels in the field of linguistics) even addressed in Japanese EFL classes? Thus, fueled by my personal and professional observations and driven by a deep desire to get to the bottom of these issues, I took my study of this topic to a deeper level and began to tackle these questions academically over the next decade. This involved countless hours, days, and years of reading and writing into this specific topic, as well as conducting various research experiments, such as the one described in this book, in an attempt to uncover the answers that have eluded researchers and practitioners up to this point. Ultimately, the impetus of the study described in this book is to help solve a real-world problem as faced by Japanese L2 English speakers such as Mr Takaya Ishida, the Japanese business man that stood trial in the USA in 1983 in the IBM-Hitachi-Mitsubishi case because, according to his lawyers, he did not understand differing backchannel conventions across cultures, as well as the many foreign EFL teachers in Japan who may have felt confused at one time or another by the seemingly mixed signals coming from their students' listener responses.

In addition to the issues discussed above, this book offers readers a window into the following six topics:

(1) Descriptive and explanatory knowledge about conversational behaviour: From the perspective of Japanese EFL/ESL speakers, this book provides readers with an opportunity to learn about how conversational and listening styles differ, and why miscommunication and negative perceptions occur across cultures.
(2) More specifically, since the end of WWII, there has been great interest in (mis)communication between Japanese and Americans, and this book is sure to inform readers who are specifically interested in this aspect of the topic.
(3) Knowledge pertaining to sound research design: This book offers young researchers a chance to learn about some of the methodological considerations and issues involved in conducting a longitudinal study involving cross-cultural communication in the field of Applied Linguistics.
(4) The state of English education in Japan: This book provides a synopsis of English teaching in Japan, explaining its failures and discussing potential areas for reform in the future.
(5) Practical applications: The findings of this study are directly relative to what happens in the foreign language classroom. The study described in this book shows that pragmatic targets such as listener responses can and should be taught in EFL/ESL classes and also provides language practitioners with detailed information on how to go about doing this.

(6) Theoretical applications: In a much broader context, this book sheds light on current theoretical issues in SLA and Pragmatics, such as the role of consciousness in language teaching (Krashen's Input Hypothesis vs. Schmidt's Noticing Hypothesis), the interpretation of Grice's maxims across cultures, and the degree to which Brown and Levinson's politeness theory, and specifically the aspect that deals with face theory, can be applied to Asian contexts.

I sincerely hope readers find this book useful in some capacity and are able to relate its contents to their studies and/or experiences as I did. On a final personal note as I reflect on my life and the journey I have travelled to get to this point, I feel extremely fortunate to have crossed paths with so many wonderful people along the way, and I remain forever in debt to my family and friends in Japan and abroad for their encouragement and support through the years in times both good and bad to keep me focused on my goals. Earning my doctorate is the culmination of a life-long dream, and the consequent publishing of this book truly provides the proverbial icing on the cake. In closing, I would like to express my deep and enduring gratitude to Cambridge Scholars Publishing for, first, noticing my PhD thesis and, subsequently, for guiding me through its transition into the book you are now reading. It goes without saying that none of this would have been possible without you.

CHAPTER ONE

THE BACKGROUND OF THIS STUDY

1.1 Introduction

With the increasing prominence of globalisation, intercultural communication is becoming increasingly common around the world. As English is generally regarded as the international language for communication used in such fields as international politics, academia, business and science, more people around the world are studying EFL/ESL every day. Perhaps no country has expended greater resources encouraging its citizens to study English than Japan, yet the results to date have been largely unsatisfactory, particularly concerning oral skills. An important part of effective oral communication is being able to give effective feedback to one's interlocutor (O'Keeffe, McCarthy & Carter 2007), and this is a specific area in which the writer contends that Japanese EFL learners (JEFLs hereafter) have experienced problems (Cutrone 2005). It is becoming increasingly clear that what constitutes effective feedback seems opens to interpretation, and there is potential for cross-cultural pragmatic failure and misunderstanding when listening styles differ. In an attempt to inform language pedagogy in the JEFL context, the general aims of this book are to gain a better understanding of how and why JEFLs produce L2 backchannels the way they do and, subsequently, to determine how to improve this aspect of JEFLs' English.

Before issues concerning listening behaviour are presented in Chapter 2, it is necessary to first set the background for the study described in this book. To this end, Chapter 1 provides an examination of Japanese learners of L2 English. The first part of this chapter, Section 1.2, focuses on the JEFL context in which this study takes place. To help explain how the current situation came to be, this section consists of a historical overview of English education in Japan. The final part of this section explores the status of language learning in Japan compared to other Asian settings. The next section, 1.3, provides a description of JEFL speakers, while Section 1.4 considers the L1-L2 language transfer that Japanese learners experience. Section 1.5 examines some of the affective factors that influence JEFL learners' oral output, which include language anxiety and willingness to communicate. Section 1.6 examines how the term culture is used in this study, while Section 1.7 looks at aspects of Japanese culture thought to influence the communication style of individuals in this group. Addressing issues involved in communication across cultures, Section 1.8 includes subsections which define Intercultural Communication (IC) and Intercultural Communicative Competence (ICC). Section 1.9 examines the four maxims included in Grice's (1975) cooperative principle as a framework to identify sources of miscommunication across cultures, and, lastly, Section 1.10 concludes the chapter by providing an overview of its contents.

1.2 The Japanese EFL context

1.2.1 A Brief History of English Education in Japan

The first Japanese contact with English likely occurred in 1600 when an Englishman, William Adams, was swept ashore on the southern island of Kyushu (Ike 1995; Hughes 1999). Japan's relationship with English has traversed numerous peaks and valleys since this time. Regarding the latter, there were periods in Japanese history when the study of English and contact with foreigners were forbidden, such as when Japan adopted a strict isolationist policy from 1638 to 1853 and at the time of political upheaval leading up to and during World War II. In terms of peaks, the study of English in Japan reached new heights during the Meiji Restoration in the mid to late 1800s and again after the Allied Forces defeated Japan to end WWII in 1945. However, even when English was being studied in earnest in Japan, there was not often much emphasis on mastering communicative abilities. While the study of English in Japan was initially seen as a gateway to communicating with the outside world during the Meiji Era, it soon became just one of the many non-communicative subjects of study in Japan and was mainly learnt in order to be able to read written texts in such areas as technology, science, architecture and medicine (Kitao & Kitao 1982).

While there have been various debates and discussions regarding the direction of English education in the Japanese school system over the past fifty years, little has changed in terms of classroom practice as the entrance examination system continues to define English education in Japan to this day. This is a prototypical example of the phenomenon known in education as the 'washback effect' in which testing methods have a major influence on teaching and learning in the classroom (Gates

1995: 101). Since mandatory education is completed in Japan upon graduating from junior high school, all senior high schools and most universities, both public and private, have entrance examinations, which include an English component. The English section of the examinations demands knowledge of grammar and vocabulary, which are taught in Japanese. Due to the make-up of the entrance examinations, the nature of the curriculum and instruction during these years has for the most part not been communicative. Rather, it has generally focused on the rote learning of grammatical rules, translation, some listening skills and the ability to develop reading skills.

1.2.2 EFL in Japan Compared to Other Asian Settings

Recently, in the age of globalisation in which we now live, the reasons for Japanese citizens to learn and be able to function in English have expanded greatly as English has grown in modern times to become the international language for communication used in such fields as international politics, academics, business and science (Ammon 2003; Yano 2001; Yashima 2002). Further, English proficiency has become a common requirement for jobs in Japan and is considered to be important in building a successful career (Kitao & Kitao 1995; Nikolova 2008). This is evidenced by the fact that many companies in Japan offer their employees incentives for achieving designated scores on various English proficiency tests such as the Standard Test of English Proficiency (STEP), Test of English for Intercultural Communication (TOEIC) and Test of English as a Foreign Language (TOEFL).

Although the Japanese seem to have many good reasons to study English, and despite the fact that English education in Japan has had a relatively long history, the learning outcome has been markedly inadequate, particularly where speaking skills are concerned. While Japan has expended vast resources as a nation on the study of English, Japanese citizens continue to rank near the bottom among Asian countries in English language proficiency tests (Clark 2000; Nikolova 2008) such as TOEFL (Kwahn 2002; Takahashi 2005) and TOEIC (ETS 2000, 2006). While the general failure of English language education in Japan has been highly documented in the literature and continues to generate a lot of discussion, most analysts agree that oral skills are what JEFLs have the greatest trouble with (Ellis 1991; Farooq 2005; Helgesen 1987; Hughes 1999; Okushi 1990; Matsumoto 1994; Yano 2001; Reesor 2002; Roger 2008; Takanashi 2004). For instance, Ellis (1991: 123) and Okushi (1990: 65) have noted that the regular Japanese high school and/or university graduate is seriously incompetent as an English speaker, particularly where sociolinguistic competence is concerned. Farooq (2005: 27) describes JEFLs as having 'extreme difficulties in interacting with native speakers in real-life situations even at a survival level'. The term false beginner is often used to describe JEFLs in current course books and/or teacher instructional manuals designed for university classes (Helgesen, Brown & Mandeville 2007; Martin 2003). According to Peaty (1987: 4), who describes the JEFL university student as the 'prototype false beginner', false beginners have a background in English based on their study of grammar and translation in junior and senior high school, but have very little, if any, communicative abilities. Recent scores on the newly adopted TOEFL iBT, which was made to include a speaking section for the first time, also suggest that JEFL/ESLs have difficulty with the oral tasks therein (ETS 2007, 2008, 2009).

Many reasons for the Japanese failure to learn English have been put forward. First, the independent and/or insular attitudes that may have evolved from Japan's self-imposed isolation (1638-1853), and the fact that Japan remains an island country, are among the most commonly cited reasons to explain the struggles of the Japanese to learn to communicate in English (Hughes 1999; Reischauer 1988). Several scholars have gone so far as to say that Japanese society and culture, which favours reticent and passive students, is as much to blame for this failure as anything else (Anderson 1993; Matsumoto 1994; McVeigh 2002). The role that Japanese culture plays in English communication will be explored in Section 1.7. Hidasi (2004: 3) provides the following list of potential factors that may contribute to the low efficiency in varying degrees:

1. Large class-sizes
2. Lecture-type class arrangements
3. Not-sufficient English language skills of the Japanese native teachers
4. Overall ageing of the teachers' population
5. The lingua-typological difference of Japanese from English
6. Fluctuation of native English language teachers
7. Not-sufficient number of English native teachers (sic)
8. Rigidity of the curriculum
9. Non-stimulating textbooks
10. Writing-reading oriented teaching methods
11. Exam-oriented content of the teaching
12. Lack of students' motivation
13. Lack of exposure to real-life intercultural communication
14. No real need to know a foreign language within Japan

15. Relatively old age of students when first exposed to foreign language learning
16. Difference in mental programming that manifests itself in communication behaviour

Most of the reasons listed above are related to inadequate classroom methods and instruction. As noted previously, EFL instruction in Japanese schools has not been very communicative and has employed primarily approaches which rely heavily upon reading, memorising grammatical rules and translation.

1.3 A Brief Description of JEFL Speakers

There exists a strong stereotypical view of JEFL learners and speakers as reticent, hyper polite, and compliant to the group's needs over their own, which is supported by general observation and/or anecdotal evidence. While there may be some truth to some of these depictions, great care must be exercised in arriving at generalisations because they do not take account of the variation in communicative behaviour that results from contextual factors and individual personalities (Scollon & Scollon 2001). Also, it should be noted that many of the studies assessing JEFLs' oral abilities involve elicited data rather than naturally occurring data, and, thus, it cannot be said with any certainty that the linguistic behaviour observed in such activities as Discourse Completion Tests (DCTs)[1] and/or role-plays corresponds to behaviour in authentic communicative situations. With this in mind, this section seeks to provide a general description of JEFL speakers and to show how their communication styles may sometimes differ from Native English Speakers (NESs) in various respects; however, due to reasons stated above, the picture which seems to emerge from the literature must be treated with circumspection.

In an article in which he discusses Japanese learners' failure to acquire sociolinguistic competence in English, Ellis (1991) provides us with a starting point. By drawing on considerable research (Barnlund 1974; Beebe & Takahashi 1989; Beebe, Takahashi & Uliss-Weltz 1990; Clancy 1990; Fukushima & Iwata 1985; Graham 1990; Hill 1990; LoCastro 1987; Loveday 1982; Takahashi & Beebe 1987; Tanaka 1988; Wolfson 1983, 1989), Ellis (1991: 116) offers the following generalisations of the Japanese communication style as compared to NESs (Australian and

---

[1] This is a technique often used in interlanguage pragmatics research, which asks learners to write responses according to hypothetical situations.

American):

1. Japanese are less verbal, more inclined to use silence in intercultural interactions.
2. Japanese are inclined to use more backchanelling devices.[2]
3. Japanese can be more direct in some situations, in particular those where a lower-status person is being addressed, and less direct in others.
4. Japanese may lack the politeness strategies needed to successfully perform face-threatening speech acts such as invitations and requests.
5. Japanese are less explicit in giving reasons for their verbal behaviour.
6. Japanese tend to be more formal.
7. Japanese tend to give recognition to status relationships between speakers rather than to level of familiarity.

Much of the research centres on particular speech acts and is cross-sectional in design. Barnlund (1974), who administered questionnaires to elicit the Japanese perspective regarding interpersonal relationships, reports that the Japanese participants in his study emphasised the need to keep conversations pleasant by behaving smoothly and avoiding disagreement. While this may be a common human trait, there is mounting evidence to suggest that it may exist to a higher degree in Japanese culture (Loveday 1982; Kenna & Lacy 1994; Matsumoto & Boyè Lafayette 2000). Loveday (1982) describes the Japanese conversational style as markedly different from the western style, in that the latter seems to involve a type of logical game with continuous positive and negative judgements. Loveday (1982) also claims that NESs often perceive JEFL speakers to be distant and cool because of their reluctance to talk about their personal feelings. While it is impossible to generalise the communicative behaviour of any group in this way, it is interesting to see that a great deal of cross-cultural literature is littered with such conjecture.

---

[2] While this definition will be expanded upon in Chapter 2, backchannelling devices can be defined for the time being as the responses and/or reactions that a listener gives to the primary speaker when the primary speaker is speaking (Yngve 1970).

1.4 Language Transfer in the JEFL Context

Relative to the scope of this study, this section considers the degree of pragmatic transfer experienced by JEFL learners. Beebe, Takahashi and Uliss-Weltz (1990: 56) define pragmatic transfer as the 'transfer of L1 sociocultural communicative competence in performing L2 speech acts or any other function of language, where the speaker is trying to achieve a particular function of language'. Pragmatic transfer is most likely to occur in speech acts that require delicate interpersonal negotiation as learners seek to alleviate or avoid face-threatening behaviour in ways they understand best. There are numerous studies demonstrating varying degrees of L1 Japanese to L2 English pragmatic transfer involving the speech acts of refusals (Takahashi & Beebe 1987; Beebe, Takahashi & Uliss-Weltz 1990; Robinson 1992), requests (Takahashi 1996) and apologies (Maeshiba et al. 1996).

Nonetheless, it is difficult to come to any concrete conclusions regarding the variables impacting on the development of pragmatic competence due to the somewhat conflicting findings, as well as some of the methods used to collect data. Particularly, the relationship between linguistic proficiency and pragmatic transfer remains unclear. Whereas some studies found evidence of greater L1 pragmatic interference in more proficient learners (Takahashi & Beebe 1987; Maeshiba et al. 1996), other studies found less (Schmidt 1983; Takahashi 1996). Some researchers have suggested that development may follow a bell-shaped pattern, in which learners first show increased pragmatic transfer as they acquire the linguistic competence to encode native-like patterns and later less as they develop pragmatic competence in the target language (Ellis 1991; Takahashi & Beebe 1987). In other words, pragmatic interference would not be expected to simply disappear as a result of linguistic development; rather, in the case of some learners, it may temporarily increase at times. According to Ellis (1991: 119), 'linguistic competence is not sufficient to guarantee the development of pragmatic knowledge, but it is probably necessary'.

Furthermore, as Takahashi (1996) asserts, learners' level of sociolinguistic competence in the L2 may be a more crucial factor than their linguistic proficiency in the L2 in determining the extent of pragmatic transfer they might experience. Another factor that may cause researchers to be cautious in arriving at any conclusions is that most of the aforementioned studies described in this section used some type of DCT. There have been concerns regarding the reliability and validity of the data DCTs produce (Gass & Neu 1996). That is, as responses are elicited on the

DCT and learners generally have time to weigh their options, many argue that this type of data is unnatural as the responses produced may bear little resemblance to the spontaneous responses produced in natural settings, as evidenced by Beebe and Takahashi (1989).

1.5 Individual Differences:
A Focus on Affective Variables

As Individual Learner Differences (IDs) have been shown to influence learning outcomes on various levels (Ellis 2008), the study of IDs continues to be an area of SLA inspiring a great deal of research attention and scholarly discussion (Fewell 2010). IDs generally include, among others, factors classified under the following three areas: learning styles, learning strategies and affective variables (Ehrman, Leaver & Oxford 2003). Relative to the study described in this book, IDs thought to have particularly strong influences on the oral abilities of JEFLs include the interrelated affective variables known as Foreign Language Anxiety (FLA) and Willingness to Communicate (WTC). The latter, as Section 1.5.2 discusses, is a particularly useful construct for researchers in that it has been shown to encompass various other affective IDs, such as FLA, self-confidence, motivation, intergroup dynamics, social context, communicative competence and personality.

While the following subsections describe FLA and WTC in greater depth, it is useful to briefly touch upon two other variables of relevance to this study: the extraversion/intraversion dimension of personality (see Section 3.3) and language proficiency. Extraversion is of particular importance as it has traditionally been thought to be at the centre of Personality models (Eysenck 1992), and, similar to the WTC construct, it has been shown to influence L2 use (Dewaele & Furnham 2000). Regarding language proficiency, various researchers have attempted to use IDs to create profiles of successful JEFLs (Heffernan & Jones 2005). Concerning pragmalinguistic features of language, it is not yet clear how L2 proficiency affects the learning of such targets (see Section 2.9.2.4). Thus, in attempting to piece together profiles of performance associated with listening behaviour, the influences of L2 proficiency, extraversion, and/or WTC require examination.

1.5.1 Foreign Language Anxiety

Several researchers have commented on the Japanese learner's disposition towards reticent behaviour (Anderson 1993; Ellis 1991; Greer

2000; Townsend & Danling 1998). In observing the oral abilities of a group of Japanese university EFL learners, Helgesen (1993) reported that his learners rarely initiated conversation, avoided bringing up new topics, did not challenge the teacher, seldom asked for clarification, and did not volunteer answers. There exists a great deal of research attributing this type of reticent behaviour to FLA (Cutrone 2004). While the concept of FLA and efforts towards defining it in precise terms are part of a continuing process, Gardner and MacIntyre (1993: 5) provide a useful starting point in describing FLA as 'the apprehension experienced when a situation requires the use of a second language with which the individual is not fully proficient'. Some of the symptoms include nervousness, tension, apprehension and introversion. Using Horwitz, Horwitz and Cope's (1991) 33-item Foreign Language Classroom Anxiety Scale (FLCAS) in his oral EFL classes in a Japanese University, Burden (2004) reported that approximately half of the 289 learners in his study suffered from FLA in some way.

1.5.2 The Development of the WTC Model

While the presence of FLA may certainly have something to do with JEFL learners' reticence, the relationship between anxiety and achievement may not be a linear one. Many other factors such as motivation, personality, experience and self-confidence also seem to play a role to varying degrees, and researchers have developed various models to account for the interplay between these variables. Recently, a promising model, which has emerged in the affective constructs to account for many of the IDs in L2 communication, is the WTC model. WTC, first developed in L1 communication by McCroskey and Richmond (McCroskey 1992; McCroskey & Richmond 1987) was applied to L2 communication by MacIntyre and Charos (1996). WTC can be generally defined as the tendency of an individual to initiate communication when free to do so (McCroskey & Richmond 1987, 1990). MacIntyre et al. (1998) have noted that WTC in the L1 does not necessarily transfer to the L2 and have, thus, defined WTC in L2 communication more suitably as the willingness to engage in L2 communication. In L1 communication, WTC was considered to be a fixed personality trait stable across situations; however, when WTC was extended to L2 communication, limiting WTC to a trait-like variable was thought to be unnecessary as the use of the L2 introduces potential for significant situation differences based on wide variations in intergroup relations and competence (Hashimoto 2002; MacIntyre et al. 1998). The concept of WTC was meant to include communication in written forms, but most of the early research has focused on face-to-face interaction or, more specifically, speaking in an L2 (Yashima 2002). Since much language development is thought to occur through interaction, it can be assumed that more interaction leads to more language development and learning. Thus, many scholars advocate that WTC, which has been found to strongly and directly influence the frequency of communication (Clément, Baker & MacIntyre 2003; MacIntyre & Charos 1996; Yashima, Zenuk-Nishide & Shimizu 2004), can greatly impact second language acquisition (SLA) and needs to be emphasised in L2 pedagogy.

Building on the earlier work of MacIntyre and Charos (1996), MacIntyre et al. (1998) proposed a multi-layered pyramid model of WTC in which they postulate that social and individual contexts, affective cognitive contexts, motivational propensities, situated antecedents and behavioural intentions are interrelated in influencing WTC in an L2 and L2 use (see Appendix A). This heuristic model of variables influencing WTC has received a great deal of research support as it has been successfully applied to second and foreign language contexts on several occasions (Burroughs, Marie & McCroskey 2003; Hashimoto 2002; MacIntyre & Charos 1996; MacIntyre, Clément & Donovan 2002; Yashima 2002; Yashima, Zenuk-Nishide & Shimizu 2004). Many of these studies examined how personality traits (MacIntyre, Babin & Clément 1999; MacIntyre & Charos 1996; Matsuoka 2004, 2005), attitudes and motivation (Hashimoto 2002; MacIntyre, Clément & Donovan 2002; Yashima 2002) influenced differences in WTC.

1.5.3 WTC in Japanese Contexts

Recently, the Japanese Ministry of Education, Culture, Sports, Science and Technology (MEXT) guidelines have placed a greater emphasis on communication in L2 (Monbusho 1989, 1999a, 1999b); thus, a greater portion of materials and classroom activities have begun to focus on face-to-face communication in hypothetical intercultural encounters. This emphasis on communication as a goal for language instruction in Japan has led to a concentrated research effort focusing on the affective variables that influence communication outcomes such as language anxiety, self-confidence, motivation and attitude towards the people or group that learners will communicate with, WTC, perceived competence and intercultural postures (Hashimoto 2002; Matsuoka 2005; Matsuoka & Evans 2005; Yashima 2002; Yashima, Zenuck-Nishide & Shimizu 2004). Despite the stated goals and objectives in MEXT's guidelines, several scholars have wondered how realistic these goals will be to achieve whilst

Japan remains mired in the current entrance examination washback cycle (Caine 2005; Reesor 2003; Sakui 2004). Further, as Ellis (1991) and Fujita (2002) have pointed out, many students involved in compulsory English education in the Japanese school system may not have much intercultural contact in their lives and, thus, despite MEXT's desire to produce learners with communicative competence, there seems to be no clear and practical purpose of learning English in Japan for many students.

1.6 Examining the Term *Culture* as Used in this Study

The impact of culture on language has been widely acknowledged for many years (Vygotsky 1962) and is one of the issues concerning this study, which seeks to examine how Japanese culture may influence JEFLs' communication strategies. At this point, it is necessary to begin to define more clearly what the term *culture* means in this study. As evidenced by Kroeber and Kluckholm's (1952) earlier attempt to define culture, which accounted for approximately two hundred definitions, there is often 'little agreement on what people mean by the idea of culture' and the very mention of the term can cause more problems than it helps solve (Scollon & Scollon 2001: 138). In an attempt to specify what is meant by culture here, this study begins with Haslett's (1989: 20-21) working definition, which describes culture as a 'shared, consensual way of life' which 'provides the shared tacit knowledge that enables members to understand and communicate with each other'. Keesing (1974) contends that culture provides its members with an implicit theory about appropriate behaviour in different situations and how to interpret the behaviours of others in these situations. Examination of communication processes in different cultures is integral to finding a definition of culture given that communication is not only an essential part of culture but also, according to Hamnett and Brislin (1980), the primary means whereby culture is transmitted.

The concept of culture, as well as cultural differences, can pose great dilemmas to researchers embarking on studies such as this one, which compares the communication styles of two national groups. A common categorisation of culture is based on nationalities, as evidenced by Hofstede's (1991) oft-quoted study in which he compared the cultural values of citizens from over 50 different countries across four dimensions: Power Distance, Collectivism vis-à-vis Individualism, Femininity vis-à-vis Masculinity and Uncertainty Avoidance. While Hofstede's (1991) study is indeed interesting in that it points out various national differences, it is problematic to view cultures purely from the perspective of nationalities as there is sure to be a wide range of subcultures within any nation, particularly one as heterogeneous as the United States (Blommaert 1998). Accordingly, while part of this research seeks to investigate how Japanese culture could potentially influence JEFLs' performance, it is important to proceed with extreme caution in arriving at any conclusions and/or generalisations where culture is concerned, so as to not fall into the culturist trap of reducing individuals to less than they are. *Culturalism*, as defined by Holliday, Hyde and Kullman (2004: 24), is the practice of 'reducing the members of a group to the predefined characteristics of a cultural label'.

Relating to the previous section, some have argued that the L2 WTC model, which was originally formed based on studies administered in Western contexts, should be revised to include a culture-specific interpretation. In their examination of WTC in the Chinese EFL context[3], Wen and Clément (2003) conclude that Chinese communicative behaviour is deeply rooted in Confucianism and its aspects of interpersonal relations which involve other-directed self and face-protecting mechanisms. In addition, Wen and Clément (2003) suggest that the submissive way Chinese people have become accustomed to learning may explain the reluctance of Chinese EFL learners to verbally engage. Some scholars have observed similar societal and cultural factors shared in Japanese contexts and have, thus, proposed that this revised model be used in Japanese contexts (Matsuoka & Evans 2005; Simic & Tanaka 2008). Presently, while Wen and Clément's (2003) inclusion of culture has provoked great interest, particularly among Asian scholars, the new model remains theoretical and has yet to be validated empirically. It can be argued that culturalism is evident in Wen and Clément's (2003) rationale that Chinese EFL learners lack WTC due to their subconscious following of Confucianist doctrine. While the influence of Confucianism may very well run deep in the lives of many Chinese people and may indeed adversely affect some Chinese EFL/ESL learners' WTC, it seems like a major leap, and somewhat convenient, to conclude that Chinese people's behaviour and L2 WTC are determined by Confucianism, when there are likely many other contributing factors to varying degrees.

This is not to focus my criticism on the work of Wen and Clément (2003) since this type of *essentialism*, which is defined by the notion that

---

[3] Wes and Clément (2003) seem to be identifying the context of their analysis as ESL, though according to other definitions put forth by Benzhi Magazine (2008) and Bhaskaran (1997) studying English in a place such as China, where English is not the native tongue or a language of wider communication within the country, would be classified as an EFL context as referred to in this book.

there is a universal essence, homogeneity and unity in a particular culture, is ubiquitous and can be found to exist in academia, advertising, media reports, natural discourse, etc. (Holliday, Hyde & Kullman 2004). In the Japanese context, the strong images and depictions of 'Japaneseness' used in international commerce as marketing ploys to promote exoticness may play a strong role in foreign generalisations of the Japanese (Moeran 1996: 77). Further, various stereotypes of Japanese people may have been perpetuated by the voluminous literature attributing the supposed uniqueness of Japanese culture and its core principles to producing shy, quiet, passive, obedient, indirect and ambiguous speakers (see Section 1.3). According to Sugimoto (1997), much of the literature seems to have four underlying presuppositions. First, it is often assumed that all Japanese share the attribute(s) in question regardless of their stratification variables such as class, gender and occupation. Second, the descriptions in the literature often do not seem to reflect the varying degrees to which Japanese people may possess a given trait, as well as the behavioural changes that an individual may incur over time. Third, the characteristic in question is thought to be uniquely Japanese and thought to exist only marginally in other societies, particularly in the West. Lastly, the fourth assumption presupposes that the trait in question has existed in Japan for an indefinite amount of time, independently of historical circumstances.

As Koyama (1992: 5) asserts, 'in the analysis of cultural issues, it must be remembered that there is no such thing as an absolute representation. Cultural rules are not immutable like the rules of physics'. Thus, it is problematic to view culture solely from the perspective of what people have in common in such facets as history, language and geographical location, and so too is it difficult to imagine culture as a static entity with any hard boundaries at all. Similar to the cultures of other complex societies, Japanese culture is multifaceted and comprises many subcultures, or groups, influencing individual behaviour in given dimensions. In Japan, this may involve the management subculture in the occupational dimension, the large corporation subculture in the firm-size dimension, the male subculture in the gender dimension, the Nagasaki subculture in the regional dimension, to name a few. Cultural entities can be overlapping as individuals continue to negotiate their personal identities, and are constantly evolving through the process of communicating with others. In other words, cultures, which can be described as having blurred boundaries, 'have the ability to flow, change, intermingle, and cut across and through one another, regardless of national frontiers' (Holliday, Hyde & Kullman 2004: 5). Thus, considering culture as a shifting reality as expressed in post-modern research and discourse, individuals are free to conform to certain behaviours associated with any of their cultural groups or to discount other aspects based on their individual preferences and the image they wish to project to others at any particular point in time. In this way, the creation and negotiation of cultural and personal identity can be seen, in essence, as the same thing.

1.7 Important Values Pertaining to Japanese Culture

While it would be imprudent, and a vast overgeneralisation, to suggest that all Japanese people adhere to any one set of cultural principles or values, it is not a great leap to surmise that cultural influences do indeed affect the behaviour of many Japanese people to varying degrees. Hence, this section considers some of the values attributed to Japanese culture which may influence the communication styles of individual learners.

1.7.1 Group Harmony

Much has been written portraying the Japanese in an essentialist light as being group oriented and having a tendency towards avoiding confrontations in order to achieve the desired outcome of social and group harmony (Clancy 1986; Lebra 1976; White 1989; Matsumoto & Boyè Lafayette 2000). Although most of the research supporting this view has been anecdotal, there have been a few empirical studies that seem to suggest there may be a basis for making this argument in some cases. For instance, in an earlier study in which he used questionnaires to elicit students' views, Barnlund (1974) confirmed that the Japanese participants in his study emphasised the need to keep a conversation pleasant by behaving smoothly and avoiding disagreement. In the study mentioned in Section 1.6, Hofstede (1991) included a dimension measuring the degree of individualism vis-à-vis collectivism of citizens from 50 countries. He found that the American participants surveyed had the most individualistic scores, while the Japanese were ranked in the middle of the pack at twenty-third. Many have attributed the Japanese desire for group cohesiveness to aspects of their culture. With this in mind, it is important to state again that the degree to which an individual adopts a cultural concept varies and is ultimately dependent on how much that individual identifies with the concept.

In Japanese, the maintenance of harmony and peace is known as *wa* (和), and, according to many scholars, *wa* is thought to be the basis of Japanese society. Historically speaking, the concept of *wa* is believed to have developed as a result of Japan's traditionally dense population as only ten percent of its land is inhabitable. Hence, having such a large number of people living in such close proximities forced people to find ways to live together harmoniously (Kagawa 1997). Like so many other of Japan's cultural concepts, it is especially difficult for Westerners to grasp because it does not have an English equivalent. *Wa* is believed to encompass many other cultural ideologies, or sub-constructs, which are integral in Japanese society such as *giri* (social and moral obligation), *gaman* (perseverance and patience), *omoiyari* (putting the needs of others ahead of one's own needs), etc. Further, in societies influenced by the principles of Confucianism such as Japan, harmony is believed to exist when everyone in the group knows precisely his/her place in the hierarchy and behaves accordingly. While conversations in Western cultures may also exhibit behaviour where many individuals adopt a cooperative principle to some degree, the behaviour conforming to *wa* is thought to have different origins and manifests itself somewhat differently in the Japanese communicative style. For instance, in Japanese schools, there has been a growing social problem known as *iijime*, in which students who stand out and do not conform to the group are bullied by other students and sometimes even the teacher (Rios-Ellis, Bellamy & Shojic 2000).

1.7.2 The Public Self vs. the Private Self

Although many scholars would agree that *wa* is a central component of Japanese society, some have argued that the blind acceptance of this group model of Japanese society leads scholars to overlook the situational variability and individuality which also exist in Japanese society (Befu 1980a, 1980b). Undoubtedly, an individual's behaviour at any point in time will also be greatly influenced by numerous variables such as personality, age, gender, class, the context of the situation, group dynamics, etc. According to Befu (1980b), the distinction between cultural concepts known as *tatemae* and *honne* can provide some insights into some of the situational variability a Japanese person may face. *Tatemae* (the public self) refers to the principle by which one is bound to the group vis-à-vis one's ranking in the vertical order of society, whereas *honne* (the private self), on the other hand, refers to one's true or inner wishes and desires (Lebra 1976). *Wa* is thought to be cultivated and maintained through *tatemae*, not *honne* (Yamada 1997). The importance of *tatemae* and *honne* in Japanese society can be seen by the numerous expressions, or related constructs, which support this ideology of the private self vis-à-vis the public self. This list includes the following paired opposing concepts: *soto* vs. *uchi* (outside vs. inside), *oyake-goto* vs. *watakushi-goto* (public matters vs. private matters), *omote* vs. *ura* (messages vs. metamessages), to name a few.

The extreme consciousness that many Japanese seem to have regarding others people's feelings towards themselves is reflected in the common expression *hito no me* (to care about the eyes of others), which is a metaphoric expression of being watched and evaluated by other people. Koyama (1992) asserts that this extreme concern regarding others' evaluation is a major factor which discourages spontaneous behaviour. Triandis (1995: 339), using the term 'tight' to describe the way in which some cultures tend to be more rigid in requiring that ingroup members behave according to the ingroup norms, has classified Japan as a collectivistic and tight culture, and according to him, cultures that are both collectivist and tight tend to produce behaviour based on the public self, rather than the private self. Triandis (1995: 329) adds that the public self is 'an assessment of the self by the generalised other', and this should lead to behaviour that is defined as proper by society. According to scholars such as Koyama (1992: 111) and Clancy (1986: 236), this type of sensitivity to 'the eyes of others' is acquired implicitly through upbringing and may be traced back to various strategies that Japanese mothers employ with their children.

1.7.3 Differing Concepts of Politeness

While there may be common underlying elements of politeness in many cultures, there is increasing evidence to suggest that politeness may be conceptualised differently across cultures (Alymursy & Wilson 2001; Ide 1989; Janney & Arndt 1993; Lee-Wong 2002; Matsumoto 1989). To begin this analysis, it is useful to differentiate between the two types of politeness identified by Watts, Ide and Ehlich (1992): first-order politeness and second-order politeness. While the distinction between first-order politeness and second-order politeness is not always easy to rigorously maintain, first-order politeness is generally thought to involve the interpretations of participants (i.e., emic), whereas second-order politeness involves the interpretations of observers (i.e., etic). In other words, first-order politeness, or 'politeness one', generally refers to a commonsense or layperson's conceptualisation of politeness and is described by Watts, Ide and Ehlich (1992: 3) as involving the 'various ways in which polite behaviour is perceived and talked about by members of sociocultural groups'. Second-order politeness, or 'politeness two', on the other hand, can be defined more specifically as a 'theoretical construct or the scientific conceptualisation of politeness one' (Felix-Brasdefer 2008: 10). In this section, the author attempts to address both types of politeness as they relate to this study.

1.7.3.1 First-order Politeness: Definitions Across Cultures

According to Haugh (2004), who investigated various definitions of politeness in English, modern definitions generally fall into four categories: politeness as behaviour avoiding conflict and promoting smooth communication (Lakoff 1989), politeness as socially appropriate behaviour (Fraser & Nolen 1981), politeness involving the consideration of the feelings of others (Brown 1980), and politeness as an evaluation of a speaker's behaviour by the addressee as polite (Eelen 1999; Mills 2003). In Japanese, the adjective *polite* is invariably translated as *teinei* and *reigi tadashi* suggesting that 'these are the nearest equivalents of the English concept' (Haugh 2004: 90). While the fundamental principles of *teinei* are similar to the English concept of politeness described above, *reigi tadashi* is more complex and can be linked to the hierarchical elements of *wa*. According to the Kojien dictionary (Shinmura 1991: 2715), *reigi*, as it relates to politeness, is generally associated with having 'manners or etiquette' which express 'vertical respect or propriety'. This involves not only repressing one's individual desires for the betterment of the group, but understanding one's own place in this hierarchy and respecting and/or revering those in higher positions. These differing conceptualisations of politeness have been evidenced in various cross-cultural studies. For example, Ide et al. (1992) found that the adjectives *polite* and *friendly* correlated highly when applied to certain behaviours in specific situations for their 219 American respondents; however, when applied to the same cross-culturally equivalent situations for their 284 Japanese respondents, the Japanese terms *teinneina* and *shitashigena* for the English adjectives *polite* and *friendly* respectively fall into different dimensions. In a pilot study in which they interviewed Japanese speakers to ascertain their conceptualisations of politeness compared to NESs, Obana and Tomoda (1994) reported that the Japanese respondents commonly associated the terms *teinei* and *reigi tadashi* with knowing where one stands in social interactions (known as *wakimae* in Japanese) and *keigo* (honorifics), which both involve upward respect (i.e., showing respect or reverence towards others of higher rank or status than oneself, and modesty about oneself), as well as horizontal distance.

In mentioning the term '*wakimae*' above, it is useful to describe the work of Hill et al. (1986: 347) who conducted a large scale quantitative analysis of Japanese linguistic politeness vis-à-vis American linguistic politeness, and found that the concept of *wakimae* is fundamental to politeness in Japanese. While no single word seems to translate *wakimae* to English adequately, the term *discernment* seems to reflect its basic sense in describing one's strict adherence to the expected norms. In other words, discernment in this sense refers to the 'almost automatic observation of socially agreed upon rules and applies to both verbal and nonverbal behaviour' (Hill et al. 1986: 348). As a counterpart to *wakimae*, Hill et al (1986: 347) use the term '*volition*', which is defined as the aspect of politeness that 'allows the speaker a considerably more active choice, according to the speaker's intention, from a relatively wider range of possibilities'. In their study, participants were presented with language expressions and potential addressees, and asked to complete questionnaires relating to the following measurements: (1) the degree of politeness of each expression, rated on a scale of one to five, (2) the appropriate politeness level corresponding to the various addresses, also rated on scale of one to five, and (3) which linguistic form they would use for each addressee. These expressions, all related to borrowing a pen, conveyed various degrees of politeness, while the potential interlocutors were distinguished by power and status. The results of their study showed that the Japanese group adopted the discernment principle to a much greater extent as shown by their clustered responses showing a high agreement on the appropriate form(s) for making a certain request, while the American group opted more often for volition as demonstrated by a more diffuse correlation between the addressee/situation features and the appropriate form of a request.

1.7.3.2 Second-order Politeness: The Concept of *Face* Across Cultures

Following the work of Grice (1967, 1975) and Goffman (1967), Brown and Levinson's (1978, 1987) theory of politeness has dominated research and discourse regarding politeness in linguistic pragmatics for the past few decades. Brown and Levinson's work consists of two parts: a fundamental theory concerning the nature of politeness and how it functions in interaction, and a list of politeness strategies, drawing on examples from mainly three languages (English, Tzeltal and Tamil). The basic premise of their theory is that politeness in any culture can be explained in terms of a limited number of universal phenomena, namely the construct of face and certain social variables (i.e., differences in power (P), social distance (D) and relative imposition of particular acts (R)). Since its publication, a great many aspects of Brown and Levinson's politeness model have been examined, applied, challenged, or modified (e.g., Eelen 2001; Mills 2003).

Brown and Levinson's (1987) theory is presented as universal; however, several researchers have criticised it as being centred on the Anglo-Saxon tradition of the model person. For instance, as mentioned in Section 1.7.3.1, debates over Eastern and Western cultures on politeness behaviour involve the distinction of discernment politeness for Asian cultures and volitional politeness for Western cultures (other examples include Gu 1990; Matsumoto 1988, 1989; Mao 1992, 1994).

Relating Brown and Levinson's (1987, 1978) theory to this study, the author examines how one of the key concepts in their theory, *face*, may be somewhat different in English vis-à-vis Japanese. In a basic sense, the ordinary use of face in English can be interpreted as a concept similar to *kao* (face) in Japanese expressions like *kao o tateru* (literally, *set up face* which means *to save face*); however, a more in-depth analysis is required to shed light on potential differences across cultures. Brown and Levinson (1978: 66) define face as 'the public self-image that every member wants for himself', and divide it into two types: negative face and positive face. Negative face refers to the desire of every competent adult member of a culture that his or her actions be unimpeded by others, whereas positive face involves the desire of every member of a culture that his or her wants be desirable to at least some others. In other words, positive face can be thought of as 'the positive and consistent image people have of themselves, and their desire for approval', while negative face, on the other hand, is 'the basic claim to territories, personal preserves and rights to non-distraction' (Brown & Levinson 1978: 61). The satisfying of positive face is called *positive politeness* and is expressed by indicating similarities amongst interactants, and by expressing an appreciation of the interlocutor's self-image. *Negative politeness*, alternatively, can be expressed by satisfying negative face in terms of indicating respect for the addressee's right not to be imposed on. This involves efforts to mitigate what Brown and Levinson (1978: 65) call a 'Face-Threatening Act' (FTA). An FTA refers to the situations that inevitably occur in social interactions which intrinsically threaten the face of the speaker (S) or hearer (H) such as when one makes a request, disagrees, gives advice, etc. For instance, when one makes a request, that person could potentially threaten the face of the other person by forcing him/her to accept an unpleasant responsibility. Conversely, if the request were rejected, this might threaten the requester's face. The potential severity of an FTA is determined by various factors which include the following: '(1) The social distance (D) of the S and the H, (2) the relative power (P) of S and H, and (3) the absolute ranking (R) of impositions in the particular culture' (Brown & Levinson 1978: 79). Consequently, strategies to save face are chosen according to the gravity of the FTA.

As mentioned above, there has been a great deal of debate regarding the universality of Brown and Levinson's (1978, 1987) theory of politeness, and Matsumoto's (1988, 1989, 1993) work on Japanese, in particular, seems to have gained recognition as the standard reference that questions the pan-cultural applicability of the notion of face. Matsumoto (1988: 405) argues that the concept of face, particularly that of negative face, is 'alien' to Japanese, and that Brown and Levinson's (1978) concept of face, which is based on Anglo-Saxon tradition and individualism, is not appropriate to account for polite linguistic behaviour in Japanese. Drawing on the work of Clancy (1986) and Lebra (1976) among others, Matsumoto (1988: 405) explains her position as follows:

> What is of paramount concern to a Japanese is not his/her own territory, but the position in relation to others in the group and his/her acceptance of others. Loss of face is associated with the perception by others that one has not comprehended and acknowledged the structure and hierarchy of the group.

Of the 18 examples used to demonstrate her point, Matsumoto (1988: 409) begins with simple introductions as follows:

(1) Doozo yoroshiku onegaishimasu.
(lit.) I ask you to please treat me well/take care of me.

Comparable to the expression *nice to meet you* in English, this expression, or some variation of it, is used when the speaker is introduced to a new person, and expresses the speaker's desire that the relationship be a good one. The beneficiary of the good relationship with the addressee need not be the speaker as the speaker could direct the following utterances to their daughter's teacher or friend (2a), and to the boss or friend of the speaker's husband (2b).

(2a) Musume o doozo yoroshiku onegaishimasu.
(lit.) I ask that you please take care of my daughter well.
(2b) Syuzin o doozo yoroshiku onegaishimasu.
(lit.) I ask you to please take care of my husband well. (Matsumoto 1988: 410)

If these expressions are analysed according to Face Theory, these speech acts would be categorised as direct requests and, thus, impositions on the addressee's negative face (i.e., FTAs). Brown and Levinson (1978, 1987) categorised the Japanese as a negative politeness culture, which suggests that they would go to great lengths to avoid imposing on others, yet it is plain to see from the everyday utterances provided in the examples above that this does not seem to be the case at all. These utterances would also seem to be in violation of Lakoff's (1973: 298) 'rules of politeness' which specify an opposition between imposition/freedom (i.e., do not impose, and give options). Corresponding to the values associated with *wa* and *wakimae*, the acknowledgement of interdependence, known as *amaeru* in Japanese, is greatly encouraged in Japanese society (Doi 1981). Juniors (*kohai*) tend to show respect to their seniors (*senpai*) by acknowledging their dependence, and seniors, in return, accept the responsibility of taking care of their juniors. In the examples above, the speaker humbles him/herself to the addressee by placing him/herself in a lower position and acknowledging that they need to be taken care of by the addressee. Since this behaviour is the norm in Japanese society, addressees of such requests consider it an honour to be asked to take care of someone as it signifies that one is regarded as holding a higher position in society. Thus, deferential impositions are thought to enhance the positive self-image of the addressee and thus, contrary to Brown and Levinson's (1978, 1987) negative politeness culture characterisation, deferential impositions in the Japanese context could be viewed as a positive politeness strategy. Further, by uttering a variant of one of the examples above, the speaker demonstrates his/her societal competence and acceptability and, thus, manages to preserve his/her own face. Conversely, failure to recognise the hierarchical ranking would reflect unfavourably on the speaker, creating an impression of ignorance or lack of self-control.

1.8 Communication Across Cultures

1.8.1 What is Intercultural Communication (IC)?

In order to clearly understand what is meant by the term Intercultural Communication (IC), it is useful to begin by defining the separate terms found within IC. First, in revisiting Haslett's (1989: 20-21) definition mentioned in Section 1.6 above, *culture* is defined in broad terms as a 'shared, consensual way of life' which 'provides the shared tacit knowledge that enables members to understand and communicate with each other'. The second term, *communication*, in its broadest sense, can be defined as 'the sharing of information between people on different levels of awareness and control' (Allwood 1976). Hence, combining this concept of culture with the definition of communication above, IC can be defined in general terms as:

the sharing of information on different levels of awareness and control between people with different cultural backgrounds, where different cultural backgrounds include both national cultural differences and differences which are connected with participation in the different activities that exist within a national unit. (Allwood 1985: 3)

Knapp and Knapp-Potthoff (1987: 8) view 'intercultural communication as taking place whenever participants introduce different knowledge into the interaction which is specific to their respective sociocultural group'. In other words, interactants in intracultural encounters are thought to implicitly share the same ground rules of communication and meaning of signals (O'Keeffe 2004), whereas interactants in intercultural encounters are likely to experience a degree of uncertainty and ambiguity concerning the ground rules by which communication will occur and the meaning of signals (Gudykunst & Nishida 2001; Gudykunst, Nishida & Chua 1986; Gudykunst, Yang & Nishida 1985). In oral/aural exchanges, the meanings of utterances are negotiated jointly by speaker and listener; thus, it is always necessary for the receiver to draw inferences about the intentions of the sender (Scollon & Scollon 1995). In this way, it is easy to imagine the potential for misunderstandings and miscommunication in IC, which will be discussed in greater detail in Section 1.9 below. First, however, it is necessary to examine what is meant by intercultural communicative competence.

1.8.2 Intercultural Communicative Competence (ICC)

1.8.2.1 Towards a Model for ICC

In order to understand what is meant by the term Intercultural Communicative Competence (ICC), this section begins with a brief review of some of the relevant competency models found in both L1 and L2 contexts. In SLA, for example, communicative competence most often refers to Hymes's (1971) seminal article outlining the skills thought to define L2 ability. This concept was further developed by Canale and Swain (1980), whose definition of communicative competence has become canonical in the field of Applied Linguistics. Canale and Swain (1980) define communicative competence in terms of four components: grammatical competence (i.e., words and rules), sociolinguistic competence (i.e., appropriateness), discourse competence (i.e., cohesion and coherence) and strategic competence (i.e., appropriate use of communication strategies). Within this framework, some researchers have focused their efforts on developing various sub-skills thought to be essential to conversing effectively. For instance, in a study involving elementary Japanese classes, Iwai (2007: 122-123) defines conversational competence as the ability to make use of conversational features that are indispensable to successful conversations such as the appropriate usage of discourse markers and 'listener responses, evaluative comments, return questions, expansions, follow-up questions, new topic initiation and repair strategies'. Similarly, in an ESL context, Riggenbach (1998: 57) labelled eight micro-skills in learners' conversational data as necessary elements of successful conversations, which include the following: 'the ability to claim turns of talk, the ability to maintain turns of talk once claimed, the ability to yield turns of talk, the ability to backchannel appropriately, the ability to self-repair, the ability to ensure comprehension on the part of the listener, the ability to initiate repair when there is a potential breakdown, and the ability to employ compensatory strategies'. These skills, which Riggenbach (1998) advocates, display learners' discourse and strategic competence in conversation, and are required elements in coherent, fluid turn-taking (i.e., discourse competence) and in successful negotiation of meaning in the case of potential communication breakdown (i.e., strategic competence).

Some of these components can also be seen in Spitzberg and Cupach's (1984) five-factor model defining interpersonal communication. In this model, components such as knowledge, skills, motivation, appropriateness, and effectiveness are seen as the main factors determining successful interpersonal communication. Byram (1997: 3) differentiates between communicative competence and ICC by arguing that communicative competence seems to be based on the successful exchange of information, whereas in ICC, the need to 'decentre and take the perspective of the listener or reader' as well as 'establishing and maintaining relationships' is given a much higher priority. As O'Dowd (2006) contends, this is evidenced in widespread intercultural perspectives that tend to highlight the interconnectedness of language and culture learning (Kramsch 1993), the need for learners to achieve a critical distance from their own cultures (Bredella 1999) and the deconstruction of stereotypes and increase of tolerance (Bredella & Delanoy 1999) as being central goals of language and culture learning. Based on these considerations, Spitzberg (2000), using Spitzberg and Cupach's (1984) research on interpersonal communication competence as a foundation, established a five-factor model encompassing intercultural communication competence. This framework identified intercultural communication as a type of interpersonal communication (Cupach & Imahori 1993), which occurs in contexts where interlocutors have saliently different cultural backgrounds (Collier 1989; Collier & Thomas 1988). The first component, *knowledge*, is defined as 'the capacity to conceptualise and articulate variables, dimensions, and issues that need to be taken into account to explain or predict effective functioning in a particular situation' (Ruben 1976: 336). Second, the term *skills* refers to the repeatable and goal-oriented 'capacity to display behaviours that are defined as appropriate and functional by others' (Ruben 1976: 336). The third component, *motivation*, is 'the set of feelings, intentions, needs, and drives associated with the anticipation of or actual engagement in intercultural communication' (Wiseman 2002: 211). The final two components of this model provide ICC with a notion of contextual dependence. *Effectiveness* can be defined as 'the accomplishment of valued goals or rewards relative to costs and alternatives' (Spitzberg 2000: 380), while *appropriateness* refers to the degree that 'valued rules, norms, and expectancies of the relationship are not violated significantly' (Spitzberg 2000: 380). Spitzberg (2000) asserts that these five components of ICC are interdependently connected and that only the knowledge of cultural rules, the skills to apply this knowledge in a given situation, and the motivation to use these skills can facilitate appropriateness and effectiveness.

1.8.2.2 Spitzberg's Expectancy Principle

Another important feature of Spitzberg's (2000) model of ICC is his expectancy principle, which encompasses dimensions of expectancy violation and compliance. Here, Spitzberg (2000) proposes that optimal conditions for competence are provided when the knowledge, skills, and motivation to succeed are aligned with meeting the other person's expectations regarding appropriateness and effectiveness. Spitzberg (2000) explicitly accounts for differences in communicator status as a filter for expectations in dyadic intercultural conversations by outlining the following systems: the individual, episodic and relational. First, the individual system refers to the personal attributes and skills inherent in each individual person that they use to achieve competent interactions. Second, the episodic system is particularly relevant to describing the native/non-native speaker dichotomy in ICC as it posits that a person who is viewed as competent in one setting, may be perceived otherwise in another context. The changes in perceptions of competency may occur as a result of certain individual characteristics, such as physical attractiveness, established levels of status, and the extent to which one fulfils another's expectations of whether the exchange will be positive or negative (Quinlisk 2004). Third, the relational system serves to sustain competent interactions throughout the entire relationship. As this theory is based on the notion that increased communicative knowledge leads to increased competence, it is also believed that, besides having an understanding of others, flexibility in self-image, self-identity, and a willingness to negotiate portions of one's identity are crucial ingredients towards achieving ICC (Hecht, Jackson & Ribeau 2003). With this in mind, ICC is not believed to be innate within us, nor is it thought to occur accidentally (Wiseman 2002: 211). Rather, ICC is thought to be an acquired quality which develops over time as a result of intercultural training and experience (Beamer 1992; Spitzberg 2000); however, this is not to say that ICC is universally attainable as certain individuals may lack the mental and/or physical capabilities, and motivational predispositions to acquire the required knowledge, skills and motivation in order to be perceived as appropriate and to act effectively (Johnson, Lenartowicz & Apud 2006). Lastly, the contextual constraints of some individuals' upbringings and/or situational circumstances may prevent those individuals from acquiring ICC (Kupka, Everett & Wildermuth 2007).

Although Spitzberg's (2000) model appears to have found wide acceptance in its entirety or in parts (Caligiuri & Di Santo 2001; Earley & Ang 2003; Gertsen 1990; Gudykunst 1992; Hammer, Nishida & Wiseman 1996; Neuliep 2003; Wiseman 2002), it has not generated much empirical support to date. Nonetheless, it is commonplace for researchers to base their descriptions of ICC around such terms as *appropriacy* and/or *effectiveness* as Guilherme (2000: 297), for example, defines ICC as 'the ability to interact effectively with people from cultures that we recognise as being different from our own'. Another precept many of these descriptions of ICC seem to have in common is the acknowledgement that there is no universal way of being communicatively competent across all circumstances. In the end, precisely what constitutes appropriate and effective behaviour is likely to differ according to the situation and the expectations of each individual, and these expectations may at times be influenced by cultural factors to some degree. The complexity involving intercultural exchanges, thus, seems to lie in the lack of shared knowledge between participants, as well as the diversity of contexts and their corresponding perceptual rules (Kupka, Everett & Wildermuth 2007).

1.8.2.3 A Model of ICC for Dyadic Interaction

Spitzberg (2000) was extremely careful to suggest that his model attempts to explain dyadic interaction only. To understand the basis for Spitzberg's (2000) minimalist approach here, the researcher examines what is meant by the term dyad in communication studies. The term *dyad* is basically synonymous with the term *pair* and refers to the fact that two people are involved in the conversation. While the study of group dynamics and behaviour is largely beyond the scope of this study, it is worth noting that the size of the group can have an effect on the participants' interactional behaviour. Regarding the content and amount of interaction, it seems fairly obvious to state that interactants in smaller groups will have greater opportunities to speak and, thus, be more involved in the conversations. In his research, the renowned sociologist George Simmel (1900, translated into English in 1990, cited in Ritzer 1992: 166) studied the forms of groups and presented a picture of the dyad as the simplest and most fundamental of the groups to be found. In the dyad, a relationship can be considered relatively straightforward, in that each interactant can present themselves to their interlocutors in a way that maintains their identity, and either party can end the relationship by withdrawing from it. The more people added to the group, the more complex and multifaceted the behavioural choices become for the interactants. For instance, in the triad, or three-person group, various strategies emerge which have the ability to alter the form of interaction. These strategies are often influenced by such factors as competition, alliances and mediation. According to Ritzer (1992), the triad is likely to develop a group structure independent of the individuals in it, whereas this is less likely to occur in the dyad.

1.9 Using a Gricean Framework for Intercultural Analysis

Having presented a framework for analysing ICC in the previous section, the researcher now examines the potential for pragmatic failure in intercultural encounters involving Japanese EFL/ESL speakers. To this end, this section demonstrates how Grice's (1967, 1975, 1989) well-known theory of conversation can serve as a useful framework for intercultural analyses. Providing the foundation for much of the literature involved in developing politeness theory by scholars such as Brown and Levinson (1978, 1987), Lakoff (1973) and Leech (1983), the assumption of Grice's theory rests on the notion that people are intrinsically cooperative in order to construct meaningful conversations. This assumption is known as the Cooperative Principle (CP). Examining the components that make up Grice's CP, and considering how members of different cultures may interpret these components differently, may shed some light on some of the misunderstandings in IC caused by differing communication styles, which include backchannel practices (see Section 2.8). As stated in Grice's (1975: 45) seminal work, *Logic and Conversation*, interactants tend to 'make [their] conversational contribution such as is required, at the stage at which it occurs, by the accepted purpose or direction of the talk exchange in which [they] are engaged'. Grice further suggests that there are a number of conversational rules, or maxims, that regulate conversation by way of enforcing compliance with the CP. These maxims, and submaxims within, are divided into categories of quantity, manner, quality and relation, which will be discussed in the following subsections.

Before discussing how Gricean theory can inform our intercultural analysis, it is necessary to acknowledge the ongoing debate over the years regarding the universality of Grice's theory of conversation. Some researchers have questioned the feasibility that the maxims can apply universally and independently of culture, style and genre (Keenan 1974, 1976), and others have focused their attacks on the universality of Grice's CP in the context of politeness (Churchill 1978; Mura 1983; Penman 1980, 1985). Regarding the former, an example can be found in Keenan's (1976) analysis which stated that the people in Madagascar tend not to give information when required, which intentionally and systematically violates Grice's quantity maxim. Conversely, other researchers have staunchly defended Grice's CP, on the grounds that many linguists continue to misunderstand what Grice was trying to do (Horn 2004; Levinson 1983, 2000; Nunn 2000). Grice (1989: 26) himself makes no explicit claims of universality, using typically modest language to refer to a 'first approximation of a general principle' and a 'rough general principle' in describing his theory. Grice (1989: 26) is equally cautious in choosing his words so as not to overstate the case for 'cooperation' in his theory as he suggests 'each participant recognises in them [talk exchanges], to some extent, a common purpose or set of purposes, or at least a mutually accepted direction'. By advancing only the existence of a general principle, it is apparent that Grice is adopting what he believes to be the appropriate degree of certainty for a conversational principle (Nunn 2000). In short, Grice's maxims can be seen to encompass the basic set of assumptions underlying verbal exchanges; however, this is not to imply that these maxims are regularly followed in every verbal exchange as critics have sometimes thought. Grice did not prescribe these maxims as laws governing conversation; rather, he fully expected people to flout, violate, infringe and opt out of the maxims. In fact, the instances when the maxims are not followed were of particular interest to Grice, as they are useful for analysing and interpreting conversation, and often generate inferences beyond the semantic content of the sentences uttered, which Grice (1975: 39) called 'conversational implicatures'.

1.9.1 Maxim of Quantity

The category of quantity consists of the following two maxims: make your contribution as informative as is required (for the current purposes of the exchange), and do not make your contribution more informative than is required. In these maxims of quantity, the phrase 'as is required' seems open to interpretation as too much and/or too little would seem to be relative concepts. While a good portion of the descriptions portraying the Japanese as valuing reticence over verbosity seems to have been anecdotal, there are several empirical studies which seem to support the notion that some Japanese may be more comfortable with silence than citizens of some Western nations such as the United States. For instance, in a contrastive study comparing the communication styles of Japanese and American businessmen, Yamada (1997) reported an average rate of silence of 5.15 seconds per minute in the Japanese meeting and only .74 seconds in the American meeting, and the longest pause in the Japanese meeting was 8.5 seconds and only 4.6 seconds in the American meeting. There seems to be a strong belief that the long pauses and brief utterances commonly found in Japanese may negatively transfer to the L2. Several studies involving the intercultural analyses of communication styles have shown that the JEFL speakers in these studies spoke less than NESs, did not elaborate as much, and were less likely to engage in small talk (Cutrone 2005; Hill 1990; Sato 2008). This seems to be contrary to what some cross-cultural interlocutors hope to encounter in an English conversation as the importance of making small talk, taking the initiative to speak, and elaboration towards making a positive impression have been documented by several sources (Cutrone 2005; McCarthy 2003; McCroskey 1992; Ross 1998; Sato 2008; Stubbe 1998; Yashima 2002). As Section 1.8.2 discussed, sometimes when fundamental behaviours are not shared and/or do not conform to one's expectations, there is a danger that those behaviours may be negatively perceived, lead to stereotyping, and, in the worst case scenario, be misinterpreted as transgressions against one's value system (Armour 2001, 2004; Chapman & Hartley 2000).

1.9.2 Maxim of Manner

The fundamental nature of the maxim of manner is clearly encapsulated in Grice's (1975: 46) super maxim 'be perspicuous', which he then divides into the following four submaxims: avoid obscurity of expression, avoid ambiguity, be brief (avoid unnecessary prolixity) and be orderly. As the previous subsection indicated, the degree to which any of the aforementioned submaxims are followed and/or preferred is open to interpretation, and individual interpretations and preferences regarding the degree of ambiguity vis-à-vis clarity in communication will vary. In this section, the researcher discusses how potential culture-specific ideologies might also influence this phenomenon. There exists a great deal of literature claiming that Japanese speakers are ambiguous communicators, who tend to avoid direct, plain statements in favour of more suggestive, indirect comments in their L1 and in English (Hill 1990; Kenna & Lacy 1994; Loveday 1982; Matsumoto & Boyè Lafayette 2000). As Haugh (2003: 157) points out, this common view 'is held by both Japanese and non-Japanese linguists' in works ranging from intercultural communication handbooks (Kitao & Kitao 1989; McClure 2000; Yamada 1997), to academic papers (Akasu & Asao 1993; Clancy 1986; Doi 1996; Gudykunst & Nishida 1993; Nakai 1999; Nittono 1999), through to dissertations (Books 1995; Day 1996; Iwata 1999; Sato 2008). Some of the oft-cited examples of Japanese indirectness and vagueness, according to Haugh (2003: 158), involve phenomena such as 'the common omission of elements of Japanese utterances that would be made explicit in English' (Akasu & Asao 1993; Donahue 1998), the common 'use of indexicals in Japanese such as *are* and *sore* (in English, *that*) in place of the topic of a subject' (Akasu & Asao 1993), 'the frequent use of hedges such as *toumo kedo* ...' (in English, *I think that* ...) to convey hesitancy and uncertainty (Okabe 1993; Sasagawa 1996), the 'tendency to use understatements rather than overstatements such as *tabun* (maybe/probably) rather than *zettai* (definitely), and the use of opaque formulaic utterances' such as *chotto yooji ga arimasu* in reply to an invitation to go out together (in English, this may be translated as *sorry I can't, I have some business to take care of*).

Various researchers have attempted to attribute vagueness and indirectness to traditional Japanese values such as the importance of preserving harmony (*wa*) and group orientation (*shuudan shugi*) (Morita & Ishihara 1989; Nakane 1970), or to the highly contextualised nature of Japanese communication (Arima 1989; Ikegami 1989) and seeming preference for nonverbal communication (Haga 1998). Although the perception of Japanese as indirect and vague speakers seems to be widespread, there are a number of problems with this view. First, much of this description comes from anecdotal accounts and has not received convincing empirical support. Regarding some of the studies that have been conducted in this area, the results appear to have been influenced by the specific speech act under investigation and/or how the data are collected (i.e., naturally occurring data vis-à-vis DCTs). While various studies have found Japanese to be more indirect and vague performing speech acts such as requesting and complimenting (Barnlund & Araki 1985; Takahashi & Beebe 1987), an equal number of studies have produced contrary results in reporting that Japanese can be more direct in some requesting, complaining and conflict situations than NESs (Rose 1992; Sato & Okamoto 1999; Spees 1994). In light of the evidence to date, the assumption that Japanese and JEFL speakers are more vague and indirect than NESs appears to be questionable. Thus, the perceptions of Japanese communication shared by many people, who include Japanese, non-Japanese, and academics in both groups, seem to be based on factors other than objective, empirical evidence (Haugh 2003). Whether these views are driven by a lack of understanding of Japanese L1 and/or misunderstanding of Japanese people is not certain; however, it is evident that these perceptions do exist and thus may influence IC.

1.9.3 Maxim of Quality

The maxim of quality contains the supermaxim: make your contribution one that is true, which encompasses the following two submaxims: do not say what you believe to be false, and do not say anything for which you lack evidence. While violations of the quality maxim can be interpreted as contradictions, irony, metaphors and rhetorical questions, they may also be construed as exaggerations, deception and dishonesty. Similar to the discussions involving the maxims of quantity and manner above, the degree to which these maxims is followed are open to interpretation and is likely to differ according to each individual's personality as well as the specific contextual factors involved in each conversation. This subsection will consider whether culture-specific ideologies also influence this phenomenon. While there have not been many empirical investigations conducted in this area concerning Japanese behaviour, one study that was conducted was that by Imai (1981). He assessed how Japanese businessmen respond to requests that they cannot or will not fulfil. As Nishiyama (1995) points out, there are many ways of saying *no* in Japanese without actually using the word and conveying the apparent negative connotation that seems to go with it in Japanese society. Imai (1981) reported that a common strategy among Japanese businessmen was to use a number of the alternatives to the explicit word *no*, including answers which sound fairly similar to those deemed deceptive by Information Manipulation Theory (IMT), which in brief, views deception as arising from covert violations of one or more of Grice's (1989) four maxims. One example from Imai's (1981) study occurred when some of the Japanese participants said *yes* and followed with long explanations, which may be equated to violating the maxims of quality and quantity. Other responses included using vague or ambiguous replies (a violation of the manner maxim), avoiding the question and changing the subject (a violation of the relevance maxim). In this way, IMT suggests that deceptive messages function deceptively because they violate the principles that govern conversational exchanges (McCornack 1992).

A study conducted by Robinson (1992) sought to investigate 12 Japanese ESL learners' (JESLs hereafter) refusals in English. One of the methodological problems that arose was that several of the JESL respondents had a particularly difficult time issuing refusals and tended to accept requests rather than refuse them. Based on the participants' verbal reports and retrospective interviews, Robinson (1992: 59) attributed this to the nature of Japanese society, which several participants contend raises children, and especially girls, 'to say *yes*, or at least not say *no*'. In another study, Nishiyama (1993) discusses deception in a cultural framework from an organisational perspective. Nishiyama (1993) examined the tactics and behaviours of Japanese negotiators and found a number of strategies and behaviours that his Japanese participants considered everyday business practice in Japan, yet were interpreted as deceptive by American businessmen. One of these practices involved the potentially differing concepts of truth across cultures.

Kenna and Lacy (1994) summarise the American concept of truth as an absolute entity that is not dependent on circumstances. In other words, a fact is either true or false, and what is true for one person is likely true for everyone. In Japanese society, conversely, Kenna and Lacy (1994) contend that truth is relative and largely dependent on the situation and the parties involved. As has been documented by several sources (Loveday 1982; Hill 1990; Matsumoto & Boyè Lafayette 2000), maintaining harmony and protecting face are generally thought to be much more important virtues than truthfulness, clarity and directness in Japanese culture. This last claim was supported by Blanche (1987) and Cutrone (2005), who discussed the tendency of JEFLs to feign understanding and agreement in order to preserve harmony and ensure smooth communication, especially as a strategy to mitigate potential FTAs. In Cutrone's (2005) study, the post-conversation comments from the JEFLs' British interlocutors suggest that this type of behaviour, when detected, had a negative influence on the conversation. According to Doi (1986), this notion of the Japanese shifting self may be at the crux of some intercultural misunderstandings with Americans. Doi (1986) suggests that in American society it is thought to be important for these two selves to remain consistent; when the private self deviates from the public self (see Section 1.7.2), an individual might be considered to be a hypocrite. In Japanese society, however, being polite and preserving harmony is given a much higher priority, and an individual's actual feelings pertaining to an action are thought to be less important (Doi 1986; Triandis 1989).

1.9.4 Maxim of Relevance

The maxim of relevance is stated by Grice (1975: 46) as 'make your contribution relevant and timely'. Adherence to this maxim prevents random, incoherent conversations lacking continuity. According to Kaplan's (1966) longstanding theory, linearity is at least a prima facie requirement of Anglo rhetorical patterning, whereas circuity is thought to characterise an East Asian rhetorical pattern. Relating this to our intercultural analysis, this subsection touches upon some of the themes outlined above in the areas concerning harmony (Section 1.7.1) and truth (Section 1.9.3). Taking somewhat of an essentialist stance, Leki (1991) asserts that rhetoric in the Asiatic tradition seems to have a historical purpose of announcing truth rather than proving it, whereas rhetoric in the Western tradition, conversely, often seems to be designed to convince people towards a certain position. Consequently, in the Asiatic tradition, the speaker/writer arranges the propositions of the announcement in such a way that it references to a communal, traditional wisdom which invites harmonious agreement, while in the Western tradition, much more prominence is placed on the speaker/writer's ability to reason and marshal evidence in order to persuade the reader/listener towards a certain position. Accordingly, Brown (1998) summarises the Asian mode of text development as deferential, anecdotal and circuitous, one which seeks to address an issue by describing the surrounding terrain. Fliegel (1987) concurs and goes on to point out three defining characteristics of this rhetoric which include an emphasis on group collectivity, the elicitation of consent and the avoidance of direct conflict.

1.10 Conclusion

Chapter 1 has served to provide a background for the study described in this book, examining the JEFL context in which this study takes place. Due to a number of interrelated factors, which include a homogeneous society, a history of isolation and noncommunicative educational practices, English education does not appear to have thrived in Japan compared to other Asian settings, particularly regarding learners' oral abilities. It also appears that there may be strong cultural influences that affect and sometimes hinder JEFL/ESL speakers' abilities, and many of these influences are linked to affective variables such as FLA, self-confidence and motivation. Understanding the process by which these variables function, and improving learners' attitudes in these areas may be necessary in improving their overall communicative abilities. While all of these variables are related to learners' listening behaviour in one way or another, an obvious and recurring theme thus far has been the descriptions of JEFL/ESL speakers/listeners' reticent behaviour and perceived unwillingness to communicate, which has negatively affected interlocutors' perceptions of them in intercultural encounters. If we consider the empirical support of the WTC model, and the fact that increasing WTC has such far-reaching consequences in IC and ELT (i.e., to make more favourable impressions across cultures and to improve overall language ability respectively), one approach to help improve this problem is to follow Yashima's (2002) advice in making WTC one of the goals of language instruction in Japan. For instruction to be successful however, it is necessary for instructors to understand why their learners, as well as members of the target language and culture, behave and/or produce language the way they do. The use of Grice's (1975) maxims as a framework to identify miscommunication between JEFL/ESL speakers and NESs is one attempt at doing so. As Chapter 2 will discuss in greater detail, many of the issues described above are manifested in the listening behaviour of JEFL/ESL speakers.

CHAPTER TWO

REVIEW OF THE LITERATURE

2.1 Introduction

In this chapter, the research literature on aspects of interactive listening behaviour is reviewed. The next four subsections of this chapter focus exclusively on defining the key term in this study: backchannel. In attempting to pinpoint precisely what is meant by the term backchannel, Sections 2.2-2.5 address the following four areas: (2.2) the identification of listener backchannel expressions, (2.3) the differentiation between a backchannel and a turn, (2.4) different types of backchannels and (2.5) the different functions of backchannels in conversations. Next, Section 2.6 investigates culture-specific differences in backchannel behaviour in terms of frequency, variability, discourse contexts favouring backchannels[1] and simultaneous speech. This section also explores how these differences in backchannel behaviour might affect IC. Section 2.7 considers some of the issues involving the development of backchannel behaviour, taking into account the acquisition of L1 backchannels, as well as the transfer of backchannel behaviour that sometimes occurs when people learn new languages. In Section 2.8, other issues concerning JEFL/ESL speakers' backchannel behaviour are explored. Beginning with a description of the miscommunication and negative perceptions that can occur when interlocutors across cultures backchannel differently, this section also examines the pragmatic use of *aizuchi*[2] in Japanese discourse relative to English backchannels, and the potential cultural ideologies influencing Japanese listening behaviour. Section 2.9 examines the instructional approaches relative to this study. This includes a discussion of explicit vis-à-vis implicit learning processes, a look at the effects of instruction on

---

[1] The term *discourse contexts favouring backchannels,* used by Maynard (1997; 1990; 1986) refers to the places or points identified in the primary speaker's speech where the non-primary speaker frequently sends backchannels.
[2] While this definition will be expanded upon in Section 2.8.2, *aizuchi* can be defined for the time being as the Japanese version of backchannel.

pragmatic development, a rationale for the teaching of listener responses, and a general framework for the assessment of listenership. Finally, Section 2.10 presents the research questions and hypotheses of this study.

2.2 Identification of Listener Backchannel Expressions

Most early research consisting of face-to-face interaction has tended to focus more on the speaker's role than on the listener's. Other than Fries (1952), Kendon (1967, 1977), Dittman and Llewellyn (1968) and Hall (1974), few studies had examined the responses of non-primary speakers in conversational interaction. Fries (1952: 49), in analysing English conversations, was perhaps the first to group together 'those single free utterances', such as as *uh huh*, *yeah*, *mm*, *I see*, that are used by the listener to show continued attention. Kendon (1967: 23) called these utterances 'accompaniment signals'. Only recently has there been an increase in research activity concerning the behaviour of listeners in conversational interaction. While there currently exist several terms to describe the utterances of non-primary speakers, the most widespread one is *backchannel*. The term was coined by Yngve (1970: 568) in his pioneering research, and he explained it as follows:

> When two people are engaged in conversation, they generally take turns....In fact, both the person who has the turn and his partner are simultaneously engaged in both speaking and listening. This is because of the existence of what I call the backchannel, over which the person who has the turn receives short messages such as *yes* and *un-huh* without relinquishing the turn.

In other words, when one person is taking a turn at speaking in the conversation, they are considered the primary speaker, and their talk is the main channel of communication. The listener is then considered the non-primary speaker and their utterances during the primary speaker's turn are backchannels, which in turn serve to provide short cues to notify the primary speaker that the non-primary speaker is listening (Hayashi & Hayashi 1991).

In addition to the multitude of different terms used to describe what Yngve (1970) classified as a backchannel, there exists a great deal of variation even within the term backchannel from one research study to the next depending on the particular definition researchers chose to apply in their analysis (Fujimoto 2007; McCarthy & O'Keeffe 2004). Following the work of several linguists (Fries 1952; Dittman & Llewellyn 1968; Kendon 1967, 1977; Yngve 1970), Orestrom (1983) and Hall's (1974) identification of backchannels included mainly minimal utterances such as *uh huh*, *yeah*, *mm*, *I see*, etc. Researchers such as Duncan (1974), Duncan and Fisk (1977) and Maynard (1986, 1987, 1989, 1990, 1997) have broadened this definition of backchannels to include sentence completions, requests for clarification, brief statements and nonverbal responses such as head nods and headshakes. In addition, Brunner (1979), Hattori (1987) and Schenkein (1972) have included other aspects of nonverbal communication such as smiles, laughter and raised eyebrows as backchannels. As the researcher tends to agree that brief utterances and nonverbal cues by the non-primary speaker are also backchannels in that they too operate as messages to the primary speaker, this broader definition of backchannels was used in identifying backchannels in an earlier study (Cutrone 2005). While there exist many issues to resolve in identifying backchannels in conversational data (see Sections 2.3 and 3.3), backchannels can be defined for the time being as the brief verbal and nonverbal responses and/or reactions that a listener gives to the primary speaker when the primary speaker is speaking.

Although the preceding definition has made a distinction between a backchannel and a primary speaking turn, it makes sense, for instructional purposes, to briefly reconsider these concepts collectively. Sections 2.2-2.5 provide a thorough and precise definition of the term backchannel from a research standpoint, which is necessary in order to compare the backchannel tendencies reported in previous studies; however, as Fujimoto (2007) and Thonus (2007) have suggested, it may be more practical from an instructional perspective to use the superordinate term *listener response*. Following O'Keeffe and Adolphs (2008: 74), the term 'listener response' is used as an umbrella term to describe any response which reacts to something that the primary speaker has said. In the context of this study, listener responses would extend beyond what is meant by the term backchannel to also encompass longer utterances which also act in response to an interlocutor's utterance. The rationale for this becomes clear in Section 2.9.4 when the framework for assessing listening behaviour is presented. As Section 2.9.4.3 describes, one of the criteria for effective listening behaviour is to be able to produce the lengthier listener responses, or conversational repair strategies, which prevent the conversations from breaking down.

Ultimately, therefore, the assessment of listening behaviour in the language classroom will have to go beyond the analysis of backchannel responses to incorporate other important and relevant features such as having the ability to pose questions and initiate conversational repair strategies. Here, though, the strategy taken by the researcher is to begin with a micro-level examination of listener responses, which focuses on the backchannel unit. This allows for various features of listening behaviour to be compared across studies. At this stage, it is necessary to provide a working definition of the term backchannel. While definitions of backchannels have been quite variable over time, the trend in more recent studies is to go beyond non-word vocalisations[3] such as *mhm* or *unn* and to include sentence completions, requests for clarification, brief statements and nonverbal responses. Including some of these longer utterances as backchannels, which Sacks, Schegloff and Jefferson (1974) identify as turns, raises the issue as to how researchers differentiate between backchannels and turns at talk, which will be discussed in the following section (2.3).

In addition to brief utterances, researchers commonly include nonverbal cues by the non-primary speaker as backchannels. Brunner (1979), Hattori (1987), Maynard (1987) and Schenkein's (1972) broadened the interpretation of backchannels to include nonverbal cues such as smiles, laughter, raised eyebrows and head movement. In the studies administered by Cutrone (2005) and Maynard (1997), the duration of smiles and laughter were only recorded when they occurred for prolonged periods (exceeding two seconds). Raised eyebrows were identified as backchannels only in instances where it was deemed that the eyebrows were raised to send a message to the primary speaker. In observing head movement, the analysis was limited to vertical head movement (head nod) and horizontal head movement (head shake). For head movement to be considered a backchannel, the interlocutor moving their head would have to return their head back to the starting position (centre). In other words, slight movements of the head in one direction were not considered backchannels.

2.3 Differentiating a Backchannel from a Turn

Following the work of Maynard (1986, 1987, 1989, 1990, 1997), Tao and Thompson (1991) and White (1989), backchannels in this study will be identified in the context of the turn-taking system. According to Maynard (1986), the most difficult aspect in identifying a backchannel seems to be in determining whether a particular behaviour constitutes a backchannel or a separate turn. Consequently, it is necessary to be able to

---

[3] Unlike Cutrone's (2005) previous study, which adopted White's (1989) term *paralinguistic ejaculation* to describe non-lexical backchannel interjections such as *mhm* and *unn*, this study uses O'Keeffe and Adolph's (2008) term *non-word vocalisation* because it was thought to be more specific and easily understood.

understand and identify specifically what constitutes a turn in this study. In their seminal work, Sacks, Schegloff and Jefferson (1974) propose a model for the organisation of turn-taking in conversations. Central to their discussion, Sacks, Schegloff and Jefferson (1974) describe a turn to consist of one or more *turn-constructional units* (TCUs). These units can range in size from a single word to sentence filled with many embedded clauses. Each unit ends at a *transition-relevance place* (TRP), which is identified as a moment in the conversation at which an exchange of turn is appropriate. TRPs are signalled by the conversation's participants to each other through various contextual cues such as *silence* or the *end of a question*. TRPs are often found in similar discourse contexts to those of backchannels (Clancy et al. 1996; Maynard 1997; White 1989), which suggests a strong link between the two that may have pedagogical implications.

While Sacks, Schegloff and Jefferson's (1974) model is useful for understanding the general set of rules that govern the turn-taking system, it is of limited use in identifying backchannels in this context, as it does not account for the concept that Edelsky (1981), Hayashi (1988) and Maynard (1986) refer to as *having the floor*. Whereas the definition of a TCU is primarily grammatical, the concept of having the floor is based on participants' sense of who has the floor and on topic, as well as the quantity and frequency of speech. This concept also has its shortcomings in terms of identifying backchannels as a speaker could continue to hold the floor while non-floor holders ask questions and/or make comments to drive the floor holder into new directions of conversations. For the practical purpose of identifying backchannels in the turn-taking context, Markel's (1975: 190) definition of turn is useful:

> A speaking turn begins when one interlocutor starts solo talking. For every speaking turn there is a concurrent listening turn, which is the behaviour of one or more nontalking interlocutors present.

Markel (1975) adds that the only time that a change in speaking turn can take place is when the non-primary speaker begins solo speaking. Solo speaking is defined here as some point or statement made which advances the conversation, and does not include the backchannel utterances we have discussed above such as *uhuh*, *mmm* and/or *I see* which seem only to serve the listening functions described below. In cases where simultaneous talk occurs, the primary speaker continues to *have the turn* if the primary speaker continues to solo speak after the simultaneous talk. However, if the non-primary speaker begins solo speaking after the simultaneous talk, then a change of primary speaker turns would have occurred.

In their studies, Cutrone (2005) and Maynard (1986, 1997) adopted Markel's (1975) definition of turn. In doing so, the position taken in these studies was to identify a brief statement as a backchannel and not a primary turn when it serves only to react to what the primary speaker is saying (listening function) and not to add any new information to the conversation (speaking function). Hence, these studies recognised brief questions such as *Is that so?* or *Really?*, which are formed in terms of requests for clarification, as backchannels. However, a question such as *Why did he go?* was interpreted as a full speaking turn because it serves a speaking function in terms of steering the conversation in a new direction. Further, responses to questions are not considered backchannels. This follows one of the tenets of Ward and Tsukuhara's (2000) practical definition of backchannels that, unlike responses to questions, backchannels are optional and not required. Additionally, answers to questions, which are sometimes quite brief and include ellipsis, would also seem to provide new information that helps drive the conversation forward constituting a change of primary speakership. Lastly, researchers have to make decisions regarding how to deal with utterances found between turns at talk, i.e., would such utterances be identified as backchannels or part of a turn at talk? Cutrone (2005) and Maynard (1986, 1997) identified utterances as backchannels only when they occurred immediately after the primary speaker stopped talking (within one second) and were followed by a substantial pause before the next turn at talk starts (exceeding one second). This decision was made because it was felt that these backchannels were produced in response to the primary speaker's speech, and they occurred before a substantial turn-transitional period starts.

2.4 Types of Backchannels

In attempting to label backchannel forms according to specific categories, it is useful to begin with Tottie's (1991) classification of backchannel and backchannel items, where the former could consist of one or more of the latter. Examples are provided in each of the three categories of verbal backchannels presented below.

A *Simple type* of backchannel such as *yeah* is sent as one backchannel item occurring in isolation. A *Compound type* of backchannel such as *yeah yeah yeah* is one in which one backchannel item exists but is repeated more than once. A *Complex type* of backchannel such as *yeah I know* consists of multiple and varied backchannel items.

To account for nonverbal backchannels, which can occur both simultaneously and independently of the three categories above, Cutrone (2005) added the following categories:

- *simple* accompanied by a head nod(s),
- *compound* accompanied by a head nod(s),
- *complex* accompanied by a head nod(s),
- isolated head nod,
- multiple head nods,
- smile,
- laughter,
- raised eyebrows, and
- two or more nonverbal backchannels occurring simultaneously.

In a study analysing the verbal feedback devices in IC involving a small sample of Maori and Pakeha listeners, Stubbe (1998: 259) uses what she calls 'the feedback continuum'. At one end of the continuum is listener feedback which is heard as being at least minimally supportive in interactional terms, but which is basically neutral in effect. That is, as Stubbe (1998: 259) surmises, 'it is possible for a listener to utter such neutral minimal responses more or less automatically and still appear sufficiently attentive to maintain the primary speaker's turn at talk'. These minimal responses are characteristic of the simple and compound backchannel types described in Tottie's (1991) classification above. At the opposite end of the continuum, lengthier verbal listener feedback consisting of multiple and varied words as characterised by Tottie's (1991) complex type above would demonstrate a listener's higher involvement in the conversation. This type of extended listener response is thought 'to be explicitly supportive, and may express a range of positive meanings such as sympathy, interest, surprise, and enthusiastic agreement' (Stubbe 1998: 259). Thus, *minimal responses* can be defined here as any simple (non-lexical) and/or nonverbal backchannel occurring in isolation. *Extended responses*, on the other hand, refer to the lengthier verbal listener feedback consisting of multiple and varied words as characterised by complex backchannels, irrespective of nonverbal backchannel accompaniment.

Another level of analysis, following Bjørge (2009), Cutrone (2005), O'Keeffe and Adolphs (2008), Tottie (1991), Uematsu (2000) and White (1989), involves the variability of verbal backchannels at the word level and beyond. To this end, backchannel forms have been examined according to the following categories: non-word vocalisations, single words (i.e., isolated content words) and multi-word phrases and/or expressions.

Concerning non-word vocalisations, some researchers have taken to creating their own supplementary subcategory of non-lexical sounds to provide an overview of some of the common non-lexical sounds participants used in conversations (Uematsu 2000). While dividing the sounds that make up minimal backchannels into clear and definitive phonetic categories seems like an especially difficult task, the inventory of common conversational non-lexical sounds outlined in Ward (2006) provides linguists with a useful tool enabling the categorisation of non-word vocalisations, as well as comparison across studies. Although non-lexical items such as *uhuh*, *mhm* and *mm* might be expected in such an inventory, other sounds such as *oh* and *ah* are also included because they also function as non-lexical items in this context (Bjørge 2009; Brinton 1996; Ward 2004, 2006). That is, according to Lee (1999: 117), discourse markers such as *oh* and *ah* are somewhat 'semantically bleached', which denotes that the 'semantics of the word has been completely erased so that the word loses any meaning it once had and does not take on any new meaning'. Similarly, in line with O'Keeffe and Adolph's (2008) analysis of listener responses, this study also includes *yeah* in the non-word vocalisation category.

Finally, as various researchers such as Bjørge (2009) and Kobayashi (1995) have shown, some of the words within verbal backchannels are uttered as repetitions of the primary speaker's speech; thus, an additional category showing the number of repetitions as compared to other words and phrases autonomously and spontaneously created by the listener would seem to be justified. This category is further warranted by Thonus's (2002, 2007) claims that L2 learners often incorrectly use repetitions as a backchannel strategy. As will be mentioned in Section 2.5.7, backchannel repetitions commonly serve to request clarification (i.e., with rising intonation); however, when L2 learners overuse repetitions and/or employ them to serve other functions in English, they may cause confusion and/or be perceived negatively. Therefore, the addition of a repetition category would have to differentiate between clarification repetitions and non-clarification repetitions.

2.5 Functions of Backchannels

Attempting to present the functions of backchannels in a structured and coherent list has proven to be a difficult task for several reasons. First, while researchers have suggested a range of functions, there has been little consensus to date. One of the reasons may be that there appear to be reliability issues in measuring this aspect of conversation. While it is not clear precisely how researchers arrived at their conclusions in many cases, it appears that several of them based their findings on conversational analyses focusing on the primary speakers' perceptions of the functions of their interlocutors' backchannels as shown by how the conversation unfolded. This may assist in piecing together part of the puzzle; however, it does not take into account what the non-primary speaker meant to convey with their backchannel utterance. As the next chapter will discuss, this study aims to take into account the observed backchannel behaviour of the participants, the non-primary speakers' stated backchannel intentions, and their interlocutors' perceptions of these backchannels. Considering the various functions of backchannels, Maynard (1997) has attempted to sum up the previous work in this area by identifying the following six categories: (1) continuer, (2) understanding, (3) agreement, (4) support and empathy, (5) emotive and (6) minor additions. The researcher has expanded Maynard's (1997) list by adding the following three categories: (7) clarification, (8) non-understanding and (9) disagreement and dissatisfaction. The following explanations and hypothetical examples demonstrate these functions.

2.5.1 Continuer

The main functions of this type of backchannel are for the non-primary speaker to signal to the primary speaker that they are indeed listening attentively, and to allow the primary speaker to continue their speaking turn. According to Schegloff (1982), this is premised on the turn-taking system and specifically on the non-primary speaker forsaking the opportunity to take a primary speaking turn. This can be seen in the following example in which B's backchannel *mm hm* signals that A should continue speaking:

A: I'll pick it up from his place
B: *mm hm*
A: at around 7 o'clock

2.5.2 Display of Understanding of Content

This is when the non-primary speaker feels it is necessary to show that he/she understands the primary speaker as in the following example:

A: You have to go two blocks
B: *mm hm*

A: then turn left at the video store
B: *uh huh*
A: It's a few stores down on the right side
B: *I see*

In this example, B sends two continuer type backchannels in *mm hm* and *uh huh* to signal to A that he/she should continue giving directions, and once B seems to understand where the place is, B signals understanding of content to A with the backchannel *I see*.

2.5.3 Agreement

This is when the non-primary speaker sends a backchannel to show agreement to some known fact or idea that the primary speaker has presented.

A: It's now a matter for the courts to decide
B: *right right*

This type of backchannel is generally observed at the end of a turn or a semantic completion point (Wannaruck 1997).

2.5.4 Support and Empathy Towards the Speaker's Judgement

This occurs when the non-primary speaker responds with a show of support or empathy to an evaluative statement made by the primary speaker. For example:

A: He quit his job again
B: I find that odd
A: *Yeah*
B: He'll have to apply...

This example could be interpreted as A feeling it necessary to provide support to B's evaluative statement *I find that odd*; however, this does not necessarily constitute agreement. As several researchers have observed (Cutrone 2005; Uematsu 2000; Maynard 1997), backchannels sent to show support and empathy appear to be far more prevalent in Japanese than in English, and thus may be a source of misunderstanding in intercultural encounters involving Japanese EFL/ESL speakers.

2.5.5 Strong Emotional Response

A strong emotional response occurs when the non-primary speaker responds emphatically to a statement made by the primary speaker, which indicates more than a simple continuer, misunderstanding, or support. This is found in the form of a laugh and exclamatory statement as in the following example.

A: I got an A+ on my Chemistry test
B: *Fantastic!*
A: I hope I can...

2.5.6 Minor Addition

This type of backchannel occurs in such instances as when the non-primary speaker corrects something the primary speaker has just uttered, or when the non-primary speaker attempts to add a word in completing the utterance the primary speaker has just made. The latter can be seen in B's addition in the following example:

A: John will be back next year...
B: *in July*
A. so we can...

Although Maynard's (1997) description of this category included clarifications, it is included as a separate category here because of the seemingly fundamental difference in how these backchannels function. A clarification functions as a request for information, whereas, in contrast, a minor addition serves to offer information.

2.5.7 Clarification

Backchannels in this category are employed when the non-primary speaker requires the primary speaker to clarify something as in the following example:

A: Her room is empty
B: *Really?*
A. Yeah, she left this morning

In this example, it is clear to see that B was surprised at A's first utterance, and B's backchannel response of *Really?* signalled B's request for confirmation. Backchannel repetitions with a rising intonation commonly function to request clarification.

2.5.8 Non-understanding

The backchannels in this category are sent to signal to the primary speaker that the non-primary speaker has not understood or has misheard something (Uematsu 2000). While the function of this category is often communicated through primary speaking turns, it can also be communicated minimally through non-primary speakers' backchannels as in the following example:

A: I heard that it is a genetic predisposition
B: *Genetic what?*
A: That means he's...

The main difference between this category and the previously mentioned Clarification category is that a backchannel in this category is a much more emphatic signal of non-understanding of content.

2.5.9 Disagreement or Dissatisfaction

In their lists of the functional categories of backchannels, Fujimoto (2007), Horiguchi (1988) and Szatrowski (1993) include a disagreement category, and Ito (2007) includes a dissatisfaction category. The researcher has chosen to adopt these into an additional category because, according to the definition of a backchannel in Sections 2.2 and 2.3, the brief strings of text making up this category do not constitute a speaking turn by themselves, and do indeed signal a message to the primary speaker allowing them to continue their speaking turn. The following example illustrates this:

A. He's really lazy
B. *Huh?*
A. I mean when he is not working

B's backchannel reaction *huh?* signalled to A that B did not necessarily agree with A's assertion that the person was lazy, and thus caused A to backtrack and explain more thoroughly and less brusquely what he/she meant. This is not to state that all instances of disagreement/dissatisfaction will be expressed by means of a backchannel. The researcher fully acknowledges that there will be instances whereby communication will break down due to the listener's disagreement/ dissatisfaction, as will there be instances when the non-primary speaker needs to take a full turn at talk to express their disagreement/ dissatisfaction. For instance, concerning the latter, a lengthier disagreement response such as *Oh, I don't go along with that at all* would be considered a full speaking turn. The basis of this category as a backchannel function is that the non-primary speaker expresses disagreement or dissatisfaction with the primary speaker's evaluative statement. Even if it alters the course of a conversation somewhat (as a clarification or non-understanding backchannel might), the primary speaker continues to provide the main channel. There might also be some confusion differentiating between this category and various aspects of the Clarification and Non-understanding categories. The difference is that in this category the non-primary speaker's backchannel will tend to have a negative evaluative connotation, while in the previous categories, the non-primary speaker's backchannel is neutral.

2.6 Backchannels Across Cultures

2.6.1 Frequency

Several studies such as Cutrone (2005), Maynard (1986, 1990, 1997) and White (1989) found that Japanese tend to backchannel more frequently than NESs. Maynard (1986, 1990) first noticed this when she compared intracultural conversations in her contrastive studies of Americans and Japanese. Subsequently, analysing intercultural conversations, Maynard (1997) discovered that the American and Japanese participants' backchannel behaviour in the intercultural conversations were similar to that within their own cultural context. On average, the Japanese participants provided backchannels every 4.5 seconds of their interlocutor's primary speaking turn, while the American participants provided backchannels every 19.25 seconds.

Similarly, White (1989) examined Japanese and Americans in intracultural and intercultural dyadic conversations and found that the Japanese participants sent more backchannels in both contexts. In the intracultural dyads, the ratio was 3:1, and in the intercultural dyads, the ratio was 1.5:1. White (1989) used audio cassettes to record her data, and thus was not able to include nonverbal communication in her observations of the backchannels. Cutrone (2005) analysed Japanese and British intercultural dyadic conversations in English and found the Japanese participants sent more backchannels than their British interlocutors at a rate of 1.14:1. Similarly, Clancy et al. (1996), who use the term 'reactive token'[4], found that in intracultural conversations, Japanese participants used slightly more reactive tokens than the Americans (1.06:1), and far more than the Mandarin speakers (3.95:1). Lastly, in a recent study comparing backchannel use in Japanese English vis-à-vis Australian English, Ike (2010) found that backchannels occurred far more frequently in Japanese English (1.95:1).

In measuring the backchannelling frequency of an individual or group, researchers need to account for the amount of input listeners were afforded. This leads to the important question as to how researchers recognise the amount that the primary speaker spoke. Conversation analysts have dealt with this primarily in one of two ways: measuring the amount of time the speaker spent talking (Ike 2010; Maynard 1986, 1997), or counting the number of words the primary speaker spoke (Clancy et al. 1996; Cutrone 2005; Crawford 2003; Ike 2010; White 1989). Both of these methods have certain drawbacks. For instance, regarding the former, it is understood that people generally have different rates of speech (Garman 1990). This difference would seem to be magnified in intercultural conversations where L2 speakers' speech, due to needing more time to plan their next utterance, might be expected to contain a great deal more non-fluencies, such as silent pauses, than NSs' speech. Similarly, concerning the latter strategy, it seems questionable to give each word the same weight in counting the total number of words used in the primary speakers' speech because some of this speech will contain words that comprise dysfluency features such as false starts, repetitions and corrections. Although the researcher acknowledges that there may be some specific projects which require the exclusion of such phenomena from total word counts, the recent trend appears to be leaning towards recognising the amount the primary speaker spoke by the number of words they uttered (Clancy et al. 1996; Cutrone 2005; Crawford 2003; Ike 2010; White 1989). Nonetheless, for the purpose of analysing backchannels and, in particular, where in the primary speaker's speech listeners choose to place them, all words the primary speaker utters are important. This is evident, for example, when a listener processes a relatively lengthy false start and acknowledges it with a backchannel before it becomes apparent that the speaker has abandoned that utterance and is beginning anew.

---

[4] It is noteworthy to point out that Clancy et al.'s (1996) definition of a backchannel is a minimal one as it identifies a backchannel as only one of the several components that make up a *reactive token*.

2.6.2 Variability

In her intercultural analysis, Maynard (1997) found that the Japanese participants' backchannels consisted mainly of brief utterances and did not vary considerably, while the American participants displayed greater variability in the types of backchannels they sent. These findings were similar to the results of Cutrone's (2005) intercultural analysis, in which the eight British participants' backchannels displayed greater variability than the eight JEFLs' in many respects. Following the different types of backchannels as outlined in Section 2.4, 12% of the backchannels that the British participants sent belonged to the *complex* category, while only 4% of the backchannels sent by the Japanese belonged to this category. Further evidence to suggest that the Japanese tend to keep their backchannels simple and repetitive was that 39% of the backchannels that they employed fell into one category: the *simple accompanied by a head nod* category. In comparison, 25.8% of the British participants' backchannels fell into this category.

From post-conversation interview responses, Cutrone (2005) discerned that some of the British participants found the lack of variability in the types of backchannels their JEFL interlocutors sent negatively affected communication. These sentiments are consistent with the observations made by Fuji (2008), McCarthy (2003) and Stubbe (1998) to the effect that minimal and/or repetitive listener responses over an extended stretch of talk run the risk of being perceived as a sign of boredom or inattentiveness. In a study examining the speech act sequence of indirect complaint/commiseration in conversational interactions between JESL learners and their English speaking peers, Boxer (1993) observed that the overuse of minimal backchannels without a more substantive response by the JESL participants discouraged rather than encouraged their interlocutor's continuation. Further, these minimal responses were characteristic of the JESL participants' replies to indirect complaints as they comprised 52.9% of the total. In comparison, these nonsubstantive replies accounted for only 2.35% of the NESs' replies.

2.6.3 Discourse Contexts Favouring Backchannels

According to Maynard (1986), grammatical completion, sentence-final particles and vertical head movement provided discourse contexts favouring backchannels in Japanese, while in American English, grammatical completion provided the single most important discourse context. In a more recent study, Maynard (1997) again found that grammatical completion, particularly in instances followed by a pause, was the most frequent discourse context of the American participants' backchannels, while the discourse contexts favouring the Japanese participants' backchannels varied considerably and the latter were generally cued by direct eye-contact, tag questions and pauses (irrespective of grammatical completion points).

Similarly, the results of Cutrone (2005) indicated that the Japanese discourse contexts favouring backchannels varied considerably, while grammatical completion points, especially coinciding with a pause, were the most frequently found discourse contexts for the native speakers of British English. Cutrone (2005) also found that both the British and Japanese groups in his study commonly sent backchannels after their interlocutors' nonverbal gestures. The British participants sent backchannels 68% of the time this discourse context presented itself, while the Japanese participants did so 80%. White (1989) did not go into great detail in this area; however, she also identified clausal boundaries and pauses as primary discourse contexts favouring backchannels in both English and Japanese. Clancy et al. (1996) further support the suggestion that grammatical completion points are places where backchannels are commonly employed in Japanese and English.

2.6.4 Simultaneous Speech

A common trend that seems to have emerged in the research is that Japanese people, regardless of whether they are speaking English or Japanese, tend to backchannel more frequently than NESs, and a great portion of these backchannels are sent during the primary speakers' speech, creating simultaneous speech (Cutrone 2005; Hayashi 1988; Maynard 1997). In her contrastive study examining simultaneous speech (SS hereafter) from the perspective of floor management of English and Japanese speakers, Hayashi (1988) reports that the 16 Japanese participants in her study simultaneously talked on average every 72.4 seconds, while the 16 American participants did so only every 182 seconds. Maynard (1997), in her study examining intercultural conversations, notes that the Japanese participants frequently sent backchannels while their interlocutor was having a turn at talk, while the American participants did not. Although she did provide several examples of this occurring, Maynard (1997) did not provide the actual number of backchannels pertaining to each group in this context as it was not the focus of her study. Cutrone (2005) found that the JEFLs sent more backchannels in this context than the NESs by a ratio of 2.67:1.

While their opinions were not based on empirical evidence, Lebra (1976) and Mizutani (1982) assert that some NESs may take these frequent interjections as a sign of the listener's impatience and demand for a quick completion of the statement. Yamada (1997) explains that the American concept of turn-taking is the likely cause of their less frequent backchannelling. Taking somewhat of an essentialist perspective, Yamada (1997) explains that Americans generally regard a speaking turn as an opportunity to show credibility and power, and speaking turns are normally held by one person at a time. Ergo, the overuse of backchannels could be viewed as invading a speaker's right to speak rather than being supportive (see Section 2.8.2 for a discussion of Speaker-Talk vis-à-vis Listener-Talk). In this framework, SS often occurs as a result of speakers' competition to gain access to the speaking floor. This would seem to be in stark contrast to the descriptions of Japanese backchannels by Hayashi (1988) and Maynard (1997) who maintain that Japanese utilise SS to show support and foster a harmonious atmosphere in the conversation.

The results in this area have been mixed and provide evidence for both sides. Cutrone's (2005) study included a correlation analysis which showed that the more frequently the Japanese participants sent backchannels, the more the British participants felt they were being interrupted, and the more they perceived their interlocutor to be impatient. Although these results were not statistically significant, the correlation coefficients regarding the items used to measure these attitudes in Hecht's (1978) modified questionnaire (Items 8 and 15) could at least be considered to be interesting as they produced correlation coefficients noticeably higher than the other items and close to the critical value which determines statistical significance (Item 8 = .50, Item 15 = .59, and critical value = .71). White (1989) also administered a similar correlation analysis attempting to determine whether backchannel conventions which were not shared across cultures contribute to negative personality attributions or stereotyping. Contrary to the results of Cutrone (2005), the NESs in White's (1989) study (i.e., ten Americans) perceived more frequent backchannels sent by their Japanese interlocutors as a positive trait. More specifically, White (1989) found that the more frequently their Japanese interlocutors sent backchannels, the more the NESs perceived them to be showing signs of comprehension, encouragement, and interest and concern (these results were statistically significant at $p<.01$, $p<.05$, $p<.001$ respectively).

Thus far, SS, as it relates to the scope of this study, has dealt only with the verbal backchannels which occur while the primary speaker is having a turn at talk. As backchannels in this context may be perceived as invasive by some yet supportive by others, it is useful to consider how this aspect of SS has been studied. According to James and Clarke (1993), the term *interruption*, as used in both ordinary speech and in academia, usually implies the violation of another's right to speak; however, not all interruptions are regarded as disruptive attempts at dominance. On the contrary, some interruptions, such as paraphrases, comments, elaborations, collaborative finishes and questions during the primary speaker's turn at talk, can be seen as signs of support and active listening (Ueno 2004). In fact, researchers such as Craig and Pitts (1990) and Furgersen (1977) have classified interruptions into two types: dominance-associated and supportive interruptions. In the same way, Stubbe (1998) uses the term Cooperative Overlaps to describe her notion of supportive interruptions. These Cooperative Overlaps can be functionally distinguished from other types of overlapping speech because they are collaborative and thus convey no sense of competition or disruption of the speaker's turn at talk. Other approaches to studying interruptions have shown that classifying interruptions is a complex process with interplay between many variables. For instance, in Beattie's (1983) study, every attempt at speaker change is marked and interruptions are identified based on three criteria: (1) success in taking over the speaking turn at talk, (2) presence of SS and (3) utterance completion. Murray (1985, 1987, 1988), having conducted numerous studies in this area, rejects any claim to the effect that interruptions can be labelled without reference to the context or the status of the interactants. Thus, as Murray (1985) advocates, the intentions of the speaker as well as the interpretation of the listener are among the many social variables that influence what might be considered an interruption at any given point in time. The fact that these aspects of interruptions have not been investigated in prior studies may signal the extreme difficulties associated with their measurement.

2.7 The Development of Backchannel Behaviour

2.7.1 The Acquisition of Backchannels

L1 backchannels are acquired as part of children's pragmatic communicative skills and language development. Research has shown that the acquisition of backchannels is a fairly slow developmental process, stretching into adolescence (Dittman 1972; Ervin-Tripp 1979; Hess & Johnston 1988; Tao & Thompson 1991). In their study examining the development of backchannel responses involving 36 normal children ranging in age from seven to eleven, Hess and Johnston (1988) showed that backchannel responses may be among the last conversational skills acquired. This was suggested due to the fact that the frequency of backchannel responses increased significantly with age. Further, the children who provided more backchannels demonstrated a significant relationship between backchannel responses and a variety of speaker cue combinations. These findings seem to suggest that the older children understood the listener role of providing collaborative feedback and also became more sensitive to appropriate points to show collaborative feedback.

Presently, not much is known about the acquisition of L2 backchannels. Schmidt's (1983) longitudinal study, which reports on the English development of a native speaker of Japanese, Wes, in an immersion setting, helps shed a little light. Upon arriving in Hawaii, Wes's English abilities were observed to be minimal in all respects. Wes's development over three years in Hawaii was largely mixed as he was able to make strides in some areas but continued to struggle in others. The area in which Schmidt (1983) noticed the greatest improvement was in Wes's backchannel behaviour in that he seemed to acquire near native-like backchannel behaviour in English. That is, as a result of increasing contact with NESs, Wes seemed to understand how to make use of backchannel responses differentially in L1 Japanese and L2 English and no longer transferred the more frequent and animated backchannel behaviour characteristic of Japanese to English (Kasper & Rose 2003).

2.7.2 L1-L2 Transfer of Backchannel Behaviour

While Section 1.4 touched upon some of the effects of pragmatic transfer on JEFLs in general terms, it remains unclear precisely how this affects L2 backchannel behaviour. Comparative studies of Japanese and English have been conducted by a number of researchers (Agawa 2002; Crawford 2003; Maynard 1986, 1990, 1997; Mizutani 1982; White 1989). In these studies, the Japanese participants consistently exhibited backchannel behaviour appropriate in their L1 Japanese in their L2 English, using the Japanese language's higher frequency of verbal backchannel cues (Crawford 2003; Maynard 1986, 1990, 1997; White 1989) and nonverbal backchannel cues such as head movements and smiles while speaking English (Agawa 2002).

In the intercultural conversations in White's (1989) study, the five Japanese participants continued to backchannel as they would in their native tongue, whereas the five Americans tended to shift their listening styles towards the Japanese. White (1989) attempted to explain this by stating that the Americans accommodated to the style of their foreign interlocutors as a means of facilitating communication. In this case, more frequent backchannelling may have been a strategy to encourage the Japanese participants to overcome their reticence and speak more. In another study, Ohira (1998) analysed one hour of each of five dinner conversations among Americans and Japanese in the United States and found that the native Japanese participants' backchannel behaviour transferred to their L2 English. Interestingly, although the Japanese participants, who had all lived in the U.S for a period of three to five years, admitted to being aware that their backchannel behaviour was different to that of the target language, they were not able to change.

Crawford's (2003) study involving four bilingual female university students revealed a pattern of preferred functional styles that carried through into second language use. That is, the two native Japanese participants continued to favour the frequent use of continuers, minor additions and requests for more information, whereas the two NESs maintained a variety of functions. Lastly, in her PhD thesis, Tsuchiya (2010) compares dyadic conversations between British tutors and British students with conversations between British tutors and Japanese students in English in order to investigate differences and similarities in their listenership. Among her conclusions, Tsuchiya (2010: 304) summarises that L1 'transfer in listenership behaviour was observed in the Japanese students' use of response tokens, such as the monotonous use of head nods and more negotiations for speaker selection'.

2.8 Issues Involving JEFL/ESLs' Listenership

2.8.1 Miscommunication and Negative Perceptions in IC

As shown in Section 1.9, misunderstandings can occur between speakers who do not share conventions in language use. With respect to conventions of listening behaviour, Sections 2.4 and 2.6.4 demonstrate the possibility that differences regarding the variability in the types of backchannels individuals or groups use, as well as the differences in how SS is employed and interpreted, can also be sources of miscommunication and negative perceptions across cultures. This section will continue this theme from the perspective of examining potential misunderstandings due to differences in backchannel functions across cultures. As outlined in Section 1.9.3, the concept of truth may be somewhat influenced by culture-specific ideologies at times. These cultural differences, as manifested through the backchannel functions people choose to employ, can have dire consequences in IC as was the case of the unfortunate Japanese businessmen (employees of Mitsubishi and Hitachi) who were arrested and indicted for allegedly trying to steal IBM trade secrets (The Japan Times 29 January 1983, p. 2). One of the defendants in the case, Mr. Takaya Ishida of Mitsubishi, claimed that he had not agreed with the undercover FBI agents when they told him he had to steal some information/documents. His defence counsellor argued that Mr. Ishida's responses of *yeah* and *uhuh* were not to show agreement, but rather to indicate he was listening and to allow the other person to continue as was characteristic of polite Japanese listening behaviour (i.e., automatic transfer of backchannel cues).

Describing a similar type of misunderstanding, Blanche (1987) observed different conceptualisations of backchannelling behaviour between Japanese students and their American English teacher, which would seem to have a negative impact on the language classroom. In this common scenario, NES teachers sometimes misinterpret students' nods coupled with vocalisations of *yes* and *mhm* at seemingly appropriate times as displays of understanding, rather than simply polite expressions of attending. When teachers discover much later on that students have not understood them, they may sometimes feel perplexed and/or even slightly annoyed by what they perceive to be mixed signals, or in extreme cases, deceptive messages, resulting in the squandering of valuable class time. This was demonstrated by the following response of a British teacher in Japan in Cutrone's (2005: 268) study:

> Victoria: The most difficult thing I find in teaching in Japan is that the students never tell you when they don't understand. Lots of times they'll just pretend they understand, but then you ask them to do something and they won't have the faintest clue what you mean.

Yamada (1997) and Mizutani (1983) also provide anecdotes of such mishaps in business negotiations and television discussions. These types of misunderstandings and miscommunications described above are consistent with other findings of Cutrone (2005). In this study, Cutrone (2005) used playback interviews [5] to explore the potential for misunderstanding and miscommunication caused by the ways that the JEFL participants in his study employed backchannels which might be considered unconventional in English. To this end, Cutrone (2005) found

---

[5] Playback interviews, as described by Johnstone (2000: 51), are a retrospective technique in which participants are interviewed while watching a conversation they had participated in.

that JEFL participants' backchannels sometimes included continuer type backchannels such as head nods, *uhum* and/or *yeah yeah* in instances when the Japanese participant disagreed and/or did not understand what the primary speaker was saying. When asked why they used backchannels in these situations, some of the JEFL respondents indicated that they were unsure but that it felt natural to do so, whereas other JEFL respondents were more aware of their backchannel behaviour and cited politeness and an unwillingness to interrupt as the main reason they used backchannels in these instances. In line with the core principles of *wa*, LoCastro (1987, 1999) explains that Japanese sometimes use continuer or agreement backchannels to mitigate potential FTAs such as disagreeing and not understanding. While this type of behaviour is thought to have different origins and manifests itself somewhat differently in the Japanese communicative style (see Section 1.7.1), this maintenance of the pretence of understanding for reasons of politeness is not confined to backchannel behaviour, or to the Japanese (Aston 1986).

Although the differences in backchannel functions across cultures stated above would seem to pose the greatest dangers in IC, there may be other functional uses of backchannels considered nonconventional in English. Relating to some of the issues concerning culture-specific ideologies regarding Grice's (1975) maxim of quantity (see Section 1.9.1), some of the JEFL participants in Cutrone's (2005) study indicated that they used backchannels as a way to avoid speaking due to shyness, lack of confidence in their English ability, and not knowing what to say. As suggested in Section 1.9.1 above, the consistent use of minimal responses and/or failure to elaborate in conversations could undermine interpersonal relationships as they may be perceived as an unwillingness to communicate and/or may even tire or bore the interlocutor. It is doubtful that using backchannels as a means to avoid speaking is what Schegloff (1982: 81) had in mind when he first described the concept of 'continuer' to allow one's interlocutor to continue speaking (see Section 2.5.1). This would seem to highlight the contrast between some functions of backchannels in an L2 context as compared to Schegloff's (1982) L1 context.

2.8.2 Understanding Japanese Backchannel Behaviour

As backchannels are an important component of any successful conversation, Heinz (2003) explains backchannel behaviour as an effect of speakers attempting to adopt Grice's (1975) CP. However, as shown in Section 2.6, there can be great variability in terms of how individuals from different cultures use backchannels. Further, due to the potentially different interpretations of Grice's maxims across cultures (see Section 1.9), the types of miscommunication and negative perceptions described in Section 2.8.1 can sometimes occur when speakers communicate across cultures. Hence, the purpose of this section is to provide insights towards understanding the backchannel behaviour demonstrated by some of the Japanese participants in the studies discussed above.

First, in an attempt to explain the greater frequency of Japanese backchannels as compared to other cultures (see Section 2.6.1), several researchers have pointed towards Japanese culture (LoCastro 1987, 1999; Kenna & Lacy 1994; Maynard 1997; White 1989). As described in Section 1.7.1, there has been a great deal of literature describing the Japanese communication style and their supposed need to keep conversations harmonious and avoid confrontations. Several linguists such as Kenna and Lacy (1994), LoCastro (1987, 1999), Maynard (1997) and White (1989) contend that Japanese use backchannelling behaviour as a way to maintain harmony in conversations. Interestingly, there appear to be few, if any, languages which have a common name for what linguists call backchannels, a term unknown in everyday English. It seems quite telling that in everyday Japanese however, the folk-metapragmatic term *aizuchi*, which literally means 'mutual hammering' (Yamada 1992: 131), is known by virtually everyone, including children (Heinz 2003). The word, *aizuchi*, is a combination of the verb, *au* (相), meaning doing something together, and the word, *tsuchi* (槌), meaning hammer. The kanji characters comprising the word *aizuchi* are derived from its original meaning which conveyed the harmonious rhythmic ensemble that two blacksmiths, master and apprentice, require as they simultaneously hammer away on a piece of iron to produce fine work. According to Maynard (1997), this type of rhythmic synchrony often exists in Japanese conversations as shown by the repetitive head movements of the Japanese participants in her study, which seem to have been distributed in such a way as to be synchronised with the tempo of the talk. Maynard (1997: 51) likens this type of behaviour to that of a 'synchronized dance' which demonstrates the constant and consistent empathy-building on the part of both participants.

This type of active listening in Japanese communication is characterised as Listener-Talk in Yamada's (1997) Listener-Talk Speaker-Talk dichotomy. While speakers from some cultures generally relegate listening to passive receiving, the Japanese are thought to attach great importance to listening behaviour. Besides showing a great deal of support and empathy to the speaker, Listener-Talk is characterised by the listener, not the speaker, assuming the critical responsibility of communication. In other words, the listener's interpretation is fundamental to the conversation moving forward, and the onus is on them to derive meaning from what the speaker has uttered. This communication style is congruent with the notion of *sassuru* (to surmise or guess) in Japanese and may contribute to depictions of Japanese as indirect and vague speakers (see Section 1.9.2). In their papers, Makino (2002) and Wilson (1998) use the common Japanese phrase *sasshi no bunka* or the guessing culture to describe the value that Japanese seem to give to listeners who can anticipate the intentions of others and are skilled at making sense of implicit messages. Yamada (1997) attributes some of the miscommunication and negative perceptions that Japanese and Americans experience in IC (as described in Section 2.7.1 above) to their contrasting communication styles highlighted by the Listener-Talk and Speaker-Talk dichotomy. Contrary to the Japanese style of communication, Yamada (1997) states that Speaker-Talk is the main mode of communication used by Americans. In Speaker-Talk, the speaker assumes the critical responsibility of communication and is responsible for monitoring the effect of their words on the listener(s). Further, a good communicator is required to clearly and quickly articulate their points. Thus, as Yamada (1997: 50) summarises, 'Americans define the ideal communicator as a speaker-in-action, while the Japanese define the ideal communicator as a listener who cares'.

While many of Yamada's (1997) assertions have been made elsewhere, it is important to note that the seemingly essentialist descriptions used in binary scales such as this (others include Hall's (1981) low-context vs. high-context scale and Hofstede's (1991) individualism vs. collectivisim scale), have come under attack by various researchers (Guest 2006; Kubota 1999; Said 1978). They argue that employing binary categories runs the risk of reducing complex realities to easy-to-control polar opposites. Moreover, an even greater danger according to Guest (2006: 8) 'can be seen in how these polarised dichotomies eventually become entrenched in later research as fixed, set, crystallised facts, not as mere tendencies existing along a continuum'.

Taking a linguistic perspective, Maynard (1989, 1997), Miller (1988) and White (1989) suggest that Japanese may use more backchannels than English speakers because the syntactic structure inherent in Japanese provides more backchannel opportunities. In comparing Japanese language to English, several linguists including Clancy (1982), Clancy et al. (1996) and Yamada (1992) agree that Japanese talk tends to be broken up into smaller units bounded by more pauses than English. As Section 2.6.3 reports, Japanese backchannels often occur in pauses in the talk. One of the reasons attributed to the frequent pausing in Japanese discourse is the existence of *joshi* (grammatical particles). Joshi, often directly followed by a pause in the primary speaker's speech, can be defined approximately as markers that show the relationship between a word, phrase, or clause to the rest of the sentence. Although some analysts have compared *joshi* to prepositions and tag questions in English, there does not appear to be a direct equivalent in English since *joshi* have a myriad of other functions and occur much more frequently in speech. Hence, Japanese particles, and the pauses accompanying them, would seem to provide an additional discourse context for backchannels which does not exist in English.

This structural-driven approach is consistent with the longstanding Sapir-Whorf hypothesis which stipulates that the structure of a language determines how its speakers view the world (Sapir 1929, referred to in Wardhaugh 1986). However, this view is not shared by all researchers. For instance, regarding Japanese backchannels, LoCastro (1999) proposes that a functional analysis may lead to more useful insights. LoCastro (1999: 379) argues that 'language behaviour is primarily the major means to communicate with others and would presumably develop over time to facilitate the playing out of that need'. In other words, she adopts a Vygotskian (1962) perspective in that she proposes that language is determined by the speakers' culture and environment rather than the other way around. LoCastro's (1999) interpretation which prioritises sociocultural and cognitive pressures on the language code has received some support regarding Japanese backchannels. For instance, Auer (1996) and Goodwin (1981) document how speaking turns are determined by the social interaction in a conversation including such cues as gaze at critical moments in the conversations, and various components of prosody. Further, Clancy (1982) suggests a cognitive explanation for the greater fragmentation of Japanese in claiming that Japanese talk may be divided into shorter units, followed by pauses, to limit the processing burden on the listener. Although Clancy (1982) does not go into detail as to why Japanese listeners should need a particularly low processing burden, one reason, as put forward by Yamada (1997), is that both the speaker and listener recognise the vital role of the listener in moving the conversation forward. In line with the principles of *wa*, as well as the empathy building behaviour identified by Maynard (1997), the speaker(s) and listener(s) in Japanese conversations could be seen to be working together to ensure that the listener(s) can interpret the primary speaker's speech and thence provide supportive feedback. While LoCastro (1999) has certainly raised an interesting point, it is difficult to arrive at any conclusions regarding it. Any decisions determining the origins of Japanese backchannels which state that a functional explanation should be adopted instead of a linguistic one will have to wait until further research is carried out. Similarly, the question of which came first, language or culture, is clearly beyond the scope of this book and will undoubtedly continue to be debated for years to come.

2.8.3 *Aizuchi* in Japanese Relative to English Backchannels

In a contrastive study of Japanese and US English backchannels, Tajima (2001) investigated the pragmatic use of *aizuchi* in Japanese discourse relative to English backchannels. An important characteristic of Japanese listening behaviour is the way in which Japanese listeners shift the style of their *aizuchi* forms to suit pragmatic elements of the conversations. While Japanese backchannel use is largely governed by hierarchical factors such as the age, gender, status of interlocutors and the formality of the conversational settings, there are also instances in which Japanese listeners attempt to mitigate FTAs by shifting the style of their backchannel forms (i.e., creating greater psychological distance in conversations). As shown in Table 2-1 below, Tajima compares some of the basic patterns of usage in Japanese backchannel forms with three common backchannel forms in English (i.e., *yeah*, *right*, and *uh-huh*). Although Tajima's presentation of common backchannel forms in Table 2-1 is somewhat limited in scope, as she does not describe in great depth some of the hierarchical elements mentioned above, it is interesting that the backchannel forms in her categories suggest a clear relationship between gender and formality. That is, backchannel forms that are considered informal in Japanese are thought to be gender-neutral, whereas feminine forms generally equate to more formal backchannels. Women who know each other well might be expected to adopt a gender neutral/informal form. Masculine forms, on the other hand, generally fall in line with the less formal backchannels. However, if a younger man were speaking to an older man, the younger man would be expected to adopt a more formal form.

Using Silverstein's (1976: 26) notion of 'indexicality' as a framework, Tajima (2001) provides some examples of 'indexical presupposition' and 'indexical creativity' from the six dyadic Japanese conversations that made up part of her contrastive study of Japanese and American English. First, relative to the description of Japanese politeness in Section 1.7.3, indexical presupposition refers here to the societal expectations that Japanese speakers choose certain *aizuchi* forms based on age, gender, status of interlocutors, and the formality of the conversational settings.

Table 2-1 English backchannels and Japanese *aizuchi* in general use

English	Japanese				
	Formal	Informal	Masculine	Feminine	Gender Neutral
yeah	hai ee	un aa	aa ou	ee	un
right	sou + sentence final particles (SFP)				
	sou desune	sou sou dane sou dayo	sou dana	sou ne sou yo	sou sou dane sou dayo
uh-huh	ee ee	un un aa aa	aa aa	ee ee	un un

(Tajima 2001: 57)

The following example, taken from Tajima (2001: 57), demonstrates how certain contextual factors from the conversation can be inferred from the *aizuchi* form the listener chooses to employ.

(1) X: Samui desu ne.
 [It's cold here]
(2) Y: ee
 [Yeah]

As shown in Table 2-1, the form *ee* suggests that speaker Y is female, speaker X has a higher status than speaker Y, and speaker X is likely an unfamiliar person to speaker Y. Tajima (2001) explains that speaker Y uttering the more informal form *un* (instead of *ee*) in this situation would be seen as showing too much familiarity between interlocutors, creating an impression of ignorance or lack of self-control.

Second, indexical creativity refers to the way listeners shift the styles of their *aizuchi* forms to mitigate FTAs. One example demonstrating this from Tajima's (2001) study occurred in an exchange between two female speakers engaged in a casual conversation. As the female speakers were friends and the same age, most of the backchannel cues in the conversation predictably consisted of plain and informal forms such as *un*, *aa* and *sou*. However, when the listener appeared to not agree with what her interlocutor was saying, the listener's backchannel cues switched from informal forms to extremely feminine forms such as *ee* and *sou yo*. By shifting to a slightly more formal and less familiar backchannel style here, the listener appears to be able to signal some level of disagreement without having to state it overtly, which would mitigate their interlocutor's loss of face. Following the principles embodied by *wa* (see Section 1.7.1), the listener seems to be manipulating their creative meaning of *aizuchi* to maintain the harmony of the conversation. Comparatively, in six dyadic conversations involving American participants, Tajima (2001) was not able to find any evidence of style-shifts of listeners' backchannel signals toward the speaker. Nonetheless, this is not to conclude that style-shifts to show listeners' psychological distance do not exist in English as Tajima (2001) did not include prosodic cues in her measurement techniques. It might be that NESs may have other ways to mitigate their psychological distance through listening behaviour such as changing their intonation, stress, pitch, etc.

2.9 Instructional Approaches Relative to this Study

2.9.1 Explicit and Implicit Learning

The context of learning/instruction underpinning the investigation of JEFL learners' acquisition of English backchannels is a central issue in this study and touches upon the more general issue of how languages are thought to be acquired. Currently, the issue regarding explicit versus implicit learning remains hotly debated within all domains of language teaching. Following the well-known skills' acquisition theory known as the Adaptive Control of Thought (ACT) theory (Anderson 1983; Anderson & Lebriere 1998), proponents of an explicit approach perceive language learning as progression from declarative/explicit knowledge through proceduralisation to final automatisation. Conversely, at the other end of the spectrum and in following the tenets of Krashen's (1982) Input Hypothesis theory, proponents of a non-interface position believe that there is no possibility of explicit knowledge being converted to implicit knowledge.

Recently, Nick Ellis (2005, 2006a,b) has made attempts to explain the dichotomy between explicit and implicit learning by drawing on the differences between L1 and L2 acquisition processes. Cognitively, by general understanding, the initial state of L2 learning is *tabula repleta*, and not *tabula rasa* as characterised by L1 learning. In other words, unlike L1 learners who are thought to acquire language implicitly, L2 learners come to the learning environment with minds already endowed with knowledge and experience of a prior linguistic system (i.e., the L1). This cognitive state seems to act as a constraint and filter in L2 input reception and output generation, two critical processes of SLA. Researchers such as Goldschneider and DeKeyser (2001) and Nick Ellis (2005, 2006a,b) have identified factors that enable features of language to be noticed and hence guide practitioners to what might need explicit instruction. In this way, explicit knowledge is thought to contribute to implicit learning. Goldschneider and DeKeyser's (2001: 34) meta-analysis of morpheme acquisition show that 'the combination of perceptual salience, semantic complexity, morphophonological regularity, syntactic category and frequency does account for a very large portion of the total variance in the accuracy scores for grammatical functors'. Goldschneider and DeKeyser (2001: 37) argue that these five factors 'can be seen as aspects of salience in a broad sense of the word, and that this salience at various levels (phonological, morphological, syntactic, semantic, and numerical) facilitates the process of induction of grammatical structure from elements of the input'.

According to Nick Ellis (2006a:19), the linguistic forms that L2 learners fail to adopt and to use routinely thereafter in their L2 processing are those which, whether available as a result of frequency, recency, or context, fall short of intake because of one of the following associative learning factors:

1. unreliable predictors of outcome,
2. not attended because of low cue salience,
3. not attended because of low functional outcome in the overall interpretation of the message,
4. not attended because they are redundant in the immediate understanding of an utterance, being overshadowed or blocked by higher salience cues which have previously been selected, and
5. ignored because L1 experience of form→meaning contingencies affects the cues and dimensions that an L2 learner's language input systems can best distinguish (perceptual learning), and L1 experience of meaning→form contingencies affects the way a L2 learner routinely expresses their meanings in language.

Although all five of Ellis's (2006a) factors listed above could be said to be detrimental to the acquisition of L2 backchannels to varying degrees, factors four and five would seem to pose the greatest hindrances. As Section 2.7.2 reported, there is a great deal of evidence showing negative transfer of backchannel behaviour from L1 Japanese to L2 English, which suggests the possibility of L1-influenced blocking. Conversational discourse features such as backchannels, despite their pervasiveness, are largely non-salient and usually pass unnoticed unless attention is drawn to them intentionally and explicitly (Brozyna 2007; Takimoto 2009). For this reason, Ellis (2006a,b) advocates explicit and conscious L2 learning as a way of supplementing or directing frequency-driven learning of patterns. It is his strong belief that consciousness is required to change behaviour in SLA as L2 learners do not seem to be equipped to notice low salient cues at a subconscious level, particularly when proficiency levels using the more obvious cues are already sufficient for everyday communicative survival. These beliefs are in line with Schmidt's (1993) *noticing* hypothesis, which stipulates that learners must consciously *notice* linguistic input in order for it to become intake.

2.9.2 The Effects of Instruction on Pragmatic Development

2.9.2.1 Form-focused Instruction: Studies Adopting a One-group Pre-test–Post-test Design

There is by now ample evidence to show that *form-focused instruction* (FFI) has a positive effect on various aspects of SLA such as grammatical development (Ellis, Rod 2002, 2005, 2008); however, the effects of FFI on L2 pragmatic development remains unclear. The results of several teachability studies, which have typically adopted a one-group pre-test-post-test design, have been largely mixed. In their study using written DCTs to assess the effects of explicit instruction on some of the finer points involved in the speech act of apologies, Olshtain and Cohen (1990) found no benefit from instruction in terms of overall frequency of semantic formulas used; however, post-test responses did contain a wider variety of apology strategies and an increased use of intensifiers compared to the pre-test, suggesting at least some benefit from the pragmalinguistic aspects of the instruction. Rose (2005) points out a possible flaw in Olshtain and Cohen's (1990) research design in that the instruction given may not have been effective in equipping learners to deal with tasks for which some knowledge of sociopragmatics was required, i.e., 'learners were presented with contexts together with a range of possible apology strategies, and asked to indicate whether they considered the various apologies acceptable, more or less acceptable or not acceptable' (Rose 2005: 391). The fact that learners' ratings did not change as a result of instruction, and remained different from those of native speakers, suggests a lack of sociopragmatic knowledge on their part. Olshtain and Cohen (1990) explain that this is a simple exposure issue, and that a long length of residence in the target language context is the solution. However, as discussed above, exposure alone does not guarantee gains in pragmatic ability. Bardovi-Harlig (2001) has demonstrated that even after lengthy periods of residence in the target language context, pragmatic infelicities can remain.

Another study apparently showing the limitations of instruction in this area was LoCastro's (1997) pedagogical intervention involving politeness strategies in group discussion, such as requesting answers, directing the talk and seeking (dis)agreement. After nine weeks of instruction, there was little change in learners' performances. However, as Rose (2005) suggests, this may have more to do with the measurement techniques she used than learners' actual abilities. For instance, LoCastro (1997) relied on the transcripts of a single group discussion conducted in a reading class to determine whether individual learners had benefited from explicit instruction on politeness strategies provided in a speaking class. Seemingly, more than a single observation would have been advisable as it is possible that participants lacked sufficient opportunity to demonstrate what they might have learnt in a single session. In another study, Liddicoat and Crozet (2001) used open role-plays to assess the effect of ten weeks of instruction on appropriately elaborated responses to the French question *T'as passe' un bon week-end?* (Did you have a good weekend?). Unlike many of the other studies described in this section, Liddicoat and Crozet's (2001) study included a delayed post-test one year after the instructional period in their measurement. Results of the first post-test showed that the instruction had a greater impact on the overall content of the responses than on use of appropriate interactive devices such as feedback and repetition. Results from the delayed post-test showed that learners retained most of the content features, but the only interactional practice they performed was feedback.

Two subsequent studies involving university students learning English in Spain by Safont (2003) and Salazar (2003) both measured the effects of explicit instruction on requests by using written DCTs, with the former focusing on the use of internal and external modification. Safont (2003) found a marked increase in her participants' use of request modification on the post-test; however, Salazar's (2003) participants displayed very short-lived effects from the instruction occurring after the first of two twenty-minute treatment sessions – by the time of the post-test, these effects had disappeared. The results of this study may have been influenced by the brevity of treatment as a mere 40 minutes of instruction does not seem to be sufficient in attempting to master a range of request strategies. Ellis (1984), measuring the effects of three hours of formal instruction on the form and meaning of *Wh* questions in 13 upper elementary school students, found no improvement for the group as a whole. Paradoxically, an additional measurement of student participation revealed that individual learners whose proficiency with these structures improved were, in fact, less involved with the instruction than the other learners.

2.9.2.2 Instruction versus Exposure Studies

In studies comparing explicit instruction to natural exposure of the target language, the results suggest that learners receiving instruction in pragmatics outperformed those who did not. For instance, in Billmyer's (1990) study on the effects of instruction on compliments and compliment responses in an ESL context, the group which received explicit instruction exhibited behaviour more closely approximating NS norms in complimenting than the group which did not. This was evident in such areas as frequency of compliments, norm-appropriate use, spontaneity, adjectival repertoire, and reply types and length. In another study, Bouton (1994) examined 64 university ESL students' ability to learn conversational implicature in English and found that the group that received explicit instruction over a 17 month period achieved results as high as those observed with previous immersion students who had spent four years living in the US. Bouton (1994) thus concluded that the process of learning conversational implicature is slow when it is not explicitly taught.

Other studies which also found evidence supporting an explicit approach were conducted by Lyster (1994), Wishnoff (2000) and Yoshimi (2001). In a study involving adolescent learners, Lyster (1994) used multiple choice tests and oral and written production tasks to examine the use of the French *tu/vous* distinction in informal and formal contexts and found that the group which received explicit instruction outperformed the group that did not on all tasks except for informal oral production, in which all learners used *tu* appropriately. These differences remained at the time of the delayed post-test three months after instruction. Wishnoff (2000) investigated the effects of instruction on L2 pragmatic acquisition in writing with a particular focus on the functions of hedges, such as modal verbs, modal adverbs and lexical verbs. Despite administering only a brief instructional period of two class sessions totalling 90 minutes, the hedging devices of the group that received explicit instruction increased five-fold, which was a statistically significant difference between the treatment and control groups. Yoshimi (2001) used written production tasks to examine the Japanese interactional markers which feature prominently in conversation of two groups of JFL learners: one that received explicit instruction for 24 weeks (i.e., a one-hour session each week) regarding this skill, and one that did not. The results showed that the instructed learners exhibited a dramatic increase in the frequency of interactional markers, while no similar increase in their use was observed by the control group.

Although explicit instruction was generally shown to be superior to exposure in the studies above, exposure alone appears to have had some effect. For instance, the control group in both Billmyer's (1990) and Wishnoff's (2000) studies demonstrated noticeable improvement using the target language during the course of these studies. As Rose (2005) explains, this may be due to the fact that both studies took place in an ESL context. Hence, the subject matter targeted in these studies seemed to be of direct and immediate relevance to the learners as they were often required to deploy the target language outside the classroom for everyday communicative survival. It is doubtful that a similar effect would have been observed in an EFL context. Regarding the acquisition of L2 backchannels specifically, Schmidt's (1983) longitudinal study is perhaps the only one of its kind to report on the development of backchannel behaviour over time. As discussed in Section 2.7.1, Schmidt (1983) describes how Wes, a native Japanese speaker, seemed to implicitly acquire L2 native-like backchannel behaviour after having lived in the United States for three years.

2.9.2.3 Explicit versus Implicit Instruction Studies

A number of researchers have conducted studies which have compared two types of pedagogical interventions known as explicit and implicit instruction. The main feature distinguishing these two instructional approaches is the general provision of metapragmatic information designed to make the target features more salient in the explicit approach. More specifically, explicit instruction commonly involves providing students with explicit metapragmatic information about L2 rules through explanations (Billmyer 1990; House 1996), metacognitive discussions (Olshtain & Cohen 1990) and corrective feedback (Bouton 1994). Gick and Holyoak (1983) add that the presentation of explicit rules is most effective in instruction when each rule is supported by concrete examples. As Rose (2005) notes, there appear to be many teachability studies in which the term explicit is not prominent, yet the instruction used in these studies tends to be characterised as such in subsequent descriptions because it is in accordance with DeKeyser's (1995) requirement that metalinguistic generalisation be part of the instruction, whether it is provided by the teacher or learner themselves. Implicit instruction, on the other hand, generally involves presenting learners with prototypical uses of the target language in meaningful contexts with or without input enhancement. The underlying assumption here is that the models of language given to learners should help raise their awareness so that they will be able to induce the rules for appropriate L2 use on their own (Bardovi-Harlig1996; Rose 1994).

In Rose and Ng's (2001) study, a control group and two treatment groups were used to investigate the effectiveness of explicit and implicit approaches to teaching compliments and compliment responses. The distinguishing feature between treatment groups was that the inductive group (i.e., implicit) was exposed to video clips and additional questionnaires on the target feature in place of the teacher-fronted metapragmatic explanations provided to the deductive group (i.e., explicit). After six 30-minute lessons, data from self-assessments, DCTs and metapragmatic questionnaires demonstrated that both groups improved in pragmalinguistic proficiency; however, only the learners that received explicit instruction effectively developed sociopragmatic proficiency. Regarding the similar improvement in both groups' pragmalinguistic proficiencies, Rose (2005) later attributed this finding to the learners' advanced proficiency levels and the relatively simplistic nature of the pragmalinguistic target features involved. Employing a more complex research design, Takahashi (2001) investigated four input enhancement conditions for Japanese learners acquiring biclausal request forms in English: explicit instruction, form-comparison, form-search and meaning-focused conditions. In the explicit instruction condition, instruction was teacher-fronted and provided metapragmatic and explicit explanations of the target feature. In the form-comparison condition, learners compared their own request strategies with those provided by NESs. In the form-search condition, learners compared request strategies of Japanese learners of English with those provided by NESs. Lastly, in the meaning-focused condition, learners listened to, read, and answered comprehension questions based on various types of input. After four weekly 90-minute treatment sessions, the data produced by the DCTs and self-reports showed that members of the explicit group learnt all of the different request strategies more successfully than the other three groups. Further, results from the immediate written retrospective and follow-up questionnaires determined that learners who received explicit instruction noticed the target forms in the input, whereas members of the other three groups did not.

As with the instruction versus exposure studies described above, several studies offer encouragement for Schmidt's (1993) noticing hypothesis (see Section 2.9.1), and have shown that learners receiving explicit instruction often outperformed those who received implicit instruction. Wildner-Bassett's (1984) study, in which 18 intermediate to advanced EFL learners received intensive instruction over a five-day period, examined the effectiveness of Suggestopedia on gambits to express (dis)agreement in a business context. The results showed that the learners who received explicit instruction outperformed those who received instruction based on the principles of Suggestopedia in terms of the quality of the gambits and in their fluent deployment in role-play interactions. House (1996) examined the effectiveness of 14 weeks of explicit and implicit instruction on the pragmatic routines and discourse strategies used by 32 advanced EFL learners at a German university. Interpreting data collected from pre- and post-instruction interviews, audio-taped conversations and three pragmatic tests done as role-plays at equal intervals throughout the program, House (1996) found that the group that received explicit instruction outperformed the group that received implicit instruction in terms of using turn-internal gambits with interpersonal focus, managing discourse transitions, and topic initiation and change. Still, despite considerable progress, the explicit group continued to show negative transfer from German in terms of reliance on content-oriented and self-referenced gambits instead of interpersonal gambits, overuse of *yes* in various interactional slots surrounding turn-taking, and especially problems in producing well-aligned responding turns.

The studies described directly above suggest that learners with higher proficiencies would seem to benefit from instructional intervention. By using beginner-level learners in their studies, Wildner-Bassett (1994) and Tateyama et al. (1997) address the important question of whether pragmatics is teachable to beginners or whether there needs to be some threshold of linguistic L2 competence first. Both of these studies, which involved the teaching of languages other than English (i.e., German and Japanese respectively), demonstrated that pragmatic routines are teachable to beginning foreign language learners. Wildner-Bassett (1994) investigated the effects of one year of instruction on the use of conversational routines by 19 beginner-level learners of German as a foreign language, and found that learners improved considerably in their ability to use routine formulas after having received explicit instruction. Tateyama et al. (1997) examined how beginner-level learners of Japanese as a foreign language developed Japanese pragmatic proficiency under both explicit and implicit instructional treatment. Targeted pragmatic features were the three functions of the routine formula *sumimasen* as an attention-getter, an apology and an expression of thanks. In the group that received explicit instruction, learners discussed the different functions of *sumimasen*, received explicit teacher-fronted explanations, and watched short video clips of examples of the pragmatic routines. The group that received implicit instruction, on the other hand, watched the same video clips as the explicit group but did not engage any explicit metapragmatic activities. After only 25 minutes of instruction, the results of quantitative and qualitative instruments, including role-play, multiple-choice test and self-reports, demonstrated that learners who had been taught explicitly outperformed the ones who had been taught implicitly. Interestingly, a subsequent replication of this study by Tateyama (2001) which increased the instructional period to four sessions spread over eight weeks found no differences across groups. Tateyama (2001) attempted to explain these results by pointing out important data obtained from the participants' background questionnaires which revealed that the members of the implicit group had more out of class contact with native speakers of Japanese. This provides a clear reminder of the significance of collecting ample information regarding the participants' exposure to the target language outside the classroom because failure to control for sociolinguistic variables across groups directly threatens the internal validity of the study.

While the studies described above generally tend to lend support for explicit instruction, there are some exceptions. For instance, in a study designed to investigate the teachability of conversational implicature to 126 JEFL university students, Kubota (1995) compared explicit and implicit instructional techniques. The results indicated that while both experimental groups significantly improved their implicature comprehension from the pre-test to the post-test, the group that received implicit instruction outperformed the group that received explicit instruction. However, by the time of a delayed post-test one month later, these differences had disappeared. It is difficult to read too much into these findings due to the apparent validity issues involved in Kubota's (1995) measurement techniques, as well as the brevity of treatment. That is, participants in the experimental groups in this study received only a 20-minute session of treatment. Moreover, this treatment occurred in the midst of a two-hour class which was also used for administering the pre- and post-tests, and the use of items on the pre-test and post-test were included as part of the treatment. In a few similar studies which produced inconclusive results, Fukuya et al. (1998) and Fukuya and Clark (2001) appealed to the brevity of treatment as an explanation for the failure to find instructional effects in both explicit and implicit groups.

In a more recent study, Takimoto (2009) examined the relative effectiveness of three types of input-based approaches for teaching English polite request forms to 60 intermediate-level JEFL learners: structured input tasks with explicit information, problem-solving tasks and structured input tasks without explicit information. The three experimental groups received four 40-minute sessions of treatment; performances were compared with that of a control group on pre-tests, post-tests and delayed post-tests consisting of a DCT, a role-play test, a listening test and an acceptability judgement test. While the findings of the post-tests showed that all of the three treatment groups performed significantly better than the control group, the delayed post-tests revealed that the group that received the structured input tasks with explicit information did not maintain the positive effects of the instruction on the listening test component. Takimoto speculated that this may have to do with the way explicit knowledge is processed and retained. That is, while explicit knowledge can remain in participants' memories at the time of an immediate post-test, it is far less likely to be retained at the time of a delayed post-test without constant explicit and implicit reinforcement.

2.9.2.4 How Does the Research Inform Practice?

While the research has been partially inconclusive in some areas, the teachability studies have generally shown that pragmatic features of language are indeed teachable. Moreover, a comparison of instruction versus non-instruction studies seems to present a clear advantage for instruction. Hence, the area which remains unresolved involves the potential approaches to instruction: explicit vis-à-vis implicit. As described above, the results of several recent studies in pragmatics such as House (1996), Rose and Ng (2001), Takahashi (2001) and Tateyama et al. (1997) seem to be leaning towards an explicit approach. Even so, in several of the studies that showed the benefits of an explicit approach (House 1996; Liddicoat & Crozet 2001; Yoshimi 2001), participants continued to exhibit some lingering problems, particularly in terms of sociopragmatic competency (Takahashi 2001). These types of problems may be attributed to limitations in control of processing, and, thus, the effectiveness of an explicit or implicit approach may depend on the type of linguistic material being learnt and the characteristics of the individual learner (Ellis, Rod 2008: 893). For instance, Liddicoat and Crozet (2001) noted that the content features in their study are more amenable to conscious attention and manipulation than their features of form, which are unconscious and automatic, making the latter a seemingly more difficult instructional target. Clearly, there is a complex relationship between the learner proficiency level, length of instruction and difficulty of learning targets, which must be considered in assessing the effects of instruction on pragmatic learning.

Regarding proficiency level, studies conducted by Tateyama (2001), Tateyama et al. (1997) and Wildner-Bassett (1994) demonstrate that short pragmatic routines are teachable to beginner-level learners, indicating that such material can be learnt before learners develop analysed L2 knowledge. Likewise, for advanced-level learners, there have been documented cases in the literature which show advanced-level learners not successfully acquiring various L2 pragmatic skills without support through targeted instruction (Bardovi-Harlig 2001). The results for intermediate-level learners have been largely mixed. In some studies, intermediate-level learners clearly benefited from instruction (Billmyer 1990; Wildner-Bassett 1984), while in others, the pre-test and post-test outcomes differed on only a few of several measures (Rose & Ng 2001), only one of many treatments made a difference (Takahasahi 2001), or initial gains had disappeared at the time of the delayed post-test (Kubota 1995). Another area requiring further exploration concerns the level of difficulty in learning targets. Various researchers have commented on the relative ease or difficulty with which certain pragmalinguistic features are learnt; however, it has not yet been made clear exactly how complexity levels are determined. Generally, researchers have used beginner-level learners in studies involving pragmatic routines (Tateyama 2001; Wildner-Bassett 1994) and have used more advanced learners in interventions involving less salient pragmalinguistic features such as discourse markers (House & Kasper 1981) and conversational implicature (Bouton 1994).

Upon examining several studies in L2 academic writing, Ortega (2003) surmised that longitudinal studies that cover less than a year of instruction may yield almost negligible results in terms of language gain. Various researchers in studies focusing on spoken discourse have attributed their inconclusive findings to the brevity of the treatment, such as Fukuya & Clark (2001) whose study contained only 48 minutes of treatment. Although there appears to be a widespread belief that lengthier instructional periods will yield more positive outcomes, this is not always the case. For instance, in Tateyama's (2001) replication of the study conducted by Tateyama et al. (1997), she increased the instructional period from one 25-minute session to four sessions spread over eight weeks and found no significant improvements (see Section 2.9.2.3). Undoubtedly, more research in this area is needed; however, conducting this research is not without its share of challenges. First, the inevitable loss of control over experimental conditions in longer-duration treatments may be one of the reasons that many studies to date have involved shorter instructional periods. In addition, it is difficult to compare the lengths of instructional periods across studies due to a number of interrelated variables that also would appear to affect outcomes. That is, observed differences in shorter-term versus longer-term treatment effects can be attributed to the relationship among a number of study variables such as the interaction of length and intensity of instruction with target structures, the interaction between treatment and type of outcome measure, and other moderator variables.

Lastly, while this current study does not examine age as a variable, it is helpful to consider how this learner characteristic may influence the effects of instruction. With the exception of studies conducted by Ellis (1984) and Lyster (1994), most of the reported interventional studies to date have involved adult language learners. As Rose (2005) advocates, interventional classroom research for younger learners is urgently needed since these learners may require different instructional measures to support their learning of L2 pragmatics, and it is not clear whether younger learners in an L2 context even require organised instructional intervention (Schmidt 1993). Regarding the study of listener responses specifically, this current study, which involves young adults at approximately an intermediate level of English proficiency, would seem to have suitable conditions for effective instruction. Thonus (2007) draws on research into L1 acquisition to support her contention that instruction is best begun at intermediate levels, regardless of age. Since listener responses are thought to be acquired very late in both L1 and L2 development (as reported in Section 2.7.1), the optimum age for their acquisition tends to occur post adolescence. More important, as Hess and Johnston (1988) point out, L1 and L2 speakers are required to reach certain stages of readiness in order to acquire the backchannels of the target language. These stages can be understood by considering the underlying combination of abilities that these listener responses reflect, which include linguistic, communicative and social mechanisms. Linguistically, listeners/speakers require experience and practice with all varieties of forms in the target language to acquire backchannels. It seems necessary to first achieve sufficient automaticity in message comprehension to free attentional resources to reflect on one's own comprehension state. Communicatively, concerning the diverse discourse schemes against which a given message can be evaluated, it is imperative that interactants have the skills necessary to sustain topic development and turn-taking. Socially, listeners/speakers must have developed the notion of reciprocity and the ability to reflect on one's own thoughts and feelings, as well as those of their interlocutors. Finally, backchannel responses to adequate messages are essentially metacommunicative, and those providing listener responses must have the skills necessary to 'move beyond message comprehension to the evaluation of message adequacy, beyond expression of ideas to comments on the clarity of expression, and beyond reciprocity to facilitation' (Hess & Johnston 1988: 332).

2.9.2.5 The Teaching of Backchannels

While there have been several calls for research examining the teachability of backchannel behaviour, there have been few, if any, published studies to date that have informed pedagogy in this area. Although he does not provide specific details, Sasajima (2000) advocates an instructional approach that focuses on cultural differences in turn-taking. Ward and Tsukuhara (2000) and Ward et al. (2007) have experimented with CALL methods as a means of teaching the timing of backchannels in English and Arabic respectively. Examining the intricacies of backchannel behaviour from a phonetic perspective, Ward and Tsukuhara (2000) created an interactive instructional software application designed to help learners mimic the general backchannelling habits of NESs. The backchannel trainer they devised for EFL/ESL students was based on the following three observations: backchannel responses in English occur about half as frequently as in Japanese, the cue to backchannels in English is a region of low pitch lasting 110 milliseconds or more (similar to Japanese), back-channels in English are not given as swiftly after the cue as in Japanese (i.e., backchannels in English commonly are given approximately 700 milliseconds after the period of low pitch). Believing that a reflex behaviour could be developed by providing immediate rewards, backchannels given at appropriate timings were flagged with a blue rectangle on the screen, inappropriate ones with a green rectangle, and missed opportunities with a red rectangle. Efficacy of the treatment was determined by comparing learners' performance pre and post training, on the same dialogue. Although nine of the 13 learners showed some improvement in their unpublished pilot study, none of the results were statistically significant and, thus, further larger-scale studies would seem to be warranted before this type of instruction can be considered (Ward et al. 2007).

Although the concept of using CALL methods to teach backchannel behaviour is certainly an interesting one, a major issue involving this type of instruction is the seemingly narrow focus of teaching the appropriate timing of English backchannels without giving attention to other crucial elements of backchannel behaviour such as form, function and contextual variables. In fact, mastering the skills to produce backchannels at appropriate times, whether they understand what the primary speaker is saying or not, may actually reduce learners' overall L2 communicative ability. That is, as discussed in Sections 1.9.3 and 2.8.1, there exists evidence of IC being negatively affected by instances of JEFL speakers producing continuer or agreement type backchannels even when they disagree or did not understand what the primary speaker was saying. A backchannel trainer that focuses solely on timing would, in essence, be helping learners to fake understanding, which has already been identified as a potential problem area that warrants instructional attention to remedy. Nonetheless, there may be extraordinary circumstances where it is advantageous to keep a person talking, even when the listener does not understand some/all that their interlocutor is saying. For instance, considering that Ward et al.'s (2007) Arabic backchannel trainer research was sponsored by the US military, this would seem to be a useful tool for American military personnel with limited Arabic language skills whose goal was to collect and record intelligence from local people in the Middle East.

Although Schmidt's (1983) longitudinal study demonstrated that target-like L2 backchannel behaviour can be acquired implicitly (see Section 2.7.1), various researchers such as Brozyna (2007) and Thonus (2007) have advocated an explicit approach towards the teaching of English backchannels. Since backchannel behaviour tends to differ significantly across cultures (see Section 2.6), and many learners may not even be conscious of this skill, Thonus (2007) believes that the first step, as in many language learning tasks, is raising awareness of this area. Gilewicz and Thonus (2003) suggest that close vertical transcriptions of NS-NS and NNS-NNS conversations are an excellent means of raising awareness, as analysis of transcripts permits focused study of backchannel variations and functions. To this end, Thonus (2007: 145) recommends the following four pedagogical strategies:

- Contrasting listener responses across languages
- Creating opportunities for students to become conversational researchers
- Providing multiple examples of listener responses in varying contexts
- Coaching listener response use in fluency-focused exercises

Thonus (2007), recognising that the acquisition of listener responses is a process that takes time, points out some of the problems that learners may need to overcome. For instance, learners may progress through stages of underuse to overuse (i.e., flooding), and may also fixate on one backchannel form to the exclusion of others, in time broadening their repertoires. Further, the incorrect use of learners' repetition-as-backchannel is also common (Thonus 2002, 2007).

In her unpublished Master's dissertation, Brozyna (2007) was perhaps the first to empirically assess the teachability of backchannels in a study that also sought to investigate the effects of instruction on discourse markers functioning as hedges and fillers. Basing her study on the awareness raising methodology of Illustration-Interaction-Induction (Carter & McCarthy 1995, 2004) and on the 'noticing the gap' (Schmidt & Frota 1986: 311) potential for learning activation, Brozyna (2007) compared the performance of a control group (attending regular English classes four hours per week), with two treatment groups receiving an additional two hours of experimental instruction over 12 weeks. One of the experimental groups was given rich exposure to target features as well as explicit instruction in terms of metalinguistic information regarding backchannels and discourse markers, whereas the other experimental group received the same treatment with the addition of opportunities for intensive and focused practice. Brozyna (2007) reported a significant improvement in the group that received practice opportunities, but not in the group that did not receive practice opportunities or the control group.

Although practical constraints may have played a role, and it is clear that Brozyna (2007) intended this project to be a pilot study for future research, there are a number of issues associated with the design as well as findings of her study. First, the six participants in each of the treatment groups consisted of male and female high school students, whereas the four participants in the control group were all adult females, aged 24-26, in full-time employment. The fact that the sociolinguistic variables such as age, gender and socioeconomic status of the members of the control group were markedly different to those of members of the treatment groups makes the results difficult to compare between these groups. Second, the brevity of the method of analysis, which was limited to counting the number of backchannels in one two-minute extract pre instruction and another two-minute extract post instruction, would also seem to bring into question the validity of the results. There would also appear to be some validity concerns involving the fact that these two-minute extracts appear to have involved all six participants conversing at once. Besides not considering the ramifications of how group dynamics might influence backchannel behaviour (see Section 1.8.2), it is easy to imagine how one or two members of a particular group, with potentially divergent and/or altered backchannel behaviour, could skew the results of such a small-scale study. Moreover, concerning studies that measure the effectiveness of instruction on a particular language feature, it is difficult to give findings any credence without a delayed post-test to demonstrate whether the treatment had any sustained effects. Lastly, and perhaps most problematic, it appears that Brozyna (2007) has based her evaluation of the efficacy of the instruction solely on the quantity of interactional features used, thus neglecting important aspects of quality such as form and function. Regarding backchannel behaviour, the fact that the group that received full treatment increased the amount of backchannels they uttered from 3 to 12 (or from .012 to .04 / number of primary speaker words) after instruction seems to have provided the foundation for stating that these participants had improved. As discussed throughout this chapter, the relationship between backchannels and discourse is not a linear one. Rather, it is complex and multifaceted, with frequency comprising only one of the many interrelated and overlapping components in this skill-set.

Lastly, a recent study conducted by Sardegna and Molle (2010) investigated the learnability of English listener responses in five JEFL students after a two-hour video conference lesson. Although Sardegna and Molle (2010) claim that this pedagogic intervention had a positive short-term effect on the production of students' listener responses, it seems difficult to give too much weight to this finding based on the data presented, as well as the brevity of the treatment and analysis. It appears that these researchers are basing their conclusion solely on the limited amount of data presented in a short post-treatment conversational excerpt involving the five JEFLs and the teacher, which the researchers hand-picked. Further, besides the problems associated with analysing all the JEFLs together discussed above, the criteria for assessing listening behaviour again appears to be oversimplified as the lone determinant of success was the observation that the JEFLs used fewer backchannel forms common in Japanese and more that are common in English. Lastly, due to technological limitations associated with the video conferencing set-up, this study was forced to exclude nonverbal backchannels in its analysis.

2.9.3 Practical Reasons for this Study

The research presented in this chapter has shown that JEFL speakers' backchannelling behaviour differs from that of NESs in many respects, and these differences can sometimes lead to miscommunication, negative perceptions and stereotyping. Considering the importance of backchannels in intercultural conversations, it would seem that the next logical step in the research is to determine how this elusive aspect of sociolinguistic competence can be better acquired by JEFL learners. As O'Keeffe,

McCarthy and Carter (2007) have noted, backchannels appear to be employed systemically in language and would thus seem to warrant some principal treatment in syllabus design. In Japan, the teaching of listener responses has been largely neglected in EFL pedagogy (Capper 2000; Cutrone 2010; Okushi 1990), and only recently has there been any mention of listener responses in teacher education materials and learner textbooks globally. These references appear to be limited in number and recognise listener responses in varying degrees of detail. For instance, as Thonus (2007) observes, various descriptions of English such as the popular teacher's reference book titled *Learner English* (Swan & Smith 2001) includes lengthy explanations regarding basic linguistic categories such as phonology, grammar, etc. but fails to provide information about features of conversational interaction that might transfer into English such as backchannel behaviour. Similarly, Numrich's (2005) widely used student textbook *Tuning in: Listening and Speaking in the Real World* lacks attention to this important feature of conversation. While investigating a dialogic/fluency model of academic speaking in a laudable manner, Folse (2006) never mentions listener responses at all. Carter and McCarthy (1997), however, do include listener responses in their transcriptions and thus make some brief comments about them, while Eggins and Slade (1997) code *oh* and *really* as *registering responses* but do not transcribe other backchannels cues. According to Thonus (2007), NESs, including teachers, may themselves often fail to provide adequate models for appropriate use of listener responses. Lindemann (2006), for instance, cited withholding acknowledgement as one method that NESs use to reject the communicative burden. Cutrone (2005), conversely, found evidence that some of the NESs in his study felt the need to provide more backchannel cues than they normally would because they wanted to reassure their Japanese interlocutor and encourage them to speak more. Thonus (2005, 2007) found evidence of teachers accommodating to learners' backchannel behaviour, which she emphasised would further increase the likelihood of students failing to learn this feature of language.

2.9.4 Assessing Backchannel Behaviour

The fact that backchannel behaviour is an especially difficult skill-set to measure may be one of the main reasons why it has been rarely taught and studied (Thonus 2007). While some research has been done examining specific features of backchannel behaviour in various cultures, no researcher to date has been able to provide a coherent description of the backchannel behaviour of a group with potential application in the language classroom. Based on descriptions of NESs' backchannel behaviour, as well as on the documented problems some JEFLs have experienced in this area, this section proposes the following instructional goals for JEFLs: (1) approximating the observed backchannel behaviour of NESs, (2) increasing WTC, (3) developing conversational micro-skills and (4) increasing ICC.

2.9.4.1 Approximating the Observed Backchannel Behaviour of NESs

Without the focus on backchannel behaviour per se, there has been a great deal of discussion in recent times regarding the creation of a common standard of English as an International Language (EIL), which most often proposes either the promotion of a prestigious standard (e.g. British or American Standard), or the creation of a common core for everyone to access and acquire. Although promoting a current variety of English would seem to be the most convenient option, it has been met with various levels of resistance as outlined in Caine's (2008) article. One of the main arguments is that, since the spread of English as the global lingua franca has created a world in which the number of non-native speakers greatly exceeds that of native-speakers, a modern model of English used in ELT should reflect the way English is currently used around the world (Widdowson 1994, 1997). Thus, the second option, establishing a common core, has attracted some research attention, as Seidlhofer (2001, 2003, 2004) has worked towards providing modern descriptions of ELF (English as Lingua Franca) and Jenkins (1998, 1999, 2000, 2003) has attempted to describe the phonetics of a core language. However, as research in this area as a whole is still in its infancy, a great deal more time and investigation will be required in order to provide a clear and comprehensive description for the world to consider adopting, especially when it comes to the socio-pragmatic features of language such as backchannels (Ellis 1991; Yamaguchi 2002). Presently, there appears to be no general consensus as to exactly what EIL entails, with practitioners commonly describing EIL, rather vaguely, as a form of English that represents the many varieties that NESs use around the world (Torghabeh 2007).

As the researcher described in an earlier paper (Cutrone 2010), a model of backchannel behaviour that can be used in the Japanese EFL classroom at the present time is that of American English. This is in no way intended to promote American hegemony and/or to discount the importance of learning other varieties of English for use in the international community. American English discourse models are considered suitable in this present study because American English is recognised as a prestigious standard of English, is learnt in many parts of the word, and is currently a normative variety of English studied in Japan (Suzuki 2010). Moreover, in the current global economy, many JEFLs will need to communicate with NESs and/or with NNSs who have adopted NES norms of discourse. Thus, the value of this study at the present time is that it examines the teachability of discourse markers such as backchannels in a context where a particular target interlocutor audience is envisaged. Furthermore, in practical terms, it also helps that there is a substantial amount of literature describing backchannel behaviour in American English, which does not seem to exist for other varieties of English. With this in mind, it is important to point out that the instructional goals for EFL backchannel behaviour in this study will have more to do with the recognised tendencies and idiosyncracies of Japanese learners (see Section 2.6) than following the norms of any one NES variety. Thus, irrespective of which English model were used, many of the general goals for JEFLs would remain the same, such as sending minimal backchannels less frequently (especially while one's interlocutor is speaking), with greater variability (but at context-appropriate moments), while asking questions and taking the primary speakership in the conversation more often (see Section 2.9.4.2), and initiating conversational repair strategies when they do not understand and/or disagree rather than feign understanding and agreement (see Section 2.9.4.3).

Before a description of backchannel norms in English can be presented, a few important points need to be made. First, it is necessary to mention again that, while identifying the general backchannel practices of a target group or culture may be beneficial for instructional purposes, there can exist a great deal of individual differences in backchannel behaviour within the culture or group. Second, the descriptions of American English backchannel behaviour in the literature provide practiioners with certain benchmarks for assessing the quantifiable aspects of backchannel behaviour; however, it is important to keep in mind that, due to the complex nature of this skill-set, there are various facets of backchannel behaviour below that cannot always be quantified in precise terms. Taking this into account, the targets in the following list provide general goals for JEFLs to strive for.

Overall Frequency

As discussed in Section 2.6.1, various studies have reported Japanese speakers of English uttering backchannels significantly more than American NESs. A target pace for sending backchannels according to the American model is approximately every 30-40 words. This is based on the results of the following studies. In intracultural dyadic conversations involving American NESs, White (1989) found that the participants sent backchannels every 37 words, and Maynard (1997) found that the participants provide a similar response every 19.25 seconds. While it is useful to have a target based on NES discourse, it is highly unlikely that interactants involved in NS-NNS intercultural conversations will approach such a high number of words between backchannels as NSs have been shown to adjust their conversational behaviour to facilitate communication with NNSs (Cutrone 2005).

Variability

JEFLs are required to develop a more diverse repertoire of backchannels to use in their intercultural encounters in English (see Section 2.6.2). While previous studies have not provided specific numerical targets in this regard, positive outcomes, as discussed in Section 2.4, are assoiated with increasing the number of extended backchannels and decreasing the number of minimal backchannels the JEFLs produce. The former objective operates in tandem with increasing WTC, which is discussed in Section 2.9.4.2.

Discourse Contexts

As Section 2.6.3 reported, grammatical completion points and pauses (especially occurring simultaneously) have been identified as primary discourse contexts favouring backchannels in American English. This is another area in which setting a numerical target may be difficult, as several other discourse contexts including self-adaptors and gesticulation (Duncan & Fiske 1977), gaze (Kendon 1977) and prosodic features (Ward 2000) have also been suggested in the research. Hence, backchannels that are sent in discourse contexts other than the primary ones mentioned above are not necessarily considered incorrect and their acceptability is largely dependent on the context of the conversation and the function that the non-primary speaker desires to convey. Moreover, since JEFL speakers' backchannels have been shown to occur much more frequently and their discourse contexts tend to vary considerably, it is likely that many of the backchannels they send, even without any training, will occur at the discourse contexts that are prevalent in American English.

Simultaneous Talk

Maynard (1997) and Hayashi (1988) have noted that Japanese tend to frequently send backchannels that co-occur with the primary speaker's speech creating simultaneous talk, while Americans do not. Although

Maynard (1997) provided examples of this type of simultaneous talk in the Japanese data, she did not report the proportion of backchannels as simultaneous talk. Hayashi (1988), on the other hand, showed that the Japanese participants talked simultaneously more than twice as frequently as the Americans, every 72.4 seconds as compared to every 182.0 seconds; however, her analysis included any talk which continued to be simultaneous for more than one second and was, thus, not limited to backchannels. For this reason, it is difficult to settle on any specific target in terms of frequency. Nonetheless, while simultaneous talk only occurring every 182 seconds seems an ambitious goal in intercultural dyadic conversations, this does at least provide an initial direction to strive for regarding this type of behaviour. Another potential consideration for success in this area involves examining the improvements of the JEFLs' rate of simultaneous talk from a ratio of more than 2:1 with the primary speaker, to a ratio closer to 1:1.

Form and Function

Learning about the functions of backchannels of the target group, along with forms that correspond to each function, may have the greatest impact towards helping JEFLs develop their ICC towards the target group norms. With this in mind, it is important to understand that, like many of the features of backchannel behaviour outlined above, the backchannel forms non-primary speakers choose to convey a particular function are highly dependent on speakers' individual personalities and conversational intentions, as well as the specific context of the conversation. Success in this area will be extremely difficult to measure as there exists no previous research to use as a barometer regarding backchannel functions, and as various researchers have noted (O'Keeffe, McCarthy & Carter 2007; Maynard 1997), the overlap between forms and functions is considerable (i.e., one form may serve more than one function, and one function may be served by more than one form). Thus, in this regard, one can see that comparisons of raw data can sometimes be misleading. While there clearly exists some variation in how researchers choose to identify their categories regarding the functions of backchannels, Cutrone's (2010) overview offers an inventory of backchannel forms according to the functional categories presented in Section 2.5. While this inventory of forms corresponding to specific functions is not meant to be exhaustive nor mutually exclusive, it does provide ELT practitioners with a place to begin. Relative to the study described in this book specifically, the main instructional objective is to develop the JEFLs' ability to convey their feelings with appropriate backchannel forms, and for these intentions to be recognised accordingly by their interlocutors.

2.9.4.2 Increasing WTC

As Section 1.9.1 reported, Japanese reticence and minimal responses have been cited by NESs as reasons negatively affecting IC. Therefore, it appears that size and variation do indeed matter when it comes to producing backchannel forms. Consistent with the ideas incorporated in Stubbe's (1998) feedback continuum scale (see Section 2.4), McCarthy (2003) agrees that it is socially advantageous to include more of the lengthier backchannel forms, possessing one or more content words rather than a single discourse marker, as the former tend to have a positive influence on attitudes and perceptions. For instance, as Cutrone's (2005) research demonstrated, people who respond with lexical items such as *How true* or *I agree*, rather than non-word vocalisations such as *mm* or *unn* to indicate agreement, may be seen in a more positive light by the primary speaker as they would appear to be putting a greater effort into the conversation. Regarding the latter, such minimal responses could undermine interpersonal relationships as they may be perceived as an unwillingness to communicate. Active listenership, as Bjørge (2009) calls the ability to give consistent and varied verbal and nonverbal feedback, including the use of verbal signals like *oh yes* and nonverbal strategies like smiling, making intensive eye contact and nodding, in addition to asking questions and summarising, is not only a useful trait in casual conversations but can also be a key aspect of the negotiation process involved in ELF (English as Lingua Franca) business interactions. According to Ulijn and Strother (1995), active listening skills are among the greatest attributes distinguishing between skilled and average negotiators in these interactions. Besides making explicit that one is paying attention and contributing towards a common understanding of the topics being debated, active listening contributes to rapport management (Spencer-Oatey 2000; Planken 2005), and is an aspect exhibiting interlocutors' pragmatic competence (House 2002).

While providing learners with the ability to use a diverse repertoire of English backchannels in various situations would certainly seem to be a useful instructional goal to start, it is also imperative that JEFL speakers exhibit more of a willingness to communicate (WTC) in L2 English. As Section 1.5 discussed in great detail, increasing WTC in language learners has many benefits. Besides serving the all-important functions of increasing confidence, reducing anxiety and facilitating future language development in the learner, increasing WTC also increases the amount learners actually speak in conversations, which, in turn, positively influences the perceptions their interlocutors have of them and their communicative abilities in any conversation. With this in mind, it is important to understand that, from a pedagogical perspective, teaching backchannel behaviour and teaching learners how to speak more (i.e., increasing WTC) are not isolated endeavours. As Section 2.5.1 indicated, there is an inextricable link between producing a backchannel and producing a speaking turn. As Schegloff (1982) observed, when non-primary speakers provide backchannels, they are essentially forsaking the opportunity to take a primary speaking turn. This is evidenced by the fact that TRPs (i.e., moments in the conversation at which an exchange of turn is appropriate) in Sacks, Schegloff and Jefferson's (1974) turn-taking system (see Section 2.3 above), are often found in similar discourse contexts as backchannels, which suggests a strong link between the two that would seem to have pedagogical implications. This was evident in Cutrone's (2005) study as several of the JEFL participants admitted that they often provide backchannels as a way to avoid taking primary speakership, yet still contribute to the conversation.

Thus, from a pedagogical perspective, it may be necessary to examine backchannel behaviour in tandem with other aspects of listener behaviour such as the ability to take over primary speakership of the conversation and/or ask follow-up questions, etc. It is for this reason that the more comprehensive term, listener response, is used to encompass all forms of listener utterances including backchannels, full turn utterances and questions, and conversational repair strategies (see Section 2.2). As the next subsection describes in greater detail, one of the ways to increase WTC among learners is to help them develop conversation management techniques. Other strategies that have been suggested to engender WTC in learners in the Japanese context include the following: enabling learners' interest in foreign affairs and foreign cultures to grow, removing learners' anxiety and building their confidence in using the L2, building on learners' knowledge, having learners perform tasks in pairs or small groups before progressing to large-group settings, using authentic materials in the classroom, and using a wide array of activities and tasks designed to stimulate learners (Yashima 2002).

2.9.4.3 Developing Conversational Micro-skills

As increasing WTC has been identified as an instructional objective, learners are required to develop their discourse and strategic competence to reach this goal (see Section 1.8.2). That is, learners need to develop the cohesive devices necessary to help keep the conversation flowing (discourse competence) and the repair strategies to avoid communication breakdown (strategic competence). While the former relates directly to strategies that can help JEFLs maintain more active involvement in conversations, the latter deals specifically with the issue of sending continuer backchannels when one does not understand or disagrees with what the interlocutor is saying. Following the definitions of conversational competence provided by Iwai (2007) and Riggenbach (1998) as discussed in Section 1.8.2, the following micro-skills would seem to be a logical place for teachers to focus in this area of instruction: appropriate usage of discourse markers and listener responses, evaluative comments, return questions, follow-up questions, new topic initiation, expansion techniques, the ability to ensure comprehension on the part of the listener, and the ability to initiate repair when there is a potential breakdown. These skills are consistent with what some interlocutors might hope to encounter in an English conversation, as the importance of making small talk, taking the initiative to speak, and elaboration have been documented by several sources (Cutrone 2002, 2005; McCarthy 2002, 2003; McCroskey 1992; Ross 1998; Sato 2008; Stubbe 1998; Yashima 2002). According to Widdowson (1989: 135), a large part of communicative competence is simply a matter of knowing how to employ such conventionalised expressions, or as he terms them, 'partially preassembled patterns' and 'formulaic frameworks'. These expressions and formulae comprising conversational micro-skills would seem to lend themselves ideally to explicit teaching, and can serve as useful language input for conversation classes (Dörnyei & Thurrell 1992, 1994).

2.9.4.4 Increasing ICC

The final aim regarding the teaching of backchannel behaviour is to increase ICC. Despite developments in the theoretical foundation of ICC, there currently does not exist any type of standard measurement to assess ICC. Various scholarly efforts have been attempted, such as the Intercultural Development Inventory by Hammer, Bennett and Wiseman (2003), the Cross-Cultural Adaptability Inventory by Kelley and Myers (1999), the Overseas Assignment Inventory by Tucker (1999), the Multicultural Awareness-Knowledge-Skills Survey by D'Andrea, Daniels and Heck (1991), and the Culture General Assimilator by Cushner and Brislin (1996), but these inventories have failed to grasp ICC comprehensively, theoretically and/or psychometrically. Reviewing

Spitzberg's (2000) model of ICC (see Section 1.9.2), components such as knowledge, skills, motivation, appropriateness and effectiveness are theorised to be the main factors determining successful ICC. Relating these components to the teaching of backchannel behaviour in JEFL/ESL contexts, learners are required to possess the following proficiencies in order to produce adequate and effective backchannel behaviour in English: the knowledge regarding how backchannels are employed in English, the skills to apply this knowledge in various situations and the motivation to use these skills. The terms appropriate and effective may not be entirely clear in this context, and it is, thus, useful to revisit Spitzberg's (2000) expectancy principle to help explain this. This principle is based on the dimensions of expectancy compliance and violation in conversations. According to Spitzberg (2000), the optimal conditions for successful ICC are provided when the knowledge, skills and motivation are aligned with meeting the other person's expectations regarding appropriateness and effectiveness. Accordingly, any measurement striving to assess appropriate and effective backchannel behaviour (as well as overall communicative behaviour) in IC must take into account the perceptions of the cross-cultural interlocutor. Hence, to produce appropriate and effective backchannels, JEFL/ESL learners are required to exhibit backchannel behaviour according to the norms and expectations of those belonging to the target culture. This would seem to overlap with the general objective stated in Section 2.9.4.1, which is to emulate the observed backchannel behaviour of the target culture. A measurement instrument that has been useful over the years in assessing interlocutors' conversational satisfaction and perceptions of one another after conversing is Hecht's (1978) Interpersonal Communication Satisfaction Inventory. This questionnaire has been used extensively to assess perceptions of listening behaviour specifically (Cutrone 2005; Saito 1994; White 1989), as well as other facets of interpersonal communication (High & Caplan 2009; Punyanunt-Carter 2008; Johnstone, Pecchioni & Edwards 2000).

2.10 Research Questions and Hypotheses

Research into the area of backchannel behaviour, and particularly its effect on IC, is in its infancy and, thus, many questions remain. Most of the research to date has focused on detailing the patterns of the backchannel output of various groups in terms of frequency, discourse contexts favouring backchannels, variability and backchannels creating simultaneous speech. Research Question (RQ) 1 thus aims to corroborate the findings of previous studies involving Japanese speakers of English and NESs such as the American participants in this study. Considering an area of backchannel behaviour only previously touched upon by White (1989) and subsequently re-examined in greater depth by Cutrone (2005), RQ 2 seeks to examine the extent to which differences in backchannel conventions across cultures affect IC. If the results confirm that backchannels are used considerably differently across cultures, and these differences are found to have a negative effect on IC, then Cutrone's (2005) conclusion that backchannels should be given a higher priority in EFL teaching in Japan will be justified.

In light of the research to date, the following RQs and Hypotheses (Hs) have been formulated (N.B. To provide a more convenient method for readers to refer to the RQs, a condensed version of the six RQs has been provided on the final page of this book, i.e., Appendix S).

RQ 1: How do participants from each culture, Japanese and American, use backchannels differently in terms of frequency, variability, use in different discourse contexts, and use during their interlocutor's primary speaking turn at talk (i.e., creating simultaneous speech)?

In light of previous findings (see Section 2.6), the following Hypotheses are formulated.

H 1: In terms of frequency of use, the JEFL group will send noticeably more backchannels than the NESs.

H 2: In terms of variability of use, the NESs will exhibit greater variability in the types of backchannels they employ than the JEFL group. More specifically, the NESs will use noticeably more content words and extended responses, while the JEFLs will use noticeably more minimal responses and non-word vocalisations.

H 3: Regarding discourse contexts favouring backchannels, the NESs will send noticeably more backchannels at final clause boundaries, and particularly those which are accompanied by a pause, whereas the JEFL participants' backchannels will vary considerably.

H 4: In terms of simultaneous speech, the JEFL group will send noticeably more backchannels while their interlocutor is taking a primary speaking turn than the NESs.

RQ 2: Will the differences in backchannel behaviour across cultures affect communication and/or lead to miscommunication, and if so, how will this occur?

Regarding RQ 2, Hypotheses 5 and 6 have been formulated.

H 5: The backchannel conventions which are not shared between the two cultures will contribute to negative perceptions and stereotyping.

H 6: The backchannel conventions that are not shared between the two cultures will cause misunderstandings and/or miscommunication.

Reporting on the instructional approaches relative to the study described in this book, Section 2.9 highlights some of the research gaps in this area. While there is evidence to suggest that pedagogical intervention can facilitate some elements of pragmatic development, little is known about how learners acquire L2 listener responses over time, as well as what effect different types of instruction might have on development in this area. Relative to the questions raised in Section 2.9.2, RQ 3 seeks to answer the more general question of whether pedagogical intervention addressing discourse features of language can have a positive effect, while RQ 4, more specifically, seeks to shed light on the Explicit-Implicit debate where listener responses are concerned.

RQ 3: Will instructional treatment help facilitate the JEFL learners' conversational skills according to the backchannel assessment criteria outlined in Section 2.9?

RQ 4: If so, will explicit treatments be more effective than implicit ones (a) in the short term and (b) in the long term?

Furthermore, little is known about the characteristics belonging to successful or unsuccessful learners in terms of producing listener responses. As discussed in Section 1.5, the effects of WTC and extraversion may influence this process and are worthy of investigation. Additionally, concerning the four assessment criteria for backchannels (see Section 2.9.4), it is not known if success or failure in one area will correlate to success or failure in others. To fill these gaps, RQ 5 attempts to bring to light in more detail some of the features associated with different levels of performance and development concerning listener responses.

RQ 5: What are some of the common characteristics pertaining to the JEFL learners that exhibited competent backchannel behaviour and/or improvement in this area compared to those that did not?

Lastly, like RQ 5, the objective of RQ 6 is also to contribute to the profile of successful and nonsuccesful learners, and their development, in terms of listener responses. To this end, RQ 6 examines L2 proficiency as a moderator variable. Various researchers such as Thonus (2007) have speculated that instruction on using listener responses is best begun at intermediate levels; however, to date, this hypothesis has not been tested. Further, there may be a general assumption of a relationship between L2 proficiency and proficiency in producing adequate listener responses that requires empirical validation. To shed light on these issues, RQ 6 has been formulated.

RQ 6: Do student L2 proficiency levels, according to the TOEIC, correlate to their levels and gains in listening behaviour?

2.11 Conclusion

In summary, the review of the literature in this chapter has provided an in-depth analysis of backchannel behaviour in various contexts. In conclusion, a number of studies have showed that JEFL/ESL speakers' backchannelling behaviour differs to that of NESs in many respects, and these differences have, at times, contributed to miscommunication and negative perceptions across cultures. In attempting to bridge the gap between research and practice, the objectives of this study, as linked to RQs 1-6, are as follows: (RQ 1) first, to provide a comprehensive description of how the Japanese and American participants in this study employed backchannels across cultures and to gain insights into potential culture-specific ideologies associated with backchannel use, (RQ 2) second, to examine how differences in listening behaviour across cultures may affect IC, (RQ 3) third, to determine if pragmatic targets such as backchannels, which are thought to be non-salient, are even teachable at all, (RQ 4) fourth, to measure how different types of instruction, explicit and implicit, may influence backchannelling behaviour in the JEFL context, (RQ 5) fifth, to attempt to piece together a profile of successful versus non-successful learners where listenership is concerned, and (RQ 6) sixth, to determine the extent to which levels and gains in the area of listening behaviour are associated with overall L2 proficiency levels.

Having a better understanding of how backchannels operate in conversations, why JEFL/ESLs employ backchannels the way they do, and what teaching practices might work, ELT practitioners would be in a much better position to design lessons tailoring to the specific needs of their learners.

Looking ahead to the remainder of this book, a brief outline of the following chapters is given as follows. The next chapter describes the methodology used in this study which includes the demographics of the sample used, the methods of administering the study, and how the data were gathered and analysed. Chapter 4 is divided into two parts addressing the cross-sectional aspects of this study (i.e., comparing the backchannel behaviour of the American NES conversational participants with the JEFL participants prior to treatment). Part one reports the results shown by the data collected, while Part two provides a discussion of these findings. Chapter 5 comprises two parts dealing with the longitudinal aspects of this study (i.e., comparing the backchannel behaviour of the control group and two experimental groups pre and post treatment). Part one presents the results over time, whereas Part two discusses the implications of these findings as they pertain to EFL pedagogy in Japan. Finally, Chapter 6 concludes this study. This will include a review of the study as a whole, an identification of its limitations, implications of the study's findings and recommendations for future research.

Chapter Three

The Methodology of this Study

3.1 Introduction

As the research questions were complex and multifaceted in nature, various methodological frameworks were considered in conducting this study. Ultimately, it was decided that the most valid and reliable approach in collecting data involved a combination of the three methods being considered: observations, questionnaires and interviews. It was thought that using methods of triangulation would not only serve to strengthen the reliability and validity of the data but also provide for a broader view with multiple perspectives of the researched topic. To this end, this chapter aims to provide a description of the methodology adopted in this study. Methods are presented in terms of participant selection, the procedural steps involved in carrying out the experiment, data collection, the handling of spoken data in the transcriptions, and the data analysis techniques involved in this study.

3.2 Participants

This study involved a total of 46 participants, of whom 30 were JEFL learners and 16 were American NESs. Participating of their free will and understanding the nature of the study, all participants read and signed a Participation Consent Form (see Appendix B) and were given explicit instructions (i.e., verbal and written) regarding this study and their role in it (see written instructions in Appendix C). All forms were typed in English with Japanese translations provided to the native Japanese speakers in this study to ensure these participants had a full understanding of the contents in each form. To protect participants' privacy, pseudonyms are used when referring to participants in this study. For the sake of mnemonicity, Japanese names were given to the Japanese participants and English names were given to the American participants. The following subsections will describe how the participants in each group were selected.

3.2.1 Japanese EFL learners

This study involved 30 Japanese participants, who resided in Nagasaki Prefecture and were second and third year EFL students in the Department of Multi-Cultural Exchange at the University of Nagasaki (UoN). 20 of these participants comprised the students enrolled in an EFL course called Oral Communication 3 (from October of 2007 until February of 2008), while the other ten participants were not enrolled in this course. As the Oral Communication 3 course was taught by the researcher and the other ten participants were in various other classes taught by the researcher within the department, the 30 JEFL learners in this study constituted an opportunistic sample. Considering the potential participants that were available to the researcher, the following conditions were sought:

(a) The Japanese participants and their parents were required to have been born in Japan. Also, it was required that these participants have only limited experiences abroad. This was judged to be less than 100 days throughout the course of their lives, and never for a period of more than 20 days at one time.
(b) Although it was understood that the JEFLs participating in this study, as students in the Department of Multi-Cultural Exchange at the UoN, would likely be attending other EFL classes at the time of this study, it was required that no participant in this study take part in a class taught by a NES and/or involving a focus on spoken discourse.
(c) It was desired that the JEFL learners' proficiency levels be similar, and beyond a beginner proficiency level, i.e., between 500-650 on the TOEIC test and/or at an intermediate-level on the ACTFL (American Council on the Teaching of Foreign Languages) Guidelines for Speaking (Breiner-Sanders et al. 2000).
(d) An equal, or at least similar, number of male and female participants were preferred.

While these conditions were met for the most part, there were some noteworthy exceptions. First, concerning (a), one of the JEFL participants has a Japanese mother and an American father. As the father's involvement in the student's life was limited to early infancy, and since the learner's L2 English ability does not appear to have been affected by this (i.e., at an approximate low- to mid-intermediate level at the time of this study), this participant was allowed to remain in the study. Second, regarding (b), nine students were enrolled in English writing classes, and three others were enrolled in CALL courses, which also focused on writing. As the other aforementioned courses did not involve spoken discourse and were not taught by NESs, it seems reasonable to assume that the instruction provided in these courses did not greatly influence acquisition of listener responses. Nonetheless, these students were divided equally across the three groups in this study. Third, concerning (c), there was some variation regarding learners' proficiency levels. 17 of the participants were within the desired 500-650 TOEIC range, ten participants ranged from 350-499 and three participants ranged from 651-700. While such discrepancies in TOEIC scores were not considered optimal initially, they do allow for the researcher to investigate how higher and lower proficiencies affect levels and gains in listening behaviour. Lastly, due to the great gender imbalance that exists within the department, the participants in this study consisted of 24 females and six males.

3.2.2 Native English Speakers

This study involved 16 American NESs, who served in one of two capacities: interlocutor or observer. Six of the NESs acted as interlocutors for the JEFL learners in intercultural dyadic conversations, while ten NESs participated by subsequently observing the video-recorded conversations and then assessing the JEFLs' listening behaviour in these conversations. The selection criteria for each group were somewhat different. First, in an attempt to control for sociolinguistic variables such as age, gender and social status in the intercultural conversations used in this study, NESs that had similar characteristics as their Japanese counterparts were sought. Hence, with this in mind, the six NES interlocutors were recruited from a pool of exchange students that visit universities in Nagasaki Prefecture every year. These NES participants were compensated monetarily for their time. It was required that the NES interlocutors all belong to the same speech community. The researcher used American participants for two simple reasons. First, compared with other national varieties of English, a great deal of literature describing American backchannel behaviour exists, which provides for an established model to use in the classroom. Second, in terms of practicality, Americans were the most accessible group to the researcher in Nagasaki Prefecture at the time of the study. To ensure that participants were native speakers of American English with minimal foreign culture experience, this study included only those whose parents were born in the United States. In addition, NES interlocutors were chosen who had lived in Japan for less than a year prior to the study, in order to reduce the possibility of acculturation to Japanese norms of backchannel behaviour (LoCastro 1987; White 1989). A final variable that the researcher considered is the extent to which the participants in each intercultural dyad knew each other. On one hand, it would be beneficial if participants were familiar with each other because it would promote the casual conversational register this study was seeking to observe. On the other hand, unfamiliarity between the participants in each dyad would ensure that perceptions would not be influenced by each interactant's prior knowledge of the other's personality traits. Taking both arguments into account, this study allowed for some participant contact prior to the study but made every effort to pair dyads together that were less familiar with each other (see Section 3.4.1 for conversation details).

Regarding the second group of NESs, the observers, participants were recruited from a pool of people acquainted with the researcher, who could fulfil the following criteria. Unlike the previously described group of NES interlocutors, it was required that the NES observers reside in an English speaking country at the time of the study and have had limited contact and exposure with native Japanese people and their language. Although initially 14 acquaintances volunteered to participate and were subsequently sent the materials to analyse, four of the 14 did not return their completed questionnaires and were, thus, eliminated from this study. The function of the NES observers, comprised of ten American nationals, was to observe and assess the JEFLs' listening behaviour in the video-recorded conversations. These participants ranged in age from 22-48 and were from various parts of the United States, which included four participants from Massachusetts, two from New York, two from California, one from Tennessee and one from Minnesota.

3.3 Procedures

Describing the procedures of this study, this section examines the steps undertaken to carry out this project.

Step 1: Pre-test

All of the JEFLs in this study received identical pre-tests occurring within three days of each other and consisting of three types of analyses: observations of them conversing with a NES (i.e. by means of videotaped data), a conversational satisfaction questionnaire filled out by both them and their NES interlocutor, and retrospective interviews with both them and their NES interlocutors regarding their intercultural conversations (Section 3.4 details these methods).

Step 2: Group formation

The 30 JEFL participants in this study were divided into three groups of ten. These groups comprised the two experimental groups (Groups A and B) and one control group (Group Z). The main objective in grouping the participants in this study was to attempt to create comparable and thus equally balanced groups in terms of gender, proficiency, WTC, personality and age. To determine English proficiency levels, this study used learners' TOEIC scores. The TOEIC was chosen as the primary proficiency measure in this study for two reasons: (1) it is an internationally recognised test for measuring English language proficiency, and (2) it has been adopted as the basis by which the EFL students at the UoN in this study are placed in their classes; thus, learners' TOEIC scores were easily accessible to the researcher. Additionally, as a supplemental tool used to describe learners' oral functional competencies specifically, this study refers to the ACTFL Guidelines for Speaking (Breiner-Sanders et al. 2000). To determine JEFL learners' WTC in interpersonal conversations in English, the researcher administered McCroskey's (1992) widely used WTC scale (see Section 3.6.2 for details).

While WTC is thought to be influenced by personality dimensions (see Section 1.5.2), the researcher decided to also include a personality measurement scale in this study as a means of further ensuring the groups were balanced. The most comprehensive instrument to measure personality is Costa and McCrae's (1992) 240-item NEO Personality Inventory, Revised (NEO-PI-R), which permits the in-depth measurement of five global personality dimensions (known as the Big-Five): Extraversion, Agreeableness, Conscientiousness, Emotional stability and Openness to new experiences. As personality dimensions were not among the major foci of this study, the 240-item NEO-PI-R was found to be too lengthy and time-consuming. Hence, faced with the choice of using an extremely brief measure of the Big-Five personality dimensions or using no measure at all, the researcher administered Gosling, Rentfrow and Swann's (2003) Ten Item Personality Inventory (TIPI, see Appendix D). Although this brief measure of the Big-Five personality dimensions may seem to be inferior to the standard of multi-item instruments, the TIPI, in fact, has been shown to reach adequate levels in terms of the following: '(a) convergence with widely used Big-Five measures in self, observer and peer reports, (b) test–retest reliability, (c) patterns of predicted external correlates and (d) convergence between self and observer ratings' (Gosling, Rentfrow & Swann 2003: 504). Further, recent studies comparing a revised version of the TIPI with the larger inventories mentioned above, supported the reliability and validity of the TIPI in the Japanese context (Oshio, Abe & Cutrone 2011, 2012). Nonetheless, overall personality scores, comprised of the combined sum of the scores of the five personality domains, would seem to do little to inform this study as higher scores on one of the five variables would negate lower scores on other variables. Thus, for the purposes of this study, it seemed practical to prioritise and choose only the personality dimension(s) that would seem most likely to affect backchannels. In the case of this study, the choice to use the Extraversion category was made for two reasons. First, the bipolar factor, Extraversion vis-à-vis Introversion, summarises several specific facets (e.g., Sociability) and subsumes a large number of even more specific traits (e.g., talkative, outgoing) that would appear to greatly influence backchannel behaviour as well as the amount one speaks in a conversation. Further, the Extraversion personality domain was consistently found to be the most reliable category in the TIPI in terms of correlating to the 240-item NEO-PI-R, while the ones that were demonstrated to correlate the least were the Agreeableness and Openness to new experiences categories. Lastly, considering the potential for divergence in self- and observer- ratings, the researcher decided to also have an objective observer, who was quite familiar with the learners, complete the TIPI regarding the learners' personality. The JEFL learners' seminar teacher filled this role. Final scores were determined by averaging the learners' self-ratings with those of their seminar teacher. Discrepancies between the two sets of scores were minimal.

Tables 3-1, 3-2 and 3-3 illustrate the characteristics of each group showing that each group was comprised of eight females and two males, with six second-year students and four third-year students (gender also divided evenly in this subcategory as second and third year students were comprised of 1 male and 4 females in each group). The average TOEIC score was 529 for Group A, 525 for Group B and 566 for Group Z (raw scores relating to all 10 items of the TIPI are provided for each group in Appendices D1, D2 and D3). Regarding the WTC measurement, the average score was 48.4 for Group A, 50.4 for Group B and 56.2 for Group Z. Lastly, the average score of the Extraversion/Introversion component of the personality test was 4.35 for Group A, 3.9 for Group B and 4.75 for Group Z (raw scores relating to all 20 items of the WTC scale are provided for each group in Appendices F1, F2 and F3). The results of an independent sample t-test indicate that there were no significant differences in scores between any of the three groups. Nonetheless, while the average scores for Groups A and B were quite similar in all categories, the average scores of Group Z were noticeably higher than the other groups regarding the TOEIC and WTC scores. This might be explained by the fact that the learners belonging to Group Z, unlike the other learners participating in this study, were openly recruited to participate in this study. That is, learners in Groups A and B volunteered to participate in the project as a part of their class (i.e., with the knowledge that they would ultimately be receiving class credit), while learners in Group Z, who were not members of the same class, volunteered to do this as a supplemental project in their own free time (i.e., with the knowledge that they would not be receiving class credit). Presumably then, it stands to reason that learners in Group Z would be more intrinsically motivated learners of English, which might, in turn, explain higher TOEIC and WTC scores.

Table 3-1 Characteristics pertaining to members of Group A

Pseudonym	Gender	TOEIC Scores	L2 WTC	Personality (Extraversion)	Age	Year
Michiko	F	700	65	6.5	20	3rd
Hika	F	650	60	6	20	3rd
Aria	F	625	44	2	19	2nd
Haruna	F	555	61	6	19	2nd
Miya	F	500	54	4	19	2nd
Saya	F	470	45	4.5	19	3rd
Chieko	F	445	34	3	20	2nd
Ayuka	F	360	42	5	19	2nd
Takanori	M	504	40	4	20	3rd
Kazuya	M	480	39	2.5	19	2nd
AVG.		528.9	48.4	4.35	19.4	

Table 3-2 Characteristics pertaining to members of Group B

Pseudonym	Gender	TOEIC Scores	L2 WTC	Personality (Extraversion)	Age	Year
Rika	F	685	50	5	20	2nd
Shio	F	630	49	3	20	3rd
Mayumi	F	585	35	2	20	3rd
Meo	F	550	52	2.5	20	3rd
Madora	F	500	60	4.5	19	2nd
Sachi	F	475	59	5	19	2nd
Keiko	F	460	39	4.5	19	2nd
Mika	F	390	51	3.5	19	2nd
Taro	M	525	58	5	19	2nd
Kouki	M	450	51	4	20	3rd
AVG.		525	50.4	3.9	19.4	

Table 3-3 Characteristics pertaining to members of Group Z

Pseudonym	Gender	TOEIC Scores	L2 WTC	Personality (Extraversion)	Age	Year
Yukari	F	695	64	6	20	3rd
Mikki	F	645	63	4	20	3rd
Akie	F	595	60	5	20	2nd
Yuki	F	565	53	4.5	19	2nd
Tomomi	F	540	61	5.5	20	3rd
Yoko	F	516	48	5	19	2nd
Misako	F	485	54	5	19	2nd
Yukiko	F	445	41	6	19	2nd
Akanori	M	610	58	1.5	19	2nd
Hiro	M	560	60	5	20	3rd
AVG.		565.6	56.2	4.75	19.6	

Step 3: Treatment

The three groups of JEFL learners in this study consisted of two experimental groups (Groups A and B) and one control group (Group Z). As such, these groups received different types of treatment as the following describes (see Appendix E for lesson by lesson details).

Group A: Receiving Explicit Instruction

Treatment in this study occurred by means of formal instruction, which took place over the course of two months, i.e., one 90-minute lesson a week for eight weeks. Following some of the strategies outlined in Section 2.9.2.5, members of Group A received explicit instruction, which began with a focus on overtly raising learners' awareness of the use and dimensions of listener responses in English as compared to Japanese. To this end, the following pedagogical strategies were implemented: (1) the form, function and perception of listener responses, as well as other communicative behaviour thought to be relevant, were compared across languages and cultures, (2) with input enhancement from the teacher, learners were given opportunities to become conversational researchers by analysing, interpreting and discussing how the form, frequency, placement and function of backchannels in varying contexts might influence IC, (3) learners were provided with explicit descriptions and concrete examples of how NESs use listener responses and conversational micro-skills in varying contexts, (4) learners completed exercises and tasks to reinforce the newly learnt conventions of listening behaviour, and (5) learners were given opportunities to practise listener response use in fluency-focused exercises in simulated contexts, and were given feedback based on their performances. This final step involved videotaping learners' performances, and subsequently having the teacher and learner(s) analyse the re-play of the conversation in an attempt to pinpoint areas for improvement.

Group B: Receiving Implicit Instruction

Members of Group B received implicit instruction (as set out in Section 2.9.2.3) over the course of two months. While the overall amount of instruction and the eight-week time line was identical to that received by Group A, the lesson parameters were somewhat different. The lessons involving classroom interaction and discussion amongst peers, which took place in Weeks 1, 4 and 8, were each administered in one 90-minute sitting; however, the sessions in which the JEFL learner conversed with a native speaker of English, which occurred in Weeks 2, 3, 5, 6 and 7, took place twice a week and were 45 minutes in duration each. Similar to the objectives of the explicit instruction above, raising learners' consciousness regarding the use and dimensions of listener responses across cultures was among the primary goals of implicit instruction in this study; however, the methods used to achieve this were quite different. Unlike the treatment Group A received, learners in Group B were not provided with explicit metapragmatic information about listener responses through explanations and concrete examples. Although the participants of this group were asked initially to consider the general qualities belonging to good conversationalists and listeners alike, they were not instructed to focus on listening behaviour as part of this treatment. The role of the teacher here was limited to that of facilitator in that learners in Group B were required to induce rules and meaning on their own based on exposure to prototypical uses of the target language in meaningful contexts. To this end, members of Group B received the following pedagogical interventions. First, learners were provided with models of conversations in three categories: (1) NS-NS discourse in Japanese, (2) NS-NS discourse in English and (3) NNS-NS intercultural conversations in English. Second, with limited input enhancement from the teacher, learners were given the opportunity to reflect upon and discuss their observations of communicative behaviour across languages and cultures in journal-writing entries and small group discussions. Third, making up the greater part of the treatment Group B received, learners were given the opportunity to communicate with NESs face-to-face in authentic contexts on 12 separate occasions. Each conversational session was followed by a brief period of reflection in which learners recorded their thoughts in their journals. In addition, after every three conversational sessions, student-led group discussions took place, affording them the opportunities to further reflect and share their general observations regarding their own as well as their intercultural interlocutor's communicative style(s), what they might have learnt, and what they hope to change or modify about their own behaviour in future intercultural conversations in English.

Group Z: No Treatment

The participants in this group, the control group, received no formal treatment regarding listener responses. This was feasible because Group Z consisted of JEFLs who were not members of the Oral Communication 3 class that all other members were attending. Like other students in the Department of Multi-cultural Exchange at the UoN, these learners were enrolled in other classes at the time of this study. Four of the participants in this group were enrolled in EFL writing classes, one of which used a CALL medium. Not related to EFL study, many of the members of this group were taking other elective classes consisting of physical education, law and history. Members of this group were enrolled in a seminar class focusing on the research interests of a Japanese faculty member, whose specialties involved Japanese literature, economics in Asia, international politics and Japanese film studies.

Step 4: Post-test 1

Post-test 1 was given to all JEFLs within three days of their last treatment, and followed the same procedure as the Pre-test outlined in Step 1 above. The only difference regarding this test was that the NES interlocutor in the intercultural conversations was a different person. While it could be argued that using the same NES interlocutor to rate the JEFL speakers' performances before and after would better achieve a baseline measurement, different NESs were used for two main reasons. First, from a practical standpoint, most of the exchange students had returned home after their brief sojourn to Japan; thus, it was not possible to use the same NESs in most cases. Hence, in an effort to make all post-tests comparable, different NESs were always used in this study. To address the problem of inconsistencies among the raters, this study added an additional measurement, which will be discussed in Step 6 below. Second, using different interlocutors would also seem to have some research design advantages. That is, it was thought that pairing the same NES-JEFL interlocutors might influence the communicative behaviour in the conversations. Not only might the interactants' familiarity with each other affect communication, but there is also a danger of interlocutors bringing possible preconceptions into the conversation stemming from the previous test's conversation and playback interviews (i.e., a common cognitive bias known as the halo effect), which would ultimately affect their ratings of the second conversation.

Step 5: Post-test 2

In an attempt to determine if the treatment had any sustained effects, a delayed post-test was given. Following similar procedures undertaken in the Pre-test and Post-test 1, Post-test 2 was administered approximately eight weeks after Post-test 1, which also marked eight weeks since the experimental groups received any instruction regarding listener responses. During the eight weeks between Post-test 1 and Post-test 2, the 20 learners in the OC 3 class were reassembled to continue on with the remaining coursework necessary to complete the course. This involved six additional 90-minute class sessions that were held weekly during the first six weeks of this period. These sessions did not involve instruction in conversation skills and/or listener responses in any way. Rather, during these sessions, these students engaged in an independent study project, which was designed to help them develop content knowledge regarding foreign countries and travelling abroad. This project involved students going through a step-by-step process of researching, recording, and ultimately presenting information regarding the country of their assignment. This project followed the model set forth in the course book entitled, *Travel Abroad Project* (McMahon 2005). Moreover, during the eight weeks between Post-test 1 and Post-test 2, all 30 of the JEFL participants in this study continued with their regular classes (as outlined in Step 3 pertaining to the control group). As mentioned above, the content of this instruction was not thought to have any direct effect on conversation skills and/or listener responses.

Step 6: NESs' Observations

While the method used to determine the NESs' assessment of their JEFL interlocutors will be discussed in Section 3.4.2 below, it is necessary to briefly touch upon how various issues have directed the researcher's implementation of procedural Step 6 in this project. Although ratings pertaining to the JEFLs' conversational performances were provided by their NES interlocutors in the Pre-test, Post-test 1 and Post-test 2, these ratings were associated with a number of concerns. First, as Step 4 mentioned above, circumstances dictated that different NES interlocutors were used across the board (i.e., cross-sectionally and longitudinally); thus, as various individuals may have different interpretations regarding appropriate conversational and/or listening behaviour, it would be ill-advised to use these ratings to compare JEFL speakers' performances cross-sectionally, as well as to track each JEFL speaker's progression over time. Second, after having engaged in a 30-minute casual conversation with the JEFL speaker, there is a chance that the NESs will have developed a personal rapport with their interlocutor, which might lead to potentially biased and misguided positive impressions regarding their interlocutor's conversational abilities. Lastly, the fact that NES interlocutors were in Japan at the time of the study would imply that they have an affinity for Japan, or at the very least, have some knowledge and understanding of Japanese culture. This might affect the ratings that they give to their JEFL interlocutor. For these reasons, the researcher thought it necessary to create a supplementary group of observers/assessors, consisting of ten American NESs who were not linguists, did not live in Japan or have an affiliation with Japanese language and culture, and did not take part in the videotaped conversations and/or earlier pilot studies. The role of this group was to watch each of the 90 videotaped conversations and subsequently provide impressions of the JEFLs' conversational and listening behaviour by filling out a questionnaire (see Section 3.4.2 and Appendix I for details). Although there is a possibility of a halo effect operating in the ratings of these NES observers, who did remain constant, this seems less likely since, unlike the NES interlocutors, they were not personally involved in the conversations (see Step 4).

3.4 Methods of Collecting Data

The Pre-test, Post-test 1 and Post-test 2 in this study each involved three methods of collecting data: observations, questionnaires and interviews. While Section 3.3 briefly touched upon how these methods were incorporated into the procedural steps of this study, this section describes each method in greater detail.

3.4.1 Observations

The first of these three methods, observations, involved the videotaping of intercultural dyadic conversations between JEFLs and American NESs.

These conversations took place in an office at the UoN in the timeframe outlined in Section 3.3. The location was a small, quiet and comfortably furnished room. The video recording equipment used was a Sony digital video camera, which was placed unobtrusively in the corner of the room. While the conversation was being videotaped, only the participants were present in the room. Initial conversational prompts (i.e., involving peer mentoring) were offered to help stimulate conversation; however, it was made clear to all participants that they were free to talk about anything they liked. Conversations were video recorded for a period of thirty minutes, of which only the middle three minutes of each conversation were included as data to be transcribed. This followed the work of White (1989), Maynard (1986, 1987, 1990, 1997) and Cutrone (2005), who also transcribed brief segments in the middle of the conversation as data. It was thought that the participants would become less conscious of the camera as the conversation progressed, and that the middle part of the conversation would be the most natural as it avoids the awkwardness which often occurs at the beginning and end of conversations between people who do not know each other well.

3.4.2 Questionnaires

The second method of data collection involved questionnaires. There were two types of questionnaire used in this study: one type was completed by the JEFL participants and used to measure their WTC over time, and the other type, which contained versions specifically designed for the JEFLs, NES interlocutors, and NES observers, sought to measure perceptions of the participants based on observations of their conversational performances. Each version of this questionnaire, including the language variants used therein, will be described below. First, regarding the WTC questionnaire, the researcher followed Yashima's (2002) study, which also involved JEFLs, in using the WTC scale published in McCroskey (1992). This WTC scale has been widely used in L2 studies (see Section 1.5.2) as it has previously been demonstrated to have a high degree of reliability (Asker 1998) and strong content, construct and predictive validity (McCroskey 1992). The WTC scale (see Appendix F) is a 20-item, probability-estimate scale. Eight of the items are fillers and 12 are scored as part of the scale. While this scale yields a total score, it also produces sub-scores which account for some of the contextual dimensions of conversations. This includes three sub-scores based on the types of receivers (i.e., strangers, acquaintances, friends) and four sub-scores based on the types of communication contexts (i.e., public, meeting, group, dyad). Considering the scope of this study, the sub-score pertaining to interpersonal communication was used in the assessment of performances. The WTC questionnaire was one of the two questionnaires given to each participant in the dyad directly after their videotaped conversation. Participants completed these questionnaires simultaneously in separate rooms.

The second type of questionnaire used in this study included modified versions of Hecht's (1978) widely used Interpersonal Communication Satisfaction Inventory. While this inventory may at first appear dated, it is still widely used in linguistic research pertaining to both listening behaviour and ICC (see Section 2.9.4.4) due to its high degree of reliability and validity when used to measure interaction satisfaction in actual and recalled conversations (Harrington 1995). Consistent with the expectancy principle in Spitzberg's (2000) model of ICC, Hecht (1978) proposed that communication satisfaction depends on the fulfilment of expectations. Three variations of Hecht's (1978) questionnaire were used in this study, each designed for a different group of participants and, thus, with a different perspective in mind. As part of the Pre-test, Post-test 1 and Post-test 2, the first two variations of Hecht's (1978) questionnaire were administered to the intercultural conversational participants: one version of the questionnaire was given to the NESs (see Appendix G), while a slightly different version was given to the JEFL participants (see Appendix H). First, regarding the similarities of the questionnaires designed for the conversational participants, both groups' questionnaires consisted of the same fifteen-item inventory and one open-response question at the end in case the participant wanted to add something that had not been addressed in the other questions. Except for the final item on the questionnaire, all questions were closed-ended, consisting of statements to which subjects responded using a Likert-scale of degrees of agreement ranging from one to seven. Further, this study, following Cutrone (2005), used slightly modified versions of Hecht's (1978) questionnaire because an earlier pilot study revealed that participants were confused by some vocabulary and some of the statements containing double negatives. For instance, participants of the pilot study had problems rating yes or no on the Likert-scale because of negatively worded statements such as *He/she didn't seem to care* and *He/she did not interrupt me*. Consequently, the negatively worded statement *He/she didn't seem to care* was excluded from the questionnaire because its positive counterpart *He expressed a lot of interest in what I had to say* already existed in the questionnaire, and similarly, the negatively worded statement *He/she did not interrupt me* was replaced with the positive statement *He/she interrupted me.*

Additionally, touching upon a key issue as discussed in Section 2.8.1, Item 15 *My conversation partner seems to want to avoid speaking* was added to Hecht's (1978) original questionnaire. The JEFL participants' questionnaires included Japanese translations underneath each of the items typed in English to ensure comprehension.

A few other alterations were made specific to the questionnaire objectives for each of the two groups. For instance, Item 2 on Hecht's (1978) original questionnaire *I felt I was able to present myself favourably during the conversation* was altered for both groups. On the JEFL participants' questionnaire, the adverb *favourably* was changed to *fairly* as the focus here was to determine whether these participants felt that they represented themselves adequately, sincerely, and as they had intended (i.e., this need not necessarily be favourably). This was made specific in the Japanese translation. Conversely, on the NESs' questionnaire, the original Item 2 was changed in its entirety to *The feelings that my partner expressed by means of listening feedback during the conversation seemed authentic and sincere*. The focus here was to explore whether the NESs could sense their JEFL interlocutor feigning understanding and/or agreement.

As described in Section 3.3, Step 6, the third variation of Hecht's (1978) questionnaire was given to the NES observers (see Appendix I). This questionnaire essentially followed the same 16-item inventory as the one given to the conversation participants save for a few additions and modifications. Regarding the former, NES observers' questionnaires included two supplemental items (Items 16 and 17) designed to pinpoint areas of relevance to the study of JEFL conversationalists' backchannel behaviour that were not covered in the original questionnaire. These consisted of Item 16 *When the Japanese person did not understand something, they were able to clearly convey this to their conversational partner with their listening feedback* and Item 17 *The Japanese person's listening behaviour seemed inadequate in some ways*. For participants expressing agreement (i.e., 1, 2, or 3 on the Likert-scale) to Item 17, an open-item response was subsequently solicited asking them to explain their answer. Moreover, since the members of the NES observer group did not participate in the conversations, referent nouns, subject pronouns, object pronouns and possessive adjectives were changed accordingly.

Lastly, while the other methods of data collection described in this section were collected at deliberately timed intervals corresponding to the Pre-test, Post-test 1 and Post-test 2, this third variation of Hecht's (1978) questionnaire was administered in the weeks following the completion of Post-test 2. The process by which this questionnaire was administered was as follows. First, all 90 of the videotaped intercultural conversations were copied to Digital Video Discs. These conversations were presented in random order on the DVDs; thus, the NES observers did not have any knowledge as to the time line of the conversations (i.e., pre versus post treatment versus delayed post treatment) and which group each JEFL belonged to (i.e., explicit, implicit, or control). Subsequently, a packet including the following items was air mailed to the NES observers' homes in the United States: a consent form, written instructions (verbal instructions were also given by telephone), 90 videotaped conversations on three DVDs and 90 copies of the questionnaires (i.e., one for each conversation). In brief, NES observers were instructed to watch each three-minute conversation and subsequently provide their impression as to the adequacy of each JEFL's conversational and listening behaviour by completing the corresponding questionnaire. The NES observers were instructed to be as critical as they liked in their analyses as their standard for good conversational and listening behaviour should reflect what they might desire and/or expect from people residing in their country.

3.4.3 Interviews

The third method of data collection entailed oral interviews with each of the conversational participants. As part of the Pre-test, Post-test 1 and Post-test 2, these interviews were the third and final part of each test, taking place directly after the participants of the intercultural dyadic conversations completed their conversations and subsequent questionnaires. Participants of each dyadic conversation were interviewed separately and in succession, starting with each NES. The interviewee's interlocutor waited in another room while the interview took place. The interview consisted of the researcher playing back the three-minute portion of the videotaped conversation used as data and asking the participants questions pertaining to the listening behaviour and communication styles displayed in the conversation. Open-ended and closed-ended questions were used in the interviews, and all interviews were audio recorded.

The interviews were semi-structured in that the interviewer had a general plan for the interviews, but did not enter with a predetermined set of questions as some questions were guided by the circumstances in the videotaped conversations and the responses of the interviewee. As suggested by Brown (2001), questions were sequenced in a way that began with general questions and gradually led to more specific and potentially sensitive questions in an effort to make participants feel more comfortable and thus provide more honest data. Upon asking a few general questions such as *How was the conversation?* and *How did you feel about being in front of the camera?*, the researcher explained to each interviewee that the study was primarily examining the conversational performances and listener responses of the Japanese participant. The interviewer attempted to be cautious in reactions to responses and in the wordings of questions so as not to lead the interviewees in any way.

The main aim in the interviews with NESs was to learn how they perceived their Japanese interlocutors' conversational and listening behaviour. This involved playing back the videotape and asking the NES to comment on what they were seeing and hearing, and specifically, what functions they perceived their JEFL interlocutors' backchannel responses to be serving. To assist with the latter, each NES was provided with a list of potential functions recognised in the research (see Appendix J) at the beginning of the interview. This list was used periodically throughout the interview to check on the functions of specific examples of backchannels. In instances singled out for analysis (i.e., where some miscommunication was thought to have occurred), the interviewer stopped the videotape and asked specific questions such as *What function do you think that head nod serves?*, *Do you think he/she understands what you are saying here?*, and follow up questions such as *Why do you think so?*. The researcher made note of any data he thought could be useful in the subsequent interview with the Japanese participant of the dyad.

In the subsequent interview with the JEFL, the researcher wanted to learn as much as possible about how and why Japanese EFL speakers use backchannels the way they do, and bring to light any misunderstandings caused by differing conventions in backchannel behaviour. One of the specific goals of the researcher in this part of the interview was to discover what the JEFLs were doing when they did not understand, i.e., were they showing their non-understanding in some way (such as by employing a conversational repair strategy as Section 3.6.3 describes, or through silence), or were they using what might be deemed as an unconventional backchannel type in this situation (such as one that typically functions as a continuer, understanding, agreement, and/or support and empathy type)? Thus, a major part of the interview with the JEFLs consisted of the interviewer asking JEFLs to comment on what they were feeling at certain points in the conversation, as well as the intended functions of their backchannel responses. The list of possible backchannel functions was again used as a reference. The researcher documented any notable differences between the JEFLs' backchannel intentions and their NES interlocutors' perceptions on a data record sheet (see Appendix K). Through this process, the researcher was able to bring to light any misunderstandings caused by the JEFLs' backchannels in the videotaped conversations and ask the participants about them. In instances singled out for analysis (where some of the Japanese participants' backchannels may have been misunderstood), the interviewer paused the videotape and attempted to delve deeper by asking specific questions such as *What function does that response serve?*, *What is the reason for saying yeah yeah here?*, *Do you understand what he/she is saying here?* and *Do you agree with what he/she is saying here?* and *Do you think he/she knows that you do not understand here?* In the cases where the Japanese participants' backchannel explanation differed greatly from their NES interlocutor's interpretation, the interviewer asked potentially sensitive follow-up questions such as *Why did you nod if you did not understand what he/she was saying here?* and *Why did you say yeah if you disagreed with what he/she was saying?* In cases where the interviewee seemed uncomfortable in answering, the interviewer did not persist with this line of questioning and instead shifted to a less sensitive area.

Although they were in no way the foci of these interviews, the researcher additionally used this time to delve into two issues concerning IC and videotaped conversations respectively: the extent to which the NESs accommodated to their intercultural interlocutors, and the effect that Observer's Paradox played in the conversations. Regarding the latter, some participants seemed to be conscious of the video camera initially as they looked towards the camera and made metamessage comments such as *we can start now* and *I probably shouldn't say that in front of the camera*. As researchers such as Johnstone (2000) and Maynard (1986) have come to accept, these types of actions are generally predictable when participants are being videotaped.

3.5 Methods Used to Transcribe

The data collected in the observation phase of this study were transcribed for purposes of analysis. As Maynard (1986), Ochs (1979) and Tottie (1991) have stated, the act of transcribing is somewhat subjective as the use of any transcription system will foreground various aspects of data and background others. Consequently, it is important to consider that the transcriptions in this study were designed with several purposes in mind. First, the researcher's main goal was to strive for consistency and the production of simple and unambiguous guidelines. Second, the transcriptions served to provide a framework for identifying the various types of backchannels occurring in the data. Quantitatively, this enabled the researcher to establish the frequency of backchannels across cultures according to various categories which include overall frequency, frequency of various types and frequency in a range of discourse contexts favouring backchannels. The transcriptions also served a qualitative function as some attention was paid to describing the conversations and examining them for patterns (see Appendix L for a sample of a transcribed conversation and a description of the symbols used).

Regarding the way various items were presented in the transcribed data, there were several issues which needed to be addressed, i.e., first and foremost, how this study identified backchannels, and particularly how backchannels were differentiated from full speaking turns at talk. Similar to the recent work of Cutrone (2005) and Maynard (1997), this study also adopts Markel's (1975) definition of turn and a broader definition of backchannels as outlined in Sections 2.2 and 2.3. The end of Section 2.3 also describes how pauses, and their varying lengths, aid the researcher in determining whether utterances found between turns at talk would be identified as backchannels or part of a turn at talk. While examining the length of pauses in relation to the identification of backchannels is a necessary course of action in this study, it also important to consider how pauses were identified within the primary speaker's turn at talk since pauses have been shown to be among the most frequent discourse contexts favouring backchannels. In marking the pauses in the transcriptions, distinctions were made between pauses of various lengths. As linguists have noted that short pauses of .4 seconds or less occur frequently in NS speech (Deese 1980; Fillmore 1979), and pauses of .5 seconds or more represent a clearly noticeable pause (Foster, Tonkyn & Wigglesworth 2000), the researcher has thus decided to use .5 seconds as a dividing line. Although all silent pauses were identified in the transcriptions, only pauses of .5 seconds or greater were given a numerical representation; all other pauses under .5 seconds, which Riggenbach (1991) recognises as either hesitations or micropauses, were simply marked with a period in between parentheses as (.). This was consistent with Riggenbach's (1991) assertion that short pauses are within the normal range of speech and, thus, not indicative of a lack of fluency or of breakdowns in speech.

Lastly, regarding the conventions used in the transcriptions in this study (see Appendix L), many of the transcription symbols were adopted from the work of Sacks, Schegloff and Jefferson (1974) and the revised Conversation Analysis (CA) conventions of Jefferson (2002). To ensure the precise timing of pauses, as well as the accurate mark-up of stress and intonation, in the transcriptions, all of the avi video files corresponding to the 90 conversations were converted into audio wav files, which were then analysed using the well-known phonetics software called Praat (Version

5.0.18). Although the prosodic aspects of backchannels were not the foci of this study, the transcriptions included demarcations of salient instances of intonation, stress, stretching and volume. In conclusion, to strengthen the internal reliability of the transcriptions, the researcher analysed the videotaped conversations with the assistance of a colleague. The colleague, who was trained by the researcher to recognise the transcription conventions used in this study (see Appendix L), assisted in two ways. First, concerning some of the words and/or actions that were not entirely clear to the researcher in the conversations, the researcher sought out the colleague's opinions so as to make a more informed choice in transcribing the word(s) or action in question. In addition, the colleague double-checked the researcher's initial transcriptions to ensure that the conventions showing the features of language were accurately presented in the transcriptions.

3.6 Overview of Data Analysis Procedures

This section begins by describing how the methods of data collection, which involved observations, questionnaires and interviews, combine to inform judgements within the following four assessment categories of backchannels: (3.6.1) observed backchannel behaviour, (3.6.2) WTC, (3.6.3) conversational micro-skills and (3.6.4) ICC. This level of analysis provides a micro examination of how the components within each of the three tests (see Section 3.3) are broken down and analysed. Subsequently, Section 3.6.5 deals with an analysis of levels and gains, while Section 3.6.6 discusses cross-sectional vis-à-vis longitudinal analysis, and, lastly, Section 3.6.7 describes the statistical analysis used in this study.

3.6.1 Observed Backchannel Behaviour

The first phase of analysing data involved a thorough examination of the transcribed conversations. This involved identifying specifically what each of the following areas entailed: frequency, variability, discourse contexts, the characterisation of linguistic units and simultaneous speech. Regarding the first of these categories, frequency, some clarification as to what this term encompasses is required. Frequency, as an independent category, refers to the overall frequency of backchannels and should not be confused with its partial inclusion in subsequent subsections where the frequency of backchannels within categories, such as variability, discourse contexts and simultaneous speech are also measured and compared as part of the data analysis. Another issue which requires some initial clarification involves the assessment and interpretation of raw data collected from the intercultural conversations. In measuring the features of backchannel behaviour described below, it is important to note that, in many cases, an unequal number of opportunities were provided to each listener and each group. Ergo, any comparisons between listeners and/or groups must first take into account the number of opportunities afforded to them before certain features can be adequately compared.

3.6.1.1 Frequency

In calculating the overall frequency of backchannels attributed to a person or a group, a number of issues need to be addressed. For instance, the amount of input afforded to each listener must be considered. That is, comparing raw data such as the overall number of backchannels sent by each group would do little to inform this study as it would not account for how much the primary speaker spoke. Hence, the overall frequency of listener backchannels has been analysed and compared according to the amount of input listeners were afforded (i.e., how much their interlocutor spoke), which, as Section 2.6.1 explains, is based on the number of words their interlocutors uttered in a primary speaking role.

3.6.1.2 Variability

The variability of backchannels will be examined broadly in terms of the type of verbal and nonverbal backchannels and the extent of backchannels provided as outlined in Section 2.4. First, concerning verbal backchannels, this study follows Cutrone (2005) and Maynard (1990, 1997) in measuring the frequency of types corresponding to Tottie's (1991) categories listed below.

Types of Verbal Backchannels:

- Simple (isolated)
- Simple with head nod(s)
- Compound (isolated)
- Compound with head nod(s)
- Complex (isolated)
- Complex with head nod(s)
- Japanese
- Minimal Response
- Extended Response

Similar to the aforementioned studies, it should be noted that the list above includes categories for both isolated verbal backchannels and those accompanied by head nod(s). Further, a category of Japanese backchannels was thought to be justified by the findings of Cutrone's (2005) study, which showed the Japanese participants' frequent use of Japanese backchannel expressions in the English intercultural conversations. There is also justification in the literature for superordinate categories based on McCarthy's (2003) observations and Stubbe's (1998) Feedback Continuum. Hence, in order to demonstrate a listener's involvement in the conversation, this study recognises minimal responses vis-à-vis extended responses.

Regarding nonverbal backchannels, this study followed Cutrone (2005) and Maynard (1990, 1997) in measuring frequencies of types listed below.

Types of Nonverbal Backchannels:

- Single head nod (isolated)
- Multiple head nods (isolated)
- Smile (isolated)
- Smile with verbal backchannel
- Laughter (isolated)
- Laughter with verbal backchannel
- Raised Eyebrows (isolated)
- Raised Eyebrows with verbal backchannel
- ≥ 2 nonverbal backchannels occurring simultaneously (isolated)
- ≥ 2 nonverbal backchannels occurring simultaneously with verbal backchannel

Lastly, this study examines the variability of verbal backchannels at the word level and beyond, which categorises the constituents that make up backchannel forms as follows:

- non-word vocalisations
- isolated content words
- multi-word backchannel phrases and/or expressions
- repetitions

Concerning the final category of repetitions, the inclusion of a repetition category would have to differentiate between clarification repetitions (with rising intonation) and non-clarification repetitions. In this study, as described in Appendix L, pitch contours containing rapid rises of

600 Hertz or more are marked in the transcriptions, and, thus, repetition backchannels as clarifications are easily distinguishable from non-clarification repetition backchannels, which contain a steady or falling intonation.

A final point worth mentioning in this analysis involves the comparing of raw frequencies of various types of backchannels across groups and/or individuals. The major concern with the comparison of overall frequency above was that the amount of input afforded to the listener be taken into account. In comparing the variability of a specific type of backchannel, however, the focus is somewhat different. What is of particular interest here is how many backchannels of a particular type, a listener, or group of listeners, is sending, as compared to other types of backchannels. Therefore, the number of backchannels within each of the categories described above was calculated as a percentage of the total backchannels given by that group and then compared across cultural groups. In this way, one could see, for instance, that the JEFLs sending 99 extended responses is actually not as prolific as the NESs sending 72 because the 99 sent by the JEFLs only made up 7.95% of their total backchannel output, whereas the 72 sent by the NESs made up 35.38% of their total.

3.6.1.3 Discourse Contexts Favouring Backchannels

While Sections 2.6.3 and 2.6.4 point out specific distinctions between contexts as being more or less favourable to backchannels for each cultural group, this study examines broadly the discourse contexts that were suggested in prior research for both groups as shown in the following list.

Discourse Contexts:

- At or directly after a pause

Clausal Boundaries:

- At or near any clausal boundary
- At or near an internal clause boundary
- At or near a final clause boundary

At or directly after points in which both clausal boundaries and pauses occur together:

- At or directly after any clausal boundary accompanied by a pause

- At or directly after an internal clause boundary accompanied by a pause
- At or directly after a final clause boundary accompanied by a pause

Gesticulation:

- After the primary speaker's nonverbal gesture
- After the primary speaker's head nod(s)

To compare results between individuals and groups, the number of backchannels within each aforementioned discourse context category was calculated relative to the number of opportunities presented to each cultural group. Hence, for instance, ten backchannels sent in a discourse context which offered fifteen opportunities would be seen to occur more regularly than ten backchannels sent in a discourse context that offered a hundred opportunities.

3.6.1.4 The Characterisation of Linguistic Units

This section now examines the characterisation of linguistic units in this study, which are important insofar as they are relevant to grammatical completion points. These grammatical completion points – or potential completion points – need to be identified, in spoken language, from a listener's perspective. Having identified clausal boundaries as a discourse context of particular interest to this study, the researcher now describes the complexities involved in the identification of such units in dynamic, real-time conversations. Given that location refers to a text string which is developing and open to modification rather than static and complete, categories of structure selected to identify location only reflect the status of the unit at a particular point in the construction of the text (Spelman-Miller 2000). For this type of analysis, Garman's (1990) concept of text units is useful. This approach begins by 'making appeal to verbs as the centres of clausal constructions, treating formal connective devices such as *and, if* and relative pronouns as initiating new units, and recognising unconnected phrases and minor elements as constituting independent units' (Garman 1990: 149).

Using text units as a basis, various types of higher order units may be identified as necessary. Within this framework, two types of potential or emergent clause boundaries are identified as discourse contexts favouring backchannels: final and internal clause boundaries (i.e., both with and without a pause). A final clause boundary occurs at points in the primary speaker's speech where the text unit is structurally and semantically acceptable as a clause, but is not bounded by terminal punctuation (Spelman-Miller 2000). These text units are fully meaningful, make complete sense and could end the utterance there (i.e., terminative). In the transcriptions, as well as the examples below, final clause boundaries are marked by two slashes side by side (//). An internal clause satisfies the grammatical structure of a clause but not the semantic condition. In other words, internal clauses are marked because the meaning of the clause is not complete, and there is a requirement for the utterance to go on in order for the meaning to be complete (i.e., continuative). A single slash (/) marks the grammatical completion point of an internal clause boundary. Taken from data used in this study (see Appendix L), Example 1 below illustrates the difference between the two boundaries.

1. it makes me very nervous/ to to handle that much money//

In this case, an internal clause boundary is located after the main clause *it makes me nervous* because the subordinate clause *to handle that much money* is required to make the utterance fully meaningful. Accordingly, a final clause boundary is marked after the word *money*. Although this analysis was fairly straightforward, there were numerous instances in the data which involved a great deal of discussion between co-transcribers. Clearly, context plays a major role in determining whether or not a potential clause completion point has been reached, and the examples below serve to demonstrate how difficult it is to work with fragmentary and elliptical data which is common in oral samples, particularly involving the speech of L2 learners. It is important to keep in mind that the identification of boundaries in the JEFLs' speech was relevant to establishing the nature of backchannel placement by their NES interlocutors in the cross-sectional comparison. Example 2 below offers a more problematic illustration because it not only contains ellipted elements but also L2 syntactical errors.

2. if you mistake/ very very big problem//

Following Foster, Tonkyn and Wigglesworth (2000), this study recognises independent sub-clausal units at clause boundaries only when they could be elaborated to a full clause by means of recovery of ellipted elements from the context of the discourse. In this way, syntax errors, which include the erroneous omission of clause elements, function similarly to ellipsis in oral data, and defective clause-functioning strings are, thus, recognised as functioning as clauses in this analysis. As a framework for this analysis, ellipsis was identified according to Quirk et al's (1985: 888) description of Situational Ellipsis, which requires the following three criteria: the missing expression is precisely recoverable, the elliptical construction is grammatically defective, and the insertion of the missing words results in a grammatical sentence (with the same meaning as the original sentence). Hence, recovering the ellipted elements from Example 2, this extract is interpreted as a subordinate clause and an independent clause making up the sentence *if you make a mistake, it is a very big problem*. From the context of the situation, as well as a basic understanding of the cause and effect nature of if-clauses, it was determined that the speaker's initial utterance is clearly representative of the final interpretation. In recognising unit boundaries, the connectivity of utterances is not limited to one person's speech. Example 3 below shows how clausal boundaries are interpreted in interactive discourse.

3. A: is it a type of money// (.)
   B: yeah//

In the dialogue shown in the example above, B's response of *yeah* is interpreted from A's preceding question *is it a type of money*. In this way, based on the preceding sentence, B's utterance of *yeah* is reconstructed to its full form *yeah it is a type of money*, which marks a final clause boundary.

Another issue related to highly interactive discourse involves how listener interjections are treated. As this study focuses on the listener's perspective, discourse contexts favouring backchannels are identified based solely on the primary speaker's speech and, thus, listener backchannels cannot be considered to complete, or be a part of, the primary speakers' units in any way. As Section 2.3 explains, answers to questions as shown in Example 3 are considered speaking turns and not backchannels. Examples 4 and 5, which are reconstructions of the more natural and interactive state of how examples 1 and 2 occurred in the data respectively, illustrate how backchannels are treated in this study.

4. A: it makes me very nervous/ (.62) [(to to)] handle that much money//aaa
   B: *[(mm)]*

5. A: if you (.) mistake/ very =   = very big (.) problem//
   B: *= (A) =*

Similarly, in cases where backchannels comprise lengthier forms, they continue to not count as separate units nor influence the clausal boundary markings in the primary speaker's speech. Example 6 below illustrates how clausal boundaries were not affected by the listener's minor addition backchannel.

6. A: i made a mistake of (1.07) sixty five dollars// (.)   (.) which is
    B: _ (at work)
    A: about nana sen en//

Shifting the focus away from interactive discourse, the following example demonstrates an instance in the data whereby a string of words was not found to comprise a complete or fully comprehensible clause.

7. so (1.30) so (.65) she said (.90) maybe (.51) _ (she said) (.) me maybe (1.22)

In Example 7, no clausal boundaries have been marked. While the fragments *she said (.90) maybe* and *_(she said) (.) me maybe (1.22)* might, at first glance, appear to function as clauses, it is not clear from the context what the speaker was trying to say. The verb *to say* appears to function as a transitive verb, and the word *maybe* appears to function as an adverb and not as a direct object. Ergo, the co-transcribers interpreted *she said* as requiring an obligatory direct object and, thus, as being incomplete.

Directly after the extract illustrated in Example 7, the same speaker uttered the following:

8. i saw¿ (.) i saw every day that brown paper money//

From the speaker's subsequent utterance, the fragments discussed in Example 7 would seem to fit the criteria required of a false start. This is characterised 'as an utterance which is begun and then abandoned altogether or reformulated in some way' (Foster, Tonkyn & Wigglesworth 2000: 368). Other dysfluency features found in the data include repetitions and self-corrections. Examples 7 and 8 show instances where repetition is used as s*he said* in Example 7 and *i saw* in Example 8 appear to be repeated either as strategies to hold the floor, or to allow time for planning on-line. Example 9 below illustrates an instance where self-correction was used.

9. you get (.) you make lots of money//

In this extract, the speaker begins with *you get* and then chooses to reformulate the utterance to *you make*, seemingly to clarify that the person receiving the money had, in fact, earned it. While these types of dysfluency features are prevalent in the data, they have not been shown to be discourse contexts favouring backchannels in previous research and are, thus, not priorities in this study. The main reason for distinguishing them here is to demonstrate what does and what does not constitute a clausal boundary in this study, and it is clear that these types of fragments do not constitute a clause. As such, when false starts, repetitions and self-corrections occur in the data, there is nothing demarcating them.

Another issue concerning the fragmentary nature of oral speech is the independent topical noun phrase satellite units commonly found in speech (Bygate 1988). Example 10 demonstrates how this study deals with these types of occurrences.

   10. you can only use cash// (.) so like real money// paper money//

This extract contains three potential final clause boundaries. While the first one after the word *cash* is fairly straightforward and its type has been described above, the second two after the word *money* in both cases require some explanation. The speaker's utterances of *real money* and subsequently *paper money* are examples of synonymy and anaphoric references to the word *cash* in the first clause. It seems that the speaker is using these references to clarify precisely what is meant by the term *cash*. In this way, these topical noun phrases or 'tails' as Carter and McCarthy (1997: 18) call them, function as clauses in that they take on the constituents of the first clause. These tails can be reconstructed as *you can only use real money//* and *you can only use paper money//* respectively. In some cases, however, a direct relationship from the tail to the preceding clause is not easy to establish. Besides containing a topical association, it is necessary that the noun phrase satellite units occur in close temporal proximity to the preceding clause. Following some of the general principles included in Foster, Tonkyn and Wigglesworth's (2000) analyses, topical noun phrases are treated as separate units. Furthermore, units which are separated from subsequent topical noun phrases by falling intonation and a pause of ≥ .5 seconds are not considered to have any topical association. Thus, if Example 10 was altered as shown in Example 11 below, the clausal boundaries would be marked as follows:

   11. you can only use cash¿// (.96) so like real money paper money and so they hand it to me//

Since the intonation at the end of the first clause is falling and a pause of ≥ .5 seconds occurs, the ensuing noun phrases *so like real money* and *paper money* are not recognised as being connected to the preceding clause and are, hence, not marked as being followed by final clause boundaries.

Next, considering other post-clausal text strings as text units, this section now discusses concluders such as *I think, ya know, you see, right* with a rising intonation, and tag questions. When these types of text strings occur after a final clause boundary, they are seen to be connected to the preceding clause and, therefore, the point after which they occur is marked as another final clause boundary as follows:

12. i'm the only research student// i think//

13. they're boyfriend and girlfriend// ya know//

However, in instances when parenthetical phrases such as *you know* and *i think* are pre-clausal or clause-internal and *kind of* is clause-internal, they will be recognised as not constituting a clause on their own as shown in the following examples:

14. i think it looks very nice//

15. they're kind of a new group//

16. so she showed (.) ya know the man that guards the gate// (.)

Finally, it is necessary to explain how minor utterances such as *hello* and *thank you* are interpreted in the data sets. While these types of formulae do not conform to the regular patterns of clause structures or to the variations of those structures in the major syntactic classes, they are generally referred to as clause-level lexical concepts or minor utterances/sentences (Evans 2009). Similarly, concerning lengthier utterances, there exist several holophrastic utterances such as *the more, the merrier* and *on with the show*. Therefore, concerning the identification of clause boundaries, this study recognises the class of 'Irregular sentences' and 'Nonsentences' identified by Quirk et al. (1985: 838-53) that are recognised to function as whole sentences.

3.6.1.5 Simultaneous Speech Backchannels

In Section 2.6.4, variations in the interpretations of *simultaneous speech* (SS) were discussed, while Section 2.9.4.1 considered how this aspect of backchannel behaviour might be assessed in EFL/ESL pedagogy. The purpose of this section is to outline how *simultaneous speech backchannels* (SSBs) are identified in this study. SSBs are recorded when a backchannel is uttered during the primary speaker's speech, and, thus, backchannels which occur during pause periods in the primary speaker's speech are not considered SSBs. SSBs include laughter; however, as SSB laughter may influence perceptions differently than non-laughter SSBs, these two types of SSBs will be broken down into additional subcategories for analysis. Instances in which SSBs occur after a pause $\geq .5$ seconds are not identified as SSBs in this study. That is, the point after such a lengthy pause would seem to provide an equal opportunity for both speakers to speak (i.e., for the primary speaker to resume the primary speakership, and for the non-primary speaker to take it over) and, thus, could not be interpreted as any type of infringement. Further, there are various points in the data in which SS occurs due to the interactants' prolonged negotiation for the primary speakership. Since these occurrences of SS did not occur during one member's turn at talk, they cannot be identified as SSBs.

Lastly, concerning the interpretation of findings in this area, it is important to note that any results relying only on raw frequencies would not provide a competent assessment of this phenomenon as they would not take into account the number of SSB opportunities given (i.e., in terms of the number of turns their interlocutor took, as well as the length of each turn). In studies such as this, it would be difficult to compare raw frequencies of SSBs across cultural groups as the JEFLs had a much greater opportunity to produce SSBs due to the fact that their NES interlocutors spoke much more. Therefore, to accurately represent how often a person and/or group employed SSBs as compared to backchannels uttered during pauses, the number of SSBs was calculated as a percentage of the total backchannels that the person and/or group uttered.

3.6.2 WTC

The examination of participants' WTC is based on two main sources: McCroskey's (1992) self-report WTC questionnaires and behavioural observations. Regarding the former, WTC sub-scores were calculated according to the type of communication context and audience involved in this study, which focused on interpersonal communication and acquaintanceship respectively. This WTC construct has been shown to have strong face validity and evidence of construct and predictive validity (Asker 1998; McCroskey 1992). According to McCroskey's (1984) earlier assessment of self-report measurement, WTC and Communication Apprehension measurements are well suited to self-report measurement because these constructs are directed towards the cognition of the individual. Nonetheless, it seems wise to include an element of observation to strengthen the findings since the way people prefer to behave may not always be consistent with the way they actually behave. Hence, to determine if the WTC self-ratings were borne out in the conversational data, the amount that each person spoke (i.e., in terms of how many words they uttered) was also included in this analysis. Relative to engendering WTC, the next section describes how conversational micro-skills, which include strategies designed to stimulate conversation, are analysed.

3.6.3 Conversational Micro-skills

Drawing on the results of oral discourse theory and conversation analysis, linguists such as Dörnyei and Thurrell (1992), Iwai (2007) and Riggenbach (1998) have described a similar set of conversational micro-skills. These micro-skills, which include conversational repair strategies, are designed to help learners communicate more effectively with other people. Relative to backchannel behaviour, there is evidence of Japanese EFL/ESL speakers employing backchannels in situations when conversational repair strategies or expansion techniques may have been better options in terms of preventing communication breakdown or misunderstanding. This includes the JEFL tendency towards sending unconventional backchannel forms (i.e., continuer, understanding, agreement, and/or support and empathy types) when they do not understand or agree with what their interlocutor is saying (see Sections 1.9.3, 2.8.1 and 2.9.4.3), and also the tactic of employing backchannels as a means of avoiding primary speaker incipiency (see Section 2.8.1). Accordingly, relative to RQ 3 (see Appendix S), the teaching of specific conversational micro-skills, as they relate to backchannel behaviour, are examined in the longitudinal aspect of this study.

These micro-skills include conversational repair strategies such as the ability to self-repair, the ability to ensure comprehension on the part of the listener (e.g., comprehension checks), the ability to initiate repair when there is a potential breakdown (e.g., clarification requests), and the ability to employ compensatory strategies (e.g., paraphrasing, circumlocution, and the use of fillers and hesitation devices). Other micro-skills focus on stimulating conversation by using return questions, follow-up questions, strategies designed to initiate new topics and expansion techniques. These features, which were covered in the instructional aspect of this study, are analysed in various ways. Regarding the identification of return and follow-up questions in the transcriptions, this is recognised in accordance with WTC (see Section 3.6.2 above), which considers one's level of involvement and participation in a conversation (Fuji 2008).

Analysis of conversational repair strategies, however, was delimited to the specific contexts relevant to the central issues in this study, such as situations when JEFLs did not understand or agree with their interlocutor. In addition to documenting the number of times JEFLs use potentially unconventional and/or inappropriate backchannels in these situations, this analysis also examines the instances in which they use conversational repair strategies. Conversational repair strategies are divided into two types of listener response: minimal backchannel expressions such as those described in the functional categories outlined in Sections 2.5.7, 2.5.8 and 2.5.9, and longer expressions that could be either complex backchannels or full speaking turns. The latter are often realised in conversations by means of a specific set of typical conversational phrases and routines such as *I beg your pardon* or *what does that mean*. As a basis for identifying expressions that make up these repair strategies, this study acknowledges text strings that correspond to and are similar to the examples set forth in two language teacher's resource books that have been entirely based on these structures: *Function in English* (Blundell, Higgens & Middlemiss 1982) and *Conversation and Dialogues in Action* (Dörnyei & Thurrell 1992).

3.6.4 ICC

As Section 2.9.4.4 discussed, a fundamental requirement of ICC is for conversational participants to be seen as competent by members of the target culture. The data collection methods used in this study to determine this are questionnaires and interviews. Regarding the former, modified versions of Hecht's (1978) Interpersonal Communication Satisfaction Inventory (as outlined in Section 3.4.2) were used to determine how participants, and their respective groups, felt about each other as a result of their conversations. Furthermore, these questionnaires were also used to determine whether there was any correlation between JEFL participants' backchannel behaviour and NES observers' perceptions of them. Specifically, the researcher examined whether the frequency of the JEFLs' backchannels, including the frequency of minimal/extended and SSB subtypes, in the conversations influenced the NES observers' ratings on the questionnaire. Details of the statistical procedure used to determine this are provided in Section 3.6.7.

The data produced from the interviews were analysed both quantitatively and qualitatively. One of the goals here was to ascertain whether there were any key differences in the functions of backchannels between the NESs and JEFLs. The texts of the interviews were transcribed verbatim, and then examined for emergent themes based on two considerations: first, the various patterns found in the interviews, and second, in answer to questions pertaining to key concepts in this study as stated in Section 3.4.3. Regarding the latter, the discrepancies between the JEFLs' backchannel intentions and the impressions of their NES interlocutors recorded on the data record sheet (see Appendix K) in the successive interviews were points of further enquiry. The implications of these differences as they affect cross-cultural communication between the two groups were the focus of this part of the investigation. One aspect that was examined specifically was the types of backchannels the JEFLs sent when they admitted that they did not understand or agree with what their interlocutor was saying. Instances when the JEFLs uttered a continuer, understanding, agreement, or empathy/support type of backchannel were duly noted in this analysis because these types of backchannels often seemed to convey sentiments contrary to what the JEFLs were feeling. That is, the discrepancy was not necessarily between the JEFLs' backchannel intentions and the NESs' impressions, but rather between the JEFLs' comprehension/opinions and their actual backchannel behaviour – and thence between the JEFLs' comprehension/opinions and the NESs' perception of these things. In such cases, the JEFL participants were asked to explain their rationale.

3.6.5 Analysis of Levels and Gains

While the major focus of this study is to determine whether treatment leads to improved listening behaviour over time, other factors contributing to levels and gains are explored. A micro-level analysis of the data here was designed to bring to light in more detail some of the features of listening behaviour which were associated with varying levels of performance, and to identify potential patterns of development. Levels of performance were judged according to the four criteria specified in Section 2.9.4. JEFLs who exhibited particularly strong and weak listening behaviour as identified by these criteria were profiled, and the extent to which overall L2 proficiency (according to TOEIC scores) reflected levels and gains in listening behaviour was also explored. Finally, in an attempt to shed further light on what places performances in a particular category, the typical patterns and anomalies found in the JEFLs' conversational performances were analysed.

3.6.6 Cross-sectional vis-à-vis Longitudinal Analysis

An overview of the data and the types and purposes of each analysis is presented in Table 3-4 below.

Table 3-4 Summary of data, and types and purposes of analyses

Data (A: Quantitative, B: Qualitative)		Type of Data	Type of Analysis	Purposes of Analysis
				Relevant RQs (see Appendix S)
CROSS-SECTIONAL				
Transcriptions of videotaped intercultural conversations	A. Frequency	A	A, B	RQ 1
	B. Variability	A	A, B	RQ 1
	C. Discourse Contexts	A	A, B	RQ 1
	D. SSBs	A	A, B	RQ 1
Post-conversation ques. ratings		A	A	RQ 2
Post-conversation inter. comments		B	A, B	RQ 2 (other)[1]
Analysis of levels		A, B	A, B	RQ 5 & RQ 6
LONGITUDINAL				
Transcriptions of videotaped intercultural conversations	A. Frequency	A	A, B	RQ 3 & RQ 4
	B. Variability	A	A, B	RQ 3 & RQ 4
	C. Discourse Contexts	A	A, B	RQ 3 & RQ 4
	D. SSBs	A	A, B	RQ 3 & RQ 4
Post-conversation ques. ratings		A	A, B	RQ 3 & RQ 4
Post-conversation inter. comments		B	A, B	RQ 3 & RQ 4 (other)
NES Observer ques. ratings/comm		A, B	A, B	RQ 3 & RQ 4
Analysis of gains		A, B	A, B	RQ 5 & RQ 6

Following the basis established in Section 2.9.4, listener behaviour is analysed according to the following criteria: (1) observed backchannel behaviour, (2) WTC, (3) conversational micro-skills, and (4) ICC. In this study, this framework is applied to two levels of analyses: a cross-

---

[1] An additional purpose of post-conversation interviews is to determine the effects of Observer's Paradox and the extent of accommodation.

sectional analysis and longitudinal analysis. The cross-sectional analysis involves an examination of the differences between the two cultural groups prior to any treatment. That is, data collected in the Pre-test from all of the members of the JEFL group (N = 30) were compared to data corresponding to the American NES interlocutor group (N = 3). The longitudinal aspect of this study, however, measures the effectiveness of different types of instruction over time in this study. That is, conversational performances of members of three groups of JEFLs (i.e., the Explicit, Implicit and Control groups; N = 10 in each group) were analysed at three points in time, with each point in time constituting one of the three tests used in this study: the Pre-test, Post-test 1, or Post-test 2 (as described in Section 3.3).

3.6.7 Statistical Analysis

As much of the data collected by the observation phase described in Section 3.4.1 and the questionnaires described in Section 3.4.2 involved a quantitative analysis, it is necessary to describe how statistics informed this study. Descriptive statistics were used at various points to describe some basic features of the data in this study, whereas inferential statistics were also included at various points to determine the probability that an observed difference between groups was a significant one or one that might have happened by chance. Both parametric and non-parametric statistical tests were used depending on the type of data analysed. The Statistical Package for the Social Sciences (SPSS), version 14.0, was used to analyse the data in this study. In all inferential statistical tests used in this study, two-tailed tests were used, and alpha levels (α) were set at 0.05. However, as the groups in this study were small, probability statistics have to be viewed with caution. Thus, considering the possibility of Type 1 errors (i.e., the false rejection of the null hypothesis) occurring, probabilities less than the more stringent 0.01 level will also be shown and discussed.

In total, there were four different statistical tests applied to the data collected in this study: the Wilcoxon Signed Rank test, the Paired Sample T-test, the Spearman Rank Correlation Coefficient test (i.e., Spearman rho) and the Pearson Product-Moment Correlation Coefficient (PPMCC). Each of these statistical tests was used to analyse different components, as well as dimensions, of data. Before discussing how these statistical tests were used in this study, this section addresses the one area in which applying inferential statistics (i.e., both parametric and non-parametric) was not deemed appropriate: the cross-sectional data. The reason the

Paired Sample T-test or the Wilcoxon Signed Rank test were not applied in comparing key differences between the two groups (i.e., the JEFL group vis-à-vis the NES group) was that the cross-sectional data violated the basic assumption of independence, which requires the observations within each treatment condition to be independent. That is, inside each treatment, it is necessary for the scores to be obtained from different individuals and to be independent of one another (Gravetter & Wallnau 2008). In the case of the cross-sectional data in this study, the JEFL group consisted of 30 participants making up 30 sets of data, whereas the 30 sets of data corresponding to the NES interlocutor group were generated by only three NES participants, who each participated in multiple conversations. Thus, due to this violation of independence between the conversations, only descriptive statistics were used to illustrate some of the differences between two groups in the cross-sectional data.

Regarding the longitudinal data in this study, inferential statistics were applied because these data did not violate the assumption of independence. That is, each of the three groups of JEFL participants involved ten participants comprising ten individual data sets, which were compared before and after treatment. Within the inferential framework, it was necessary to choose between parametric and non-parametric statistical tests. It was also necessary to choose which statistical tests to apply to the data produced by the two types of questionnaires in this study: (1) the WTC questionnaires and (2) the three versions of Hecht's (1978) modified conversational satisfaction questionnaire. Considering the assumptions of parametric tests, different statistical analyses were applied to each type of questionnaire. To analyse the WTC questionnaires, the Paired Sample-T test was used to determine whether the differences between the means of the two groups were significant. This test was chosen because this segment of data met all four data requirements. Concerning the various versions of Hecht's (1978) modified questionnaire, it is useful to subdivide these questionnaires into the following two groups: (1) those involving NES interlocutors and (2) those involving NES observers. Since the data produced by the NES interlocutors' questionnaires involved an experimental design which violated the basic assumption of independence, it is not prudent to use inferential statistics to compare these ratings longitudinally, as well as cross-sectionally, in both matched-pair and correlational analyses. As a result, descriptive statistics were used to show some of the central differences over time.

Conversely, the data collected from the NES observers' questionnaires did not violate the basic assumption of independence, and, thus, inferential statistical tests were used to examine the two types of analyses in these questionnaires: matched-pairs and correlations. In this aspect of the study, matched-pairs are referring to the NES observers' perceptions before and after treatment. However, one of the data requirements of parametric testing was not met. Namely, these data were not drawn from a normal distribution as demonstrated by an exploratory data analysis that included Q-Q plot graphs, a normal curve superimposed over histograms of the data and the Shapiro-Wilk normality test. Consequently, the Wilcoxon Signed Rank test was used to compare the mean rank (or median) between the NES observers' perceptions of the JEFL participants' conversational performances at various points before and after treatment.

The final segment of data to be discussed involves the correlation analyses in this study. First, involving the NES observers, the main aim here was to ascertain whether there was an association between NES responses and backchannel behaviour, and specifically, whether there was an association between the NES observers' ratings on any of the 18 items in Hecht's (1978) modified conversational satisfaction questionnaire and the observed frequency of the JEFLs' backchannels in the intercultural conversations. To determine a connection, the researcher conducted a correlation analysis using the Spearman rho. This is a numerical representation of the degree to which two sets of numbers are related, and, in this study, will measure the degree to which the frequency of a particular conversational feature in the JEFL participants' speech in each conversation (one set of numbers) correlates to the NES observers' responses of each item on the questionnaire (the other set of numbers). The non-parametric Spearman rho was chosen over its parametric counterpart, the Pearson Product-Moment Correlation Coefficient (PPMCC), because exploratory data analyses revealed that this portion of the data was not distributed normally, and the use of the PPMCC test assumes both linearity and a normal distribution. However, concerning the data used to examine whether the JEFLs' WTC, Extraversion and TOEIC scores were correlated to a number of sub-skills associated with backchannel performance, the assumptions for parametric testing were met, and, thus, the PPMCC was used.

3.7 Conclusion

In conclusion, this chapter has served to provide a description of the methodology adopted in this study. This involved an examination of the participant selection, the procedural steps involved in carrying out the experiment, methods of collecting data, methods used to transcribe, and the data analysis techniques undertaken in this study. Methods involving both quantitative and qualitative data collection and analysis were used. Although using a wide array of methods and analyses would seem to help strengthen the reliability and validity of the findings, there are a few issues which require further discussion. First, while the intercultural conversations recorded in this study were designed to simulate the freedom, spontaneity and complexity of natural communication, they cannot be said to constitute naturalistic data since the context of the conversations was predesigned as part of a university course (Garman 1990). Moreover, there are many linguists who question the reliability and validity of analysing conversations at all. Mills (2003), for instance, challenges the notion of objective language analysis and believes it to be rather ambitious to surmise that analysts can grasp the full fluidity of conversations that they were not a part of. Furthermore, she also finds it disconcerting to see analysts continue to analyse extracts of conversations in isolation (i.e., seemingly as a final product), without discussing the context (i.e., what came before and what comes after) and the way that the event was processed, recycled and problematised.

To counter this and to give the interactants a voice in the analyses, the present study follows Cutrone (2005) in using retrospective interviews as a supplementary measure to determine the participants' intentions in the conversations. Since the use of what Johnstone (2000: 51) calls 'playback interviews' has not, to the researcher's knowledge, been conducted by other analysts when studying backchannels, this type of analysis would seem to offer the possibility of previously untapped and novel insights. However, according to Mills (2003: 45), such data 'is getting no nearer to the data of what really went on, as it is simply another text, another conversation, only this time the conversation is with the analyst'. As post-structuralist theorists contend, retracing the true intentions of the interactants in a conversation is a post-hoc rationalisation by the analyst. Motivations and intentions are often formulated in the process of interacting with someone else and can be especially difficult to recover in conversations because they can be mixed and occur on varying levels, with many at play in any given interaction. With regard to asking a speaker about their intentions in an utterance retrospectively, there are several problems associated with this. First, since the intentions of particular utterances in a conversation are discussed after the interaction has taken place, it seems likely that the interactants will have been influenced by what happened later in the conversation. Moreover, as Mills (2003) mentions, there is a certain degree of self-justification that takes place when people are asked about their intentions in an utterance. In other words, people tend to put their intentions retrospectively in a positive light. However, rather than dispensing with intentionality altogether, Toolan (1996) suggests approaching it as a working hypothesis which each speaker and hearer formulates and revises in the light of subsequent utterances. Although one cannot assume to ever accurately recover one's own or others' intentions and motivations in interactions, the notion of intentionality can be useful as an organising principle in the sense-making process of conversation. In this way, it serves the greater purpose of shedding light into misunderstanding in IC, which is at the centre of this study's analytic model. Having described the methodological elements of this study in this chapter, the next chapter reports and discusses the results of the cross-sectional data collected in this study.

CHAPTER FOUR

CROSS-SECTIONAL RESULTS AND DISCUSSION

Part I: The Cross-sectional Results
4.1 Introduction

This chapter has been divided into two parts. The first part will present the results of the cross-sectional aspect of this study, while the second part will discuss these results as they pertain to previous research in this area. The findings are presented and discussed as they correspond to the three methods of data collection in this study: observations, questionnaires and interviews. Each method contributes to answering some of the research questions of this study (see Appendix S). First, in response to RQ 1, the data gathered by the observation phase describes how the JEFL and NES conversational participants used backchannels (BCs) differently in terms of frequency, variability, discourse contexts favouring backchannels and simultaneous speech. Second, providing some of the initial groundwork for answering RQ 2, Hecht's (1978) conversational satisfaction questionnaire reveals how participants felt about each other after the conversations. Third, the interviews were able to shed further light on the dynamics of listening behaviour and perceptions across cultures, which were useful in providing a more complete answer to RQ 2. To this end, the interviews were designed with several objectives in mind, namely, to delve deeper into the findings of the observations and questionnaires, to provide insights explaining why participants used backchannels the way they did and, ultimately, to determine the degree to which differing backchannel conventions across cultures affected IC and perceptions in this study. Lastly, in partial answer to RQs 5 and 6, a micro-level analysis of the cross-sectional data is presented in order to bring to light in more detail some of the features of listening behaviour which were associated with varying levels of performance, and to identify potential patterns of development. It is necessary to point out that statistics in this study have been rounded off to the nearest hundredth decimal point, and the

130   Chapter Four

limitations on numbers described in Section 3.2.1 precluded giving separate reports on the gender sub-groups in this study.

4.2 Frequency

As reported in Table 4-1, the conversational data show that the Japanese participants provided considerably more backchannels than the American participants (1265 and 289 respectively). Taking into account how much opportunity each group had to send backchannels, the results show that the Japanese provided a backchannel every 6.46 of their interlocutor's words, whereas the Americans provided a backchannel every 7.38 words. Appendix M provides the individual performances of members of each cultural group. While the NESs showed a slightly greater range in average frequency of backchannel per interlocutor word (+2.28) and higher SD (+.76) as reported in Table 4-1 below, an analysis of the individual frequencies shown in the table provided in Appendix M did not reveal any outliers influencing the results disproportionately. There was only one performance in either group that showed an increase in frequency of more than one point from the next closest participant in their group, and this was a modest increase of 1.5, which was not thought to have a great impact on the group's score overall. As described in Section 3.6.7, Spearman rho correlation analyses were conducted to determine whether there was a possible association between the frequency of a particular feature of the JEFLs' backchannel behaviour and the NES observers' responses of each item on the conversational satisfaction questionnaire (see Appendix N). A statistically significant correlation was found between the number of backchannels the JEFLs sent and the NES observers' ratings on Item 2 ($p<.029$), Item 5 ($p<.023$) and Item 6 ($p<.003$). Thus, as the number of JEFL backchannels increased, (Item 2) the more the NES observers believed the JEFLs to be showing understanding, (Item 5) the more the NES observers felt the conversation went smoothly and (Item 6) the more the NES observers believed the JEFLs to be encouraging their interlocutor to continue speaking.

4.2.1 Involvement in the Conversation

In addition to backchannel frequency, Table 4-1 has shown the willingness of each group to speak and carry the conversation in terms of the amount of words each group uttered. It is clear to see that the NESs spoke a great deal more, averaging 263.77 words per conversation, while the JEFLs averaged 62.43 words. Using Spearman rho, a statistically significant relationship was found between the number of words the JEFLs uttered and the NES observers' ratings on Items 1, 2, 7, 15 and 16 (see Appendix N). The direction of the significant correlation for all these items shows that greater word outputs were associated with positive ratings. Another important consideration involving this issue is the number of full-turn questions each group asked. As Table 4-2 illustrates, the NESs averaged 2.33 questions per conversation compared to 1.27 questions posed by the JEFLs. As described in Section 3.6.7, the PPMCC test was used to determine whether there was a possible association between JEFLs' Extraversion, WTC and/or TOEIC scores with the frequency of a particular feature of the JEFLs' backchannel behaviour (for cross-sectional data, see Appendix O, Pre-test). Regarding involvement in the conversation, a strongly significant positive correlation (at the .01 level) was found between the JEFLs' TOEIC scores and both the number of words they uttered and questions asked, and a moderately positive correlation (at the .05 level) was found between the JEFLs' WTC scores and the number of questions they asked.

Table 4-1 Differences in frequency of backchannels across cultures

JEFLs = 30 NESs = 3	Total Backchannels		Total Words		Average number of interlocutor's words between backchannels	
	JEFLs	NESs	JEFLs	NESs	JEFLs	NESs
Overall Total	1265	289	1873	7913	—	—
Mean ($\bar{x}$)	42.16	9.63	62.43	263.77	6.46	7.38
SD	13.18	6.11	31.39	247	1.36	2.12
Median	39.5	8	56.5	63.68	6.31	6.92
Range	47	289	114	192	5.5	7.78

Table 4-2 Number of questions across cultures

JEFLs = 30 NESs = 3	JEFLs				NESs			
	Total	$\bar{x}$	SD	Median	Total	$\bar{x}$	SD	Median
Number of Questions	38	1.27	.87	1	70	2.33	1.88	2

4.3 Variability of Use

Table 4-3 distinguishes the frequency of specific subtypes of verbal backchannels across cultures. From the mean percentage of total backchannels constituting each category, it can be seen that both groups favoured the Simple with head nod type (NESs: 37.49%, JEFLs: 35.71%). Other similarities between the two groups included Compound isolated (NESs: 1.03%, JEFLs: 1.77%), and Compound with head nod(s) (NESs: 2.74%, JEFLs: 4.55%) types. The main difference concerning verbal backchannels was the frequency by which each group uttered Complex backchannels. The mean percentage of the NESs' backchannels constituting the Complex with head nod(s) type was 20.83%, and, for Complex (isolated), it was 11.15%. In contrast, the means for the JEFLs were only 5.11% and 2.79% in these categories respectively. The large discrepancies in the standard deviations corresponding to the Simple with head nod(s), Complex (isolated) and Complex with head nod(s) categories suggest considerably more variability within the performances of the NES group.

Table 4-3 Types of verbal backchannels across cultures

Type	Japanese Backchannels N = 30				American Backchannels N = 3			
	Total	x̄ % of Total BCs	SD	Median	Total	x̄ % of Total BCs	SD	Median
Simple (isolated)	147	13.21	9.27	11.51	25	7.81	12.96	0
Simple with head nod(s)	476	35.71	16.77	37.85	112	37.49	34.06	35.42
Compound (isolated)	14	1.03	1.84	0	5	1.77	4.8	0
Compound with head nod(s)	39	2.74	2.18	2.74	15	4.55	8.53	0
Complex (isolated)	31	2.79	4.46	1.96	22	11.15	13.98	7.14
Complex with head nod(s)	68	5.11	4.05	4.44	50	20.83	17.08	16.67
Japanese	11	1.11	4.56	0	0	0	0	0

Concerning differences in nonverbal backchannels, Table 4-4 shows that the mean percentage of backchannels constituted by nonverbal backchannels (without verbal backchannel accompaniment) was much greater for the JEFLs (JEFLs: 36.79%, NESs: 19.45%). Furthermore, the mean percentage of backchannels constituted by head nod(s) was much greater for the JEFLs: 15.75% and 10.75% in the single head nod (isolated) and multiple head nod(s) categories respectively for the JEFLs, whereas the mean in these categories was only 12.25% and 4.37% respectively for the NESs. The proportion of laughter (isolated) was also noticeably higher for the JEFLs (JEFLs: 8.31%, NESs: 1.07%). Other subcategories involving nonverbal backchannels did not show great disparity between the two groups.

Table 4-4 Types of nonverbal backchannels across cultures

Type	Japanese Backchannels N = 30				American Backchannels N = 3			
	Total	x̄ % of Total BCs	SD	Median	Total	x̄ % of Total BCs	SD	Median
Total isolated nonverbal BCs	479	36.79	17.98	34.52	60	19.45	18.10	17.42
Single head nod (isolated)	222	15.75	12.4	16.33	36	12.25	16.39	2.38
Multiple head nods (isolated)	163	10.75	11.02	7.33	17	4.37	6.25	0
Isolated Smile	0	0	0	0	1	.56	3.04	0
Smiles with verbal BCs	31	2.38	3.7	.82	4	2.26	7.6	0
Laughter (isolated)	93	8.31	6.86	6.11	4	1.07	3.37	0
Laughter + verbal BCs	38	2.6	4.2	0	3	1.55	5.43	0
Raised Eyebrows (isolated)	0	0	0	0	1	.24	1.3	0
Raised Eyebrows + verbal BCs	19	1.53	2.39	0	4	1.15	3.26	0
≥ 2 nonverbal BCs occurring simultaneously (isolated)	1	.08	.45	0	1	.29	1.1	0
≥ 2 nonverbal BCs occurring simultaneously + verbal BCs	6	.5	1.62	0	2	.32	1.74	0

As Sections 2.4 and 3.6.1.2 explain, some of the above-mentioned categories combine to form two separate and distinct superordinate classes of backchannel responses: extended responses and minimal responses. As Table 4-5 illustrates, the mean percentage of backchannels constituted by minimal responses was much greater for the JEFLs (JEFLs: 75.96%, NESs: 62.88%), whereas that constituted by extended responses was much greater for the NESs (NESs: 35.38%, JEFLs: 7.95%). Using Spearman rho, a strong statistical significant relationship (at the .01 level) was found between the number of extended responses the JEFLs sent and the NES observers' ratings on Items 1, 2, 4, 6, 7, 11, 13, 15 and 17, while a significant relationship (at the .05 level) was observed for Items 5 and 16 (see Appendix N). The direction of the significant correlation for all these items shows that more frequent extended responses were associated with more positive ratings. Further, using the PPMCC to measure the relationship between variables (see Appendix O, Pre-test), significant positive correlations were found between both the JEFLs' TOEIC and WTC scores and the percentage of backchannels constituted by extended backchannels (at .01 and .05 levels respectively), and a significant negative correlation (at the .05 level) was observed between the JEFLs' TOEIC scores and the percentage of backchannels constituted by minimal backchannels.

Table 4-5 Minimal responses and extended responses across cultures

	Japanese Backchannels N = 30				American Backchannels N = 3			
Type of BC	Total	x̄ % of Total BCs	SD	Median	Total	x̄ % of Total BCs	SD	Median
Minimal Responses	1008	75.96	17.52	79.77	190	62.88	35.97	66.67
Extended Responses	99	7.95	5.59	8.39	72	35.38	30.53	32.58

4.3.1 Non-word vocalisations, content words and phrases

Examining the different constituents that make up backchannels (see Section 2.4), this section divides backchannel forms into the following three groups: non-word vocalisations (shown in Table 4-6), isolated content words (shown in Table 4-7) and multi-word backchannel phrases and/or expressions (shown in Table 4-8). To be included in any of the three data sets below, it was required that the item occur at least twice in the conversations. Supporting the overall findings presented in this section, the results here further display the NESs' greater variability and range in backchannel forms, while demonstrating the JEFLs' reliance on minimal responses as backchannel forms.

Table 4-6 Variability in non-word vocalisations

	uu/unn hm/um mm	mhm uhum	uhuh	aa/ah	oo	oh	eee	yeah yes yeah yep	Total
JEFLs	209	27	14	71	46	0	21	96	**484**
NESs	37	40	20	7	0	0	0	34	**138**

Table 4-7 Variability in isolated content words

	ok	no	really	right	wow	nice	cool	great	good	Total
JEFLs	8	0	4	0	2	0	1	0	0	**15**
NESs	9	2	5	2	2	2	1	3	2	**28**

Table 4-8 Variability in multi-word backchannel phrases/expressions

	oh/ah really	that's/ you're right	ah/oh yeah	that's interesting	that's /very nice	I know	me too	I see	Total
JEFLs	7	1	0	2	0	0	1	0	**11**
NESs	8	2	5	2	3	2	3	2	**27**

The subcategories presented in Tables 4-7 and 4-8 did not include backchannel forms which involved repetitions (REPS) of the primary speaker's speech. As described in Section 3.6.1.2, backchannels as repetitions are distinguished by two types: clarifications (CLARS) and non-clarifications (NON CLARS). Table 4-9 reports on each group's use of repetitions in the intercultural conversations. The mean percentages of backchannels constituted by repetitions were fairly similar overall (JEFLs: 3.3%, NESs: 2.19%); however, the NESs employed a greater proportion of backchannels constituted by clarification (JEFLs: .5%, NESs: 1.64%), while the JEFLs sent a greater proportion of backchannels constituted by non-clarification (JEFLs: 2.82%, NESs: .56%).

Table 4-9 Use of repetitions as backchannels across cultures

x̄ = x̄ % of Total BCs (M) = Median	Total REPS	x̄	SD (M)	Total CLARS	x̄	SD (M)	Total NON CLARS	x̄	SD (M)
JEFLs	40	3.3	1.6 (.9)	6	.5	1.1 (0)	34	2.82	1.5 (2.9)
NESs	5	2.19	1.2 (.6)	4	1.64	5.1 (0)	1	.56	3 (0)

4.4 Discourse Contexts Favouring Backchannels

Table 4-10 reports two main statistics regarding the discourse contexts of each group's backchannels (BCs): (1) the mean percentage of opportunities (Opps) that each discourse context attracted backchannels (with SDs), and (2) the mean percentage of backchannels constituted by each discourse context (with SDs). Concerning (1), the results show that the completion of a grammatical clause (i.e., at or near a final clause boundary), and particularly one accompanied by a pause, provides the single most significant contextual cue for backchannels for both cultural groups (JEFLs: 63.87%, NESs: 56.8%). However, the mean percentage of internal clause boundaries attracting backchannels (irrespective of pause) was noticeably higher for the JEFLs (JEFLs: 27.33%, NESs: 11.67%). Regarding other discourse contexts, JEFLs also had a markedly higher mean percentage of pauses attracting backchannels (JEFLs: 42.87%, NESs: 23.37%), as well as after the primary speaker's head nod(s) attracting backchannels (JEFLs: 42.73%, NESs: 22%). Regarding (2), the proportion of backchannels constituted by each discourse context category is fairly similar across groups, except in the case of clausal boundaries. Irrespective of pauses, the mean percentage of backchannels constituted by final clause boundaries is noticeably greater for the JEFLs (JEFLs: 56.87%, NESs: 35.07%). In the following table, the expressions *at or directly after a pause* and *at or near clausal boundary* have been shortened to *at pause* and *at CB* respectively.

Table 4-10 Discourse contexts of backchannels across cultures

Discourse Contexts	JEFLs N = 30			NESs N = 3		
	Total	x̄ % of Opps (SD)	x̄ % of BCs (SD)	Total	x̄ % of Opps (SD)	x̄ % of BCs (SD)
At pause	576	42.87 (12.95)	46.56 (18.69)	150	23.37 (9.91)	55.72 (23.07)
Clausal Boundaries						
At CB	779	60.13 (12.19)	60.26 (14.43)	121	43.03 (22.56)	37.87 (21.18)
At internal CB	42	27.33 (30.13)	2.88 (2.01)	7	11.67 (28.77)	1.69 (4.17)
At final CB	733	61.83 (15.03)	56.87 (14.26)	110	46.57 (24.28)	35.07 (20.86)
When CBs and pauses occur together						
At any CB accompanied by a pause	419	62.03 (16.16)	33.64 (13.65)	72	53.13 (33.05)	23.95 (18.86)
At internal CB accompanied by a pause	19	26 (38.18)	1.4 (2.5)	2	6.67 (25.37)	.34 (1.29)
At final CB accompanied by a pause	415	63.87 (16.12)	33.64 (13.75)	71	56.8 (32.59)	23.76 (18.9)
Gesticulation						
After primary speaker's nonverbal gesture	79	28.5 (20.21)	7.13 (7.64)	31	20.57 (19.89)	12.59 (14.2)
After primary speaker's head nod(s)	104	42.73 (22.52)	8.94 (7.18)	27	22 (24.02)	14.34 (21.05)

4.4.1 Simultaneous Speech Backchannels

This section examines the number of backchannels produced during the primary speaker's turn at talk creating simultaneous speech (SSBs). Table 4-11 shows that the JEFLs provided 242 SSBs, while the NESs produced only 29. Whereas there was a large discrepancy in raw frequencies, the mean percentages of backchannels constituted by SSBs were not as divergent (JEFLs: 18.1%, NESs: 10.77%), which was most notable in the non-laughter subcategory (JEFLs: 13.99%, NESs: 9.21%). Using Spearman rho, a strong significant relationship (at the .01 level) was found between the number of non-laughter SSBs the JEFLs sent and the

NES observers' ratings on Items 1, 2, 4, 5, 6, 7, 11, 13 and 17, while a significant relationship (at the .05 level) was observed for Items 3, 8, 12, 15 and 16 (see Appendix N). The direction of the significant correlation for all these items indicates that more frequent non-laughter SSBs were associated with more positive ratings. Lastly, a significant positive correlation (at the .05 level) was observed between the JEFLs' TOEIC scores and their number of non-laughter SSBs.

Table 4-11 SSBs across cultures

	Japanese N = 30			Americans N = 3		
SSB Types	Total	x̄ % of BCs	SD	Total	x̄ % of BCs	SD
Non-laughter	189	13.99	8.56	25	9.21	12.61
Laughs	53	4.11	5.18	4	1.56	4.2
Total SSBs	242	18.1	10.98	29	10.77	12.74

4.5 Questionnaires: Examining Participants' Conversational Satisfaction

To examine the conversational satisfaction of each group in this study, Hecht's (1978) modified questionnaire, as described in Section 3.4.2, was given to each participant directly upon completion of their conversations (see Appendix G for NES version and Appendix H for JEFL version). Table 4-12 shows the results across cultures as they pertain to each of the 15 items in the questionnaire (N.B. Item 2 was slightly different for each culture). Overall, the results from the questionnaire were comparatively similar across cultures, and indicated that participants generally had positive impressions from their conversations with their cross-cultural interlocutors.

Nonetheless, a few notable exceptions in which the JEFLs expressed substantially less satisfaction (>1) were found in Items 2, 3, 5 and 6. First, concerning Item 2, the JEFLs' score of 4.2 demonstrates that they felt that they may not have represented themselves fairly in the conversations (see Section 3.4.2 for an explanation of the word *fairly*). The NES interlocutors' score of 1.87 in Item 2, conversely, indicates the general perception that their JEFL counterparts expressed themselves in a way that seemed sincere and authentic. This considerable difference between the groups' scores (2.33) in parallel items would seem to highlight a gap in the IC that took place. Moreover, the JEFLs were markedly less convinced that the NESs were understanding them (difference of 1 in Item 3), were interested in what they had to say (difference of 1.3 in Item 5), and that the conversation went smoothly (difference of 1.95 in Item 6). Although the primary focus in this study is to examine how aspects of listening behaviour affects perceptions in IC, the researcher acknowledges that feelings of conversational satisfaction may have owed a lot to other factors, i.e., namely, the JEFL proficiency factor.

Table 4-12 Participants' conversational satisfaction

Items on the Questionnaire Scale ranges from 1 (strongly agree) to 7 (strongly disagree).	JEFLs N = 30 x̄ (SD)	NESs N = 3 x̄ (SD)
1. S/he let me know that I was communicating effectively.	2.27 (1.05)	1.68 (.86)
2. I felt I was able to present myself fairly during the conversation (for JEFLs only).	4.2 (1.57)	—
2. The feelings that my partner expressed by means of listening feedback during the conversation seemed authentic (for NESs only).	—	1.87 (1.49)
3. S/he showed me that s/he understood what I said.	2.4 (1.1)	1.4 (.86)
4. S/he showed me that s/he listened attentively to what I said.	1.33 (.71)	1.3 (.84)
5. S/he expressed a lot of interest in what I had to say.	2.67 (.88)	1.37 (.96)
6. The conversation went smoothly.	3.53 (1.48)	1.58 (1.12)
7. S/he encouraged me to continue talking.	1.37 (.56)	1.43 (1.17)
8. S/he seemed impatient.	6.53 (1.2)	6.73 (6.9)
9. S/he seemed cold and unfriendly.	6.97 (.18)	6.83 (.59)
10. S/he was polite.	1.57 (1.55)	1.1 (.31)
11. S/he appeared warm and friendly.	1.17 (.38)	1.77 (1.05)
12. S/he was impolite.	6.83 (.91)	6.93 (.25)
13. S/he appeared interested and concerned.	1.97 (1.3)	1.4 (1.07)
14. S/he interrupted me.	6.83 (.59)	6.53 (1.01)
15. My conversation partner seemed to want to avoid speaking.	6.27 (1.34)	6.53 (1.25)

4.6 Interviews

Based on the considerations outlined in Section 3.6.4, the interview findings are organised into three subsections which include the factors reported to affect participants' behaviour (4.6.1), the different functions of backchannels reported by informants in each culture (4.6.2), and the differing perceptions of backchannel behaviour across cultures (4.6.3). Where omissions or grammatical errors had the potential to cloud the sentiments below, words in parentheses were added to facilitate understanding.

4.6.1 Factors Affecting Backchannel Behaviour

While the main focus of the interviews was to gain insights into participants' backchannel behaviour, this initial section reports on some of the experimental and/or design issues that may have influenced participants' behaviour in the conversations. To this end, the researcher sought to determine the extent to which Observer's Paradox affected the videotaped conversations, and the degree to which the NESs accommodated to their intercultural interlocutors. Concerning the presence of Observer's Paradox in this aspect of the study, the overwhelming majority of the participants (all three of the NESs and 27 of the 30 JEFLs) indicated that they were not conscious of the camera once the conversation developed. Some of the most common responses included the following:

Michiko: The camera did not bother me at all.

Yukari: At first, it was little strange, but once (I) talked, I forgot all about (it).

Akanori: I was too busy thinking what I am going to say next to even notice camera.

Betty: The camera didn't affect me whatsoever as I just like talking in any situation really.

Jerry: As the conversation ensued, I didn't even notice the camera in the room, and I don't think my partner did either.

Of the three JEFLs who were conscious of the camera, one would not elaborate on her feelings, and the other two stated the following:

> Shio: I could not relax and feel comfortable because I can always feel camera is watching me.
>
> Keiko: I think I will not change my speak if camera not there, but I can't forget it, and I don't want to see myself after on video because I'm shy.

Further, considering the extent to which the NESs accommodated to their intercultural interlocutors, the interviewer asked the NESs whether they altered their behaviour and/or speech in any way to facilitate cross-cultural communication with their JEFL interlocutor. All three NESs interviewed in this phase of the study reported that they did indeed modify their behaviour and speech in various ways to better communicate with their JEFL interlocutors. Some of the responses below refer specifically to the conversations in this study, while others refer to general communication with Japanese people in English.

> Jerry: When I speak to Japanese people in English, I find myself subconsciously slowing down my speech and always stopping after a few words to make sure they understand me.
>
> Betty: I knew that I would have to do most of the talking because I was the native speaker in the conversation, which suits me fine cuz I love talking. Also, in the rare instances that my partner spoke, I had to provide her with extra reassurances that I understood what she was saying.
>
> Jason: I really had (to) slow down my speech and be very careful to use words and ideas that he would understand. I also find myself using a lot more gestures.

One major theme to emerge from this line of questioning is that all NESs admitted that they generally have much more patience and tolerance for misunderstandings in cross-cultural communication than they would have communicating with other NESs. In addition to Betty's response above, the following statements also support this claim.

> Jerry: I don't mind waiting for them (JEFLs) to process what they want to say because they aren't native speakers, so it's tough for them I know.
>
> Jason: I find I have a lot more patience when I talk to Japanese people. I am more willing to carry the conversation and explain things to them because they aren't native speakers.
>
> Betty: She (Ayuka) was quite low, but I didn't really mind cuz I knew she was trying hard. It might be different in another setting like work or

school. Even socially I guess I mean I doubt I'd try that hard with someone I just met if I was sitting on a bench at a bus stop back home.

The data also showed that some of the JEFLs modify their behaviour when speaking across cultures, albeit in a different way. Many of the JEFL respondents indicated that, while they would like to accommodate towards the NESs, their behaviour and performance in intercultural encounters is mostly affected by the anxiety they feel, which stems from not knowing how to act in these situations. The following responses demonstrate this:

Aria: I am nervous speaking to foreigners because, even I know the English I don't know what to say.

Mayumi: When I speak to gaikokujin (foreigners), I feel so scared because they speak so fast and look straight at my eyes. My mind goes blank, and I don't know what I should say.

Mikki: Betty was so nice, but I was so nervous when I couldn't understand her. I wish I could understand perfectly, so we can be good friends.

Kazuya: Japanese nature is to not speak a lot I think, so is difficult for we Japanese to speak to foreigners because foreigners mostly love big conversation.

4.6.2 Functions of Backchannels Across Cultures

When asked about the function of a specific backchannel during playback of the conversation, participants' responses from both cultures indicated that the functions of most backchannels were largely determined by the context of the conversation at that time. The most frequently cited functions by both groups included backchannels to allow the primary speaker to continue his/her speaking turn, to show comprehension, to show agreement, and to show empathy and support. Some functional differences between the two groups began to emerge, however, when participants were asked to explain their thought processes behind some of these common backchannels. While the three NESs described their continuer backchannels in terms generally associated with Schegloff's (1982) definition (see Section 2.5.1), the far-reaching dynamics involved in the JEFLs' concept of continuer appeared to be markedly different. All 30 of the JEFLs reported that they often employ backchannels as a means to ensure continued participation and inclusion in the conversation, and 19 of them acknowledged that they also sometimes employ backchannels as a way to avoid speaking due to shyness, lack of confidence in their English ability, and not knowing what to say next. These feelings are expressed in the responses below, of which Meo and Taro's excerpts point directly to Japanese culture as the basis for this type of behaviour.

> Haruna: My English is not good, so I give many aizuchi (the Japanese word for backchannel) so I can still be a part of the conversation.

> Meo: I think foreigners love speaking and attention, and Japanese are very shy and like mostly listening and not speaking, so we give lots of aizuchi. It's Japanese nature, I believe.

> Yuki: Of course, I want to talk more if possible, but my English is not good. I don't know what to say or do, so I just nod.

> Taro: I think Japanese try to (be) polite and let the other person talk. We give many aizuchi to support the other person when they speak.

> Yukari: It is much easier to give aizuchi than to speak; so I do that instead. [when asked later to clarify her response, Yukari explained that she responded as above because she feels her English was not good enough to be able to make significant speech contributions to the conversation. She also added that being a passive listener suits her personality type].

Another important functional difference emerged in situations when participants did not understand or agree with what their interlocutor was saying in the intercultural conversations. JEFLs often used backchannel types that conveyed different sentiments to what they were actually feeling. Specifically, relating to the unconventional use of backchannels in non-understanding situations discussed in Section 3.4.3, JEFLs used continuer, understanding, support and empathy, and agreement backchannels in 71% of the cases they reported not understanding what their interlocutor was saying (98 unconventional backchannels were sent during or after the 139 instances of non-understanding). In comparison, the NESs did not provide any of these types of backchannels during or after the 11 instances they reported of not understanding and the one instance of disagreement. Non-understanding situations, and how JEFLs behaved therein, may have owed a great deal to proficiency levels as significant negative correlations (at the .05 level) were found between the JEFLs' TOEIC scores and both the number of non-understanding situations they encountered and the percentage of these situations in which they produced unconventional backchannels (see Appendix O, Pre-test). Further, concerning the two instances the JEFLs felt disagreement with their interlocutor, they provided continuer type backchannels both times (100%).

Overall, a great majority of the JEFLs' backchannels in these contexts were reported to serve a continuer function; however, some of the other functions were also mentioned, sometimes overlapping with continuers. When asked to explain why they had employed continuer, understanding, agreement, or empathy/support type backchannels in situations when they did not understand and/or disagreed with what their interlocutor was saying at the time, some JEFLs again alluded to cultural factors and issues concerning politeness. As shown in the following excerpts, several respondents seemed to place a much greater emphasis on preserving harmony and ensuring smooth communication rather than communicating absolute truth.

Saya: I sometimes give aizuchi when I don't understand because it's polite.

Sachi: I said *yeah yeah* but didn't really understand anything.

Kouki: It is rude to interrupt, so I fake understanding sometimes.

Tomomi: It is Japanese way to listen until speaker is finished even (if) I don't understand.

Madora: Even (if) I don't understand, I nod and give aizuchi because (I) don't want to lose nice atmosphere.

Akie: I think interrupt partner is no good even (if) I disagree. Nice communication is most important for us Japanese. I don't want partner to lose the face.

Takanori: I am scared if I don't understand my partner will think I stupid, so I just say *un un* and nod always, even (if) I don't know his saying.

Similar to Takanori's response above, several other JEFL respondents stated that they sometimes used backchannels when they did not understand to avoid embarrassment. This can be seen in the following responses:

Madora: If she knows I don't understand, maybe she will think I am not intelligent, so I try to fake it and hide my bad English.

Hiro: Yes, I often do aizuchi when I don't understand. I do this because I don't want him to think I am stupid and to know that my English level is poor.

Keiko: I will feel ashamed if she knows I am not clever, so I let her do most (of the) talking.

Lastly, another potential function of the JEFLs' backchannels may be to allow additional processing time. As shown in the following responses, some of the JEFLs stated that they sometimes employ backchannels as a means to allow themselves a few extra seconds to process information and decide what they will say next.

Ayuka: Conversation was so fast, and I can't think what (to) say next, so I give aizuchi so I can have time to think more.

Madora: Sometimes, I don't understand at first. I nod and say yes and hope I can figure out main meaning later.

Hiro: I need time to translate in my head, so I give aizuchi for time and to keep partner talking until I am ready.

When the NESs were asked about this, all three replied that they did not employ backchannels to gain additional processing time, or at least were not conscious of it if they did.

4.6.3 Perceptions of Backchannels Across Cultures

As Table 4-12 reported, each cultural group in this study generally had favourable post-conversation impressions of their cross-cultural interlocutors. When responding in the interviews, the NESs offered both their general opinions of IC with the Japanese based on their brief time in Japan, as well as their specific perceptions of their JEFL interlocutor's performance in the dyadic conversations. When asked about their impressions of the NESs' backchannel behaviour, none of the JEFLs had any concrete ideas or opinions to share about this. The only minor theme to surface was that, while not committing to saying that it necessarily detracted from their enjoyment of the conversation, a few of the JEFLs recognised that the NESs' listener responses were much more exuberant and variable than their own. This is evidenced by the following excerpts:

Ayuka: Foreigners always give many big reactions, but Japanese only give small ones.

Kazuya: Japanese often say the same kind of aizuchi; not like Americans, they say so many different things and give big and livelier reactions.

> Yoko: I think it is unnatural for Japanese to give big reactions, but it is ok for foreigners because it is their culture.

In contrast, when asked about their impressions of the JEFLs' backchannel behaviour, the NESs all mentioned the JEFLs' lack of variability and exuberance as a source that might negatively affect IC. The following extracts illustrate this view:

> Jerry: I know it's tough speaking a second language, but I wish their reactions would better fit the situation. For instance, if I told them I had won a million dollars, I want to hear *wow* or *that's great* rather than just see a little head nod or hear a little grunt.

> Betty: It was difficult to tell if a few of them were really listening and getting it cuz, ya know, all the reactions were kinda similar. I wanted more enthusiasm I guess.

> Jason: Many of the reactions didn't feel very natural. I kind of got the impression that he may have been just going through the motions. I wasn't even sure if he understood what I was saying because all the responses were the same.

Related to Jason's point directly above, the NESs also expressed confusion and/or minor irritation when they sensed that the JEFLs employed backchannels in ways that seemed unconventional in English such as when they do not understand. The following examples convey the feelings of Jerry and Betty:

> Jerry: I have a hard time telling if Japanese people are really understanding me. For instance, when my partner said *mhm* here (points at the screen), I still don't know if he knows what character I was talking about. This always used to happen when I first got here a few months ago. People would just nod away even though they haven't (the) faintest clue what I'm saying.

> Betty: I sometimes feel that my partner was just nodding and laughing to be polite whether she understood or not; Americans would never do that.

Regarding the more frequent backchannelling style of the JEFL group, the NESs' responses were mixed. While one NES was not conscious of any disparity in backchannel frequency, the other two NESs had conflicting opinions. That is, Betty stated that she enjoyed the rather large amount of listener feedback, while Jerry thought it excessive and interruptive, particularly while he was speaking.

Betty: My partner nodded a lot and, generally, I like getting a lot of responses when I'm talking. I couldn't tell if she understood everything, but at least she was trying. For me, the more (responses), the merrier.

Jerry: It was difficult to know if he wanted to talk or what. I mean sometimes he would interrupt me with grunts or words I had just said, and I'd try to let him talk and he wouldn't take it any further and we'd have these awkward silences. If that was supposed to be listening feedback, then it felt a little strange to me. Laughs are fine, but it was the other stuff that I didn't really get. I guess I prefer the feedback after I'm done speaking and not during (my speech).

Finally, the fact that the Americans would have to carry the conversation was generally accepted by them as touched upon in Section 4.6.1. The following excerpts however seem to imply that it may have detracted from their enjoyment of the conversation:

Jerry: In my case, I don't mind carrying the conversation because I'm pretty outgoing and love to talk, but back in the States where I'm from, I doubt people would make such an effort to keep a conversation going if the other person didn't reciprocate.

Betty: It was hard to tell if she was interested because she didn't speak much or ask any questions. I really wanted to hear what she thought, and of course, I wish she would have asked me more questions.

Jason: It seemed like he didn't really want to talk and was counting the seconds to get out of the conversation. He was very curt in his replies. In the few times he did say something, his English was fine, so that wasn't it. Maybe he just found me or the topic boring.

All three NESs expressed a desire for their JEFL interlocutors to be more involved in the conversations, and the JEFLs' perceived lack of involvement seems to have caused the NESs to question how interested the JEFLs were in the conversation. This lack of JEFL involvement in the conversations, and its negative effect on IC, appears to be a recurring theme in this study and will be revisited in the second part of this chapter (see Section 4.8), which will discuss these findings in relation to previous research, as well as corresponding themes and RQs of this study.

Part II: Discussion of Cross-sectional Results

4.7 Frequency

The findings presented in Table 4-1 showed that the JEFLs sent noticeably more backchannels than the NESs. Taking into account the number of backchannels per interlocutor word, the ratio of 1.14:1 between cultural groups in this study was identical to that found in Cutrone's (2005) earlier intercultural analysis, which involved British NESs conversing with JEFLs. Other cross-sectional studies such as Clancy et al. (1996) and White (1989) also found that Japanese speakers of English provided more backchannels than their American NES counterparts in intercultural conversations by a ratio of 1.06:1 and 1.5:1 respectively. This disparity might have been even greater if the backchannels had been identified in broader terms. Unlike the present study, these studies used minimal definitions of backchannels as Clancy et al. (1996) identify a backchannel as only one of the several components that make up a reactive token, and White (1989) did not include nonverbal backchannels in her analysis. Maynard's (1997) intercultural analysis, which included a broader identification of backchannels as adopted in this study, was difficult to compare to the other studies in terms of frequency since she used timed measurements rather than the number of interlocutor words (see Section 2.6.1). Nonetheless, Maynard's (1997) finding that the Japanese participants provided backchannels every 4.5 seconds of their interlocutor's primary speaking turn, while the American participants provided backchannels only every 19.25 demonstrated the great disparity between the two groups.

While there are several studies providing evidence of Japanese speakers of English employing backchannels more frequently than NESs, it is not certain what effect this has on IC. Previous studies such as Cutrone (2005) and White (1989) have used correlation analyses to test Lebra (1976) and Mizutani's (1982) hypothesis that NESs may take such frequent interjections as a sign of the listener's impatience and demand for a quick completion of the statement. This view was supported by the results of Cutrone (2005), who found that as JEFL backchannels increased, the more the British NESs felt they were being interrupted and the more they perceived their interlocutor to be impatient. The findings of this current study, however, were similar to those reported in White (1989), who found that more frequent JEFL backchannels were associated with positive ratings given by American NESs (observers in this study) on multiple items in the questionnaire (see Section 4.2). The overall positive ratings that the NES interlocutors gave to their JEFL counterparts (shown in Table 4-12 above) also suggest that the disparity in backchannel frequency did not greatly influence perceptions in a negative way. These contrary findings also highlight the fact that there may be considerable differences in how NESs of different varieties such as British English and American English perceive backchannels.

4.8 Involvement in the Conversation

As Sections 2.5.1 and 2.9.4.2 discussed, conversational listeners are thought to have a choice between producing a backchannel and taking a primary speaking turn at talk. Thus, it is not surprising to observe the large number of backchannels produced by the JEFLs compared to how little they actually spoke in the intercultural conversations. Although it is difficult to say with great certainty what effect the frequency of backchannels had on the intercultural conversations in this study, it is clear that lack of involvement, and/or perceived lack of involvement, in the intercultural conversations played a major role in the NESs' perceptions of their JEFL interlocutors. While many of the JEFLs commented that they were generally more comfortable in a listener's role (see Section 4.6.2), all three NESs indicated that they would have liked their JEFL interlocutors to participate more in the conversations in terms of speaking more and asking more questions. The results presented in Table 4-1 show that the NESs spoke more than four times as many words as the JEFLs (264 and 62 words per conversation respectively) and asked nearly twice as many questions (2.33 and 1.27 questions per conversation respectively).

Although the NESs generally expected and accepted that they would have to carry the conversation in their NS-NNS exchanges (see Section 4.6.1), they also admitted that this onus detracted from their conversational satisfaction and enjoyment (see Section 4.6.3). Predictably, as reported in Appendix N, Spearman rho analyses showed the following significant correlations at the $p<.01$ level: as word output increased, the more the NES observers believed JEFLs' listening feedback to be authentic (Item 7); as word output decreased, the more the NES observers perceived the JEFLs to want to avoiding speaking (Item 15) and the less they believed the JEFLs were able to convey that they did not understand (Item 16). These results were consistent with the findings of Cutrone (2005) and Sato (2008), who also found JEFLs' reticence as a source that would negatively influence cross-cultural perceptions and conversational satisfaction. These findings would seem to support the notion of divergent interpretations of Grice's (1975) maxim of quantity across cultures as described in Section

1.9.1. It was also suspected that the JEFLs may not have spoken as much as the NESs due to a preference for implicit communication, which would lend credence towards a culture-specific interpretation of Grice's (1975) maxim of manner (Section 1.9.2); however, such a correlation was only mildly corroborated in the interviews.

From the perspective of NESs, this desire for greater participation and more elaboration from their interlocutor appears to be a recurring theme in this study (see Sections 1.9.1, 2.6.2 and 2.9.4.2). These findings would seem to warrant a renewed emphasis on developing conversational micro-skills and expansion techniques in the EFL curriculum in Japan. This approach may prove effective for the learners who wanted to speak but did not because of their limited linguistic skills; however, it may be of little help to learners who did not speak due to other reasons. As Sections 4.6.1 and 4.6.2 reported, some of the JEFLs attribute their reticence directly to the influence of Japanese culture. This finding seems to have touched upon a much larger pedagogical issue, which goes beyond this study's scope. That is, to what extent should the language instructor intervene in this regard? In situations where cultural inhibitions are involved, EFL teachers need to proceed with extreme caution and keep in mind that the degree to which a learner wishes to acculturate to the target culture is largely up to him or her. Accordingly, in cases where Japanese provide backchannels because they are afraid to speak, teachers would be well advised not to force the issue. It may be that learners just need more time in getting acclimatised to the norms of the target culture. Teachers' aggressive attempts at persuading learners to speak more would likely only exacerbate learners' cultural inhibitions (Cutrone 2005, 2009). However, in situations where learners would like to speak but employ backchannels because they do not have the linguistic skills to realise other options, teachers can certainly assist these learners. More often than not, learners in elective EFL classes in Japan are more than willing to embrace the target culture in their efforts to learn English, and their problems speaking have more to do with lacking the skills necessary to do so than an unwillingness to communicate (Matsuura, Chiba & Hilderbrandt 2001). This appears to have been the case for several of the JEFL participants in this study who explained that they generally preferred to be in a listener's role and sometimes avoided speaking because they did not understand and/or did not know what to say in certain situations. Instruction in this area should include the development of conversational micro-skills such as expansion and repair strategies to help prevent communication breakdown (see Section 2.9.4.3). Lastly, the findings here also support the idea that EFL teachers should look for creative and unobtrusive ways to engender WTC in their learners (see Sections 1.5.2 and 2.9.4.2). Such a strategy does not necessarily need to focus on backchannel behaviour per se, as a holistic approach emphasising learners' WTC can have a more profound impact on language development and perceptions in interpersonal communication than any narrow attempts towards improving one language feature in isolation.

4.9 Variability

The results presented in Section 4-3 demonstrate that the NESs exhibited greater variability, overall, in the types (see Tables 4-3, 4-4 and 4-5), as well as the forms (see Tables 4-6, 4-7, 4-8 and 4-9), of backchannels they employ as compared to the JEFLs. Consistent with the recurring theme mentioned in the preceding section, the JEFLs mainly relied on producing minimal responses and were not prone to elaboration, whereas the NESs employed noticeably more extended responses (27.43% difference in mean percentage of total backchannels). While what this means in a conversation is likely to vary depending on the form and function of each backchannel in its specific context, it is clear from the NESs' post-conversation interview responses in Section 4.6.3 that the JEFLs' perceived lack of variability and exuberance was generally thought to affect IC in a negative way. This is consistent with the finding that more frequent JEFL extended responses were associated with positive ratings given by NES observers on multiple items in the questionnaire (see Appendix N), while no such correlations were found for minimal responses. These findings seem to support the observations made by Boxer (1993), Cutrone (2005), McCarthy (2003) and Stubbe (1998) that NESs tend to prefer extended and/or varied listener responses over minimal and/or repetitive ones.

Examining individual aspects of variability, the findings are able to shed further light on tendencies associated with verbal backchannel forms. While the NESs employed a much greater percentage of isolated content words and multi-word phrases in their backchannels, minimal backchannels were still found to be the most common type of backchannel produced by both cultural groups. This was not a surprise as various researchers such as McCarthy (2003) and Schegloff (1982) have alluded to a certain economy which seems to be built into spoken communication. Thus, it is not at all uncommon for speakers to utter no more than the bare minimum response. However, as McCarthy (2003) points out, speakers do not seem to economise when it comes to sociability. Generally speaking, varied responses coming at context-specific moments of the primary speaker's speech would perhaps go the farthest towards establishing active listenership and a positive effect in the conversation (Cutrone 2005; Stubbe 1998). On the other end of the spectrum, minimal and/or repetitive listener responses over an extended stretch of talk run the risk of being perceived as a sign of boredom or inattentiveness (McCarthy 2003), which is what some of the NESs perceived in this study (see Section 4.6.3).

As shown in Table 4-4, overall, the JEFLs sent a far greater percentage of backchannels constituted by nonverbal backchannels than the NESs (36.79:19.45). This seems to have been a product of the JEFLs' lower proficiency. The most noticeable disparities between the JEFLs and NESs' nonverbal backchannels were found in two subcategories: head nods (1.6:1) and laughter (4.2:1). The former was expected as Cutrone (2005) and Maynard (1986, 1990, 1997) have shown that Japanese tend to nod much more frequently than NESs in intercultural conversations. Regarding laughter and its relationship with backchannel behaviour, this has not been studied previously in any great detail; however, Cutrone (2005) and Maynard (1997) found that the Japanese speakers of English in their studies produced relatively similar amounts of laughter as the NESs. One way to explain the disparity in laughter between the two cultural groups in this study is to consider the possibility that the JEFLs may have employed laughter at times as a means of allaying their anxiety and helping create a comfortable atmosphere in the conversation (see Section 4.6.1). This would seem to be consistent with the Japanese cultural concept *wa* (introduced in Section 1.7.1), as well as what several of the JEFLs stated as conversational goals in Section 4.6.2.

4.10 Discourse Contexts

Concerning discourse contexts favouring backchannels, the results of this study were similar to previous studies in some respects but different in others. First, similar to Cutrone (2005), Maynard (1997) and White (1989), clausal boundaries, and particularly those accompanied by a pause, were the most common discourse context favouring backchannels for the NESs. It was somewhat surprising, however, that this discourse context was equally important for the JEFLs in this study since the previously mentioned studies generally reported much more variation in the discourse contexts favouring their backchannels. In terms of final clause boundaries versus internal clause boundaries (see Section 3.6.1.4), previous studies did not seem to differentiate between the two; however, this study found that both cultural groups were more prone to providing backchannels at final clause boundaries than internal clause boundaries.

While clausal boundaries, irrespective of pause, were shown to be important discourse contexts for both cultural groups, there were a few discourse contexts that were shown to be more specific to the JEFLs. For instance, the mean percentage of pauses attracting backchannels was nearly double for the JEFLs (1.8:1), as well as after primary speakers' head nod(s) (1.9:1). To a lesser extent, Cutrone (2005) also found that the JEFLs in his study provided a greater proportion of backchannels at or directly after a pause in the primary speaker's speech (1.3:1) and after the primary speaker's nonverbal gesture (1.2:1), which included raised eye brows, laughs and smiles, as well as head nods. Although there does appear to be some moderate variability in terms of discourse contexts favouring backchannels between the two cultural groups, there was no evidence showing that the variability in discourse contexts negatively affected the conversations from the post-conversation interviews.

The wide range of discourse contexts favouring the JEFLs' backchannels seem largely to be a by-product of the great frequency by which they employ backchannels in conversations. That is, compared to the NESs, the JEFLs' backchannels were found to occur frequently and their discourse contexts favouring backchannels varied considerably; thus, it should be no surprise that many of the JEFLs' backchannels were found at discourse contexts also prevalent in American English. Conversely, backchannels that are provided in discourse contexts other than the ones NESs commonly use are not necessarily considered inappropriate and are largely dependent on the context of the conversation and the function that the non-primary speaker desires to convey. Lastly, several other discourse contexts including self-adaptors and gesticulation (Duncan & Fiske 1977), gaze (Kendon 1977) and prosodic features (Ward 2000) have also been suggested in the research but were not represented in this study due to practical constraints.

4.11 Simultaneous Speech Backchannels

The results presented in Table 4-11 demonstrated that the JEFLs' mean percentage of backchannels constituted by SSBs was noticeably greater than that of the NESs (1.7:1). These findings were generally consistent with the results of Cutrone (2005) and Hayashi (1988), who found slightly greater ratios of 2.7:1 and 2.5:1 respectively. As Sections 2.6.4 and 4.7 discussed, previous studies have considered the effects of overall backchannel frequency rather than focusing on SSBs specifically. Nonetheless, it was somewhat surprising, in light of Lebra (1976) and Mizutani's (1982) hypothesis that frequent interjections uttered by

Japanese L2 English speakers are often ill-received by NESs, that more frequent non-laughter SSBs were associated with positive ratings on multiple items of the NES observers' questionnaire (see Appendix N). While the correlation analyses showed that SSBs may have actually had a facilitative effect on the conversations, the three NES interlocutors reported quite mixed feelings regarding this issue in the interviews. One NES was not even cognisant of SSBs existing in the conversations, and the other two offered opinions that were polar opposites. As reported in Section 4.6.3, one NES conversational participant preferred a great deal of listener feedback, while the other felt too much listener feedback to be intrusive and confounding, especially when he was in the midst of speaking. In light of the mixed findings of this and previous studies, it is impossible to draw any firm conclusions supporting or refuting Lebra (1976) and Mizutani's (1982) hypothesis at the present time. The great disparity in the three NESs' opinions regarding this issue seems to lend further credence to the notion that backchannel behaviour and how it is perceived are highly individualistic and context-specific matters.

Nonetheless, in one of the comments in Section 4.6.3, the exception to his admitted aversion to SSBs singled out by Jerry warrants further examination. In his statement, Jerry mentioned laughter as the only SSB form he found acceptable, while other forms, and especially repetitions, were not at all appreciated while he was in the midst of speaking. As the definition of *simultaneous speech* has not always been clear and/or consistent in previous studies, there may be a rationale for including SSB Laughter as a separate category as discussed in Section 3.6.1.5. That is, as Jerry points out, SSB laughter may influence perceptions differently than non-laughter SSBs. In this study however, the ratio of NES SSBs to JEFL SSBs only decreased by .2 when Laughter was taken out of the equation (from 1.7:1 to 1.5:1), and, thus, it is doubtful that such a minor difference had any great impact on conversational satisfaction and perceptions. Moreover, Jerry's mention of repetition SSBs as inappropriate may also be telling as this supports Thonus's (2002) position that non-clarification repetition-as-backchannels should be avoided.

4.12 Examining Participants' Conversational Satisfaction

4.12.1 Analysing Positive Results

Overall, the ratings from the questionnaires reported in Table 4-12 were similar across cultures, and indicated that members of each culture generally had positive impressions from their cross-cultural conversations. This finding was similar to other studies such as Cutrone (2005) and

White (1989) that also incorporated Hecht's (1978) conversational satisfaction questionnaire into an intercultural analysis of Japanese L2 English speakers and NESs. A few factors may have contributed to these positive ratings. First, as Section 4.6.1 reported, the NESs acknowledged that they were more tolerant of misinterpretations in the conversations because they attributed them to the fact that their Japanese interlocutors were less competent in English. As White (1989) points out, misunderstandings between native speakers are far more likely to bring about negative feelings as they would be attributed to the personalities of the participants, not their linguistic skills. Second, the fact that the register of the conversations was casual may be an important factor in explaining the positive ratings in the questionnaire. A casual register is one which involves no stakes and, thus, the participants feel no pressure to communicate. One can speculate on how different these results might be if the conversational register were more rigid and/or more demanding as one might find in the workplace or school. Comments made by Betty in Section 4.6.1, as well as Jerry's final excerpt in Section 4.6.3, show that some of the NESs lowered their expectations in the conversations in this study.

In addition, it is reasonable to assume that the JEFLs and NESs in this study already had positive feelings towards the cross-cultural group at the outset of the study for some obvious reasons. First, participants volunteered to participate in a study that involved conversing with a member of another culture. Accordingly, Japanese learners choosing to major in English studies would be expected to have a positive attitude towards conversing with NESs, and the fact that the NES interlocutors chose to travel to Japan in their university's exchange program suggests that they have some interest in Japan and its culture. Relative to this last point, there may be other ramifications beyond an affinity for Japan and an extended tolerance of conversational differences across cultures. Although it was required that the NESs in this part of the study live in Japan for a period less than a year, it is possible that they had already begun to adopt Japanese communication habits in order to be better understood by their hosts. Consequently, it seems necessary to consider the possibility that the NESs' behaviour, as well as their perceptions, may have been influenced to varying degrees by their acculturation to Japanese society.

Lastly, this subsection attempts to explain some of the positive findings which were somewhat unexpected. Rather than being perceived negatively (as discussed in Section 4.11), more frequent backchannels and non-laughter SSBs were significantly associated with positive ratings on multiple items of the NES observers' questionnaire (see Appendix N).

Returning to a common theme in this study, one possible explanation is that the NES observers preferred active listenership, and, thus, more backchannels of any type would be preferred to silence. This desire for active participation is consistent with the responses of the NES interlocutors (see Section 4.6.3) and the findings of other studies (see Sections 1.9 and 2.9.4.3). Still, minimal responses, overall, were not associated with any positive significant findings; however, the fact that more frequent JEFL extended responses were associated with positive ratings given by NES observers on multiple items in the questionnaire supports the notion that elaboration was preferred by the NESs.

4.12.2 Analysing Negative Results

Although the impressions across cultures were generally positive overall, there were a few notable exceptions, reported in Table 4-12, in which the JEFLs expressed substantially less satisfaction than the NESs (greater than 1 point difference on the rating scale). First, the JEFLs were noticeably less confident that the NESs were understanding them (difference of 1 in Item 3), were interested in what they had to say (difference of 1.3 in Item 5), and that the conversation went smoothly (difference of 1.95 in Item 6). While the generally positive ratings across cultures were expected, it was somewhat of a surprise to find that the NESs did not express substantially less satisfaction on any of the items in the questionnaire than their cross-cultural counterparts had. It was thought that the NESs would have more of a precise, and perhaps more rigid, idea of what constitutes appropriate behaviour and conversational satisfaction as it pertains to their native tongue, English. Negative results may also have been influenced by the age and learner status of the participants in this study. Unlike the adult Japanese L2 English speakers in Cutrone (2005) and White (1989), the participants in this study were EFL learners in their late teens, and much of the contact they would have previously had with NESs was restricted to a formal instructional context in the foreign language classroom. Thus, it is possible that, subconsciously at least, the JEFLs may have felt as though they were being evaluated in conversing with NESs. Accordingly, this potential evaluation anxiety combined with a lack of experience communicating with NESs may have played a role in creating unnecessary pressure and expectations, which negatively influenced their ratings on various items of the conversational satisfaction questionnaire. The lack of confidence described here is consistent with the comments made by several JEFLs in their post-conversation interviews expressing an extraordinary amount of self-doubt and worry concerning their oral English abilities (see Section 4.6.1).

Compared to the other studies incorporating conversational participant satisfaction questionnaires, the results of this study contain various similarities and overlap with the findings of White (1989), but were markedly different from the findings of Cutrone (2005). In White's (1989) study, there were several items on the questionnaire in which the Japanese L2 English speakers exhibited considerably less satisfaction: the Japanese participants felt less satisfied that their interlocutor was letting them know they were communicating effectively (difference of 1.1), the Japanese participants felt less confident that they were able to present themselves favourably (difference of 2.3), and the Japanese participants perceived their American interlocutors to be less patient (difference of 1.1), polite (difference of 1) and attentive (difference of 1.3). Conversely, in the study administered by Cutrone (2005), it was the NESs, not the JEFLs, who reported noticeably less satisfaction on several items on the questionnaire. Specifically, the British participants felt their Japanese interlocutor expressed less interest in the conversation (difference of 1.5), felt less encouragement to continue talking (difference of 1.88), and perceived their interlocutors to be less warm and friendly (difference of 1.12). Thus, the results of the various studies using Hecht's (1978) conversational satisfaction questionnaire appear to be conflicting. While the findings of Cutrone (2005) seem to support the general expectation that differing conversational styles lead to misinterpretation of meaning, the results here and those reported in White (1989) invite the possibility that conversational differences, at times, may actually positively influence perceptions across cultures. However, these findings may have more to do with the method of collecting data and the general type of information sought than the in-depth feelings of the participants. Although White (1989) followed up her questionnaires with brief interviews, it appears that the questioning may have lacked the depth and direction necessary to obtain valuable insights. The interview consisted of only two questions: *How do you feel about the conversation,* and *What do you think of your partner?* Besides being brief, the questions in the interviews seem to have forced the participants into the unenviable task of evaluating other people. It may be the case that with all other things being equal, people are inclined to give each other positive ratings, especially in conversations of a casual register.

158   Chapter Four

4.12.3 Analysis of Key Issues, Inconsistencies and Other Influences

One of the goals of this study was to examine the extent and reasons that miscommunication took place in the intercultural conversations. The JEFLs' scores on Item 2 of the conversational satisfaction questionnaire showed that the JEFLs generally felt that they had not represented themselves in a sincere and authentic manner. This notion was corroborated by several of the JEFLs admitting in the playback interviews that they often employed continuer, understanding, agreement, and/or support and empathy type backchannels in situations when they did not understand and/or when they disagreed with what their interlocutor was saying. As discussed in Sections 1.9.3 and 2.8.1, this lends support to the idea that Japanese L2 English speakers may sometimes feign understanding and/or agreement in order to keep conversations pleasant.

Concerned with the way the JEFLs represented themselves, as well as how they were perceived by their NES interlocutors, the researcher included parallel items in each group's questionnaires to investigate this. Thus, unlike how the JEFLs rated themselves on Item 2, the NESs' scores on their parallel item suggested a general belief that their JEFL interlocutors had represented themselves in a sincere and authentic manner in the conversations. However, in post-conversation interviews, two of the three NESs' responses demonstrated that they were indeed aware that their JEFL interlocutors were sometimes feigning understanding and found this type of behaviour to be somewhat confusing and mildly irritating (see Section 4.6.3). This discrepancy in the findings collected by questionnaire vis-à-vis interviews would seem to highlight the advantages of using (semi-structured) interviews to supplement questionnaires, as the former enables greater depth with opportunities for interviewees to clarify and explain their responses.

Furthermore, while the studies presented above have provided some insights concerning the differing perceptions of backchannel behaviour, any concrete comparisons between these studies should be treated with circumspection for many reasons. First, as Mills (2003) points out (see Section 3.7), the analysis and interpretation of features of conversations is a highly subjective, individualistic and context-driven endeavour. In other words, behaviours and perceptions in these simulated naturalistic conversations may be influenced by a number of factors beyond the control of the researcher. Moreover, it is difficult to compare and draw conclusions from such small sample groups, particularly with disparities in age and ethnicities between the participants in each study. That is, the cross-sectional part of this study involved three NESs in their late teens, while the studies administered by Cutrone (2005) and White (1989) consisted of eight and ten adult NESs respectively. Furthermore, Cutrone's (2005) study involved British NESs, while this study and that which was conducted by White (1989) both involved American NESs. As Tottie (1991) explains, there can be important differences in the backchannel tendencies between British and American NESs. Lastly, this study and Cutrone's (2005) were conducted in an EFL context, while White (1989) administered her study in an ESL context. Undoubtedly, the amount of exposure to the target language and culture would have a major impact on the Japanese participants' conversational behaviour in English.

4.12.4 Culture Influences and their Impact on Instruction

Consistent with the findings of Cutrone's (2005) study, the interview responses given by Jerry and Betty (see Section 4.6.3) highlight the IC issue raised in Section 1.9.3 concerning Grice's (1975) maxim of quality which explored the notion of truth as a relative concept across cultures. Compared to the NESs' stated preference for clarity, directness and sincerity in conversations, many JEFL respondents in this study and Cutrone (2005) seemed to place a much greater emphasis on preserving harmony and ensuring smooth communication, which many attributed to Japanese culture. The apparent link between culture and listenership, as well as potential differences in this area across cultures, is something that EFL teachers in Japan need to consider. While instructional goals in this area should involve encouraging JEFLs to represent themselves accurately (i.e., convey what they indeed intend to convey), cases in which individual speakers choose to represent themselves disingenuously would seem to be a personal choice and, thus, beyond the reach of the language instructor in the classroom. Like the results of Cutrone (2005), several JEFL respondents in this study, who feigned understanding and agreement in the intercultural conversations, attributed this type of behaviour to a cultural norm which stresses being polite, keeping conversations harmonious and avoiding confrontations (see Section 4.6.2). As discussed in Section 2.8.1, however, this desire to avoid confrontations is a human tendency, and, while it may manifest itself somewhat differently in the Japanese communicative style, it is certainly not restricted to Japanese society. As Aston pointed out (1986), less proficient L2 speakers of all nations will tend to feign understanding in order to avoid conversational difficulty and embarrassment.

Another aspect of Japanese culture which may be related to this type of behaviour involves the Japanese concept of politeness and face as described in Section 1.7.3. While there is evidence suggesting that JEFLs sometimes backchannel rather than interject when they do not understand or agree out of politeness and as a way to allow the primary speaker to save face, another dynamic to this face-saving mechanism, which may not be entirely clear to westerners, is that the Japanese person may backchannel when they do not understand to save their own face. Consistent with Cutrone's (2005) findings, several of the JEFL respondents stated that they sometimes provided backchannels when they did not understand to avoid humiliation (see Section 4.6.2). Besides giving further credence to LoCastro's (1987, 1999) cultural explanation of Japanese backchannels (see Section 2.8.1), the belief that Japanese society and culture plays a role in JEFL learners being afraid to make mistakes and feeling ashamed when they do has been well documented (Conlan 1996; Nevara 2003; Thompson 1987).

Although differing functional objectives of backchannel behaviour may certainly contribute to miscommunication in cross-cultural encounters, EFL teachers would be well advised to not push or force their learners to use and/or avoid using backchannels in ways where they may feel uncomfortable. According to Apltekin and Apltekin (1984), Brumfit (1980) and Kramsch (1998), aggressive attempts at making EFL learners bicultural are often met with resistance and can result in their disengagement from the target culture. Kramsch (1998) offers insights into the sensitivity of this issue by explaining that people forge their identities and beliefs through their culture, hence any attempts by teachers or anyone else for that matter to change their behaviour in this way may feel like a personal attack. Thus, as far as culture is concerned, the degree to which learners choose to conform to the backchannel practices of a target culture is entirely up to each individual (Farr 2003). Nonetheless, many learners are more than willing to embrace the target culture in their efforts to learn English, and for those who hold back initially, it is likely that their comfort levels will increase gradually over time as they become more acclimatised to the target culture.

4.13 Micro-level Analysis of Students' Levels

As presented in Appendix S, RQs 5 and 6 each address two areas of backchannel behaviour: levels and gains. While gains are discussed on the basis of the longitudinal data presented in the next chapter, levels prior to treatment are addressed here. This section aims to provide an answer to the first parts of RQs 5 and 6 respectively, which seek to uncover some of the common characteristics pertaining to the JEFLs that exhibited competent backchannel behaviour as compared to those that did not, and to investigate the degree to which proficiency levels (according to TOEIC scores) were associated with performance involving backchannel behaviour. Concerning the latter (RQ 6), the correlation analyses (PPMCC) reported in Sections 4.2-4.6 have shown, overall, that higher proficiency levels were, to some extent, associated with a number of qualities corresponding to good listening behaviour (see Appendix O). In an attempt to bring to light in more detail some of the features associated with different levels of performance concerning backchannel behaviour, this section now examines the data in a more fine-grained way. Providing a partial answer to RQ 5, this analysis will present the following:

- Profiles of performance for JEFLs who exhibited higher and lower levels of listenership, as identified by the four assessment criteria outlined in Section 2.9.4.
- Patterns of performance which are associated with some of the higher and lower level JEFLs in this study.

4.13.1 Backchannel Behaviour

4.13.1.1 Frequency

Based on the descriptions provided in Section 2.9.4.1, JEFLs who provided fewer backchannels per interlocutor word might appear to be in more accord with NESs' backchannel behaviour. Regarding less frequent backchannelling, the JEFLs to backchannel an average of less than every eight words were Madora, Yuki, Sachi and Haruna. It was thought that less frequent backchannelling might be correlated to more primary speaker words; however, in the case of these participants, less frequent backchannelling seemed to be indicative of less involvement in the conversation overall as Madora, Yuki and Haruna spoke substantially less than the average of the JEFL group (while Sachi was only slightly below the JEFL average). Besides their overall reticence, the profiles of these participants did not contain any noteworthy features. Compared to the other 26 JEFLs, these participants generally had near average TOEIC scores and slightly higher than average scores on the Extraversion dimension of the personality scale. On the other end of the spectrum, the JEFLs to backchannel most frequently (i.e., an average of more than every five words) were Hika, Ayuka and Kazuya. While Hika's TOEIC score was markedly higher than the JEFL average (+110), Kazuya (-60) and

Ayuka's (-180) scores were noticeably lower. Regarding the Extraversion scale, Hika scored the highest (6) of the three, followed closely by Ayuka (5), while Kazuya (2.5) was found to be among the least extraverted JEFLs. English proficiency levels, as well as scores on the Extraversion scale, seemed to reflect to some extent how much these three JEFLs spoke. That is, Hika's word output (57) was near the JEFL average (62), while the number of words uttered by Kazuya (41) and Ayuka (49) were observed to be considerably lower.

4.13.1.2 Variability

While the JEFLs overall exhibited limited variability in the type of backchannels they employed as compared to the NESs, a few such as Yukari (46:25), Tomomi (71:15), Shio (62:13), Aria (68:13) and Hiro (75:15) provided a ratio of minimal to extended backchannels more congruent to that of the NESs in this study. In fact, one of the JEFLs, Yukari, had a better ratio than the NES average of 66:22. This ability to produce lengthier and more complex backchannels seems to be associated with proficiency levels. All five of these JEFLs scored better than the JEFL average on the TOEIC test (i.e., 540), and the scores of three were exceptionally high (>620). Further, of the seven JEFLs on the other end of the spectrum who exhibited an exceptionally high ratio of minimal to extended backchannel responses, five of them had below average TOEIC scores. These participants included Chieko (93:0), Ayuka (95:3), Madora (89:3), Keiko (89:3) and Kazuya (89:3). Akanori (85:0) and Rika (91:2), however, scored better than average on the TOEIC proficiency test.

4.13.1.3 Discourse Contexts and Simultaneous Speech

The most important discourse context favouring backchannels in English has been identified as clausal boundaries, and particularly those accompanied by a pause (see Section 2.6.3). As the JEFL output (based on the number of opportunities) was similar to the NESs in this context, it was observed that most of the JEFLs performed in a NES-like way in this area. Hence, it was not possible to single out exceptional performances in this area. However, two of the JEFLs, Saya and Aria, produced percentages of backchannel frequency in this discourse context which were noticeably lower than the JEFL average (<25%). As was discussed in Section 2.9.4.1, it is difficult to ascertain the extent to which a lower percentage of backchannels in a particular discourse context influences IC. Shifting the focus, this subsection now examines backchannels occurring as simultaneous speech (SSBs), which some researchers believe can have a negative effect on IC (see Section 2.6.4). In this sense, less frequent SSBs are thought to be a measure of success in this area because this behaviour would be compatible with that of the NESs in the intercultural conversations. While the average number of non-laughter SSBs per intercultural conversation for the JEFL groups was 6.3, various JEFLs produced less than half that many. This list includes Takanori (1), Kouki (2), Taro (2), Madora (3), Mayumi (3) and Shio (3). Of this group, only Madora was also included in the list of infrequent backchannellers above. While Mayumi and Shio had above average TOEIC scores, the remaining four JEFLs had TOEIC scores well below the average (<505). Conversely, the two JEFLs, Rika and Hika, who produced notably more non-laughter SSBs (>20) than any other JEFL were also among the most proficient JEFLs according to TOEIC scores, and both were reported to have extraverted personalities (>4.5). Hence, a high proficiency level overall does not necessarily translate into success in terms of limiting one's SSBs.

4.13.1.4 Functions

In Section 4.6.2, some unconventional uses of backchannels in English were brought to light, namely, the JEFLs' tendency to employ continuer, understanding, agreement, and/or support and empathy type backchannels in situations when they did not understand or agree with what their interlocutor was saying. Regarding the latter, as there were only two instances of disagreement in all 30 conversations, it was not possible to discern any patterns of behaviour. Concerning the former, there were 139 instances of a JEFL not understanding the gist of what their interlocutor was saying; thus, there were ample opportunities for participants' tendencies to be uncovered in this area. While the average number of times the JEFL produced an unconventional backchannel in this type of situation was 71%, it is important to keep in mind that the number of times that participants did not understand the gist of the conversation was going to fluctuate depending on each participant's listening comprehension ability. The three JEFLs who had both a high number of instances when they did not understand and a high percentage of unconventional backchannels in these situations were Kazuya, Ayuka and Kouki. Kazuya had eight instances of non-understanding in which he used eight unconventional backchannels (100%), Kouki had seven instances of non-understanding in which he provided seven unconventional backchannels (100%), and Ayuka had 13 instances of non-understanding in which she employed 11 unconventional backchannels (85%). Predictably, the TOEIC scores for these participants were among the lowest in the JEFL group, and they were among the least talkative in terms of words uttered. Their scores on the extraversion scale were wide-ranging. Hence, it appears that the main factor associated with the JEFLs' unconventional backchannel behaviour was low proficiency level. This finding was generally consistent with the overall analyses provided in Section 4.13.1, in which most of the subcategories therein found an association between TOEIC scores and performance related to backchannel behaviour. Nonetheless, as will be discussed in a broader scope at the end of Section 4.13.4, a great deal of individual variation in the features of backchannel behaviour was observed.

4.13.2 Conversational Repair Strategies

The ability to use conversational repair strategies is directly linked to the aforementioned discussion of the JEFLs' tendency to employ unconventional backchannels when they did not understand or agree with what their interlocutor was saying. Rather than feign understanding or agreement in these situations, JEFLs may choose to convey their true feelings in one of two ways: by providing a minimal backchannel expression with a rising intonation such as those described in the clarification, non-understanding and disagreement functional categories outlined in Sections 2.5.7, 2.5.8 and 2.5.9 respectively, or by employing a longer expression or phrase as a conversational repair strategy (see Section 3.6.3). It was difficult to identify participants who performed adequately in this area because no JEFL used a conversational repair strategy while their interlocutor was engaged in a primary turn at talk. A few of the JEFLs, however, used a greater percentage of minimal backchannel expressions conveying clarification, non-understanding and/or disagreement. Of the participants who experienced at least five separate instances of non-understanding in their conversations, only Michiko, Yukiko, Misako, Hiro and Taro conveyed their non-understanding more than 50% of the time by employing one of the minimal backchannels described above. There does not appear to be any relationship between this behaviour and participants' TOEIC and Extraversion scores, which were found to be wide-ranging. Interestingly, however, it was noticeable that four of the six JEFL males in the study conveyed their non-understanding more than 50% of the time, while only five of 24 JEFL females did. This would seem to support Robinson's (1992) finding that Japanese females are often more apt to conceal their true feelings (see Section 1.9.3). However, due to the limited number of males used in this study, it is difficult to reach any definitive conclusions where gender is concerned.

Overall, there were only two instances of a conversational repair strategy used by the JEFLs, and both instances were used by the same participant in response to a question in the following sequence:

Conversation Excerpt 1

11. Betty;	( ) (.91)	= and on thanksgiving if you eat a lot of turkey/ [you] just want to sleep// (.) (.)
		^ ^ ^
	eeee =	[mm] L

12. Betty;	(so) L (.) (.80) (.) are there foods/ in japan?/ (.) that make you sleep// (1.44)
	L ( )

13. Yoko;	_sorry// (.) one more please// (.)

14. Betty;	is (.) are there foods/ in japan/ that make you sleepy// (.) when you eat them// (.)

15. Yoko;	eee (.) sleepy (1.44) eeee (1.74) i don't know// (.) = so[rry] = yeah (.77) mmm (2.09)
	> > ^ ^
	mm = [may]be not =

16. Yoko;	_i don't know// (.) (sorry) (2.65) eee what's your (1.71) unlike food?// (.98)

17. Betty;	(food) i don't like? (.) (.) aaa (.) beef// (.) = pork// = (.) and tomatoes// = (.)
	G ^ G ^ ^
	uhuh beef = = pork = tomatoes

In line 13, Yoko's first speaking turn shows her using a conversational repair strategy. Here, she asks her interlocutor to repeat the question because, as she later admits, she did not understand it. After her interlocutor repeats the question, Yoko replies *I don't know* and attempts to steer the question in a new direction with a question of her own. *I don't know* seems to function as a conversational repair strategy initially because Yoko is admitting that she does not know the answer. However, in her post-conversation playback interview, Yoko acknowledges that even after hearing the question repeated, she was still not clear as to what her interlocutor was asking, though she knew a response by her was expected. In this way, it seems as if the response *I don't know* was used much the same way that the aforementioned unconventional backchannels are used, i.e., to help the non-primary speaker save face by navigating the situation without their non-understanding being exposed.

This example highlights the potentially differing dynamics involved in using conversational repair strategies in response to a question as compared to during one's interlocutor's primary speaking turn at talk. That is, if the non-primary speaker does not understand the question that is posed to them, they would seem to have only a limited number of options available to them: silence (i.e., ignore the question), answer incorrectly, or use a conversational repair strategy. While all three options may involve some degree of losing face and/or loss of *wa* in the conversation, the first two options pose potentially the greatest threats as they could easily be detected by the participants' interlocutors and would seem to have the most chance of leading to subsequent awkwardness, embarrassment, and, ultimately, communication breakdown. In this way, the JEFL had very little choice but to use a conversational repair strategy if he or she could. However, in situations where questions were not posed and the JEFLs did not understand the gist of what their interlocutor was saying, there was no pressure and/or expectation for the JEFL to respond. Consequently, none of the JEFLs initiated a repair strategy in the many instances these situations presented themselves. An earlier segment of Yoko's conversation provides an example of this.

Conversation Excerpt 2

8. Betty;   my mom cooks chi- (.) turkey that's very [that's] very dry// =   (.) _( ) (.)
                                            ^
                  [(nn)]   = dry (.) uuuun

9. Betty;   and turkey makes you sleepy// (.59) there's a special (.) chemical// (.)
            ^   ^
                                                                chemical =

10. Betty;   = and you eat it// (.)   = and then you get sleepy// (.94)   (1.12)
                              ^   ^ ^ ^
                  Aaa =   really¿

In the sequence leading up to lines 11-17 shown above, Betty focuses her discussion in the conversation on the dryness of cooked turkeys. While Yoko knows that Betty is talking about culinary turkeys in general, she does not quite understand the concept of a dry turkey which makes one sleepy. Rather than using a minimal backchannel expression or a conversational repair strategy to convey non-understanding here, Yoko initially adopts a backchannel as repetition strategy (in lines 8 and 9) in hopes of staying with the line of conversation long enough to eventually make sense of it. As Betty had perhaps sensed that Yoko did not completely understand what she was talking about from these repetitions, she attempted to further explain why eating turkeys make people feel sleepy. In line 10, after hearing Betty's explanation, Yoko's backchannel of *really* (with a falling intonation) was her most definitive attempt to feign understanding. It seemed believable to Betty, who subsequently began to pose questions specifically related to this topic. Hence, it was at this time that Yoko's non-understanding was exposed. Fortunately for her, she was able to use a conversational repair strategy initially (in line 13) and then skilfully navigate her way out of the situation by asking a question of her own. Her question served to alter the focus of the conversation to another, and more simpler, aspect of food talk when she uttered *what's your unlike food* in line 16.

4.13.3 Involvement in the Conversations

The JEFLs' involvement and WTC in the conversations was measured in three ways: (1) WTC scores, (2) how much they spoke in the conversations and (3) the number of questions they asked their interlocutor. First, concerning McCroskey's (1992) WTC scale described in Section 3.6.2, the following participants scored noticeably higher than the JEFL average of 51: Michiko (65), Yukari (64), Mikki (63), Akie (60), Hika (60), Sachi (60) and Hiro (60). Second, regarding the number of words uttered in each conversation, the following participants spoke substantially more than the JEFL average of 62 words: Chihiro (126), Shio (121), Taro (113) and Yukari (109), Hiro (101) and Yoko (100). Lastly, several participants posed greater than the JEFL average of 1.3 questions per conversation. Yukari posed three questions, while Michiko, Hika, Mayumi, Meo, Madora, Yukari, Mikki, Akie, Misako and Akanori posed two questions each. From these results, the only JEFL participant to achieve high ratings in all three areas in this category was Yukari. As might be expected, Yukari was also one of the most proficient JEFLs in terms of TOEIC scores (695), one of the most extraverted students in terms of the Extraversion scale (6), and was also able to display exceptional skills relating to the variability of backchannels she employed, as discussed in Section 4.13.1 above. Three other JEFLs, Mikki, Akie and Hika, scored highly in two of the three categories, WTC scores and number of questions asked. In taking a closer look at the number of words they spoke in their conversations, Mikki's output (86) was above the JEFL average, while Akie and Hika were well below it. Similar to Yukari, Mikki was also found to be a highly proficient and extraverted participant.

Other aspects of backchannel behaviour discussed above, such as conversational repair strategies, were largely irrelevant to Yukari and Mikki due to their strong listening comprehension skills. Yukari and Mikki only found themselves in one situation each where they did not understand what their interlocutor was saying. Still, in their one instance of non-understanding, they both provided one of the backchannel types deemed unconventional above, but were able to recover the gist of the conversation as it progressed. In this way, proficiency seems to be linked with how much risk a listener can take in their backchannel behaviour. That is, similar to NESs, highly proficient JEFLs may be able to get away with feigning understanding initially because they can often grasp the gist of the conversation later on as their interlocutor continues talking. Lower to mid-level learners, on the other hand, seem far more likely to run into problems later on as shown by Excerpts 1 and 2 in the previous section above. Lastly, to complete the picture on Yukari and Mikki, they employed five and ten SSBs respectively, which was near the average for the JEFLs but believed to be somewhat too frequent for NESs.

On the other end of the spectrum, this subsection now examines the JEFLs who were least involved in the conversations. Some of the lowest scores on the WTC scale belonged to Chieko (34), Mayumi (35), Keiko (39), Kazuya (39), Takanori (40) and Ayuka (42). Regarding the number of words uttered in the conversations, the following participants were well below the JEFL average of 62: Miya (12), Haruna (20), Akie (25), Kouki (28), Mika (29) and Yukiko (29). Finally, Arisa, Ayuka, Takanori, Sachi and Yukiko did not pose a single question to their interlocutor in the conversations. From this data, the researcher was not able to identify any participants who rated low in all three categories. However, Ayuka and Takanori both scored low in two of the three categories, WTC scores and number of questions asked. Examining the number of words they spoke in their conversations, Ayuka and Takanori's output was identical at 49 words, which was below the JEFL average of 62. It was not surprising to find that these students who were less involved in the conversations were also below average in proficiency according to TOEIC scores. In Ayuka's case, she was by far the least proficient JEFL, and, predictably, scored quite low in other areas measuring features of backchannel behaviour such as frequency (i.e., average of one backchannel every 4.42 interlocutor word), variability (95:3) and functional use of backchannels (85% of non-understanding situations constituted unconventional backchannels, and there were not any conversational repair strategies employed). While a link between proficiency level and competent backchannel behaviour appears to exist on some levels as Yukari and Ayuka have demonstrated above, it is not always the case. For instance, while many of the JEFLs who spoke a great deal also appear to have the highest TOEIC scores (i.e., Chihiro, Shio, Taro and Yukari); this did not always hold true as Rika had a very high TOEIC score (685) yet only spoke near the JEFL average number of words. Taro, with a TOEIC score 160 points lower, uttered more than twice as many words as Rika.

4.13.4 ICC

As is discussed in Sections 2.9.4.4 and 3.6.4, a fundamental requirement of ICC is for a foreign language speaker to be seen as a competent conversationalist by members of the target culture. In this study, the NESs were able to share their perceptions of their JEFL interlocutors in Hecht's (1978) Interpersonal Communication Satisfaction Inventory, as well as in post-conversation playback interviews. From the responses given in the questionnaires (see Table 4-12) and interviews (see Section 4.6.1), it can be seen that the NESs' perceptions of their JEFL interlocutors were generally positive; in fact, near perfect ratings were given in 11 of 30 questionnaires. Concerning this analysis of levels, the fact that the NES interlocutor, Betty, was universally generous in rating her 24 JEFL interlocutors makes it difficult to single out any JEFLs exhibiting exceptional ICC. For instance, Yukari, who performed well in most areas associated with backchannel behaviour, scored only a slightly higher rating on the conversational satisfaction questionnaire than Ayuka, who struggled in most areas. In one of Betty's interview responses, however, she remarked that Yukari's English proficiency seemed much more natural than any other JEFL and was someone she could see herself becoming friends with outside the study. Regarding Ayuka, though, Betty's comments in Section 4.6.1 suggest that she may have had a more lenient and compassionate standard in communicating with non-native speakers in the course of this study than she might have in other contexts. As mentioned in Section 4.12, a casual conversational register, which has no stakes, would seem to be conducive to mutual goodwill in the conversations.

The only JEFL to receive more negative ratings than positive ratings on the 17 items in the conversational questionnaire was Kazuya, who scored well below average on both the TOEIC test (480) and Extraversion scale (2.5). In terms of backchannel behaviour performance, Kazuya generally scored low in all areas as he was observed to backchannel frequently (i.e., average of one backchannel every 4.97 interlocutor word), have limited variability (89:3) and poor functional use of backchannels (100% of non-understanding situations constituted unconventional backchannels, and there were not any conversational repair strategies employed). Further, while he was not named as one of the least involved JEFLs, the meagre 41 words and 1 question he uttered, as well as his score of 39 on the WTC scale, were all below the JEFL average.

From the findings analysed above, some general observations can be made. Addressing RQ 5 (see Appendix S for RQs), the JEFLs who performed well or poorly in one area of the four assessment criteria of backchannel behaviour tended to perform in the same way in other areas.

Further, no consistent association between the JEFLs' scores on the Extraversion scale and their performances regarding backchannel behaviour was found. In response to RQ 6, there appears to be an association between proficiency level and performances relative to backchannel behaviour on many levels. Along with these general trends emerging in the data, several exceptions were also discovered. First, the patterns revealed in answer to both RQ 5 and RQ 6 above were found not to apply to the Frequency and Simultaneous Speech subcategories outlined in Section 4.13.1.1 and to the Conversational Repair Strategies category described in Section 4.13.2. Second, within single subcategories, there were instances contrary to the general trends, which make it impossible to draw any concrete and comprehensive conclusions regarding the patterns described above. Clearly, a great deal of individual variation has occurred in these conversations, and output has been influenced to varying degrees by the specific contexts of each conversation, the personality and demeanour of the participants, and the chemistry between the participants in the dyadic conversations, as well as seemingly peripheral variables such as the amount of sleep the participants had the night before and the mood of the participants at the time of the conversations. In short, this section has served to provide an answer to the first parts of RQs 5 and 6, which consider factors associated with varying levels of performance concerning backchannel behaviour. The next section, the conclusion, will summarise the findings of the cross-sectional aspect of this study by answering RQs 1 and 2.

4.14 Conclusion

In summarising the findings corresponding to the cross-sectional part of this study, the following RQs will be answered: (1) How did the two cultures use backchannels differently in this study, and (2) How did differences in backchannel behaviour affect IC? In answer to the first question, this study found that the JEFLs provided more than four times as many backchannels, while the NESs uttered more than four times as many words. Thus, in relative terms, the findings demonstrate that the JEFLs employed slightly more backchannels per interlocutor word than the NESs. Regarding the variability of the types of backchannels used by each culture, this study found that the NESs' backchannels contained more variability, and there were several differences in the forms making up these backchannels as they pertain to each culture. Many of the discourse contexts favouring backchannels were similar between the two groups; however, it was observed that the JEFLs provided noticeably more backchannels than the NESs in three contexts: at or directly after a pause in the primary speaker's speech, at or directly after the primary speaker's head nod(s) and during the primary speaker's turn at talk creating simultaneous speech. Lastly, many situational and functional differences were brought to light. While the NESs were generally found to employ backchannels consistent with Maynard's (1997) functional list provided in Section 2.5, the JEFLs used backchannels in a number of different ways. First, several of the JEFLs admitted to providing supportive backchannels (i.e., continuer, understanding, agreement, and/or support and empathy types) even when they did not understand and/or agree with what their interlocutor was saying. The common reason given for this behaviour was that it was thought to be polite and culturally important. Other functions of backchannels specific to the JEFLs were to avoid speaking, to keep the other person talking to allow themselves additional time to process information, and out of habit.

Before answering the second question, it is important to mention again that the NESs were generally accepting of the miscommunication which occurred as they largely attributed it to their interlocutor's weaker proficiency level in English. With this in mind, the NESs acknowledged that some of the ways their interlocutors used backchannels (and JEFL speakers generally for that matter) could have a potentially negative effect on IC. Some specific irritants they mentioned included the JEFLs' tendency to use backchannels as a way to avoid speaking, to not focus on the communication because they were worried about their English, and their lack of variability and exuberance in the types of backchannels they employed. Related to this last point, some of the NESs specified the JEFLs' lack of awareness in using situation-specific backchannels as a source to negatively influence IC. Further, at times when the NESs were cognisant of the JEFLs employing backchannels when they disagreed and/or did not understand, the NESs expressed displeasure and/or confusion at this. In summary, the results of this study provide further evidence that JEFL speakers' backchannelling behaviour differs from that of NESs in many respects, and these differences sometimes lead to miscommunication and negative perceptions across cultures. These findings, generally consistent with the conclusions of Cutrone (2005), reaffirm the recommendation that backchannels warrant more attention in EFL classes in Japan. The following chapter will present and discuss the results of the longitudinal aspect of this study, which seeks to determine the effects of implicit and explicit instruction on JEFL learners' backchannel behaviour over time.

CHAPTER FIVE

LONGITUDINAL RESULTS AND DISCUSSION

Part I: The Longitudinal Results

5.1 Introduction

This chapter has been divided into two parts. The first part will present the findings of the longitudinal aspect of this study, while the second part will discuss these findings as they relate to RQs 3-6 (see Appendix S) and other key issues discussed in the literature review of this study. In part one, the results of the JEFL groups' performances at each of the three points of measurement are presented in the following areas of backchannel behaviour: (5.2) frequency, (5.3) involvement in the conversation, (5.4) variability, (5.5) discourse contexts favouring backchannels, (5.6) simultaneous speech backchannels, (5.7) conversational satisfaction, (5.8) the quantitative and qualitative data produced by the interviews and, lastly, (5.9) an analysis of common learner characteristics that were associated with varying performances over time, and the degree to which L2 proficiency levels were associated with gains.

5.2 Frequency

The subsections below demonstrate the observed frequency of the backchannel (BC) occurrences of Group A (Explicit), Group B (Implicit) and Group Z (Control) at the three points of measurement in this study.

5.2.1 Group A (Explicit)

Table 5-1 presents Group A's total backchannel output, number of their interlocutor's words, and the number of backchannels per interlocutor word during the Pre-test, Post-test 1 and Post-test 2. Since the average number of backchannels between interlocutor's words takes into account the backchannel opportunities afforded each participant, paired-samples t-tests were conducted for these figures only. The differences between the means of the Pre-test and Post-test 1 and the Pre-test and Post-test 2 were found to be strongly significant.

Table 5-1 Differences in frequency of BCs over time for Group A

N =10	Total Backchannels			Interlocutor's Words			Average # of interlocutor's words between backchannels		
	Pre	Post 1	Post 2	Pre	Post 1	Post 2	Pre	Post 1	Post 2
Total	450	290	371	2700	2874	3217	—	—	—
Mean ($\bar{x}$)	45	29	37.1	270	287.4	321.7	6	9.91** (p<.001)	8.67** (p<.001)
SD	15.23	11.12	12.33	21.83	12.39	18.14	1.19	2.45	1.94

($\bar{x}$ difference of Pre-test → Post-test 1, and Pre-test → Post-test 2 significant at p<.05 level = *; significant at p<.01 level =**)

5.2.2 Group B (Implicit)

As shown in Table 5-2, Group B provided a backchannel every 6.84 of their interlocutor's words during the Pre-test, 8.79 during Post-test 1, and 7.98 during Post-test 2. A paired-samples t-test found the difference in the means of the Pre-test and Post-test 1 just reached significant.

5.2.3 Group Z (Control)

As Table 5-3 illustrates, the frequency rate of Group Z's backchannels did not change greatly throughout the course of this study. Control group members provided a backchannel every 6.55 of their interlocutor's words in the Pre-test, 7.51 in Post-test 1, and 7.19 in Post-test 2.

Table 5-2 Differences in frequency of BCs over time for Group B

N = 10	Total Backchannels			Interlocutor's Words			Average number of interlocutor's words between backchannels		
	Pre	Post 1	Post 2	Pre	Post 1	Post 2	Pre	Post 1	Post 2
Total	370	268	391	2530	2355	3120	—	—	—
Mean ($\bar{x}$)	37	26.8	39.1	253	235.5	312	6.84	8.79* (p<.046)	7.98
SD	10.7	4.83	9.78	15.3	20.16	15.79	1.52	1.87	1.29

($\bar{x}$ difference of Pre-test → Post-test 1, and Pre-test → Post-test 2 significant at p<.05 level = *; significant at p<.01 level =**)

Table 5-3 Differences in frequency of BCs over time for Group Z

N = 10	Total Backchannels			Interlocutor's Words			Average number of interlocutor's words between backchannels		
	Pre	Post 1	Post 2	Pre	Post 1	Post 2	Pre	Post 1	Post 2
Total	445	317	474	2914	2381	3408	—	—	—
Mean ($\bar{x}$)	44.5	31.7	47.4	291.4	238	340.8	6.55	7.51	7.19
SD	13	9.15	12.9	18.23	10.5	11.24	1.37	1.26	.89

($\bar{x}$ difference of Pre-test → Post-test 1, and Pre-test → Post-test 2 significant at p<.05 level = *; significant at p<.01 level =**)

5.2.4 Differences in BC Frequency Across Groups Over Time

Analysing the data of the three groups collectively, Figure 5-1 shows that the general trend for the experimental groups was for JEFLs to backchannel much less frequently in Post-test 1 vis-à-vis the Pre-test and then, in Post-test 2, revert to a level closer to their original Pre-test level, while the Control group only showed a slight decrease from the Pre-test to Post-test 1. Noticeably, from the Pre-test to Post-test 1, the 3.91

backchannel per interlocutor word decrease shown by the Explicit group was found to be strongly significant ($p<.001$), and the 1.95 decrease for the Implicit group was significant at the .05 level ($p<.046$). Further, while all three groups had reverted back to providing more frequent backchannels in Post-test 2, there was some variability between the frequencies in each group. For instance, the Control group provided backchannels only slightly less frequently in the Pre-test than in Post-test 2 (difference of only .64 backchannels per interlocutor word), whereas the Implicit group provided backchannels noticeably less frequently in the Pre-test than Post-test 2 (difference of 1.14 backchannels per interlocutor word). The Explicit group, however, was the only one to sustain statistically significant changes ($p<.001$) in frequency from the Pre-test to Post-test 2 (difference of 2.67 backchannels per interlocutor word).

Figure 5-1 Comparing BC frequencies of the three groups over time

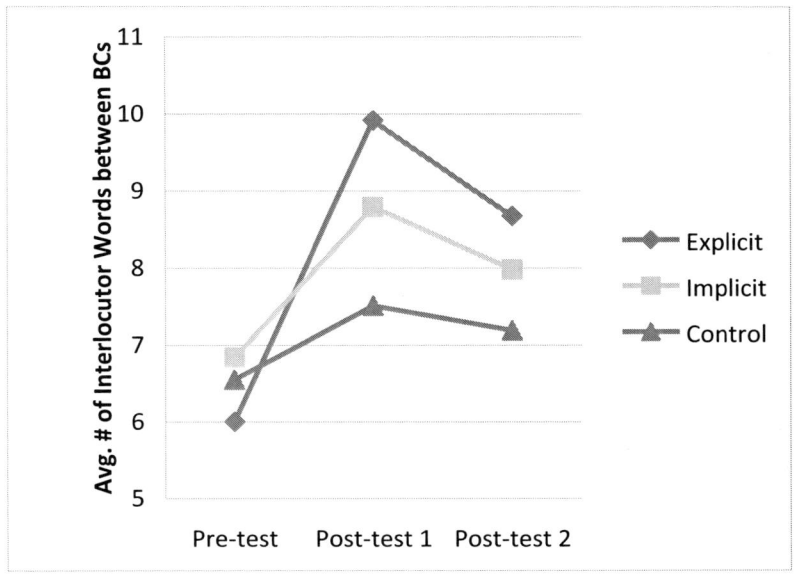

5.3 Involvement in the Conversations

The JEFLs' involvement and WTC in the conversations was measured in three ways: (1) WTC scores, (2) how much they spoke in the conversations and (3) the number of questions they asked their interlocutor. This section reports the results of these features of conversations as they pertain to each of the three groups, and, subsequently, a comparison of the results of the three groups collectively is presented.

5.3.1 Group A (Explicit)

Table 5-4 below demonstrates the average WTC scores, number of words and number of questions pertaining to members of Group A at the three points of measurement in this study. The WTC scores rose significantly from 48.4 in the Pre-test to 70 in Post-test 1 and 57.7 in Post-test 2. Paired-samples t-tests showed these differences from the Pre-test to be statistically significant in both Post-tests. The overall word count for the Explicit group was 583 words during the Pre-test, 973 during Post-test 1, and 567 during Post-test 2. A paired-samples t-test showed the difference in means between the Pre-test and Post-test 1 to be statistically significant. Regarding questions, Group A asked an average of .08 questions in the Pre-test, 2.1 questions in Post-test 1, and 1.6 questions in Post-test 2. Paired-samples t-tests revealed the difference in means between the Pre-test and Post-test 1 to be statistically significant, as well as the Pre-test and Post-test 2.

5.3.2 Group B (Implicit)

Table 5-5 below shows the differences in WTC scores, number of words, and number of questions corresponding to members of Group B at the three tests. While there were noticeable increases in the number of words and questions Group B uttered from the Pre-test to Post-test 1, only their increases in WTC scores from the Pre-test to Post-tests 1 and 2 were found to be statistically significant.

Table 5-4 Group A's involvement in the conversation over time

N = 10	WTC		Words			Questions		
	x̄	SD	Total	x̄	SD	Total	x̄	SD
Pre	48.4	10.74	583	58.3	32.82	8	.08	.79
Post 1	70** (p<.001)	6.79	973	97.3** (p<.007)	35.87	21	2.1** (p<.001)	.88
Post 2	57.7** (p<.001)	9.12	567	56.7	26.37	14	1.6* (p<.011)	.70

(x̄ difference of Pre-test → Post-test 1, and Pre-test → Post-test 2 significant at p<.05 level = *; significant at p<.01 level =**)

Table 5-5 Group B's involvement in the conversation over time

N = 10	WTC		Words			Questions		
	x̄	SD	Total	x̄	SD	Total	x̄	SD
Pre	50.4	8.14	650	65	32.33	12	1.2	.63
Post 1	60.6** (p<.002)	6.08	901	90.1	31.19	16	1.6	1.17
Post 2	56.6* (p<.022)	8.21	705	70.5	23.01	11	1.1	1.29

(x̄ difference of Pre-test → Post-test 1, and Pre-test → Post-test 2 significant at p<.05 level = *; significant at p<.01 level =**)

5.3.3 Group Z (Control)

As Table 5-6 shows, Group Z's WTC scores remained fairly constant; however, the number of words they uttered increased noticeably from the Pre-test to Post-test 1 and then reverted back to their near Pre-test level in

Post-test 2, and the number of questions they posed consistently declined at each measurement. Regarding the latter, the decline in questions from the Pre-test to Post-test 2 was found to be statistically significant.

Table 5-6 Group Z's involvement in the conversation over time

N = 10	WTC		Words			Questions		
	$\bar{x}$	SD	Total	$\bar{x}$	SD	Total	$\bar{x}$	SD
Pre	56.2	7.27	640	64	32	18	1.8	.92
Post 1	57.3	7.42	963	96.3	30.63	14	1.4	.84
Post 2	58.5	7.37	641	64.1	33	9	.9* (p<.041)	.74

($\bar{x}$ difference of Pre-test → Post-test 1, and Pre-test → Post-test 2 significant at p<.05 level = *; significant at p<.01 level =**)

5.3.4 Conversational Involvement Across Groups Over Time

Examining the data of the three groups collectively, the differences in WTC scores, number of words and number of questions asked at the three tests are shown in Figures 5-2, 5-3 and 5-4 respectively. First, as shown in Figure 5-2, the Explicit group showed the greatest increase in average WTC score from the Pre-test to Post-test 1 (+21.6), as well as the greatest sustained increase from the Pre-test to Post-test 2 (+9.3). Both of these increases were found to be significant at the .01 level. The path of the Implicit group largely mirrored that of the Explicit group but without the same range in scores. The 10.2 increase in this group's average WTC score from the Pre-test to Post-test 1 was found to be strongly significant (at the .01 level), and the 6.2 increase from the Pre-test to Post-test 2 was significant at the .05 level. For the Control group, the average WTC scores remained fairly constant over time, only showing minor increases of 1.1 and 2.3 from the Pre-test to Post-tests 1 and 2 respectively.

Figure 5-2 Comparing WTC scores of the three groups over time

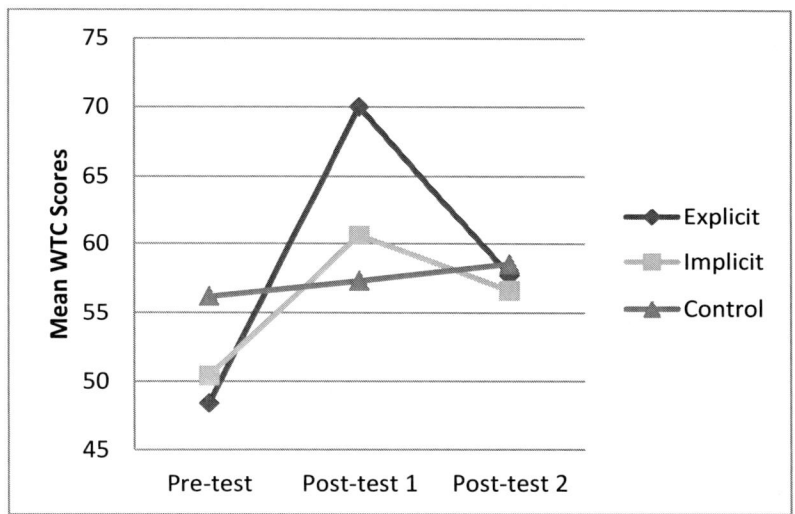

Second, as Figure 5-3 demonstrates, the three groups followed a similar path in terms of word output over time. As with the findings shown in Figure 5-1 concerning frequency, the general trend, regardless of which group they belonged to, was for the JEFLs to speak much more frequently in Post-test 1 compared to the Pre-test and then, in Post-test 2, revert to a level closer to their original Pre-test level. The mean increase exhibited by the Explicit group (39 words) was the only one found to be statistically significant from the Pre-test to Post-test 1 ($p<.007$); however, the differences for the Implicit (25.1) and Control groups (32.3) were also salient.

As Figure 5-4 illustrates, the path that each group followed in terms of the average number of questions posed was somewhat different. The Explicit group showed the greatest initial increase in questions from the Pre-test to Post-test 1 (+1.3), as well as a sustained increase from the Pre-test to Post-test 2 (+.8). Paired-samples t-tests found both of these increases to be statistically significant ($p<.001$ from Pre-test to Post-test 1, and $p<.011$ from Pre-test to Post-test 2). In comparison, the Implicit group showed only a modest initial increase from the Pre-test to Post-test 1 (+.4), and ultimately a slight decrease overall from the Pre-test to Post-test 2 (-.1). The Control group was the only group to decrease in both measurements after the Pre-test, i.e., (-.4) from the Pre-test to Post-test 1 and (-.9) from the Pre-test to Post-test 2. The latter decrease was found to be statistically significant at the .05 level.

Figure 5-3 Comparing word output of the three groups over time

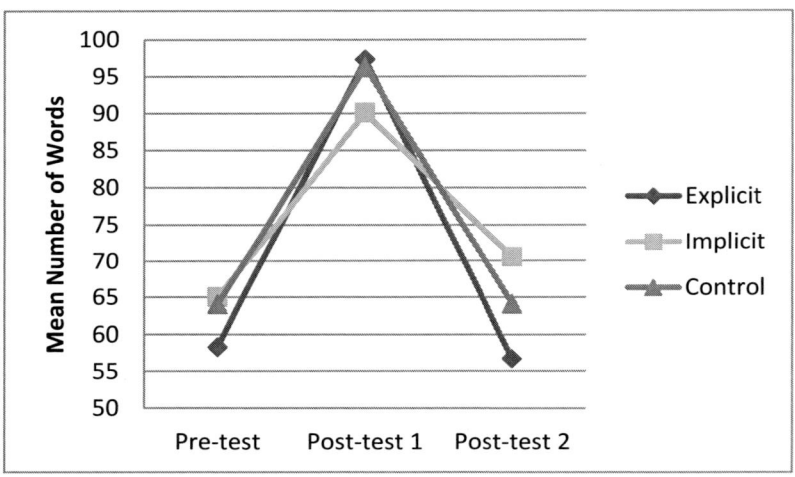

Figure 5-4 Comparing the number of questions of the three groups

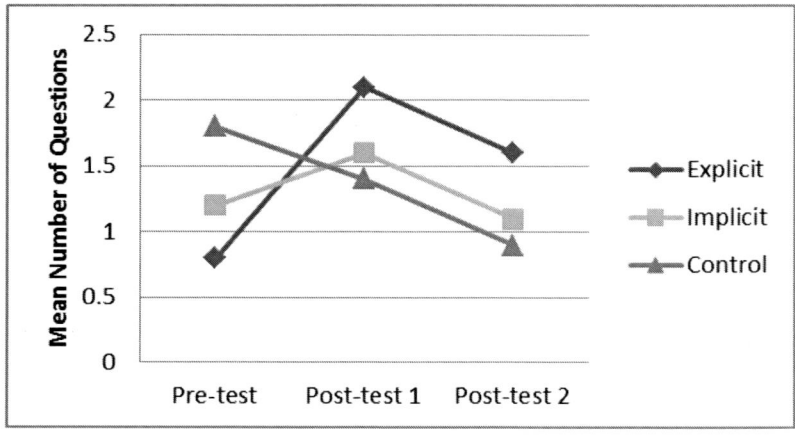

5.4 Variability of Use

Sections 5.4.1-5.4.3 report on the variability of each group's backchannels (BCs) at the three points of measurement in this study. The final subsection, 5.4.4, compares the main findings in this area across groups.

5.4.1 Group A (Explicit)

Reporting on the variability of Group A's verbal backchannels, Table 5-7 demonstrates findings in which the differences in mean percentage of total backchannels were statistically significant between tests. Paired-samples t-tests found the difference between the means of both subcategories of the Compound backchannel type to be statistically significant from the Pre-test to Post-test 2: Compound isolated and Compound with head nods. In addition, the means of the Complex backchannel type were found to be statistically significant in the following subcategories: Complex isolated from the Pre-test to Post-test 1, Complex with head nod from the Pre-test to Post-test 1, and, lastly, Complex with head nod from the Pre-test to Post-test 2. For various categories, such as Compound (isolated) and Compound with headnod(s) in Post-test 1 and the Complex (isolated) in Post-test 2, the high variability around the mean, shown by the SDs, was the cause of lack of significance in the differences.

Table 5-8 reports on the variability of Group A's nonverbal (NV) backchannels over time. Paired-samples t-tests found the differences between the mean percentage of total backchannels across tests to be statistically significant in the following categories: Multiple head nods isolated from the Pre-test to Post-test 1 and from the Pre-test to Post-test 2, Smiles with verbal backchannel from the Pre-test to Post-test 2, and Raised eyebrows with verbal backchannels from the Pre-test to Post-test 1.

Table 5-7 Variability of Group A's verbal backchannels over time

N = 10	Pre-test			Post-test 1			Post-test 2		
Type of Backchannel	Total	x̄ % of Total BCs	SD	Total	x̄ % of Total BCs	SD	Total	x̄ % of Total BCs	SD
Simple (isolated)	55	14.6	10.38	55	19.4	11.3	51	14.7	12.82
Simple with head nod(s)	152	30.5	16.92	85	29.2	14.41	82	21.7	11.74
Compound (isolated)	1	.2	.63	7	2.7	3.62	10	2.9* (p<.011)	2.6
Compound with head nod(s)	10	1.9	1.85	13	5.7	5.9	21	6.2** (p<.007)	3.52
Complex (isolated)	7	2.3	3.02	18	7.2* (p<.045)	8.5	24	8.8	12.34
Complex with head nod(s)	21	4.3	4.97	36	11.5* (p<.019)	7.2	54	15.6** (p<.008)	11.34
Japanese (all complex)	1	.2	.63	0	0	0	0	0	0

(x̄ difference of Pre-test → Post-test 1, and Pre-test → Post-test 2 significant at p<.05 level = *; significant at p<.01 level =**)

Table 5-8 Variability of Group A's nonverbal BCs over time

N = 10	Pre-test			Post-test 1			Post-test 2		
Type of NV BC	Total (T)	x̄ % of Total BCs	SD	T	x̄ % of Total BCs	SD	T	x̄ % of Total BCs	SD
Single head nod (isolated)	87	20.4	14.05	31	10.6	18.09	79	18.2	17.52
Multiple head nods (isolated)	78	16.6	14.79	11	4.2* (p<.021)	4.32	19	5.5* (p<.049)	5.52
Smile (isolated)	0	0	0	1	.3	.95	0	0	0
Smile + verbal BC	6	1.6	.67	8	3.2	1.48	18	5.4* (p<.027)	1.79
Laughter (isolated)	37	9.6	7.78	36	11.8	9.07	33	8.9	7.34
Laughter + verbal BC	18	3.6	5.64	14	4.1	3.96	18	5.5	4.53
Raised Eyebrows (isolated)	0	0	0	2	.5	1.58	1	.3	.95
Raised Eyebrows + verbal BC	3	.7	1.16	8	2.6* (p<.045)	2.5	4	1.4	2.46
≥ 2 NV BCs occurring together (isolated)	0	0	0	3	.9	1.91	0	0	0
≥ 2 NV BCs occurring together with verbal BC	0	0	0	0	0	0	2	.5	1.08

(x̄ difference of Pre-test → Post-test 1, and Pre-test → Post-test 2 significant at p<.05 level = *; significant at p<.01 level =**)

As explained in Section 2.4, some of the different types of backchannels mentioned above can be grouped together to form two larger categories: minimal responses and extended responses. Table 5-9 shows that the mean percentage of Group A's backchannels that were minimal responses was 82.1% in the Pre-test, 62.1% in Post-test 1 and 60.4 in Post-test 2. Paired-samples t-tests confirmed that the difference between the mean percentages of total backchannels in the Pre-test and Post-test 1, and the difference between the means of the Pre-test and Post-test 2, were statistically significant. In comparison, the mean percentage of Group A's backchannels that were extended responses was 7% in the Pre-test, 18% in Post-test 1 and 23% in Post-test 2. The differences between the means from the Pre-test to Post-tests 1 and 2 were also found to be strongly significant.

Table 5-9 Group A's use of minimal versus extended BCs over time

N = 10	Pre-test			Post-test 1			Post-test 2		
Type of BC	Total (T)	x̄ % of Total BCs	SD	T	x̄ % of Total BCs	SD	T	x̄ % of Total BCs	SD
Minimal Responses	372	82.1	10.6	182	62.1** (p<.003)	8.49	232	60.4** (p<.002)	13.02
Extended Responses	29	7	4.37	62	18** (p<.009)	9.04	78	23** (p<.004)	13.49

(x̄ difference of Pre-test → Post-test 1, and Pre-test → Post-test 2 significant at p<.05 level = *; significant at p<.01 level =**)

Shifting to a micro perspective, the next part of this subsection reports on the variability that members of Group A exhibited in terms of the individual constituents that comprise backchannel forms. Following the categories outlined in Section 3.6.1.2, Tables 5-10, 5-11 and 5-12 demonstrate respectively how often members of this group used non-word vocalisations, isolated content words, and multi-word backchannel phrases and/or expressions at the three tests (N.B. For an item to be included in the data sets showing backchannel forms, it was required that the item occur at least twice in the conversations).

Table 5-10 Variability of Group A's non-word vocalisations over time

	uu unn hm um mm	yeah yes yeah yep	mhmu hum	uhuh	aa ah	oo	oh	eee	so	**Total**
Pre	58	34	3	1	18	14	6	8	0	**142**
Post 1	41	24	12	1	9	13	6	0	0	**106**
Post 2	25	53	4	2	12	13	9	1	0	**119**

Table 5-11 Variability of Group A's isolated content words over time

	ok okay kay	no	really	right	wow	nice	cool	interesting	**Total**
Pre	4	0	3	0	2	0	0	0	**9**
Post 1	1	0	2	1	2	2	0	1	**9**
Post 2	4	0	0	0	3	0	0	0	**7**

Table 5-12 Variability of Group A's multi-word BC phrases over time

Total = T	oh/ah really	ah/ oh ok	ah/oh yeah (yes)	that's right	oh / that's (very) nice	do you	me too	I see	I under stand	is that so	T
Pre	3	0	0	0	0	0	0	0	0	0	**3**
Post 1	4	1	0	0	0	1	1	1	0	0	**8**
Post 2	4	0	2	1	2	0	0	0	1	1	**11**

Individual backchannel forms presented in this section do not include the constituents of backchannel forms which involved repetitions of the primary speaker's speech. Reporting these separately, Table 5-13 presents Group A's use of repetitions (REPS). While there was some noticeable fluctuation in the raw frequencies of different types of repetitions used in Post-test 1 (9) compared to the Pre-test (12) and Post-test 2 (13), the mean percentage of total backchannels constituted by repetition did not greatly vary and showed only slight increases from 2.91% in the Pre-test to 3.08% in Post-test 1 and 3.32% in Post-test 2. Concerning the different types of repetitions outlined in Section 3.6.1.2, the mean percentages of non-clarifications (NON CLARS) exceeded the mean percentages of clarifications (CLARS) in all three tests. The use of clarification repetition backchannels was minimal with a mean percentage of only .19% issued in the Pre-test, 1.22% in Post-test 1, and .35% in Post-test 2, whereas non-clarification repetition backchannels were more common on the whole with a mean percentage of 2.66% in the Pre-test, 2.76% in Post-test 1, and 3.29% in Post-test 2.

Table 5-13 Group A's use of repetitions as backchannels over time

	Total REPS	x̄ % of Total BCs	SD	CLARS	x̄ % of Total BCs	SD	NON CLARS	x̄ % of Total BCs	SD
Pre	12	2.91	1.24	1	.19	.60	11	2.66	1
Post 1	9	3.08	2.34	3	1.22	1.97	6	2.76	2.79
Post 2	13	3.32	2.96	1	.35	1.09	12	3.29	1.82

(x̄ difference of Pre-test → Post-test 1, and Pre-test → Post-test 2 significant at p<.05 level = *; significant at p<.01 level =**)

5.4.2 Group B (Implicit)

Reporting on the variability of Group B's verbal backchannels, Table 5-14 shows the following categories in which the differences in the mean percentage of total backchannels were statistically significant between tests: Simple with head nod from the Pre-test to Post-test 1, Compound isolated from the Pre-test to Post-test 2, Compound with head nod from the Pre-test to Post-test 2 and, lastly, Complex with head nods from the Pre-test to Post-test 1 and from the Pre-test to Post-test 2.

Table 5-14 Variability of Group B's verbal backchannels over time

N = 10	Pre-test			Post-test 1			Post-test 2		
Type of BC	Total (T)	x̄ % of Total BCs	SD	T	x̄ % of Total BCs	SD	T	x̄ % of Total BCs	SD
Simple (isolated)	41	13.1	11.92	49	18.3	9.27	72	18.2	11.07
Simple with head nod(s)	162	44.2	17.15	77	27.8* (p<.018)	11.64	126	32.1	8.8
Compound (isolated)	2	.7	2.21	9	3.4	3.53	17	4.9* (p<.024)	3.84
Compound with head nod(s)	11	2.7	2.11	12	4.4	5.06	28	7.3* (p<.044)	6.04
Complex (isolated)	5	1.6	2.37	13	4.1	6.32	11	3.1	4.2
Complex with head nod(s)	18	5.1	3.41	34	13.1* (p<.011)	6.23	40	11* (p<.021)	6.55
Japanese (all complex)	7	2.4	7.59	5	1.8	3.55	6	2.1	3.57

(x̄ difference of Pre-test → Post-test 1, and Pre-test → Post-test 2 significant at p<.05 level = *; significant at p<.01 level =**)

The results demonstrating the variability of Group B's nonverbal (NV) backchannels over time are presented in Table 5-15 below. The only statistically significant findings were attributed to the Laughter with verbal backchannel category, which showed the differences in the mean percentage of total backchannels to be statistically significant from the Pre-test to Post-test 1 and from the Pre-test to Post-test 2.

Table 5-15 Variability of Group B's nonverbal BCs over time

N = 10	Pre-test			Post-test 1			Post-test 2		
Type of NV BC	Total (T)	x̄ % of Total BCs	SD	T	x̄ % of Total BCs	SD	T	x̄ % of Total BCs	SD
Single head nod (isolated)	57	12.9	12.04	17	6.5	9.07	42	9.9	7.51
Multiple head nods (isolated)	42	9.5	11.4	12	5.3	10.47	18	4.1	3.51
Smile (isolated)	0	0	0	1	.5	1.58	1	.3	.95
Smile + verbal BC	11	1.1	1.45	20	2	1.76	28	2.8	2.74
Laughter (isolated)	23	7.4	6.15	38	14.3	7.53	22	7.2	4.78
Laughter + verbal BC	6	1.5	2.92	19	7.3** (p<.01)	5.44	16	4.5* (p<.035)	2.91
Raised Eyebrows	0	0	0	0	0	0	0	0	0
Raised Eyebrows + verbal BC	5	1.3	.75	6	2.7	1.04	6	1.8	.77
≥ 2 NV BCs occurring together (isolated)	0	0	0	0	0	0	0	0	0
≥ 2 NV BCs occurring together + verbal BC	1	.3	.95	3	1.5	2.72	0	0	0

(x̄ difference of Pre-test → Post-test 1, and Pre-test → Post-test 2 significant at p<.05 level = *; significant at p<.01 level =**)

Concerning Group B's use of minimal versus extended responses, Table 5-16 demonstrates findings in which the differences in mean percentage of total backchannels constituted by each type were statistically significant between tests. Paired-samples t-tests showed that the differences between the means of the Pre-test (79.7) and Post-test 1 (59.1), and the difference between the means of the Pre-test (79.7) and Post-test 2 (66.9), were statistically significant. Moreover, concerning extended responses, the differences between the means from the Pre-test (7.1) to Post-test 1 (17.1) and Post-test 2 (14.5) were also statistically significant. Subsequently, in Tables 5-17, 5-18 and 5-19 respectively, non-word vocalisations, isolated content words, and multi-word backchannel phrases and/or expressions used by the Implicit group at the three tests are reported.

Table 5-16 Group B's use of minimal versus extended BCs over time

N = 10	Pre-test			Post-test 1			Post-test 2		
Type of BC	Total (T)	$\bar{x}$ % of Total BCs	SD	T	$\bar{x}$ % of Total BCs	SD	T	$\bar{x}$ % of Total BCs	SD
Minimal Responses	302	79.7	10.87	157	59.1** (p<.001)	9.09	269	66.9* (p<.022)	12.87
Extended Responses	23	7.1	4.43	47	17.1** (p<.001)	7.23	51	14.5* (p<.015)	10.01

($\bar{x}$ difference of Pre-test → Post-test 1, and Pre-test → Post-test 2 significant at p<.05 level = *; significant at p<.01 level =**)

Table 5-17 Variability of Group B's non-word vocalisations over time

	uu/unn hm/um mm	yeah yes yep	mhm uhum	uhuh	aa ah	oo	oh	ee	so	Total
Pre	69	32	8	2	21	14	2	5	0	**153**
Post 1	29	26	19	2	12	7	3	3	3	**104**
Post 2	46	51	8	1	22	10	3	5	1	**147**

Table 5-18 Variability of Group B's isolated content words over time

	ok okay kay	no	really	right	wow	nice/ cool	interesting	today	Total
Pre	2	0	0	0	0	0	1	0	3
Post 1	3	0	7	0	1	0	0	2	13
Post 2	1	0	3	0	2	0	0	0	6

Table 5-19 Variability of Group B's multi-word BC phrases over time

	oh/ah really	ah/ oh ok	ah/oh yeah	that's interesting/ good /great	very nice/ so good	me too	I understand	do you	Total
Pre	2	0	2	0	0	0	0	0	4
Post 1	3	0	3	0	2	0	0	0	8
Post 2	4	1	0	1	0	0	1	1	8

Table 5-20, reporting on Group B's use of repetitions (REPS), showed that there was not a great deal of variation within each of the three categories across tests. Similar to the results of the explicit group, the mean percentages of clarifications (CLARS) was again noticeably lower than the percentages of non-clarifications (NON CLARS) in all three tests.

Table 5-20 Group B's use of repetitions as backchannels over time

N = 10	Total REPS	x̄ % of Total BCs	SD	CLARS	x̄ % of Total BCs	SD	NON CLARS	x̄ % of Total BCs	SD
Pre	14	4.39	2.14	4	1.33	1.74	10	2.68	1.59
Post 1	12	4.43	2.88	2	.61	1.28	10	4.17	2.16
Post 2	13	3.45	1.85	3	.83	1.45	10	2.85	1.61

(x̄ difference of Pre-test → Post-test 1, and Pre-test → Post-test 2 significant at $p<.05$ level = *; significant at $p<.01$ level =**)

5.4.3 Group Z (Control)

The frequencies shown in Table 5-21 demonstrate the variability of Group Z's verbal backchannels in the three tests. Subsequently, Table 5-22 reports on the variability of Group Z's nonverbal backchannels in this study. Further, unlike the results of the experimental groups in this area, Table 5-23 demonstrates that the mean percentage of Group Z's backchannels that were minimal responses rose slightly at each point of measurement, while the percentage which constituted extended responses decreased. Regarding the latter, a paired-samples t-test showed that the decrease between the means from the Pre-test to Post-test 2 was statistically significant.

Table 5-21 Variability of Group Z's verbal backchannels over time

N = 10	Pre-test			Post-test 1			Post-test 2		
Type of BCs	Total	x̄ % of Total BCs	SD	Total	x̄ % of Total BCs	SD	Total	x̄ % of Total BCs	SD
Simple (isolated)	51	12.1	5	46	15.8	10.88	66	13.79	15.7
Simple with head nod(s)	162	36.3	9.58	96	30.4	10.82	169	35	7.5
Compound (isolated)	11	2.2	1.81	2	.8	1.75	9	1.9	2.13
Compound with head nod(s)	18	3.9	2.18	12	3.8	2.53	19	3.1	2.13
Complex (isolated)	19	4.9	6.71	6	2.1	1.97	8	2	2.06
Complex with head nod(s)	29	6.3	3.47	21	6.9	3.93	22	4.5	3.24
Japanese (all complex)	3	.7	2.21	2	.9	2.85	3	1.2	3.8

(x̄ difference of Pre-test → Post-test 1, and Pre-test → Post-test 2 significant at p<.05 level = *; significant at p<.01 level =**)

Table 5-22 Variability of Group Z's nonverbal BCs over time

N = 10	Pre-test			Post-test 1			Post-test 2		
Type of NV BC	Total	$\bar{x}$ % of Total BCs ($\bar{x}$)	SD	Total	$\bar{x}$	SD	Total	$\bar{x}$	SD
Single head nod (isolated)	78	15.9	10.15	67	19.7	12.3	104	21.6	10.36
Multiple head nods (isolated)	43	10.1	7.65	30	8.7	5.66	45	9.2	6.56
Smile (isolated)	0	0	0	1	.5	1.58	0	0	0
Smile + verbal BC	14	3	5.12	17	5.5	4.4	21	4.7	3.53
Laughter (isolated)	33	8.3	6.87	36	11.9	7.31	28	6	4.12
Laughter + verbal BC	14	3.2	3.68	13	4.1	4.12	22	4.7	5.85
Raised Eyebrows (isolated)	0	0	0	0	0	0	0	0	0
Raised Eyebrows + verbal BC	11	2.6	3.17	7	2.3	2.83	8	1.6	2.84
≥ 2 NV BCs occurring together (isolated)	1	.2	.63	0	0	0	0	0	0
≥ 2 NV BCs occurring together with verbal BC	5	1.1	2.42	4	1.4	1.9	5	1.4	2.5

($\bar{x}$ difference of Pre-test → Post-test 1, and Pre-test → Post-test 2 significant at p<.05 level = *; significant at p<.01 level =**)

Table 5-23 Group Z's use of minimal versus extended BCs over time

N = 10	Pre-test			Post-test 1			Post-test 2		
Type of BC	Total	x̄ % of Total BCs	SD	Total	x̄ % of Total BCs	SD	Total	x̄ % of Total BCs	SD
Minimal Responses	321	74.4	11.3	241	75.5	10.79	398	82.4	5.6
Extended Responses	48	11.2	6.55	27	10.8	5.41	36	7.4* (p<.04)	3.31

(x̄ difference of Pre-test → Post-test 1, and Pre-test → Post-test 2 significant at p<.05 level = *; significant at p<.01 level =**)

Tables 5-24, 5-25 and 5-26 below demonstrate non-word vocalisations, isolated content words, and multi-word backchannel phrases and/or expressions corresponding to the Control group.

Table 5-24 Variability of Group Z's non-word vocalisations over time

	uu/un nn/um mm hm	yeah yes yep	mhm uhum	uhuh	aah	oo	oh	ee	so	Total
Pre	68	30	22	11	32	17	2	5	0	187
Post 1	51	15	12	2	11	12	5	3	0	111
Post 2	85	32	13	3	11	11	8	5	0	168

Table 5-25 Variability of Group Z's isolated content words over time

	ok okay kay	no	really	right	wow	nice	cool	interesting/ today	Total
Pre	3	0	2	0	0	0	1	0	**6**
Post 1	0	1	0	1	0	0	0	0	**2**
Post 2	3	2	3	0	1	0	0	0	**9**

Table 5-26 Variability of Group Z's multi-word BC phrases over time

	oh/ ah really	that's/ you are right	ah/oh yeah	that's/ very nice/ great/ interesting	me too	I see/ know	do you	Total
Pre	3	1	1	2	1	1	0	**9**
Post 1	3	0	0	0	1	1	0	**5**
Post 2	3	0	0	1	0	0	1	**5**

As Table 5-27 shows, there was not much range in the frequency of Group Z's repetition backchannels at the three points of measurement.

Table 5-27 Group Z's use of repetitions as BCs over time

	Total REPS	x̄ % of Total BCs	SD	CLARS	x̄ % of Total BCs	SD	NON CLARS	x̄ % of Total BCs	SD
Pre	14	3.09	1.39	1	.14	.45	13	3.77	2.48
Post 1	12	4.2	3.1	1	.31	.99	11	3.72	2.88
Post 2	13	2.95	1.87	1	.23	.72	12	2.36	1.17

(x̄ difference of Pre-test → Post-test 1, and Pre-test → Post-test 2 significant at $p<.05$ level = *; significant at $p<.01$ level =**)

5.4.4 Differences in Variability of Backchannel Use Over Time

In collectively presenting some of the key findings corresponding to the variability of backchannel use exhibited by the three groups over time, this subsection focuses on the area thought to have the greatest influence on perceptions in communication: minimal responses and extended responses. The data illustrated in Figures 5-5 and 5-6 demonstrate some noticeable differences in terms of the experimental groups' performance in this area over time. First, Figure 5-5 illustrates that both the Explicit and Implicit groups showed a considerable decrease in their mean percentage of backchannels constituted by minimal backchannels from the Pre-test to Post-tests 1 and 2. The Explicit group decreased by 20% from the Pre-test to Post-test 1 and by 21.7% from the Pre-test to Post-test 2, while the Implicit Group decreased by 20.06% from the Pre-test to Post-test 1 and by 12.8% from the Pre-test to Post-test 2. Paired-samples t-tests showed that the differences between the means of the Pre-test and Post-test 1 were strongly significant for both experimental groups: the Explicit group ($p<.003$) and Implicit group ($p<.001$). The differences between the means of the Pre-test and Post-test 2 were also found to be statistically significant for both experimental groups; however, the difference for the Explicit group, at the .01 level, was again strongly significant ($p<.002$), whereas the difference for the Implicit group was significant at the .05 level ($p<.022$). The Control group was markedly different, being the only group to increase in the mean percentage of total backchannels constituted by minimal responses from the Pre-test to Post-test 1 (+1.1%) and the Pre-test to Post-test 2 (+8%). Paired-samples t-tests confirmed that these increases were not statistically significant.

Figure 5-6 also highlights some noticeable differences in terms of the experimental groups' use of extended backchannels over time. Predictably, since the experimental groups showed a noticeable decrease in the mean percentage of backchannels constituted by minimal backchannels, Figure 5-6 demonstrates the Explicit and Implicit groups exhibiting a considerable increase in the mean percentage of backchannels constituted by extended responses from the Pre-test to Post-tests 1 and 2. The mean percentage of the Explicit Group increased by 11% from the Pre-test to Post-test 1 and by 16% from the Pre-test to Post-test 2, whereas the Implicit Group increased by 10% from the Pre-test to Post-test 1 and by 7.4% from the Pre-test to Post-test 2. Paired-samples t-tests showed that the differences between the means of the Pre-test and Post-test 1 were strongly significant for the Explicit group ($p<.009$) and Implicit group ($p<.001$), and, once again, the difference was strongly significant for the Explicit group from the Pre-test to Post-test 2 ($p<.004$), while it was significant at the .05 level for the Implicit group ($p<.015$). Unlike the experimental groups, the path of the Control group, conversely, showed decreases in the mean percentage of backchannels constituted by extended responses from the Pre-test to Post-test 1 (-.4%) and the Pre-test to Post-test 2 (-3.8%). The latter was found to be statistically significant at the .05 level ($p<.04$).

Figure 5-5 Comparing the proportions of minimal BCs over time

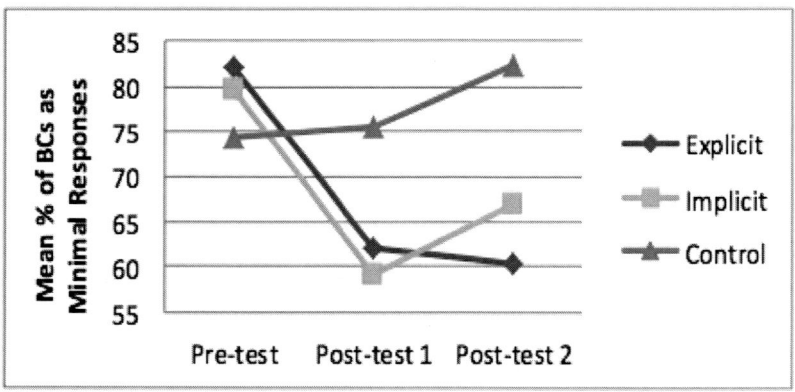

Figure 5-6 Comparing the proportions of extended BCs over time

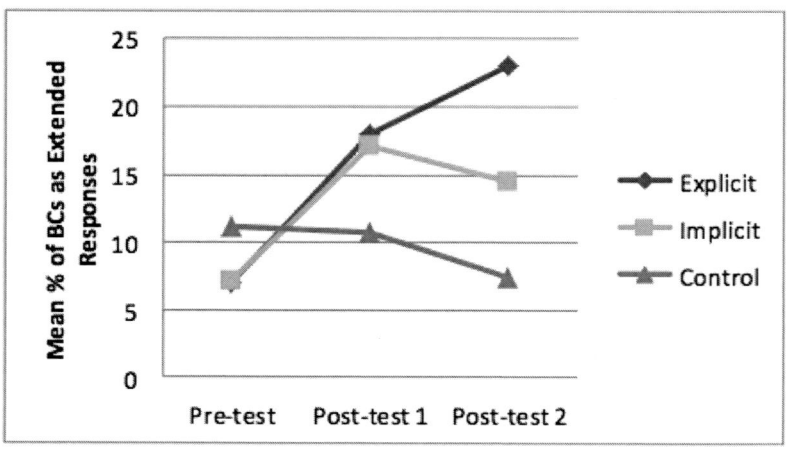

5.5 Discourse Contexts Favouring Backchannels

Tables 5-28, 5-29 and 5-30 report two main statistics regarding the discourse contexts of each group's backchannels at the three tests: (1) the mean percentage of opportunities (Opps) that each discourse context attracted backchannels (with SDs), and (2) the mean percentage of backchannels constituted by each discourse context (with SDs). In the final subsection, 5.5.4, some of the main findings concerning the three groups' discourse contexts favouring backchannels are compared.

5.5.1 Group A (Explicit)

Concerning (1), Table 5-28 shows that the mean percentage of potential backchannel opportunities which actually attracted backchannels tended to decrease for Group A from the Pre-test to Post-tests 1 and 2. With the exception of one category (i.e., At or directly after internal clause boundaries accompanied by a pause), Group A were, on average, making less use of backchannel-attracting contexts in Post-test 1 than they did in the Pre-test. The difference in means between tests was statistically significant in the following categories: At or directly after a pause from the Pre-test to Post-test 1 ($p<.031$) and from the Pre-test to Post-test 2 ($p<.045$), At or near any clausal boundary (CB) from the Pre-test to Post-test 1 ($p<.001$) and from the Pre-test to Post-test 2 ($p<.048$), At or near a final CB from the Pre-test to Post-test 1 ($p<.041$), At or directly after any CB accompanied by a pause from the Pre-test to Post-test 1 ($p<.021$), and At or directly after a final CB accompanied by a pause from the Pre-test to Post-test 1 ($p<.016$). Regarding (2), Table 5-28 also demonstrates the mean percentage of backchannels constituted by each discourse context at the three tests. The only differences to be found statistically significant in this area were the increases in mean percentage of backchannels occurring at any CB and final CB opportunities from the Pre-test to the Post-test 1 ($p<.047$ and $p<.034$ respectively).

5.5.2 Group B (Implicit)

Table 5-29 shows that the mean percentage of potential backchannel opportunities which actually attracted backchannels also tended to decrease for Group B from the Pre-test to Post-tests 1 and 2. In other words, Group B were, on average, making less use of backchannel-attracting contexts in Post-tests 1 and 2 than they did in the Pre-test. The difference in means between tests was statistically significant in the following categories: At or near any CB from the Pre-test to Post-test 1 ($p<.005$) and from the Pre-test to Post-test 2 ($p<.007$), At or near any final CB from the Pre-test to Post-test 1 ($p<.013$) and from the Pre-test to Post-test 2 ($p<.02$), At or directly after any CB accompanied by a pause from the Pre-test to Post-test 1 ($p<.002$) and from the Pre-test to Post-test 2 ($p<.009$), At or directly after a final CB accompanied by a pause from the Pre-test to Post-test 1 ($p<.004$) and from the Pre-test to Post-test 2 ($p<.026$), and After the primary speaker's head nod(s) from the Pre-test to Post-test 1 ($p<.043$). Reporting the mean percentage of backchannels constituted by each discourse context at the three tests, Table 5-29 shows that the differences in means between tests were statistically significant in the following categories: At or directly after a pause from the Pre-test to Post-test 1 ($p<.002$), At or directly after any CB accompanied by a pause from the Pre-test to Post-test 1 ($p<.001$) and from the Pre-test to Post-test 2 ($p<.001$), At or directly after a final CB accompanied by a pause from the Pre-test to Post-test 1 ($p<.001$) and from the Pre-test to Post-test 2 ($p<.003$), and After the primary speaker's head nod(s) from the Pre-test to Post-test 1 ($p<.049$).

5.5.3 Group Z (Control)

Similar to Groups A and B, Group Z were, on average, making less use of backchannel-attracting contexts in Post-test 1 than they did in the Pre-test. As shown in Table 5-30, the differences in the mean percentage of opportunities that each discourse context attracted backchannels in the following categories were statistically significant: At or directly after a pause from the Pre-test to Post-test 1 ($p<.001$), At or near any clausal boundary (CB) from the Pre-test to Post-test 1 ($p<.001$), At or near any final CB from the Pre-test to Post-test 1 ($p<.002$), At or directly after any CB accompanied by a pause from the Pre-test to Post-test 1 ($p<.037$), At or directly after a final CB accompanied by a pause from the Pre-test to Post-test 1 ($p<.02$), and After the primary speaker's head nod(s) from the Pre-test to Post-test 1 ($p<.007$) and from the Pre-test to Post-test 2 ($p<.001$). In the following table, the expressions *at or directly after a pause* and *at or near any clausal boundary* have been shortened to *at pause* and *at CB* respectively.

Table 5-28 Discourse contexts of Group A's backchannels over time

N = 10	Pre-test		Post-test 1		Post-test 2	
Discourse Contexts	x̄ % of Opps (SD)	x̄ % of BCs (SD)	x̄ % of Opps (SD)	x̄ % of BCs (SD)	x̄ % of Opps (SD)	x̄ % of BCs (SD)
At pause	43.3 (13.1)	41.81 (15.07)	29* (9.23)	36.12 (16.32)	32.9* (11.77)	52.85 (23.25)
Clausal Boundaries						
At CB	59.2 (12.36)	56.93 (9.72)	43.9** (10.31)	69* (15.05)	50.5* (10.44)	64.58 (13.96)
At internal CB	35.3 (39)	2.87 (2.42)	10.3 (14.17)	1.57 (2.06)	37.3 (30.68)	6.58 (5.51)
At final CB	57.8 (17.78)	52.68 (9.15)	45.8* (17.73)	66.27* (20)	52.5 (9.47)	58.82 (19.08)
When CBs and pauses occur together						
At any CB accompanied by a pause	58.1 (18.6)	26.73 (7.52)	41.5* (13.87)	22.06 (8.67)	57 (11.66)	33.6 (17.06)
At internal CB accompanied by a pause	10 (22.55)	.82 (1.83)	20 (42.16)	.74 (1.59)	42.7 (46.97)	4.49 (5.37)
At final CB accompanied by a pause	59.6 (16.39)	30.34 (14.47)	41.5* (16.35)	21.33 (8.39)	52.3 (13.91)	32.9 (18.77)
Gesticulation						
After primary speaker's nonverbal gesture	36.6 (23.37)	8.87 (10.68)	24.4 (19.27)	6.65 (5.21)	29.3 (16.33)	7.84 (4.53)
After primary speaker's head nod(s)	35.5 (21.85)	4.93 (3.85)	30.1 (18.94)	7.62 (5.17)	31.8 (22.75)	5.78 (4.28)

(x̄ difference of Pre-test → Post-test 1, and Pre-test → Post-test 2 significant at p<.05 level = *; significant at p<.01 level =**)

200   Chapter Five

Table 5-29 Discourse contexts of Group B's backchannels over time

N = 10	Pre-test		Post-test 1		Post-test 2	
Discourse Contexts	x̄ % of Opps (SD)	x̄ % of BCs (SD)	x̄ % of Opps (SD)	x̄ % of BCs (SD)	x̄ % of Opps (SD)	x̄ % of BCs (SD)
At pause	46.3 (14.48)	57.34 (20.6)	33.1 (13.68)	33.52* (12.2)	38.7 (10.44)	45.99 (12.12)
Clausal Boundaries						
At CB	59.3 (11.64)	66.62 (7.34)	38.9** (6.87)	60.49 (12.5)	47.2** (9.86)	57.59 (12.92)
At internal CB	22.4 (27.16)	4.15 (5.67)	19.4 (20.64)	3.58 (3.56)	20.6 (16.76)	4.52 (4.97)
At final CB	62.1 (12.85)	62.46 (8.58)	42.1* (8.91)	57.24 (12.44)	50.3* (10.14)	53.06 (14.69)
When CBs and pauses occur together						
At any CB accompanied by a pause	67.6 (14.88)	42.37 (14.91)	42.7** (10.83)	18.86** (8.45)	57.1** (13.58)	29.62** (11.09)
At internal CB accompanied by a pause	34.7 (45.76)	2.57 (3.66)	10 (21.08)	.98 (2.07)	27 (35.26)	2.14 (3.13)
At final CB accompanied by a pause	67.1 (14.88)	39.57 (13.25)	43.1** (12.42)	17.88** (9.2)	58.2* (13.13)	27.76** (9.85)
Gesticulation						
After primary speaker's nonverbal gesture	27.3 (19.74)	7.29 (7.07)	22.4 (12.33)	9.02 (6.33)	29.6 (18.05)	6.89 (5.52)
After primary speaker's head nod(s)	45.3 (27.26)	12.8 (8.85)	22.4* (15.29)	5.32* (5.35)	34 (15.80)	6.6 (3.94)

(x̄ difference of Pre-test → Post-test 1, and Pre-test → Post-test 2 significant at p<.05 level = *; significant at p<.01 level =**)

Table 5-30 Discourse contexts of Group Z's backchannels over time

N = 10	Pre-test		Post-test 1		Post-test 2	
Discourse Contexts	x̄ % of Opps (SD)	x̄ % of BCs (SD)	x̄ % of Opps (SD)	x̄ % of BCs (SD)	x̄ % of Opps (SD)	x̄ % of BCs (SD)
At pause	39 (11.37)	43.17 (10.54)	24.4** (12.04)	28.29* (17.35)	37.6 (8.22)	48.53 (10.6)
Clausal Boundaries						
At CB	61.9 (13.61)	62.08 (8.59)	40.07** (14.54)	55.56 (17.16)	52 (9.38)	55.86 (8.86)
At internal CB	24.3 (23.65)	2.31 (2.39)	13.4 (19.59)	1.88 (3.04)	34.4 (30.29)	3.22 (2.62)
At final CB	65.6 (14.57)	59.78 (9.8)	44.4** (14.44)	53.68 (17.47)	55.7 (9.33)	52.24 (8.87)
When CBs and pauses occur together						
At any CB accompanied by a pause	60.4 (15.34)	34.19 (8.33)	40.5* (17.66)	19.22** (10.67)	62.8 (11.19)	33.29 (12.1)
At internal CB accompanied by a pause	33.3 (40.82)	1.09 (1.2)	10 (21.08)	.45 (.97)	40.5 (42.05)	2.42 (2.51)
At final CB accompanied by a pause	64.9 (17.74)	33.1 (8.05)	41.7* (18.28)	18.77** (10.57)	63.6 (9.51)	28.43 (13.81)
Gesticulation						
After primary speaker's nonverbal gesture	21.6 (15.91)	5.23 (4.05)	21 (12.72)	6.36 (3.93)	27.4 (17.55)	6.48 (4.43)
After primary speaker's head nod(s)	47.4 (18)	9.21 (5.97)	21.6** (23.83)	3.23** (4.3)	31.9** (20.66)	4.41* (2.91)

(x̄ difference of Pre-test → Post-test 1, and Pre-test → Post-test 2 significant at p<.05 level = *; significant at p<.01 level =**)

Concerning the mean percentage of backchannels constituted by each discourse context, Table 5-30 shows the differences in means between tests was statistically significant in the following categories: At or directly after a pause from the Pre-test to Post-test 1 ($p<.022$), At or directly after any CB accompanied by a pause from the Pre-test to Post-test 1 ($p<.007$), At or directly after a final CB accompanied by a pause from the Pre-test to Post-test 1 ($p<.009$), and After the primary speaker's head nod(s) from the Pre-test to Post-test 1 ($p<.01$) and from the Pre-test to Post-test 2 ($p<.043$).

5.5.4 Comparing Discourse Contexts Favouring BCs Over Time

As the results in the tables above have demonstrated, the analysis of junctures attracting backchannels includes many components. The researcher focuses here on the most common discourse context favouring backchannels in English: final clause boundaries. As the results pertaining to clausal boundaries with and without pauses were similar for all three groups, the following line graphs will be presented according to overall frequencies. First, Figure 5-7 compares the three groups' mean percentages of final clause boundaries eliciting backchannels at the three tests, and, second, Figure 5-8 compares the three groups' mean percentages of total backchannels constituted by backchannels occurring at final clause boundaries. While there was some variation in the range of each group, Figure 5-7 shows that the general trend for all three groups was to send backchannels much less frequently at final clause boundary opportunities in Post-test 1 as compared to the Pre-test and then, in Post-test 2, to revert to a level closer to their original. The decrease in mean percentage from the Pre-test to the Post-test 1 was statistically significant for all three groups; however, the Implicit group was the only group to record a statistically significant decrease from the Pre-test to the Post-test 2. Concerning the proportions of total backchannels constituted by backchannels at final clause boundaries, Figure 5-8 illustrates the disparity between the Explicit group and the other two groups. The mean percentage of the Explicit Group increased by 13.59% from the Pre-test to Post-test 1 and by 6.14% from the Pre-test to Post-test 2. In contrast, the Implicit group decreased from the Pre-test to Post-test 1 by 5.22% and by 9.4% from the Pre-test to Post-test 2, and the Control group decreased by 6.1% and 7.54% respectively.

Figure 5-7 Comparing the proportions of final CBs attracting BCs

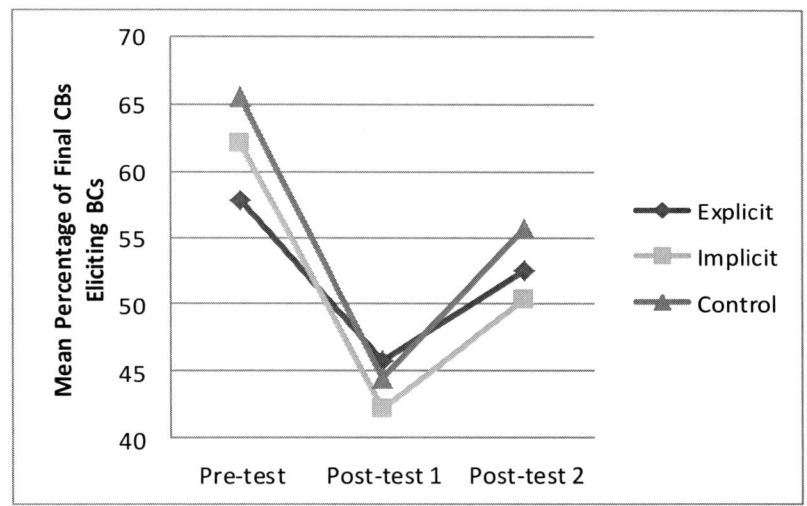

Figure 5-8 Proportions of BCs constituted by BCs at final CBs

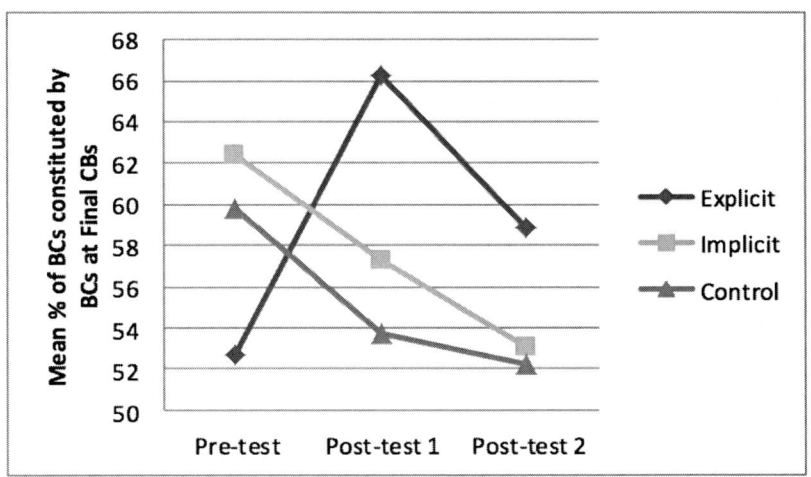

5.6 Simultaneous Speech Backchannels

Tables 5-31, 5-32 and 5-33 report on each group's use of simultaneous speech backchannels (SSBs), which include the total number of SSBs and Non-laughter and Laughter subtypes, the mean scores and standard deviations (SDs) of each group, and the mean percentage of backchannels constituted by each SSB category (with SDs) in the three tests. In the final subsection, 5.6.4, the main parts of these findings will be compared.

5.6.1 Group A (Explicit)

Reporting the mean number of Group A's SSBs in each category, Table 5-31 shows the differences in the following categories were strongly significant (at the .01 level): Total SSBs from the Pre-test to Post-test 1 ($p<.004$) and from the Pre-test to Post-test 2 ($p<.001$), and Non-laughter from the Pre-test to Post-test 1 ($p<.001$) and from the Pre-test to Post-test 2 ($p<.001$). Concerning the mean percentage of backchannels constituted by SSBs, paired-samples t-tests found the following decreases to be statistically significant (at the .05 level): Total SSBs from the Pre-test to Post-test 2 ($p<.043$), and Non-laughter from the Pre-test to Post-test 2 ($p<.049$).

Table 5-31 SSBs of Group A over time

N = 10	Pre-test			Post-test 1			Post-test 2		
Types of SSBs	Total T	x̄ (SD)	x̄ % of BCs (SD)	T	x̄ (SD)	x̄ % of BCs (SD)	T	x̄ (SD)	x̄ % of BCs (SD)
Non-laughter	77	7.7 (3.83)	17.48 (7.21)	55	5.5** (3.72)	18.69 (8.76)	51	5.1** (3.14)	14.12* (7.91)
Laughs	28	2.8 (3.15)	6.78 (8.13)	19	1.9 (2.08)	5.58 (5.36)	18	1.8 (1.62)	4.6 (4.13)
Total SSBs	105	10.5 (4.55)	24.15 (10.84)	74	7.4** (5.32)	24.27 (11.75)	69	6.9** (4.62)	18.96* (10.74)

(x̄ difference of Pre-test → Post-test 1, and Pre-test → Post-test 2 significant at p<.05 level = *; significant at p<.01 level =**)

5.6.2 Group B (Implicit)

Presenting the mean number of Group B's SSBs, Table 5-32 shows that only the increase in the Laugh SSB subcategory from the Pre-test to Post-test 1 was statistically significant ($p<.025$). Regarding the mean percentage of backchannels constituted by SSBs, Table 5-32 found the increases in the Total SSB and Laugh categories from the Pre-test to Post-test 1 were statistically significant ($p<.044$ and $p<.049$ respectively).

Table 5-32 SSBs of Group B over time

N = 10	Pre-test			Post-test 1			Post-test 2		
Types of SSBs	Total T	x̄ (SD)	x̄ % of BCs (SD)	T	x̄ (SD)	x̄ % of BCs (SD)	T	x̄ (SD)	x̄ % of BCs (SD)
Non-laughter	51	5.1 (5.45)	13.08 (9.81)	47	4.7 (3.34)	17.39 (10.83)	58	5.8 (3.01)	15.41 (8.78)
Laughs	11	1.1 (.99)	3.11 (2.6)	18	1.8* (1.55)	6.92* (6.51)	9	.9 (.88)	2.53 (2.37)
Total SSBs	62	6.2 (6.16)	16.19 (11.34)	65	6.5 (3.98)	24.31* (13.93)	67	6.7 (3.06)	17.94 (9.65)

(x̄ difference of Pre-test → Post-test 1, and Pre-test → Post-test 2 significant at p<.05 level = *; significant at p<.01 level = **)

5.6.3 Group Z (Control)

Table 5-33 shows that the mean number of Group Z's SSBs in all three categories remained fairly similar across tests. Concerning the mean percentage of backchannels constituted by SSBs however, the differences in the Total SSB and Non-laughter categories from the Pre-test to Post-test 1 were strongly significant ($p<.001$ and $p<.007$ respectively).

Table 5-33 SSBs of Group Z over time

N = 10	Pre-test			Post-test 1			Post-test 2		
Types of SSBs	Total T	x̄ (SD)	x̄ % of BCs (SD)	T	x̄ (SD)	x̄ % of BCs (SD)	T	x̄ (SD)	x̄ % of BCs (SD)
Non-laughter	61	6.1 (3.03)	13.66 (5.68)	61	6.1 (1.45)	19.86** (4.74)	75	7.5 (2.84)	15.9 (5.99)
Laughs	14	1.4 (.84)	3.14 (1.6)	19	1.9 (1.73)	6.33 (5.71)	18	1.8 (1.48)	3.73 (3.04)
Total SSBs	75	7.5 (3.31)	16.8 (5.11)	80	8 (2.06)	26.19** (7.09)	92	9.2 (3.19)	19.4 (5.03)

(x̄ difference of Pre-test → Post-test 1, and Pre-test → Post-test 2 significant at $p<.05$ level = *; significant at $p<.01$ level =**)

5.6.4 Differences in SSBs Over Time

As non-laughter and laughter SSBs are thought to influence perceptions in conversations differently (see Sections 3.6.1.5. and 4.11), the group comparison below focuses on the former due to their potentially negative effects. Further, comparing the total number of non-laughter SSBs seems to be the best way to demonstrate frequency in this area. That is, unlike some of the other discourse contexts presented above, the number of opportunities a listener has to produce an SSB is not quantifiable in clear terms (i.e., opportunities occur anytime the primary speaker is in the midst of talking). As shown in Figure 5-9, the general paths of the Implicit and Control groups mirrored one another by starting comparatively low, remaining fairly stable from the Pre-test to Post-test 1, and then sharply increasing from Post-test 1 to Post-test 2 (by 11 and 14 respectively). The Explicit group, conversely, showed a sustained decline, of 22 from the Pre-test to Post-test 1, and then another decrease of 4 from Post-test 1 to Post-test 2. As reported in Table 5-31, these decreases were found to be strongly significant ($p<.001$ and $p<.001$ respectively).

Figure 5-9 Non-laughter SSBs of the three groups over time

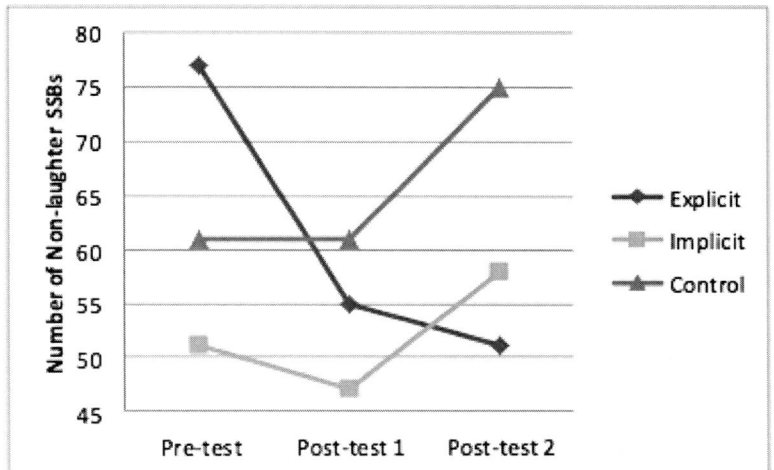

5.7 NESs Observers' Perceptions

This section reports the NES observers' perceptions of the three group's conversational performances at the three points of measurement in this study. Tables 5-34, 5-35 and 5-36 show the mean scores regarding the NES observers' ratings according to each of the 17 items in the conversational satisfaction questionnaire. To provide a general idea as to how the overall ratings compared across participant groups at the three tests, the researcher has divided the items in the questionnaire into two groups distinguished by the positive and negative connotations associated with each rating. For instance, in the items in group one (1, 2, 3, 4, 5, 6, 7, 10, 11, 13 and 16), a *low* score would indicate a desirable effect, whereas for the items in group two (8, 9, 12, 14, 15 and 17), a *high* score would convey a desirable effect. Analysing these two groups separately makes it possible to compare the sum totals of average responses to items in each group over time and between participant groups in this study. As mentioned in Section 3.4.2, the random presentation of the videotaped conversations ensured that the NES observers did not have any knowledge as to the time line of the conversations or which group each JEFL belonged to.

5.7.1 Group A (Explicit)

Table 5-34 demonstrates that the NES observers' perceptions of Group A improved after explicit instruction for all 17 items in the conversational questionnaire, and the level of improvement was generally maintained through to the delayed Post-test. The Wilcoxon signed rank test showed the observed differences in means between the ratings on the Pre-test and Post-test 1 were statistically significant for Items 1 (p<.005), 2 (p<.005), 4 ($p<.011$), 5 ($p<.008$), 7 ($p<.008$), 8 ($p<.02$), 10 ($p<.012$), 11 ($p<.013$), 12 ($p<.041$), 13 ($p<.016$), 14 ($p<.011$), 15 ($p<.005$), 16 ($p<.012$) and 17 ($p<.008$). These improved perceptions were, for the most part, sustained through to the delayed Post-test as Items 1 ($p<.018$), 3 ($p<.042$), 4 ($p<.028$), 5 ($p<.01$), 7 ($p<.009$), 10 ($p<.005$), 11 ($p<.011$), 12 ($p<.024$), 13 ($p<.014$), 14 ($p<.008$), 15 ($p<.028$), 16 ($p<.013$) and 17 ($p<.012$) were also found to have statistically significant differences from the Pre-test to Post-test 2.

5.7.2 Group B (Implicit)

Reporting on the NES observers' perceptions of Group B, Table 5-35 shows that the ratings for all 17 items in the questionnaire improved after implicit instruction, and many of these improved ratings were sustained through to the delayed Post-test. The Wilcoxon signed rank test found the differences between the Pre-test and Post-test 1 ratings were statistically significant for Items 1 ($p<.012$), 4 ($p<.05$), 5 ($p<.008$), 7 ($p<.012$), 10 ($p<.007$), 11 ($p<.011$), 15 ($p<.036$), 16 ($p<.007$) and 17 ($p<.013$). Regarding the differences between the Pre-test and Post-test 2 ratings, Items 1 ($p<.008$), 2 ($p<.025$), 3 ($p<.05$), 4 ($p<.021$), 5 ($p<.036$), 7 ($p<.007$), 10 ($p<.022$), 16 ($p<.005$) and 17 ($p<.007$) were statistically significant.

5.7.3 Group Z (Control)

Overall, the NES observers' ratings of Group Z showed some moderate improvements. As Table 5-36 shows, the Wilcoxon signed rank test found the differences in mean scores from the Pre-test to Post-test 1 to be statistically significant in Items 2 ($p<.033$), 5 ($p<.014$), 7 ($p<.009$), 8 ($p<.038$), 10 ($p<.012$), 11 ($p<.033$) and 16 ($p<.021$). Further, the differences in mean scores from the Pre-test and Post-test 2 were found to be significant for Items 2 ($p<.046$), 5 ($p<.038$), 7 ($p<.019$), 10 ($p<.028$), 11 ($p<.024$), 12 ($p<.043$) and 16 ($p<.032$).

Table 5-34 NESs' conversational satisfaction ratings of Group A

Items on the Questionnaire N = 10 Rating Scale: 1 (strongly agree) to 7 (strongly disagree)	Pre		Post 1		Post 2	
	x̄	SD	x̄	SD	x̄	SD
Group 1 items:						
1. The JEFL let his/her partner know that the partner was communicating effectively.	2.81	.80	2.23**	.66	2.24*	.47
2. The JEFL showed his/her partner that they understood what their partner said.	2.81	.84	2.2**	.69	2.4	.62
3. The JEFL showed that they were listening attentively to what their partner said.	2.21	.6	1.83	.37	1.93*	.38
4. The JEFL expressed a lot of interest in what their partner had to say.	2.64	.71	2.02*	.38	2.15*	.53
5. Conversation went smoothly.	3.28	1.13	2.2**	.57	2.52**	.56
6. The JEFL encouraged partner to continue talking.	2.82	.95	2.55	.66	2.5	.61
7. The feelings that the JEFL expressed by means of listening feedback during the conversation seemed *authentic* (i.e., what they were truly feeling).	3.22	.84	2.32**	.75	2.46**	.48
10. The JEFL was polite.	2.06	.47	1.5*	.22	1.44**	.26
11. The JEFL appeared warm and friendly.	2.34	.66	1.83*	.32	1.81*	.42
13. The JEFL appeared interested and concerned.	2.73	.72	2.18*	.39	2.13*	.34
16. When the JEFL did not understand, they were able to clearly convey this to their conversational partner with their listening feedback.	3.19	.73	2.39*	.61	2.36*	.39

Group 2 items:	Pre		Post 1		Post 2	
	x̄	SD	x̄	SD	x̄	SD
8. The JEFL seemed impatient.	6.1	.38	6.36*	.2	6.34	.28
9. The JEFL seemed cold and unfriendly.	6.41	.34	6.46	.22	6.5	.27
12. The JEFL was impolite.	6.52	.29	6.74*	.17	6.75*	.2
14. The JEFL interrupted their partner at times.	6.18	.29	6.59*	.13	6.59**	.31
15. The JEFL seemed to want to avoid speaking.	5.14	.86	5.99**	.55	5.76*	.27
17. The JEFL's listening behaviour seemed inadequate in some ways.	5.1	.72	5.89**	.54	5.7*	.69

(x̄ difference of Pre-test → Post-test 1, and Pre-test → Post-test 2 significant at $p<.05$ level = *; significant at $p<.01$ level =**)

Table 5-35 NESs' conversational satisfaction ratings of Group B

Items on the Questionnaire N = 10 Rating Scale: 1 (strongly agree) to 7 (strongly disagree)	Pre		Post 1		Post 2	
	x̄	SD	x̄	SD	x̄	SD
Group 1 items:						
1. The JEFL let his/her partner know that the partner was communicating effectively.	3.15	.79	2.49*	.49	2.52**	.52
2. The JEFL showed his/her partner that they understood what their partner said.	3.1	.81	2.59	.5	2.59*	.52
3. The JEFL showed that they were listening attentively to what their partner said.	2.54	.63	2.07	.29	2.12*	.31
4. The JEFL expressed a lot of interest in what their partner had to say.	3.06	.7	2.5*	.53	2.52*	.61

Group 1 items continued	Pre		Post 1		Post 2	
	x̄	SD	x̄	SD	x̄	SD
5. Conversation went smoothly.	3.89	.97	2.98**	.72	2.89*	.73
6. The JEFL encouraged partner to continue talking.	3.12	.65	2.63	.48	2.9	.65
7. The feelings that the JEFL expressed by means of listening feedback during the conversation seemed *authentic* (i.e. what they were truly feeling).	3.5	.84	2.56*	.52	2.71**	.6
10. The JEFL was polite.	2.06	.24	1.54**	.2	1.65*	.33
11. The JEFL appeared warm and friendly.	2.4	.58	1.9**	.33	1.97	.45
13. The JEFL appeared interested and concerned.	2.94	.68	2.41	.46	2.47	.46
16. When the JEFL did not understand, they were able to clearly convey this to their conversational partner with their listening feedback.	3.84	.82	2.69**	.65	2.88**	.58
Group 2 items:						
8. The JEFL seemed impatient.	5.97	.54	6.31	.39	6.29	.34
9. The JEFL seemed cold and unfriendly.	6.18	.33	6.34	.38	6.45	.2
12. The JEFL was impolite.	6.3	.29	6.63	.31	6.53	.35
14. The JEFL interrupted their partner at times.	6.52	.24	6.54	.14	6.56	.17
15. The JEFL seemed to want to avoid speaking.	4.91	.82	5.77*	.71	5.66	.57
17. The JEFL's listening behaviour seemed inadequate in some ways.	4.61	.9	5.76*	.48	5.59**	.51

(x̄ difference of Pre-test → Post-test 1, and Pre-test → Post-test 2 significant at p<.05 level = *; significant at p<.01 level =**)

Table 5-36 NESs' conversational satisfaction ratings of Group Z

Items on the Questionnaire N = 10 Rating Scale: 1 (strongly agree) to 7 (strongly disagree)	Pre		Post 1		Post 2	
	x̄	SD	x̄	SD	x̄	SD
Group 1 items:						
1. The JEFL let his/her partner know that the partner was communicating effectively.	2.6	.8	2.19	.57	2.19	.44
2. The JEFL showed his/her partner that they understood what their partner said.	2.71	.79	2.24*	.68	2.34*	.46
3. The JEFL showed that they were listening attentively to what their partner said.	2.55	1.17	2.04	.44	2.06	.41
4. The JEFL expressed a lot of interest in what their partner had to say.	2.6	.83	2.34	.65	2.47	.57
5. Conversation went smoothly.	3.2	1.01	2.57*	.71	2.65*	.46
6. The JEFL encouraged partner to continue talking.	2.85	.97	2.45	.73	2.75	.5
7. The feelings that the JEFL expressed by means of listening feedback during the conversation seemed *authentic* (i.e., what they were truly feeling).	3.24	.8	2.55**	.67	2.56*	.52
10. The JEFL was polite.	2.03	.4	1.59*	.24	1.55*	.23
11. The JEFL appeared warm and friendly.	2.3	.47	1.98*	.33	2.06*	.43
13. The JEFL appeared interested and concerned.	2.56	.54	2.34	.51	2.41	.48
16. When the JEFL did not understand, they were able to clearly convey this to their conversational partner with their listening feedback.	3.15	.79	2.66*	.82	2.74*	.54

Group 2 items:	Pre		Post 1		Post 2	
	x̄	SD	x̄	SD	x̄	SD
8. The JEFL seemed impatient.	6.06	.5	6.36*	.4	6.29	.54
9. The JEFL seemed cold and unfriendly.	6.22	.64	6.47	.26	6.48	.3
12. The JEFL was impolite.	6.44	.25	6.58	.19	6.63*	.13
14. The JEFL interrupted their partner at times.	6.15	.42	6.25	.53	6.31	.24
15. The JEFL seemed to want to avoid speaking.	5.33	.67	5.46	.61	5.7	.48
17. The JEFL's listening behaviour seemed inadequate in some ways.	5.35	.74	5.7	.62	5.64	.46

(x̄ difference of Pre-test → Post-test 1, and Pre-test → Post-test 2 significant at p<.05 level = *; significant at p<.01 level =**)

5.7.4 Longitudinal Differences in NES Observers' Perceptions

Figure 5-10 provides an illustration comparing the items in group one between participant groups over time. In this line graph, the figures on the y-axis represent the sum of the average ratings in response to the group of items, while the x-axis again shows the differences in performance over time. The line graph demonstrates that the general paths of the three participant groups were quite similar in that the NES observers' perceptions greatly improved from the Pre-test to Post-test 1, and then experienced a slight decrease from Post-test 1 to Post-test 2. While the Control group followed a similar path generally, the experimental groups experienced substantially greater improvements in ratings from the Pre-test to Post-tests 1 and 2. Specifically, the average NES observers' ratings improved by 7.24 from the Pre-test to Post-test 1 and by 6.39 from the Pre-test to Post-test 2 for the Implicit group, by 6.82 from the Pre-test to Post-test 1 and by 6.02 from the Pre-test to Post-test 2 for the Explicit group, and by 4.84 from the Pre-test to Post-test 1 and by 4.01 from the Pre-test to Post-test 2 for the Control group.

Figure 5-10 NESs' perceptions of three groups: Group 1 items

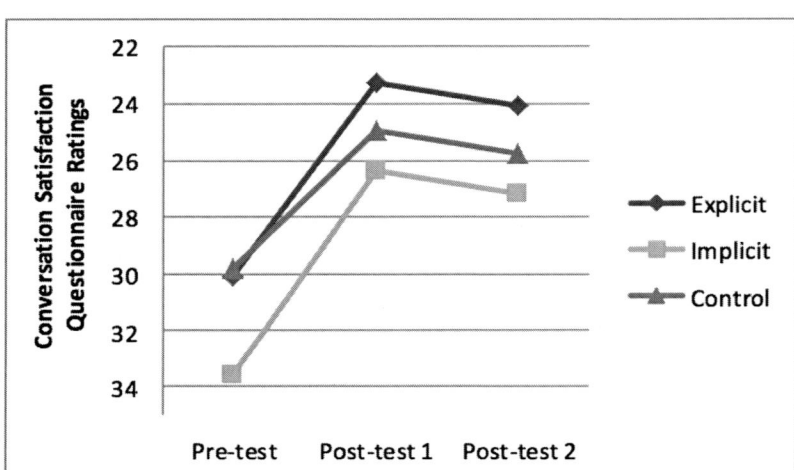

Figure 5-11 provides an illustration comparing the items in group two between participant groups over time. Similar to the findings in group one above, the line graph below also demonstrates that the NES observers' perceptions improved for all three groups from the Pre-test to Post-test 1. The experimental groups also then showed a slight decrease in positive perceptions from Post-test 1 to Post-test 2, while the Control group showed a slight increase. Overall, however, the experimental groups experienced a considerably greater improvement in ratings from the Pre-test to the Post-tests 1 and 2. Specifically, the average NES observers' ratings improved by 2.86 from the Pre-test to Post-test 1 and by 2.59 from the Pre-test to Post-test 2 for the Explicit group, by 2.54 from the Pre-test to Post-test 1 and by 2.19 from the Pre-test to Post-test 2 for the Implicit group, and by 1.27 from the Pre-test to Post-test 1 and by 1.5 from the Pre-test to Post-test 2 for the Control group.

Figure 5-11 NESs' perceptions of three groups: Group 2 items

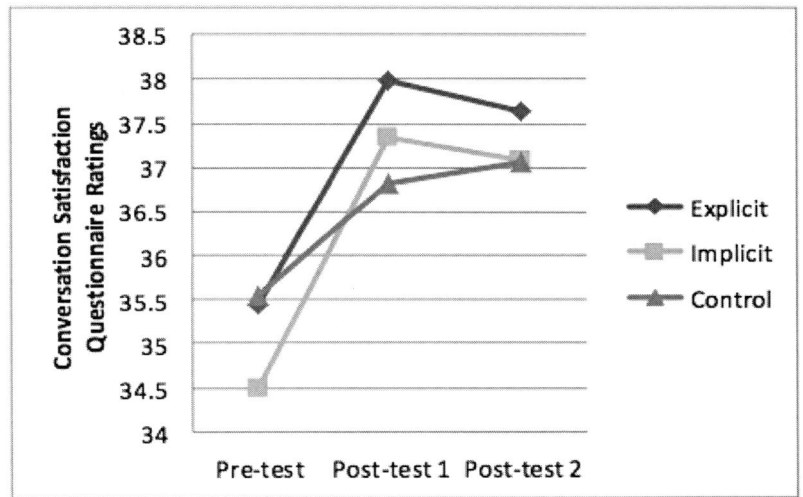

5.8 Interviews

This section presents the quantitative and qualitative data elicited by the interviews of the three groups of JEFLs at the three points of measurement in this study. These findings are divided into three subsections. The first subsection reports on the JEFLs' development in dealing with situations of non-understanding. It should be noted that disagreement situations were excluded from this analysis because they occurred only four times in the 90 conversations. Lastly, the final two subsections present the JEFLs' opinions regarding their rate of progress at the time of Post-test 1 and 2 respectively.

5.8.1 Dealing with Situations of Non-understanding

As Sections 3.4.3 and 3.6.3 described, one of the goals of the post-conversation playback interviews was to discover what the JEFLs were doing when they did not understand. Reporting on the instances of non-understanding situations where the JEFLs spoke (NONUs), Table 5-37 shows that the mean percentage of non-understanding situations in which unconventional backchannels were employed by Group A was 69.41 in the Pre-test, but only 25.17 in Post-test 1 and 31.38 in Post-test 2. Paired-samples t-tests found the difference between the means from the Pre-test to Post-tests 1 and 2 to be strongly significant ($p<.001$ and $p<.001$ respectively). Further demonstrating the benefits of explicit treatment, Table 5-37 shows that the mean percentage of non-understanding situations in which Group A employed conversational repair strategies rose in each test. Concerning minimal backchannels, the difference between the means of the Pre-test (30.6) and Post-test 1 (44) was found to be statistically significant at the .01 level ($p<.003$), and the difference between the means of the Pre-test (30.6) and Post-test 2 (50.93) was found to be statistically significant at the .05 level ($p<.033$). Similarly, regarding lengthier expressions, the difference between the means of the Pre-test (0) and Post-test 1 (30.83) was found to be strongly significant ($p<.004$), and the difference between the means of the Pre-test and Post-test 2 (19.79) was found to be statistically significant at the .05 level ($p<.02$).

Table 5-37 Reactions at points of non-understanding for Group A

N = 10	NONUs	Unconventional BCs		Conversational Repair Strategies			
				Minimal BCs		Lengthier Expressions	
		Total	x̄ % of NONUs (SD)	Total	x̄ % of NONUs (SD)	Total	x̄ % of NONUs (SD)
Pre	49	36	69.41 (11.66)	13	30.6 (11.66)	0	0 (0)
Post 1	32	10	25.17** (28.55)	13	44** (11.2)	9	30.83** (25.47)
Post 2	30	12	31.38** (22.95)	11	50.93* (30.46)	7	17.69* (19.79)

(x̄ difference of Pre-test → Post-test 1, and Pre-test → Post-test 2 significant at p<.05 level = *; significant at p<.01 level =**)

Regarding Group B's performances in this area, Table 5-38 demonstrates some noticeable improvements from the Pre-test to Post-test 1. The mean percentage of non-understanding situations in which members sent unconventional backchannels decreased (-14.34), while the mean percentage of non-understanding situations in which they sent conversational repair strategies rose (+14.33); however, these differences in means were not found to be statistically significant. In the Post-test 2, the mean percentage in all categories returned to near their original Pre-test level, showing that the initial moderate improvements had not been sustained. Lastly, Table 5-39 shows that Group Z's performances in this area were fairly stable across the three tests.

Table 5-38 Reactions at points of non-understanding for Group B

N = 10	NONUs	Unconventional BCs		Conversational Repair Strategies			
				Minimal BCs		Lengthier Expressions	
		Total	x̄ % of NONUs (SD)	Total	x̄ % of NONUs (SD)	Total	x̄ % of NONUs (SD)
Pre	46	34	73.17 (11.82)	10	23.17 (10.84)	2	3.67 (7.77)
Post 1	31	19	58.83 (31.27)	9	31.17 (19.82)	3	10 (21.08)
Post 2	29	20	68.33 (22.5)	8	28.33 (18.92)	2	3.33 (10.54)

(x̄ difference of Pre-test → Post-test 1, and Pre-test → Post-test 2 significant at $p<.05$ level = *; significant at $p<.01$ level =**)

Table 5-39 Reactions at points of non-understanding for Group Z

N = 10	NONUs	Unconventional BCs		Conversational Repair Strategies			
				Minimal BCs		Lengthier Expressions	
		Total	x̄ % of NONUs (SD)	Total	x̄ % of NONUs (SD)	Total	x̄ % of NONUs (SD)
Pre	44	28	62.83 (16.35)	14	33 (15.15)	2	4.17 (9)
Post 1	25	15	59.17 (16.87)	9	37.5 (21.25)	1	3.33 (10.54)
Post 2	27	17	62.5 (22.65)	9	32.5 (24.99)	1	5 (15.81)

(x̄ difference of Pre-test → Post-test 1, and Pre-test → Post-test 2 significant at $p<.05$ level = *; significant at $p<.01$ level =**)

218   Chapter Five

Comparing the findings across groups reported above, the line graphs below illustrate the different path each group followed regarding this issue. First, in describing Figure 5-12, the y-axis corresponds to the mean percentage of non-understanding situations eliciting unconventional responses, while the x-axis demonstrates the differences in performance over time. From this, it can be seen that the Explicit group showed the greatest initial and sustained improvement in this area. The Implicit group displayed a moderate decrease initially at Post-test 1, but this level of improvement was not maintained at Post-test 2. The performance of the Control group, in comparison, remained fairly constant throughout.

Figure 5-12 Comparing NONUs eliciting unconventional BCs

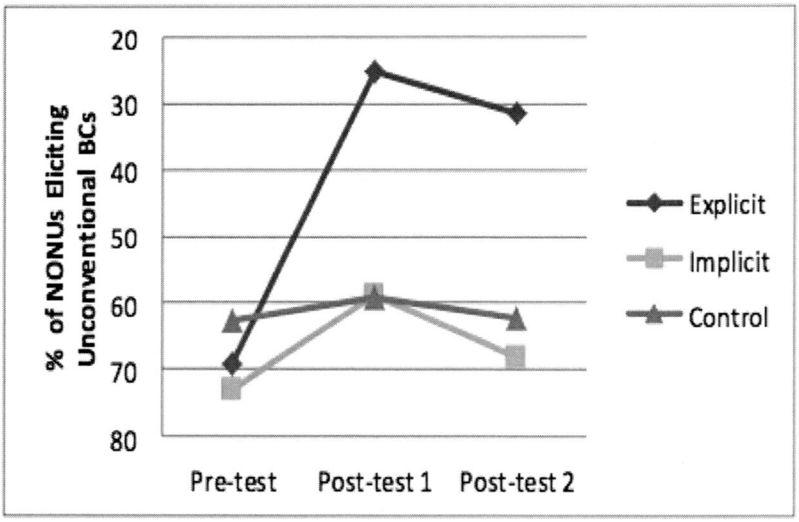

Regarding conversational repair strategies, lengthier expressions are examined here for two reasons. First, there was not much fluctuation in terms of how minimal backchannels were used in this situation by all three groups. Second, lengthier expressions as conversational repair strategies are thought to be more in line with successful conversational behaviour, and they relate directly to the materials used in the explicit treatment of Group A. Thus, in explaining Figure 5-13 below, the figures on the y-axis represent the mean percentage of non-understanding situations eliciting lengthier repair strategies for each group, while the x-axis again demonstrates the differences in performance longitudinally. Once again, it is clear that the Explicit group showed the greatest and most sustained improvement, while the Implicit group showed a modest improvement initially at Post-test 1 but then a decrease at Post-test 2. The Control group again did not show any noticeable improvement or regression.

Figure 5-13 Comparing NONUs eliciting lengthier CRSs

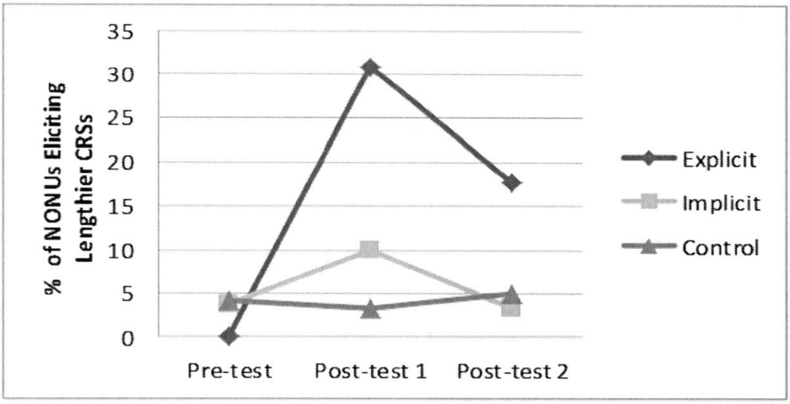

5.8.2 Perceived Development from the Pre-test to Post-test 1

One common pattern to emerge for all three groups in the qualitative data of Post-test 1 was a general feeling of improved performance due to increased confidence and/or decreased anxiety. Labelled below by group, many respondents attributed this to having participated in the Pre-test conversation with a NES.

Explicit group:

> Haruna: I was too nervous in the first conversation to speak much, but in the second my nervous mostly go away because I know more what to expect.

> Ayuka: I think experience speaking in the first conversation with Betty was good for me and helps me feel more relaxed in this conversation.

Implicit group:

> Shio: I was so scared speaking with native at first, but after speaking with native many times I got very big confidence.

220   Chapter Five

> Taro: This class is wonderful because it is only chance I can use English conversation in Japan; my English conversation skills much better now thanks to speaking with natives. We Japanese feel sometimes silly to speak to other Japanese using English.

Control group:

> Yoko: I was still little nervous but not so much as first conversation.

> Hiro: I can speak much more easier in second conversation because I know the situation everything.

Furthermore, several responses from members of the Implicit group reflected that the benefits of their contact with NESs went beyond the Pre-test and also occurred as part of the implicit instruction they received. Regarding this treatment, some members of this group pointed to some general areas of improvement and the methods they used to achieve them, as follows:

> Mayumi: The best thing that helped me was comparing what I did with what the natives did. I learnt that making mistakes is not as important as keep talking.

> Meo: I tried to copy natives as much as I could. From first conversation, I know I have to speak more and ask more questions, and I tried to do this.

> Shio: Natives make me feel relaxed and teach me that I must speak more and try to give my opinions sometimes.

> Kouki: I tried speak more like native speaker style and give bigger reactions.

It seems, then, that several members of the Implicit group were trying to adopt the conversational style of NESs, which they appeared to equate with speaking more often. When commenting on their Post-test 1 performances, many members of the Explicit group also referred to the instruction they received as a reason for their perceived improvements. What was different, however, was that the Explicit group seemed to be able to pinpoint, explain and describe specific areas of their development related to what they had learnt in class. The following responses demonstrate this group's consciousness regarding the frequency and placement by which they sent backchannels, particularly SSBs:

> Hika: During her speaking time, I careful not speaking over her like before.
>
> Aria: I tried to give aizuchi mostly only when she finished her main idea like class taught me.
>
> Saya: I knew I shouldn't aizuchi so much, especially when she is speaking, so I tried to give at the end of sentences.
>
> Kazuya: In first conversation, I did not even think about it, but now I was thinking how much aizuchi and when I should give.

This group's awareness also extended to the variability of backchannels they sent, as well as their WTC, as shown by the following statements:

> Chieko: This class was good for me because I learnt many new ways to give aizuchi. Before I only say un un or move my head like Japanese usually do.
>
> Ayuka: I practised my learning in class by speaking more than before.
>
> Michiko: The most important thing for me is I participated more actively. Before like too passive, I didn't try to speak enough, and maybe I always give same boring aizuchi. Now, I'm using different aizuchi and sharing my thinking and asking questions.
>
> Haruna: I think learning cultural differences really helped me because I now have some ideas what I should do in English conversation. In first conversation, I had English enough in my mind, but I don't know when or how I can always use it.
>
> Takanori: I feel better in second conversation because I can speak more and ask questions to my partner.
>
> Miya: As much as I could, I used the FOQ method (Statement + Fact or Opinion or Question as a response strategy) we learnt in class. It helped me keep the conversation continue.

In terms of function, several respondents indicated that learning how to use conversational repair strategies facilitated communication and, in some cases, saved them from various pitfalls experienced in their earlier conversation.

> Hika: Before when I didn't understand, the conversation stopped and I wanted to leave it. This conversation happened same thing, but I used

class sentence and it worked, was good for me, and I think can feel more confident about this situation in future.

Saya: I never changed my aizuchi at all, but in this conversation, I tried to change this and asked the person to explain more until I understand.

Aria: Big thing for my better speaking is I know better what I should say in many different situations, especially when I don't understand.

Chieko: When I didn't understand before, I did not know what to do, and conversation became broken. Because of lesson, I now had a confidence what to do and what I can say in this situation.

Kazuya: I see aizuchi style is different about interrupting. Little aizuchi don't need to give so much when he speaking, but more important time like when I need help or something, I should speak this feeling.

While the comments above suggest that many members of the Explicit group generally believed their ICC had improved after instruction, several members of this group also commented on some of the difficulties they experienced in trying to apply what they learnt in a real-time conversation.

Ayuka: It was difficult for me use different aizuchi sometimes because (Betty) was speaking so fast.

Takanori: It was hard to think what I need to say because I need to concentration on what she was saying.

Michiko: Sometimes, I forgot what I'm going to say because I waited for her to finish and then lost my thought.

Hika: The pace was too fast; I couldn't speak my ideas fast enough to keep up.

Takanori: I was thinking so many things that it was difficult to use these naturally in the conversation.

5.8.3 Perceived Development from Post-test 1 to Post-test 2

Analysing the qualitative data of the interviews in Post-test 2, the researcher found some key differences pertaining to the responses of the experimental groups as compared to the Control group. A trend to emerge in the qualitative data of Post-test 2 was a general belief among the experimental groups that their communicative competence had decreased since Post-test 1. The following responses suggest that these members

largely attributed their regression to not having had treatment for a great length of time (i.e., eight weeks).
Implicit group:

> Meo: I did not have any practice chance for this conversation, so I forget everything from before.
>
> Sachi: I forgot the habits of native speakers because I didn't have a chance to speak to someone.
>
> Kouki: It was so long since I talked to native that I became very nervous again and couldn't focus enough on the conversation.

Explicit group:

> Miya: I can't have good conversation like before because I did not study for it. I should look at my class papers.
>
> Aria: My conversation skills went down a little because I forgot so many things I learnt before. For example, when I explain something and need more time to continue, I forgot the sentence you taught that can give me more time; what is that, do you know?
>
> Kazuya: Basically, I was too slow to reaction in conversation, and my aizuchi was too simple like at beginning. I needed more different kinds like my paper I have shows.
>
> Akie: I think I probably gave too many aizuchi, maybe even a lot when we was speaking. And, I did not speak enough or ask enough questions.
> Hika: I pretended to understand like before. I should have asked for help, but it was too fast and I was too late.

While members of both experimental groups reported feeling that their conversational skills had decreased since Post-test 1, the responses of the Explicit group above again seemed to include a greater depth and understanding in explaining where they went wrong. Further, many of the Explicit group's responses implied that the information they needed to perform better could be found in one of the many hand-outs they had received in class. The final interviews conducted to complete Post-test 2 also served as a means for the JEFLs to voice their opinions regarding the treatment (or lack thereof) they received in the study. While most members of the experimental groups indicated that they had enjoyed participating in the study and that the instruction and materials had been helpful, some members of each group, ironically, expressed a desire for the type of instruction that the other group had received. That is, some members of the Explicit group stated that they would have liked more opportunities to communicate with NESs and practise what they had learnt, and some members of the Implicit group commented they would have liked more explicit advice and direction from the teacher.

Conversely, members of the Control group did not report any major changes regarding their conversational performances from Post-test 1 to Post-test 2; however, a few comments suggested slight improvements, as follows:

Control group:

> Tomomi: This was my third conversation, so I get less nervous every time.
>
> Akanori: I think I could speak more because I knew what to do from other conversations.

5.9 Profiling Performances

To bring into focus some of the features associated with different levels of performance over time, this section will profile the performances of individual JEFLs who exhibited higher and lower levels of listening behaviour, and discuss the extent to which proficiency levels are associated with gains in listening behaviour.

5.9.1 Listening Behaviour

This section now examines some of the common characteristics attributed to JEFLs who exhibited higher and lower levels of listening behaviour. Since major gains were not consistently observed with any members of the Control group over time, they are not mentioned in this analysis. While the success or failure attributed to most of the performances of members of the experimental groups also included a great deal of fluctuation between the sub-skills of listening behaviour, there were a few JEFLs who performed consistently well or badly in multiple assessment categories. Regarding gains, a micro-level analysis of the data showed that two members of the Explicit group, Chieko and Takanori, made noticeable improvements in various sub-skills of the four major areas of assessment from the Pre-test to Post-test 2 (see Appendix P for micro-analysis). First, in terms of emulating NESs, both JEFLs made noticeable gains in areas of variability and SSBs. Specifically, Chieko and

Takanori increased their percentage of backchannels made up of extended responses (by 29% and 31% respectively) and decreased the percentage of backchannels constituted by minimal backchannels (by 15% and 14% respectively), and decreased the percentage of backchannels constituted by non-laughter SSBs (by 17% and 7% respectively). In addition, while most JEFLs actually decreased the percentage of backchannels sent at final clause boundaries (see Figure 5-7), Takanori increased by 4%. Second, in terms of involvement, Chieko and Takanori's WTC scores increased by 13 and 19 points respectively, and both asked one more question in the Post-test 2 conversation. Third, regarding the ability to use repair strategies in situations of non-understanding, Chieko and Takanori did not produce a single unconventional backchannel in this situation in Post-test 2 and, in fact, uttered only full-turn conversational repairs in these situations (i.e., improvements in both sub-skills of 100% and 50% respectively). Fourth, in terms of ICC, the average ICC questionnaire ratings (associated with positive perceptions) given to Chieko and Takanori by the NES observers increased from the Pre-test to Post-test 2 by 16 and 11 points respectively.

Not surprisingly, in light of the group-specific findings presented above, a micro-analysis of individual performances revealed that the JEFLs who generally showed the least amount of development in this area, Shio, Madora, Sachi and Keiko, were all members of the Implicit group. While a micro-analysis of the sub-skills in each of the four assessment criteria is provided in Appendix P, a more important consideration here is whether any clear profiles of successful or unsuccessful learners have emerged. Statistical analyses (PPMCC) examining potential correlations that the JEFLs' WTC and Extraversion scores had with a number of sub-skills associated with backchannel performance were conducted (see Appendix O), and no strongly significant correlations (at the .01 level) were observed. However, a moderate positive significant correlation (at the .05 level) was found initially (at the Pre-test) between the JEFLs' WTC scores and both number of questions and the percentage of backchannels constituted by extended responses. In subsequent tests, positive significant correlations (at the .05 level) were found only between the JEFLs' Extraversion scores and number of SSBs and laughter SSBs in Post-test 1, and between the JEFLs' WTC scores and number of non-laughter SSBs in Post-test 2.

A closer look at the JEFLs mentioned in the upper and lower bands of improvement in listening behaviour may shed some light regarding trends in performance. Surprisingly, compared to the other 28 JEFLs, the JEFLs showing the most progress over time, Chieko and Takanori, had below average scores in all three areas examined: TOEIC scores (360 and 504 respectively), the WTC questionnaire (34 and 40), and the Extraversion dimension of the personality scale (3 and 4 respectively). In comparison, the scores of the JEFLs showing the least development over time, Shio, Madora, Sachi and Keiko, were varied. Shio, for instance, scored 90 points above the average TOEIC score (630), yet scored slightly lower than average on the WTC (49) and the Extraversion questionnaires (3). Madora, Sachi and Keiko, on the other hand, all had below average TOEIC scores (500, 475 and 460 respectively), but scored higher than average on the Extraversion questionnaire (4.5, 5 and 4.5 respectively). Regarding WTC scores, Madora and Sachi rated well above the average (60 and 59 respectively), while Keiko's score was well below average (39).

It is also important to note that there were several areas of development within individual learners that did not conform to their overall performances. For instance, Shio and Keiko, who were generally unsuccessful in their ability to improve their listener behaviour, both managed to utter 29 more words each from their Pre-test to Post-test 2. In addition, Sachi increased her percentage of lengthy backchannel expressions and backchannels produced at final clause boundaries by 14% and 12% respectively. Similarly, there were also some notable exceptions involving the JEFLs in the upper band of improvements in listening behaviour. In particular, Chieko and Takanori spoke 15 and 8 fewer words respectively in Post-test 2, and Chieko produced 15% less backchannels at final clause boundaries.

5.9.2 Proficiency

Although a general link between proficiency level and competent listening behaviour appears to exist on some levels, this is not always the case. As the exceptions in Section 4.13 demonstrated, much will depend on the individual differences of learners, as well as the particular sub-skills being learnt. In terms of analysing this effect longitudinally, it was interesting to note that the links between proficiency and various sub-features of backchannel behaviour that were found at the time of the Pre-test were largely diminished in both post-treatment tests. That is, a Pre-test correlation analysis (see Appendix O) showed strongly significant positive correlations (at the .01 level) between the JEFLs' TOEIC scores and the number of words, questions, and percentage of backchannels constituted by extended responses; at the .05 level, a significant positive correlation was found between the JEFLs' TOEIC scores and number of non-laughter SSBs, and significant negative correlations were found between the JEFLs' TOEIC scores and the number of non-understanding situations, percentage of backchannels constituted by minimal responses, and percentage of non-understanding situations constituted by unconventional backchannels. Conversely, in subsequent correlation analyses applied to Post-tests 1 and 2, no statistically significant correlations were found at the .01 alpha level. Overall, only significant positive correlations at the .05 level were observed in Post-test 1 between the JEFLs' TOEIC scores and number of words, SSBs and laughter SSBs.

A closer look at the most and least proficient JEFLs (according to their TOEIC scores) in each group shows similar levels of development longitudinally. For instance, while the performances and ratings of the highest and lowest JEFLs in the Control Group, Yukari (695) and Yukiko (445), both did not change much throughout this study, the highest and lowest members in the Explicit group, Michiko (700) and Ayuka (360), and the Implicit group, Rika (685) and Mika (390), demonstrated similar gains in most of the assessment areas outlined in Section 2.9 (see Appendix Q for micro-analyses). The one assessment area in which both higher-level students performed noticeably better in the experimental groups involved conversational repair strategies. Michiko and Rika noticeably decreased the number of unconventional backchannels they sent when they did not understand (by 60% and 34% respectively), whereas Ayuka and Mika were only slightly able to decrease theirs (by 12% and 25% respectively). In addition, both Michiko and Rika were able to greatly increase the amount they used full-turn conversational repair strategies when they did not understand (by 67% and 33% respectively); however, Ayuka demonstrated only a slight gain in this area (by 13%) and Mika's level did not change at all.

Part II: Discussion of Longitudinal Results

The discussion of the findings related to the longitudinal aspect of this study is divided into three parts: (5.10) a discussion regarding improvements in listening behaviour, (5.11) an analysis of the findings and (5.12) a chapter conclusion. Section 5.10 draws together the findings of each sub-skill of backchannel behaviour to form a broad-spectrum picture of what transpired in the study. Accordingly, Section 5.11 is able to provide answers for RQs 3 and 4 (see Appendix S for RQs) determining the efficacy of instruction on performance in the short term and the long term. This section also considers the implications of these findings relative to previous studies and from a theoretical perspective. Ultimately, aiming to answer the parts of RQs 5 and 6 that were not dealt with in Chapter 4, the final part of this section discusses some of the common learner characteristics associated with varying performances over time, and the degree to which L2 proficiency levels were associated with gains. Lastly, Section 5.12 summarises the findings of the longitudinal aspects of this study.

5.10 Improvements in Listening Behaviour

5.10.1 Approximating the Backchannel Norms of NESs

Observations of the listening behaviour of the JEFLs before and after treatment found evidence of both experimental groups adopting more native-like listening behaviour after treatment. The greatest and most sustained developments in this area belonged to the Explicit group, whose improvements were found to be strongly significant (i.e., at the .01 level) from the Pre-test to Post-test 1 and also through to Post-test 2 in areas of frequency (Table 5-1), variability (Table 5-9) and SSBs (Table 5-31). In comparison, a statistically significant improvement for the Implicit group was observed at the .05 level in the area of frequency from the Pre-test to Post-test 1; however, it was not evident at the time of Post-test 2. In the area of variability (Table 5-16), the Implicit group's improvements were found to be strongly significant from the Pre-test to Post-test 1 (at the .01 level) and significant at the .05 level from the Pre-test to Post-test 2. Regarding the Control group, no significant improvements were found as expected; however, in one of the subcategories of variability, the proportion of backchannels constituted by Extended responses (Table 5-23), the Control group's performance showed noticeable regression as their mean percentage decreased significantly (at the .05 level) from the Pre-test to Post-test 2.

Interestingly, there was one area of analysis in which a statistically significant decline was found for all three groups: backchannels provided at final clause boundary opportunities (see Figure 5-7). This was somewhat surprising because this discourse context, which has been identified in the literature as the most common discourse context in English, was explicitly taught to members of Group A in the instruction they received. However, while all three groups sent significantly less backchannels at clausal boundaries from the Pre-test to Post-test 1, this decline was only maintained for the Implicit group in Post-test 2. While the across-the-board decline between the Pre-test and Post-test 1 is difficult to explain, the fact that Post-test 2 figures (i.e., after no subsequent treatment) returned to near original Pre-test levels for two of the three groups suggests that this discrepancy may have been an aberration. Nonetheless, the fact that the three groups were starting at approximately the same point and the Explicit group consistently sent the most backchannels at this discourse context thereafter would seem to suggest that they achieved the highest degree of success in this area also. This is supported by the fact that the Explicit group showed marked increases in the proportions of total backchannels constituted by backchannels at final clause boundaries from the Pre-test to Post-tests 1 and 2, while the Implicit and Control groups showed a steady decline. Lastly, the fact that the Implicit and Control groups' performances consistently worsened in this area from the Pre-test to Post-tests 1 and 2 provides another example in which a lack of treatment may be associated with skill loss.

The overall findings, which demonstrated that explicit treatment had an extremely positive effect on the JEFLs' backchannel output, would seem to go against the conventional wisdom that L2 backchannels are especially difficult to learn in a way that is not completely implicit due to their spontaneity and automaticity in real-time conversations (Cutrone 2005; Miyazaki 2010; Ward et al. 2007). Since most, if not all, of the JEFLs had never even considered their L2 backchannels previously, it seems that raising their awareness of this all-important feature of language for the first time was enough to make a dramatic impact on their L2 conversational behaviour. However, there were some aspects of backchannel behaviour that did not appear to respond to this type of focused attention. For instance, explicit treatment did not seem to significantly affect the use of non-clarification repetitions as backchannels (see Table 5-13) as there was not a great deal of variation between the three tests for all three groups in this area. This may be one of the sub-features of backchannel behaviour that is difficult for learners to control in the midst of spontaneous real-time conversations. Nonetheless, due to the limited number of times these backchannels were uttered in this study (i.e., x̄<4.5% of total BCs for all three groups at all three tests), their impact appears largely negligible and certainly not the problem area that Thonus (2002, 2007) describes.

As expected, there was ample evidence in the JEFLs' interview data to suggest strong biases towards the English used by NESs (see Section 5.8.2). The partiality towards the speech of NESs described above is consistent with the observations of Suzuki (2010), who points out that teacher training programmes in Japan still present only standard American and/or standard British English as normative varieties of English. Many JEFLs seemed to equate conversational success and development with how well they were able to adopt the conversational styles of NESs. Further, many JEFLs attributed their perceived improvements in their post-treatment interviews to noticing differences between their own conversational output and NESs' output. While Schmidt's (1993) noticing hypothesis will be discussed in greater detail below, the fact that learners consciously perceived the difference between the feature in their target language and their own can be said to be evidence of 'noticing the gap' (Schmidt & Frota 1986: 311).

5.10.2 Involvement in Conversation

The findings show that treatment had a positive effect on the experimental groups' involvement in the conversation, and once more it was the Explicit group that displayed the greatest and most sustained benefits. Specifically, improvements corresponding to the Explicit group were found to be strongly significant from the Pre-test to Post-test 1 in all three subcategories of Involvement in Conversation (Table 5-4): WTC scores, amount spoken as primary speaker, and number of follow-up questions asked. The Explicit group's initial improvements in this area varied among the sub-skills at the delayed Post-test 2. That is, from the Pre-test to Post-test 2, the improvement in mean WTC scores was again found to be significant at the .01 level, while the increase in mean number of questions was significant at the .05 level, and the difference in mean number of words was not found to be statistically significant. In comparison, the improvements in mean WTC scores for the Implicit group were found to be strongly significant from the Pre-test to Post-test 1 and from the Pre-test to Post-test 2 (Table 5-5); however, no significant improvements were evident in the other two subcategories. Finally, no significant improvements for the Control group were found in this area; however, as was the case with the Variability category, the Control group significantly regressed (at the .05 level) in one of the subcategories of this skill-set: mean number of questions asked (Table 5-6). As discussed in Section 5.10.1 above, this further suggests that a lack of treatment may, in some cases, eventually lead to a deterioration of skills.

While some of the improvements detailed in the previous section concerning L2 backchannel output may have been somewhat surprising, it was not surprising to see the experimental groups improve in some of the areas described in this section. Regarding the Implicit group, it seems easy to understand why their WTC scores increased significantly as this project not only afforded them an opportunity to increase their L2 confidence, but it also gave them a chance to communicate in English in a natural setting with NESs, which can be difficult to do in Japan. Regarding the Explicit group, the overt teaching of conversational micro-skills certainly may have helped (see discussion of formulaic chunks of language in the next section); however, the researcher believes that making more of a concerted effort to speak and ask questions might have more to do with a larger process involving the student's attitude and increased motivation, which were reflected in their WTC scores over time. That is, once members of the Explicit group became aware of the potential misunderstandings that could transpire due to a perceived unwillingness to communicate, they seemed to make a better effort towards active participation in the conversation. This was evident from the fact that the Explicit group was the only group to ask significantly more questions from the Pre-test to Post-test 1 and Pre-test to Post-test 2. However, as the decline in number of questions from Post-test 1 to Post-test 2 suggests, this may be an area that needs to be constantly emphasised and reinforced. Further, the finding that the Explicit group was the only group to produce significantly more words directly after treatment should not be overstated for a number of reasons. First, the Explicit group's word output in Post-test 2 returned to near its Pre-test level. Second, the Implicit and Control groups also showed a similar increase in word output from the Pre-test to Post-test 1 and then a similar decrease from the Pre-test to Post-test 2 (see Figure 5-3), so the increase may have had more to do with the JEFLs, collectively, feeling more confident to speak in Post-test 1 because they knew what to expect from their experience in the Pre-test. Third, the fact that the standard deviations are quite high across groups in this category suggests considerable variability within the performances of this group.

5.10.3 Conversational Repair Strategies

The results in this category demonstrate a clear and sustainable benefit of instruction for the Explicit group that was not found in the Implicit group (see Figures 5-12 and 5-13). That is, both the increase in the amount of lengthy conversational repairs and the decrease in unconventional backchannels at situations of non-understanding employed by the Explicit group were statistically significant from the Pre-test to Post-tests 1 and 2. No significant improvements were found at any time for either the Implicit or Control groups. This part of the findings was consistent with the results of Takahashi (2001), who also found that students receiving explicit instruction were much better able to produce the set expressions needed to keep the conversation going and/or avoid communication breakdown (see Section 2.9.2.3). It may very well be that these types of linguistic expressions, which are often a part of L2 pragmatic routines, lend themselves best to overt and explicit instruction because they are formulaic and rehearsed, rather than propositional, creative, or freely generated (Fillmore 1979). In this way, it is easy to understand why the Implicit or Control group did not use a wide range of conversational repair strategies (i.e., formulaic chunks of language) since it cannot be certain that they were even exposed to them.

5.10.4 ICC

The findings of the final category show that NES observers' perceptions improved for all three groups at various points in the study (see Figures 5-10 and 5-11). Once more, however, the Explicit group displayed the greatest and most sustained improvement in this study. This was evidenced by a statistically significant improvement on 14 of 17 items on Hecht's (1978) modified questionnaire from the Pre-test to Post-test 1 (6 of which were significant at the .01 level), and 13 of 17 items from the Pre-test to Post-test 2 (4 of which were significant at the .01 level). In comparison, the Implicit group showed a statistically significant improvement on 9 of 17 items from both the Pre-test to Post-test 1 and the Pre-test to Post-test 2 (in both cases, 4 items were significant at the .01 level). Finally, concerning the Control group, a statistically significant improvement was found on 7 of 17 items from both the Pre-test to Post-test 1 and the Pre-test to Post-test 2 (only 1 item was significant at the .01 level, and this occurred from the Pre-test to Post-test 1). Concerning how the results of the previous three sections relate to the findings here, it was not surprising to observe that the JEFLs who came the closest to adopting the norms of the target group also received the highest ratings in the NESs' conversational satisfaction questionnaires. Thus, the findings would seem to bear out the hypotheses of Cutrone (2005) and White (1989) that backchannel conventions shared across cultures lead to increased levels of conversational satisfaction, and, as reconfirmed in Section 4.6, backchannel conventions which are not shared across cultures contribute to negative perceptions and stereotyping.

The findings demonstrating some level of improvement for all three groups are difficult to explain. Since the researcher provided the NES observers with the 90 conversations presented in random order, it cannot be said that ratings were affected by the NES observers lowering their expectations as they became more familiar with participants and the rating process. It is more likely that the NES observers picked up on the JEFLs' increased confidence and WTC. That is, while most of the JEFLs reported to feeling especially nervous in their first conversation with a NES (see Section 4.6.1), many of them reported a general feeling of improved performance in subsequent conversations due to increased confidence and/or decreased anxiety (Section 5.8.2). These general improvements for JEFLs in all three groups may be somewhat attributed to two factors associated with experiential learning: (1) managing to get through the first conversation with a NES seems to have made many of JEFLs less nervous in the subsequent conversations with a NES, and (2) some anxiety may have been lifted in Post-tests 1 and 2 because the JEFLs were much more familiar with what the testing process would entail.

While not directly applicable to the findings presented in the longitudinal aspect of this study, an interesting ancillary discovery came to light upon comparing the NES observers' perceptions with those of the NES interlocutors in the ICC data. Although the NES interlocutors' ratings were only used in the cross-sectional data for reasons stated in Section 3.2.2, it became obvious after comparing the ratings of the groups of NESs that the NES observers were much more critical of the JEFLs' conversational performances than the NES interlocutors had been, as the researcher had hypothesised (see Appendix R for ratings of NES interlocutors). The more positive ratings given by the NES interlocutors may be partly attributed to the rapport that they may have developed with their interlocutor in the conversations, as well as their general affinity for Japan and understanding of Japanese behaviour.

5.11 Analysis

5.11.1 Analysis Relative to Previous Research

In answer to RQ 3 (see Appendix S for RQs), the findings of this study demonstrate that instructional treatment had a positive effect on the listening behaviour of both experimental groups in this study. In answer to RQ 4, the group that received explicit treatment clearly outperformed the group that received implicit treatment in both the short term and the long term. These findings are consistent with the results of the majority of studies presented in Sections 2.9.2.2 and 2.9.2.3. As Rose (2005: 396) surmises, 'in most cases where there was not some apparent methodological (or other) flaw, learners who had been provided with metapragmatic information regarding the target feature(s) outperformed those who did not'. Nonetheless, there do appear to be exceptions as was shown by the apparent contrary findings of Takimoto's (2009) well-designed study of three types of input approaches for teaching polite request forms to 60 JEFLs (see Section 2.9.2.3). To review, Takimoto found, among other findings, that the group that received structured input tasks with explicit information was outperformed by the groups that received structured input tasks without explicit information and the one that received problem-solving tasks on one aspect of assessment, the listening test, in the long term. Since the group receiving explicit information showed significant improvement directly after treatment but not at the delayed post-test four weeks later, Takimoto attributed these findings to the short-term memory limitations of explicit knowledge, which may have been even more pronounced due to the online processing demands brought on by the listening test which did not exist for the other assessment categories (DCTs, role-plays and acceptability judgement tests).

In this way, the different results obtained by Takimoto's (2009) study and this study can be explained by the simple fact that the Explicit group in this study received a great deal more treatment (eight sessions of 90 minutes each over eight weeks as compared to four sessions of 40 minutes over four weeks) and reinforcement opportunities (multiple compared to none) than the group that received explicit instruction in Takimoto's study. Additionally, a closer look at the three experimental groups in Takimoto's study suggests that they all contained elements of what might be considered explicit instruction (see Section 2.9.2.3). According to Jeon and Kaya (2006), who described instruction as a continuum of absolutely explicit and absolutely implicit extremes, the degree to which the target feature of the instruction is made overt to the learners determines the positioning of that kind of instruction in relation to the explicit and implicit poles. Although the group said to be receiving explicit information was one of the structured input groups in his study, Takimoto emphasises that the problem-solving tasks led to more overt instruction, whereas the structured input tasks led to less overt instruction. Further confusing the explicit and implicit distinction in this study is the fact that 'participants in the three treatment groups were instructed to pay attention to those social context variables as well as pragmalinguistic features of the target structure' (Takimoto 2009: 8). In this way, it can be argued that explicit methods may have contributed to varying degrees of performance gains achieved by all three treatment groups in this study.

5.11.2 Analysis Relative to the Noticing Hypothesis

The discussion of the results now shifts to Schmidt's (1993) noticing hypothesis and the more general question of how input becomes intake in the process of SLA. As the paragraphs that follow will discuss, there are no clear-cut answers regarding these issues. As Cross (2002) and Truscott (1998) have rightly pointed out, there are many problems associated with the testability of the noticing hypothesis, not least of which includes an inconsistent and unclear interpretation of what it means *to notice* in the research literature, and the failure to recognise *noticing* as an internal process that cannot be observed directly and requires a high degree of inference from observation of behaviour. For Schmidt (1990, 1993), *noticing* appears to be equated with attention plus awareness, which is operationalised as a cognitive process that takes place both during and immediately after exposure to the input that is available for self-report. In this sense, the fact that members of the Explicit group received increased attention to form (i.e., increased *noticing*), then demonstrated a much greater improvement than the other groups in terms of actual conversational performance over time, and ultimately were able to report on specific areas of improvement by referring to what they had learnt in class (i.e., what had drawn their attention) would seem to offer some encouragement to supporters of the noticing hypothesis.

Further, the findings of this study would also seem to support Nick Ellis's (2006a) assertions that explicit instruction is helpful in dealing with acquisition issues related to lack of salience and L1-influenced blocking (see Section 2.9). That is, concerning the former, non-salient features of language such as backchannels seem to require intentionally focused attention to facilitate successful L2 learning. Regarding L1-influenced blocking, the findings of this study imply that drawing attention to backchannel behaviour may have helped change the cues that learners focused upon in their language process, which ultimately changed what their implicit learning systems were able to absorb. As evidenced by the Control group's lack of progress throughout this experiment, it is likely that without such a change in the attentional focus of cues, learners would continue to exhibit a great deal of L1 negative transfer where backchannels are concerned, perhaps only gradually showing traces of improvement after considerable L2 experience. In this way, FFI can be seen as a means of expediting the learning process (MacWhinney 1987, 2001).

In addition, while development may not have been as great or sustained as that of the Explicit group, the fact that the group receiving implicit instruction also displayed considerable improvements in several key areas of backchannel behaviour needs to be taken into account moving forward. Schmidt's (1983) case study providing evidence of the implicit learning of L2 backchannel behaviour in an immersion setting (see Section 2.7.1), and the opinions voiced by many of the JEFLs (see Section 5.8.3), would seem to lend further credence to a mixed approach. Thus, the best way forward may be a combination of these methods in which implicit methods are used to supplement an explicit approach. This would seem to be in line with Nick Ellis's (2008: 105) conception of how Schmidt's (1993) noticing hypothesis works:

> once a stimulus representation is firmly in existence, that stimulation need never be noticed again; yet as long as it is attended for use in the processing of future input for meaning, its strength will be incremented and its associations will be tallied and implicitly catalogued.

In this way, Ellis (2008), taking an interface position, has also explained how explicit knowledge is converted into implicit knowledge. Thus, as it relates to the findings of this study, this would mean that FFI may be especially helpful in facilitating the learning of listener responses at first; however, continued progress in this area will likely depend on how much the learner is able to use the newly learnt skill in authentic settings. Once consolidated into construction, new cues to interpretation of input are strengthened with each subsequent processing episode associated with repeated use and exposure. As mentioned above, the difference in reinforcement opportunities afforded to learners in this study compared to Takimoto's (2009) study may have been the primary reason for the different findings.

5.11.3 Micro-level Analysis of Students' Gains

In answer to RQ 5 (see Appendix S for RQs), it is not possible to arrive at any clear and definitive profiles regarding the students who showed improved listening behaviour versus those who did not. The findings presented in Section 5.9.1 seem to re-emphasise the individualistic nature associated with the acquisition of L2 listener responses. Although some students may be thought to be alike due to similarities in the way in which they performed some of the sub-skills, or because of their similar proficiency level in English, there appear to be too many exceptions to surmise that a student fitting a specific profile will learn backchannels more readily than a student fitting another profile. While the importance of individual differences has been well documented throughout this study, it is also important to consider that each sub-skill may have its own unique interface with individual learners, and, thus, the mastery of one, or even many, of the sub-skills involved in listening behaviour does not guarantee success in other areas of this highly complex and multifaceted skill-set.

In answer to RQ 6, the results presented in Section 5.9.2 are not sufficient to conclude that proficiency did not play any role in post-treatment performances; however, they do seem to imply that there may not always be a direct link between the two longitudinally, and that pedagogical interventions may have more to do with overall progress in this area than levels of proficiency. However, regarding the ability to produce conversational strategies specifically, the higher-level JEFLs in the experimental groups showed noticeably more improvement than the other JEFLs. It stands to reason that this specific area of listening behaviour, which requires learners to produce formulaic chunks of language at precise moments in conversations, may require a higher degree of proficiency to perform.

5.12 Conclusion

In summarising the findings corresponding to the longitudinal part of this study, RQs 3-6 are reviewed in succession below (see Appendix S for RQs). First, in addressing the effects of instruction on listening behaviour, (RQ 3) the findings of this study demonstrate that instructional treatment had a positive effect on the listening behaviour of both experimental groups in this study, and (RQ 4) the group that received explicit treatment clearly outperformed the group that received implicit treatment in both the short term and the long term. Second, in an attempt to profile successful and unsuccessful learners regarding this feature of language, (RQ 5) this study found that the characteristics pertaining to the JEFLs demonstrating competent listening behaviour and those that did not were largely varied and idiosyncratic in both groups, and (RQ 6) proficiency did seem to be linked to performance in this area for many of the JEFLs initially; however, pedagogical interventions seem to have had a much greater effect on the learners' development over time.

Although benefits of FFI in the teaching of backchannels have been shown, it is difficult to reach any firm conclusions regarding Schmidt's (1993) noticing hypothesis due to the reasons mentioned in Section 5.10.2. As Section 6.3.2 discusses, the position taken here is that *noticing* appears to be helpful in speeding up the process of learning L2 backchannels, but it remains uncertain as to whether it is actually necessary or not. While this distinction may be particularly important to theorists, it is far less relevant to classroom practitioners whose main goal is to help students learn the target language in the most efficient way possible. In this way, the researcher adopts the position taken by Swan (2005: 393) who states the following:

> The role of instruction in a typical language classroom is not, surely, to attempt the impossible task of replicating the conditions of natural acquisition, but to compensate for their absence.

The final chapter which follows will further discuss the implications of this study's findings, and also demonstrate how they comprise an original contribution to knowledge.

CHAPTER SIX

CONCLUSION

6.1 Introduction

This chapter begins with an overview of the study in Section 6.2, which comprises a discussion of the study's limitations (6.2.1), followed by a brief summary of the study's findings (6.2.2), and an explanation of how these findings make an original contribution to knowledge (6.2.3). Subsequently, Section 6.3 discusses the implications of this study, which are divided into three categories: (6.3.1) methodological implications, (6.3.2) theoretical implications and (6.3.3) practical implications. Lastly, Section 6.4 offers some suggestions for future studies in this area.

6.2 Overview of this Study

6.2.1 Limitations

Before any conclusions are presented, it is necessary to consider the limitations of this study. First, having identified what specific behaviour constitutes a backchannel in this study in Sections 2.2 and 2.3, it is important to point out now that there exist several phenomena not included in this study which may influence backchannel behaviour. For example, Kendon (1977) proposes direction and duration of gaze as factors affecting backchannels, Duncan and Fiske (1977) mention the use of self-adaptors and gesticulation as important aspects, and Koiso et al. (1998) and Ward and Tsukahara (2000) have studied the prosodic features of conversation which cue backchannels. This study's exclusion of these phenomena is in no way intended to slight their importance in regard to the study of backchannels. The decision taken here was to delimit the cases studied under backchannels because this phenomenon is too complex and varied to be studied under one heading.

Other limitations involve the research design used to produce the conversational data in this study. First, concerning the activities used within each treatment, multiple activities were packaged together, and there is no way of disentangling the contributions of each activity to the effect on learning outcomes. In addition, the conversations in this study were limited to dyadic conversations. While this may be a logical place for a linguist to begin analyses (see Section 1.8.2), it is clear that authentic communication is not restricted to dyadic interactions (Mills 2003). Undoubtedly, the group dynamics that people experience in everyday life can have a major impact on their interactional behaviour. Another limitation concerning the conversational data was the fact that the register of the conversations was highly casual and informal (see Section 4.12.1). As O'Keeffe and Adolphs (2008) demonstrated when comparing data from three corpora (CANCODE, LCIE, and an Irish radio phone-in show corpus), the type of communication event, as well as the group dynamics therein, can play a large role in the functional distribution of one's listener responses.

The final set of limitations, which have been discussed briefly in Chapter 3, involves the sample used in this study. With only 30 JEFL participants, the researcher would have preferred a larger sample size by which to assess L2 listening behaviour. Further, the demographic range of JEFLs participating in this study was quite narrow in that all JEFLs were university students living in Nagasaki Prefecture. Lastly, the gender imbalance of 24 females and six males in the JEFL sample precluded the possibility of delving deeply into gender as a potential variable affecting backchannel behaviour. Due to these limitations, one must be very cautious in generalising from this study to the wider population of JEFL speakers. The researcher fully acknowledges that individual differences in personality and language learning aptitude may have contributed to learning outcomes. Nonetheless, this is not to diminish the importance of the findings of this study as they do provide a platform for future investigation and diagnosis, and have yielded valuable insights into an area of foreign language pedagogy previously unexamined.

6.2.2 Summary of Findings

While Chapters 4 and 5 provide more detailed summaries and assessments of the cross-sectional and longitudinal results respectively, a brief review of the main findings of this study is given here. First, regarding the cross-sectional aspect of this study, the following findings support the idea that backchannels warrant more attention in EFL classes in Japan:

- Cultural differences were found in the ways the Japanese and American participants employed English backchannels in terms of frequency, variability, placement and function.
- These differences were found to contribute to negative perceptions across cultures.

Concerning the longitudinal aspect of this study, the following findings related to the effectiveness of treatment emerged:

- Explicit and implicit pedagogical interventions were both found to have a positive effect on the listening behaviour of the JEFLs in those groups.
- The group receiving explicit instruction greatly outperformed the group receiving implicit treatment in both the short term and the long term.

Lastly, the longitudinal findings also provide some insights into the profiles of successful and unsuccessful JEFLs in this area:

- This study did not find any definitive patterns involving the characteristics of learners who improved versus the ones who did not.
- Although a tenuous link between proficiency and performance was found when learners did not receive any training, pedagogical interventions had a greater influence on learner development in this area over time.

6.2.3 This Study's Contribution to Knowledge

In light of the findings presented above, the present study has expanded the scope of empirical work examining conversational behaviour across cultures, and also provides a response to the calls for research examining the teachability of backchannel behaviour in the language classroom. Thus, the main value of the present research would seem to lie in the general finding that pedagogical interventions, and most notably explicit instruction, did indeed appear to have a positive effect on L2 backchannel behaviour. This not only provides support for the incorporation of backchannel behaviour into second language pedagogy and cross-cultural communication training in the JEFL context, but also provides practitioners with some pedagogical suggestions. Beyond this fundamental conclusion, there are several other implications to consider which are discussed in the following section.

6.3 Implications of this Study

For the purpose of clarity, the researcher has divided the implications of this study's findings into categories of methodology, theory and practice. However, it is important to understand that these are not distinct and exclusive subcategories; clearly, there is a great deal of overlap, which will be evident in the subsections that follow.

6.3.1 Methodological Implications

The complicated design of this study is in large part responsible for the richness of data uncovered. The focus of this discussion is on three aspects of research design thought to be essential to future research in this area: the longitudinal design, the supplementation of observations with questionnaires and interviews, and the inclusion of video recording as a method of collecting data. First, regarding the use of a longitudinal design, Rose (2005) notes that most researchers studying the effects of instruction on a pragmatic feature of language have typically adopted a one-group pre-test-post-test design. The researcher argues here for the inclusion of both a control group and a delayed post-test to the research design of future studies in this area. Regarding the former, controls are needed to help eliminate alternative explanations of experimental results. Concerning the latter, comparing the first post-test with the second post-test can help researchers detect a delayed effect of the treatment or could reveal that the effect of the treatment wanes across time. In the case of this study, many of the positive gains exhibited by Group B in Post-test 1 were no longer evident in Post-test 2, suggesting that the effects of implicit instruction were not sustainable without continued treatment.

Second, as outlined in Section 2.10, most of the previous research examining backchannel behaviour involved linguists drawing conclusions from conversation analysis alone. While this study also included this dimension of analysis, the researcher felt it important to go beyond the observational stage and into a deeper investigation of how communication is affected by differences in backchannel behaviour. In this way, this study follows the recommendations of Mills (2003) and Scollon and Scollon (1995) to the effect that misunderstanding should be at the centre of conversation analysis. It is from this perspective that conversations are recognised as the instantiations of interactants' emotional responses to one another. Thus, the different frames of reference that interactants draw upon, which contribute to misunderstanding and miscommunication in intercultural conversations, are of particular interest to the researcher. To this end, consultation with participants was included in this study via post-conversation questionnaires and interviews. As Section 3.7 discussed, this is not to say that participants' post hoc rationalisations of the conversations should necessarily be considered the *truth* of what happened; however, it provides the researcher with an additional avenue in which to examine what participants may have been thinking. In other words, it was thought that using a multitude of data collection methods would not only serve to strengthen the reliability and validity of the data but also provide for a broader view with multiple perspectives on the researched topic.

Lastly, the researcher weighs in on the debate over whether video recordings are necessary in the study of backchannel behaviour. Heinz (2003) defends her choice to focus her analysis on audio-recorded conversations by pointing out the strong research tradition that validates the use of audio-taped phone conversations for the study of backchannel responses or turn-taking systems (e.g., Brady 1968; Drummond & Hopper 1993a,b; Ervin-Tripp 1979; Jefferson 1973). In response to Heinz (2003), studies focusing on phone conversations would seem to be justified in using audio-only recordings; however, in the researcher's opinion, any study claiming to analyse face-to-face interaction would need to include video recordings. As outlined in Section 2.2, the trend in the study of backchannel behaviour for some time has been to include nonverbal backchannels such as head nods, which requires video recording. Further, Shaw (2007), a proponent of video analysis, points out the counter argument that audio-only recording is thought by some to be less intrusive. In this study, as well an earlier one administered by the researcher (Cutrone 2005), however, this was not an issue. While a few of the participants acknowledged that they were aware of the video camera at the beginning of the conversation, they also reported that this awareness began to diminish as the conversation continued, and they did not believe they had changed their behaviour in any way because of the camera.

6.3.2 Theoretical Implications

The findings of this study have implications for theory in the fields of conversation analysis and second language acquisition. First, with misunderstanding as the focus of this analysis, the researcher found it useful to examine intercultural conversations using a Gricean (1967, 1975, 1989) framework. That is, intercultural misunderstandings and negative perceptions relating to backchannel behaviour were often associated with differing interpretations of Grice's maxims. These findings would seem to support the belief that Grice's maxims do not apply universally and independently of culture (O'Keeffe, Clancy & Adolphs 2011). In this way, Grice's maxims would seem to better serve linguists engaged in cross-cultural research as a tool for analysis rather than a set of norms expected in conversations. If researchers were seeking prescriptive laws to govern intercultural conversations, a good place to start would be with Clyne's (1994) culturally sensitive modifications and additions to Grice's maxims.

Regarding the universality of Brown and Levinson's (1987) theory of politeness, the findings of the cross-sectional aspects of this study appear to provide evidence supporting both sides of the debate. First, concerning Matsumoto's (1988) claims (see Section 1.7.3.2), the findings of this study would seem to offer some support that the concept of negative face may not play as large a role in the communication of Japanese people as Brown and Levinson (1978, 1987) had originally thought. That is, relative to their American interlocutors, the JEFLs frequently sent backchannels, many of which occurred while their interlocutor was speaking, and did not seem to consider this behaviour to be an imposition to their interlocutors. In fact, according to the reasons many JEFLs gave (see Section 4.6.2), the primary function of these frequent backchannels was quite to the contrary, i.e., to facilitate a harmonious atmosphere in the conversations. In this way, the JEFLs did not seem to see their backchannel behaviour, consisting of frequent and speech overlapping backchannels, as affecting the negative face of their interlocutors; rather, they believed such behaviour to be accentuating the positive face of their interlocutors. Backchannels may have also served this general purpose to the NESs; however, the fact that some of the NESs in this study, as well as in Cutrone's (2005) earlier intercultural analysis, mentioned the overuse of backchannels as a negative trait seems to suggest a fundamental difference from how the Japanese conceptualised backchannels.

Thus, while the researcher generally agrees with the sentiments put forward by Matsumoto (1988) that understanding one's position in the societal hierarchy and speaking and behaving accordingly is the defining feature of Japanese politeness, Matsumoto's (1988: 405) contention that negative face is 'alien' to Japanese culture seems to be somewhat overstated. The findings of this study, as well as this researcher's earlier study (Cutrone 2005), demonstrated that many of the Japanese participants were aware and sensitive to the loss of their interlocutors' negative face. Many JEFLs admitted that they often resorted to avoidance and/or feigning understanding as a way of opting out and/or redressing FTAs such as disagreeing and not understanding. As described in Section 2.8.3, Tajima (2001) also found evidence supporting both sides of the debate. While it was clear that Japanese backchannel use, like other elements of the Japanese language, was largely governed by hierarchical factors such as age, gender, status of interlocutors, and the formality of the conversational settings in her study, there were also instances in which the Japanese listeners attempted to mitigate FTAs by shifting the styles of their backchannel forms (i.e., creating more psychological distance in conversations). This is a debate that the researcher does not expect to see settled any time soon. Ultimately, the main issue seems to involve the differing interpretations of what Brown and Levinson (1987) wrote in describing their revised model of politeness. That is, while claiming that the underlying principles of their theory are universal, Brown and Levinson (1987: 57) acknowledge that 'cultural specific usages will vary'. Thus, as Gilks (2009-2010) points out, how broad these cultural specific usages can become before moving beyond the boundaries of Brown and Levinson's theoretical framework seems to be at the core of this debate.

Finally, the findings of this study relative to Schmidt's (1993) noticing hypothesis are discussed. As Sections 5.11 and 5.12 mentioned, this is another debate that the researcher does not expect to be resolved any time soon, and certainly not by the results of this study. The finding that explicit input enhancement, drawing attention to non-salient features of language such as backchannels facilitates learning, would seem to provide encouragement for the noticing hypothesis; however, it falls short of providing conclusive evidence supporting Schmidt's (1993) claim that *noticing* is a necessary condition for learning. This study cannot comment as to whether unconscious learning took place or not because the researcher did not set out to test this. In this study, *noticing* cannot be said to have been limited to the Explicit group, even if it appears that they may have *noticed* a great deal more. It seems plausible that members of both the Explicit and Implicit groups incurred some level of *noticing* of input, but, for both groups, it is not always clear as to exactly what was *noticed* and when, and how this precisely affected L2 output in subsequent conversations. The researcher is, thus, inclined to adopt a weaker position of the noticing hypothesis to the effect that *noticing* does appear to be helpful in speeding up the learning process, but it remains unclear as to whether it is actually a necessary condition for learning as Schmidt (1993) has asserted. What is certain, however, is that the members of the Explicit group outperformed the Implicit group after treatment and were better able to describe and detail some of the specific areas of their improvements. While it cannot be said with absolute certainty that the Explicit group performed better because they *noticed* more, it is possible to conclude that the Explicit group displayed more metalinguistic knowledge of the rules of backchannel behaviour after treatment. This conclusion would then, at the very least, support Truscott's (1998) reformulation of the noticing hypothesis as a claim that *noticing* is tied to the acquisition of metalinguistic knowledge but not necessarily to the development of communicative competence.

6.3.3 Practical Implications

As mentioned in Section 6.2.3, this study found that instruction did indeed help JEFL learners improve various aspects of their listening behaviour in English. Due to the vital role backchannel behaviour has in intercultural communication (see Section 2.8.1), and the fact that it is largely neglected in EFL pedagogy (see Section 2.9.3), the findings of this study suggest that listener behaviour warrants a higher priority in EFL teaching in Japan. With this in mind, the next question is how EFL teachers can best integrate this important feature of conversation into the language classroom. While the Explicit group, who received FFI, demonstrated the greatest sustained improvement overall, the Implicit group also displayed considerable improvements in several key areas. These findings seem to suggest that the best way forward may be a combination of these methods in which implicit methods are used to supplement an explicit approach. The norms of backchannel behaviour, as well as how different listening behaviours can be misconstrued across cultures, should be systematically taught, and this should be supported with teacher feedback, peer discussions and self analysis. However, in doing so, it is imperative that teachers approach issues involving cultural differences with extreme sensitivity. As O'Keeffe, Clancy and Adolphs (2011: 100) have pointed out, attempts to move between L1 and L2 pragmatic norms can feel like 'a minefield for learners of a language'. Hence, backchannel norms in English should not be presented in a rigid and prescriptive way (Farr 2003); rather, EFL teachers would be wise in taking the approach that they are merely offering their learners some alternative strategies should they choose to use them in their future encounters in English, especially in communication with NESs (this issue, as it relates to assessment, is revisited on the pages that follow). Finally, wherever possible, learners should be afforded reinforcement opportunities to communicate in the target language in meaningful and authentic contexts. This would not only give them a much-needed chance to apply their newly learnt skills, but would also allow them to develop their own strategies implicitly.

Having presented a general framework for the inclusion of backchannel behaviour in the language classroom above, the researcher acknowledges that various obstacles still remain. First, it seems unrealistic to expect teachers to go from little or no instruction in this area to suddenly dedicating entire classes and/or syllabi to it. A reasonable approach would be to start with modest goals and gradually progress to larger ones as teachers become more familiar and comfortable teaching this feature of language. A good place to introduce backchannel behaviour would be in EFL textbooks designed for oral communication classes. As researchers such as Thonus (2007) and Wannaruk (1997) have advocated, these materials need to start incorporating sections explaining how backchannels are used and activities to practise using them.

Another issue concerning listener behaviour in the classroom, as well the research arena, involves potential assessment criteria. As outlined in Section 2.9.4, this study used the following four criteria to assess listening behaviour: (1) the observed backchannel behaviour, (2) WTC, (3) use of conversational micro-skills and (4) ICC of the JEFLs. The researcher acknowledges that these criteria are a work in progress and will likely need to be modified for application, particularly in other contexts. Concerning criterion (1), some linguists may question the use of native anglophone backchannel norms as a model for EFL instruction when English is currently the global lingua franca used by many non-native speakers to communicate across national borders every day. Due to the reasons presented in Section 2.9.4.1, the researcher believes the use of the NES model to be fully justified in the present study. However, this is not to say that change in this area should not be sought in the future, even if it is sure to be a long and arduous process. Although resolving such a colossal issue as to which model of English should be used in Japan is certainly beyond the focus of this current investigation, this study has touched upon on an important issue that seems to be in dire need of re-examination in Japan. That is, as Walsh (2007) and Kachru (1998) have pointed out, the reason the NES model is used in Japan may not be due to any linguistic reason (i.e., the absence of a common standard of EIL) as much as it is an ideological one. Since Japan, a homogenous island nation, has historically endured periods of isolation from the West (see Section 1.2.1), the identity of English has long been associated with Westernisation. In the Meiji Restoration, as well as the post WWII era, this ideology has been what has driven the Japanese passion for *kokusaika* (internationalisation), which McConnell (1996: 447) describes as 'the urgent need for Japan to emerge from cultural isolation and assimilate a set of Western values'. Kubota (1999) adds to this definition by stressing that through this process of Westernisation, the Japanese believe themselves to be achieving a higher status and promoting their own nationalistic values. This is evident in Japan's thriving *Eikaiwa* industry (private English conversations with NESs) which exploits this superficial view of English for financial gains (Cutrone 2001; Heffernan 2005). At best, this ideology promotes a rather limited view of how English can be used in the world today; at worst, such ideas can be seen as a form of racism as Kubota (1998: 298) explains in the following quote:

> The non-native speaker of English, or the Other, is viewed as uncivilized and inferior to the Anglo speaker of English. Learning English, a language of the 'civilized' has been one of the means for the Japanese to identify themselves with Westerners.

As Walsh (2007) points out, this ideology seems to have prevented English from being a multilateral tool, i.e., because of their deference to NESs, the Japanese are failing to make use of English as much as they could for NNS-NNS communication. In light of the way English is used around the world today, it makes great sense for Japan to move away from the NES model and the ideologies that may be associated with it. However, adopting such a shift in ideology would likely be quite difficult to implement at first as large-scale reforms to the English education system in Japan would be needed. In addition to other problems associated with using a seemingly antiquated system of teaching that stresses rote learning and grammar translation over fluency and communicative competence, the current system in Japan employs Japanese teachers who are not wholly proficient in English (Hughes 1999; Ida 2004; Ishida 2002; Koike & Tanaka 1995), which may also be part of the problem. Besides making a concerted effort to raise the standard of its Japanese teachers of English, ELT administrators in Japan would be well-advised to rethink the prevailing ideology regarding how NESs contribute to JEFLs' language development. It is imperative that ELT in Japan goes beyond the thinking of NESs as the only sources of comprehensible input (Cutrone 2002), or, using Tajino's (2002: 30) term, as 'human tape-recorders' whose main purpose is to model pronunciation and/or provide knowledge of language based solely on their native intuition. The researcher strongly believes that more credence needs to be given to the professional skills the language teacher possesses through training and experience instead of where they happen to have been born. Clearly, there is a great deal to discuss concerning reforms in Japan's English educational system. Although calls to make ELT more communicative in Japan seem like a good place to start, it is doubtful that much will change in this regard until Japan alters its entrance examination system as described in Section 1.2.1 (Cook 2010, 2011).

Furthermore, returning to address criteria (2), (3) and (4) mentioned earlier in this subsection, the association between listening behaviour and each of these criteria has been clearly established at various points throughout this book. Although these criteria are justified in terms of assessing listening behaviour in the Japanese context, following them may not always make sense elsewhere. Moreover, some linguists may question the need to analyse these criteria collectively because each one of them, along with one's overall L2 proficiency, can greatly affect conversations independently. While this may indeed be true, and it would certainly be easier for practitioners to deal with, the researcher believes it would be illogical to ignore the inextricable links between these features of conversation when examining listenership. In other words, examining backchannel categories such as frequency, variability, placement and function independently would do very little to inform pedagogy. More importantly, it is necessary to understand the issues underpinning the tendencies of backchannel use, and to examine how differing backchannel conventions influence communication.

6.4 Recommendations for Future Research

For the findings of this study to be confirmed, there is a need to replicate this study in other settings and with other individuals. Immediate directions for future research emerge from the above discussions of limitations and implications of this study. Follow-up studies could be designed to address some of these issues by increasing sample size, and incorporating a more balanced ratio of female to male participants. Regarding the latter, the role of gender differences in backchannel behaviour could be examined by utilising mixed-sex conversations. Further, future research in this vein would do well to examine diverse groups of EFL learners, and investigate how backchannel behaviour is affected by other factors such as larger group dynamics, varying conversational registers, interlocutor familiarity, and the topic of the conversation.

Concerning pedagogical research specifically, besides the ideological problems outlined in Section 6.3.3, there are other issues that need to be resolved. First, while the use of NES norms as a model for backchannel behaviour is presently justified in this study (see Section 5.10.1), it would be a positive development to see researchers one day piece together a more thorough and representative description of English backchannel behaviour as it exists in the international community. As various researchers have pointed out (O'Keeffe & Adolphs 2008; O'Keeffe & Farr 2003; O'Keeffe, McCarthy & Carter 2007), recent advances in technology have revolotionised the way linguists approach data, and the development of corpora of English spoken in contexts where English is a lingua franca, such as the corpus development project called the Vienna-Oxford International Corpus of English (VOICE), provides linguists with a useful instrument to begin developing an EIL model of backchannel behaviour. To this end, a recent study conducted by Knight (2009) provides a glimpse of what may be possible as she uses video, audio, and textual records of interaction found in the Nottingham Multi-Modal Corpus (NMMC) to offer a brief description of the ways in which backchannels appear to function and operate in specific discursive episodes in the corpus. Nonetheless, for classroom use, practitioners will have to balance any prospective account of EIL backchannel behaviour with other related and contextual factors mentioned throughout this book such as how much learners speak, the variability of their responses, potential reasons underpinning their listening behaviour, etc.

Second, little is known about how much instruction is needed for maximum effect, and how much time elapses before superficial benefits begin to fade. Regarding the latter, clues come from studies such as White's (1991) investigation into the effects of instruction on adverb placement, which found beneficial effects remained five weeks after instruction, but were no longer present after a year. Hence, future investigations into the time effects of instruction are needed. Moreover, as explained in Section 2.9.2.4, Thonus's (2007) recommendation that instruction directed at backchannel behaviour should focus on higher-level learners appears to be well founded; however, this study observed cases in which instruction was found to be beneficial for some of the lower-level learners as well. Thus, further research examining the effects of instruction on varying levels of proficiency would be useful.

Further, as mentioned in Section 2.9.2.5, there is some recent evidence to suggest that video conferencing may be a means in which JEFLs can improve their backchannel behaviour in English (Sardegna & Molle 2010). As the research in this area has only scratched the surface, further studies exploring the viability of video conferencing as a way to improve backchannel behaviour are needed. Taking this into account, this line of investigation may have larger ramifications in the field of EFL in Japan. One of the main problems associated with EFL learning in such a homogeneous nation as Japan has been the lack of L2 practice opportunities afforded JEFL learners. In light of recent advances in making interactive technology easier to use, one possible solution is to give JEFLs more authentic practice opportunities conversing with speakers of English all over the world by using video conferencing methods. While there is a wealth of literature devoted to studies examining the technical side of video conferencing, there seems to be little concerning the human aspects of video conferencing, and more specifically in relation to conversation analysis and language learning.

Lastly, in addition to research informing classroom practice, future studies into backchannel behaviour would do well to shed light on issues concerning oral testing procedures. According to Wolf's (2008a) *backchannel output hypothesis*, the speech of L2 learners of English may be greatly affected by their interlocutor's backchannels during oral tasks, especially when interactants adhere to divergent backchannel conventions. This hypothesis was supported by small-scale studies conducted by Sasaki (2006) and Wolf (2008b). In both studies, which involved Japanese learners of English, learners were found to be more fluent when their interlocutor adopted backchannel norms they were accustomed to, and less fluent when they were less familiar with the backchannel style. Sasaki's (2006) study also found that interviewees' level of anxiety was associated with the interviewers' backchannel output in this same way. Wolf's (2008a) backchannel output hypothesis needs to be conducted in larger-scale studies, as validation would have serious implications on how students prepare for Oral Proficiency Interviews (OPI), especially those conducted by foreign interviewees. That is, learners would need to develop their awareness and tolerance of unfamiliar types, frequency, placement, and function of backchannel provision that they might ultimately encounter at test time.

Although there is clearly much work to do in the future, the present study contributes to our understanding of how backchannels operate in intercultural discourse, and also demonstrates how an explicit approach to teaching English backchannel behaviour leads to positive outcomes in the JEFL context. In the broader context of language pedagogy, the findings of this study are especially important as they suggest that explicit teaching may benefit various aspects of language which might not normally be thought of as suitable for explicit instruction. The researcher hopes the present study will serve as a platform for future investigation and diagnosis into this area, as well as the other areas mentioned above.

APPENDIX A

Heuristic Model of Variables Influencing WTC

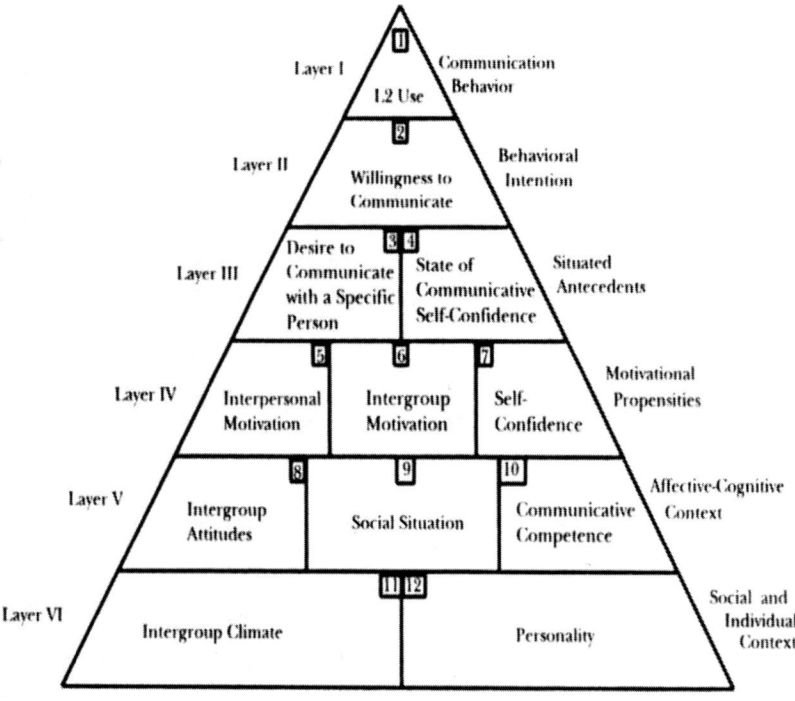

(MacIntyre, Clément, Dörnyei & Noels 1998: 547)

APPENDIX B

Participation Consent Forms for NESs (A) and JEFLs (B)

Consent Form A

Tentative Project title: An examination of the acquisition of American English backchannels by Japanese EFL learners

I have read and had explained to me by Pino Cutrone the Information Sheet relating to this project.

I have had explained to me the purposes of the project and what will be required of me, and any questions have been answered to my satisfaction. I agree to the arrangements described in the Information Sheet insofar as they relate to my participation.

I understand that my participation is entirely voluntary and that I have the right to withdraw from the project any time.

I have received a copy of this Consent Form and of the accompanying Information Sheet.

Name:

Signed:

Date:

Consent Form B 同意書 B

Project title(研究タイトル):

An examination of the acquisition of American English backchannels by Japanese EFL learners

(日本人のEFL学習者によるアメリカ英語伝達方法習得に関する調査)

I have read and had explained to me by Pino Cutrone the Information Sheet relating to this project.

(私は、ピノ・カトローニからこの調査研究に対する説明を受け、説明書も読みました)

I have had explained to me the purposes of the project and what will be required of me, and any questions have been answered to my satisfaction. I agree to the arrangements described in the Information Sheet insofar as they relate to my participation.

(この調査研究において、参加者に求められることと、その目的を聞き、私が聞いた質問にも満足いく内容で答えをもらいました。そのうえで、私がこの調査研究に被験者として参加することをここに同意します)

I understand that my participation is entirely voluntary and that I have the right to withdraw from the project any time.

(私はこの調査研究にみずから参加するものとし、また、いつでも被験者をやめることもできることも

理解しました)

I have received a copy of this Consent Form and of the accompanying Information Sheet.

(この同意書の写しと、説明書も手渡され、自分で管理します)

Name(名前):　　　　　Signed(署名):

DATE(記入日):

APPENDIX C

Information Sheets for NES Interlocutors (A), NES Observers (B), and JEFLs (C)

(N.B. Original information sheets contained the University of Reading's letterhead with the contact details of my supervisor at that time.)

Information sheet A

I, Pino Cutrone, would like to request your participation in a study I am carrying out for my PhD Thesis from the University of Reading. The study will observe cross-cultural conversations in English between Japanese and American participants, which is why you have been asked to participate. The primary goal of this study is to develop insights into the field of conversation analysis which may help Japanese learners in their study of English as a foreign language.

As part of the study, I will videotape short conversations (in English) between pairs consisting of a Japanese and an American national. Conversational prompts will be offered to help stimulate the conversations. The conversations are to be casual, and participants can feel free to take the conversation in any direction they like.

After the short conversations are complete, students will first fill out a questionnaire, and subsequently be interviewed. The questionnaire will consist of questions about the prior conversations, and the interview will involve me playing back a brief segment from the videotaped conversation and asking the participant a few questions.

If participants wish, I will provide them with a copy of my finished work. It is my hope that this project will eventually be published in an academic journal and/or book. The consent forms to be used in this project will be kept securely in the School of Language and European studies for a reasonable time after the project. All the data collected for use in this study will be stored in a locked drawer in my office at the University of Nagasaki during the project and thereafter, and only myself, my supervisor and my examiners will have access to it. All personal information will be kept strictly confidential. I promise the following assurances to protect your privacy:

- I will not let people (other than my course markers at the University of Reading) listen or see the videotaped conversations unless you give me special permission to do so.
- By using pseudonyms in writing and talking about my study, I will never use your name or any other information that could give away your identity.
- If at any point in the study you want me to erase from the videotape anything you have said, you have the right to tell me to do this, and I will erase it in your presence.

This project has been subject to ethical review by the University Ethics and Research Committee and has been allowed to proceed. Participants are free to withdraw their voluntary participation at any stage if they should so wish. By signing below, you are indicating that this research has been satisfactorily explained to you, and that you consent to participating in the ways described above. If you have any queries or wish to clarify anything about the study, please feel free to contact my supervisor at the address above.

Name:

Signed:

Date:

Information Sheet B

I, Pino Cutrone, would like to request your participation in a study I am carrying out for my PhD Thesis from the University of Reading. The study will observe cross-cultural conversations in English between Japanese and American participants. The primary goal of this study is to develop insights into the fields of conversation analysis and intercultural communication which may help Japanese learners in their study of English as a foreign language (EFL).

More specifically, this study seeks to examine the effect of different types of instruction on Japanese EFL learners' listening behaviour. A group of 30 Japanese EFL students at the University of Nagasaki will be divided into three equally representative groups, and each group will receive a different form of instruction regarding the listening behaviour that native speakers of English employ. That is, one group will receive explicit instruction, one group will receive implicit instruction, and one group, the control group, will receive no instruction. The students' listening behaviour will be assessed at various points: prior to instruction (Pre-test), directly after the two experimental groups have received eight weeks of instruction (Post-test 1), and after a subsequent eight weeks of no instruction to determine the long-term effects of the previous instruction (Post-test 2).

In order to assess the listening behaviour of the students at each phase of the study (i.e., the Pre-test, Post-test 1 and Post-test 2), I will videotape several brief conversations (in English) between pairs consisting of a Japanese EFL student and an American national. A great majority of the assessment of the Japanese learners' listening behaviour over time will involve a linguistic analysis of the conventions used in each conversation, as well as an examination of the data produced by interviewing the participants involved in the conversations. As an additional measurement, the adequacy of the Japanese EFL learner's listening behaviour will also be determined by the perceptions of native speakers of English (i.e., North Americans), who are not linguists, do not live in Japan, and did not take part in the videotaped conversations and/or earlier pilot studies. It is for these reasons that I request your participation.

Thus, in summary, your role as participant is to watch each videotaped conversation and subsequently provide your impressions of the Japanese EFL learners' listening behaviour by filling-out the "Inventory of Listening behaviour" questionnaire. Each three-minute conversation requires the same brief questionnaire to be completed (instructions are provided therein). Please feel free to be as critical as possible in your analyses as your standard for good listening behaviour should reflect what you expect from people residing in your country.

If participants wish, I will provide them with a copy of my finished work. It is my hope that this project will eventually be published in an academic journal and/or a book. The consent forms to be used in this project will be kept securely in the School of Languages and European Studies for a reasonable time after the project. All the data collected for use in this study will be stored in a locked drawer in my office at the University of Nagasaki during the project and thereafter, and only myself, my supervisor and my examiners will have access to it. All personal information will be kept strictly confidential. By using pseudonyms in writing and talking about my study, I will never use your name or any other information that could give away your identity.

This project has been subject to ethical review by the University Ethics and Research Committee and has been allowed to proceed. Participants are free to withdraw their voluntary participation at any stage if they should so wish. By signing below, you are indicating that this research has been satisfactorily explained to you, and that you consent to participating in the ways described above. If you have any queries or wish to clarify anything about the study, please feel free to contact my supervisor at the address above.

Name:

Signed:

Date:

Information Sheet C　研究説明書 C

I, Pino Cutrone, would like to request your participation in a study I am carrying out for my PhD Thesis from the University of Reading. The study will observe cross-cultural conversations in English between Japanese and American participants, which is why you have been asked to participate. The primary goal of this study is to develop insights into the field of conversation analysis which may help Japanese learners in their study of English as a foreign language.

（私、ピノ・カトローニは、レディング大学博士号論文における調査研究のために、あなたの参加を求めます。この研究は、日本人参加者とアメリカ人参加者の会話を見るもので、あなたはこの日本人参加者になります。この研究の最終的ゴールは、この研究を行なうことで、私自身が今後日本人の英語学習者に対して、特に会話分野において、より効果的な手助けができるようになることです。）

As part of the study, I will videotape short conversations (in English) between pairs consisting of a Japanese and an American national. Conversational prompts will be offered to help stimulate the conversations. The conversations are to be casual, and participants can feel free to take the conversation in any direction they like.

（調査内容として、まずネイティブスピーカーとの英語での会話をしている場面をビデオに撮影させていただきます。その会話は難しいものではなく、話しやすいテーマや言葉のサポートも適宜与えられて、気楽に落ち着いた中で自由に話すことができます。もちろん英語のレベルチェックをするものではなく、この会話の出来具合があなたの評価につながることは絶対にありません。）

After the short conversations are complete, students will first fill-out a questionnaire and, subsequently, be interviewed. The questionnaire will consist of questions about the prior conversations, and the interview will involve me playing back a brief segment from the videotaped conversation and asking the participant a few questions. This is not a test to check your English level, and I assure you that your performance in this conversation is not related to your score in this class.

(この短い会話を終えた後、参加者はまず質問紙に答え、その内容を補足するためにインタビューに答えることになります。質問紙の内容は、その前の会話の受けとめ方に対してのもので、インタビューは撮影したビデオを見ながらその時の会話の状況を聞いていくものです)

If participants wish, I will provide them with a copy of my finished work. It is my hope that this project will eventually be published in an academic journal and/or book. The consent forms to be used in this project will be kept securely in the School of Language and European studies for a reasonable time after the project. All the data collected for use in this study will be stored in a locked drawer in my office at the University of Nagasaki during the project and thereafter, and only myself, my supervisor and my examiners will have access to it. All personal information will be kept strictly confidential. I promise the following assurances to protect your privacy:

- I will not let people (other than my course markers at the University of Reading) listen or see the videotaped conversations unless you give me special permission to do so.

- By using pseudonyms in writing and talking about my study, I will never use your name or any other information that could give away your identity.

- If at any point in the study you want me to erase from the videotape anything you have said, you have the right to tell me to do this, and I will erase it in your presence.

(もし参加者が希望すれば、研究終了後に、撮影したテープのコピーや結果の写しをお渡しすることも出来ます。最終的にこの研究論文が学術雑誌に掲載されることを目標としています。この調査研究参加に対する同意書は、研究終了後に、私が所属するレディング大学に安全に保管されます。全てのデータは、研究中はシーボルト大学内の私のオフィスの施錠できる場所に、その後は、私個人が厳密に管理し、私の他に論文指導者のみがそれを見ることができるとし、それ以外に公開されることはありません。全ての個人情報が確実に守られることを以下のように保障します。

・私は、参加者から特別な許可が無い限り、論文指導者以外にビデオテープを見せたり、内容を伝えることは絶対にしません。

・参加者の名前に関しては全て仮名や記号を用い、参加者が特定できるような情報や名前を出すことは絶対にしません。

・もし参加者が、自分の内容に関して削除して欲しい箇所があれば、いつでも申し立てることが出来る権利があり、私は必ずそれに従うものとします。）

This project has been subject to ethical review by the University Ethics and Research Committee and has been allowed to proceed. Participants are free to withdraw their voluntary participation at any stage if they should so wish. By signing below, you are indicating that this research has been satisfactorily explained to you, and that you consent to participating in the ways described above. If you have any queries or wish to clarify anything about the study, please feel free to contact my supervisor at the address above.

（この研究は私の所属する大学の倫理委員会規則にのっとったものであり、参加者はいつでも研究対象から外れることが出来ます。この同意書にサインすることで、上記の内容を理解された上での自発的な参加とみなされます。研究に対しての質問や要望があれば、いつでも以下のレディング大学のアドレスに連絡をして下さい。）

Name（名前）:

Signed（署名）:

Date（記入日）:

APPENDIX D

Ten Item Personality Inventory (TIPI)

Name（名前）:_____ Date（記入日）:_____
Questionnaire　質問紙

Following the scale below, please write a number next to each statement below to indicate the degree to which you agree or disagree with that statement.（下の枠内の１から７までのスケールに従って、１から１２までの問いに対して、最も自分に当てはまる度数の数字を、問いの数字横の空欄にそれぞれ入れてください。）

Disagree Strongly（全く違うと思う）	Disagree moderately（あまりそうだとは思わない）	Disagree a little（少し違うと思う）	Neither agree nor disagree（どちらでもない）	Agree a little（少しそう思う）	Agree moderately（まあまあそう思う）	Agree strongly（強くそう思う）
1	2	3	4	5	6	7

I see myself as（私は自分のことを・・・）:

1. _____ Extraverted, enthusiastic.（外向的、社交的、熱心だと思う）

2. _____ Critical, quarrelsome.　（批判的、口やかましいと思う）

3. _____ Dependable, self-disciplined.（頼りがいがある、自立していると思う）

4. _____ Anxious, easily upset.（感情が変化しやすい、すぐいらいらすると思う）

5. _____ Open to new experiences, complex.（新しい経験や物事に挑戦する事が好き）

6. _____ Reserved, quiet.（遠慮がち、おとなしいと思う）

7. _____ Sympathetic, warm.（思いやりがある、あたたかみがあると思う）

8. _____ Disorganised, careless.（注意ミスが多い、忘れ物が多いと思う）

9. _____ Calm, emotionally stable.（おだやか、感情が安定していると思う）

10. _____ Conventional, uncreative.（新しい物事に保守的、独創性がないと思う）

(N.B. The Japanese translation of the TIPI has since been modified and renamed the TIPI-J as presented in the recent works of Oshio, Abe & Cutrone 2011, 2012.)

Appendix D1:
Group A's Raw Scores Relating to 10 Items of TIPI

GROUP A	Mic	Hi	Ar	Ha	Miy	Sa	Ch	Ay	Ta	Ka
TIPI Q1	7	6	2	6	6	5	4	6	4	3
TIPI Q2	4	2	4	3	3	6	3	4	3	5
TIPI Q3	4	4	2	5	3	6	5	3	5	4
TIPI Q4	5	4	3	3	5	5	3	3	6	6
TIPI Q5	7	7	2	7	6	7	5	5	5	5
TIPI Q6	2	2	6	2	6	4	6	4	4	6
TIPI Q7	5	5	4	6	5	5	6	5	5	6
TIPI Q8	4	5	3	4	4	6	5	5	3	2
TIPI Q9	4	4	3	5	3	2	4	4	3	3
TIPI Q10	3	2	6	4	3	3	5	4	3	4

Appendix D2:
Group B's Raw Scores Relating to 10 Items of TIPI

GROUP B	Ri	Sh	May	Me	Mad	Sa	Ke	Mi	Ta	Ko
TIPI Q1	5	5	2	2	4	6	6	3	5	5
TIPI Q2	2	2	7	1	3	3	5	2	5	4
TIPI Q3	3	4	3	5	4	2	2	2	4	4
TIPI Q4	2	3	7	4	2	4	2	2	6	6
TIPI Q5	4	5	6	6	5	7	5	4	6	7
TIPI Q6	3	7	7	5	3	4	4	4	3	5
TIPI Q7	5	6	6	5	5	4	6	4	5	4
TIPI Q8	6	2	7	5	4	6	5	6	6	6
TIPI Q9	5	6	2	6	5	4	4	3	6	
TIPI Q10	6	6	2	3	4	3	5	4	4	3

Appendix D3:
Group Z's Raw Scores Relating to 10 Items of TIPI

GROUP Z	Ya	Mik	Ak	Yi	To	Yo	Mis	Yu	Aka	Hi
TIPI Q1	5	5	6	5	6	6	6	6	5	2
TIPI Q2	5	4	1	4	2	4	4	5	2	1
TIPI Q3	4	5	6	5	3	4	5	6	2	5
TIPI Q4	5	3	1	2	2	5	7	6	5	2
TIPI Q5	6	6	7	7	6	7	7	5	6	5
TIPI Q6	2	5	4	4	3	4	4	2	3	7
TIPI Q7	4	5	6	5	2	4	4	6	4	6
TIPI Q8	5	5	3	6	2	5	3	4	6	5
TIPI Q9	3	6	6	6	2	4	2	2	6	6
TIPI Q10	2	5	2	3	4	5	1	3	3	4

(N.B. Due to space limitations, the pseudonyms above have been abbreviated.)

APPENDIX E

Explicit Instruction

Week 1 (1 Lesson: 90 minutes)

1. Plenary – Students were asked to brainstorm the traits they believed belong to good versus bad listeners. The teacher wrote students' answers on the board. (10 minutes)

2. The class was put into pairs. The teacher selected half of the pairs and put them face-to-face at the front of the classroom instructing one student in each pair to talk about a chosen topic until told to stop. The teacher instructed the second student to listen to the speaker and react naturally; listener questions and reactive comments were allowed, but listeners were instructed to not take over the primary speaking, i.e., leaving it up to the first student for the moment. The rest of the class acted as observers, each of whose job it was to focus on one of the pairs and to pay attention to the way the second student listens (i.e., what did the listener do to show they were listening, and how was it perceived by the speaker).This activity was repeated until all the students had a chance to speak, listen, observe and be observed. (20 minutes)

3. The teacher had the students sit in a circle and discuss the following questions: What did the listeners do or say while they were listening? Did you notice any difference in the behaviours of the different listeners? Did you (the speakers) feel that the listener was paying attention to you? Why or why not? Did you (the speakers) feel that the listener was interested in what you were telling him/her? Why or why not? Students were also asked to think about and discuss their own general L1 listening behaviour considering the following questions: Do you make any noises or comments, ask any questions, use any gestures or facial expressions when listening? Do you behave like any of the listeners you observed at times? Do you listen (or show that you are listening) in a different way when you are speaking to your teacher, boss, or family? Do you think you act this way because of your personality or the personality of the other speakers?

How much influence does the situation have on your listening behaviour? Do other speakers of your language act the same way? (20 minutes)

4. Plenary – The students were shown a brief video clip of a group of Japanese people conversing in Japanese. The students watched the video clip three or four times. The teacher asked the students to examine and note some of the individual differences in the listening behaviour of the participants in the conversations. Students' observations were shared and discussed with the entire class. (20 minutes)

5. Plenary – The students were shown a brief video clip of a group of American people conversing in English. The students watched the video clip three or four times and, subsequently, were asked to examine and note some of the individual differences in listening behaviour of the participants in the conversations. Students' observations were again shared and discussed with the entire class. (20 minutes)

Week 2 (1 Lesson: 90 minutes)

1. The teacher briefly reviewed the previous lesson's contents. (5 minutes)

2. The two intracultural video clips shown in the previous lesson were replayed in succession, and students were asked to make notes regarding any observed differences in listening behaviour between the two cultures. The conversations were shown two or three times. (15 minutes)

3. Subsequently, students were asked to share their observations in small groups. (10 minutes)

4. Each group shared their observations with the entire class and discussions ensued. Students were asked to consider why each culture behaves the way they do when they are listening. (15 minutes)

5. Plenary – The students were shown two brief intercultural video clips of a Japanese and an American person conversing in English. The first clip consisted of two males, and the second clip consisted of two females. The students watched the video clips three or four times. After the first viewing, the teacher asked the students to examine and note some of the individual and cultural differences in listening behaviour of the participants in the conversations. Transcriptions of these conversations were provided after the first viewing. (15 minutes)

7. Subsequently, students were asked to share their observations in small groups. (15 minutes)

8. Each group was asked to share their observations with the entire class and discussions followed. (15 minutes)

Week 3 (1 Lesson: 90 minutes)

1. The teacher briefly reviewed the previous lesson's contents. (5-10 minutes)

2. The students were shown a video clip of two Americans conversing in a casual conversation. Once students understood the main idea from the conversation, the teacher supplied them with an uncomplicated transcription of the conversation and replayed the video clip several times over the next two lessons. For each viewing, the teacher had students focus on an aspect of backchannel behaviour for in-depth analysis – see outline below. (80-85 minutes as broken down below)

A. First viewing(s): Listening Practice – Content and Vocabulary. The first viewing was designed solely to get the students familiar with the content of the conversation and the vocabulary used. Prior to watching and listening, the teacher gave students a general listening task, which included answering such question as (1) what is the conversation about, or (2) what did he mean when he said ..…? Answers were subsequently shared. (10-15 minutes)

B. Second Viewing(s): To raise awareness of backchannels in English, students were provided with a scaffolding sheet in which they had to mark the backchannel forms they heard. The teacher subsequently gave students the answers to the task. (10-15 minutes)

C. Third viewing(s): The teacher gave the students a transcription of the conversation and allowed them one or two viewings while they followed along with the transcription. After answering any remaining content and/or vocabulary questions, the teacher had students underline the backchannels in the conversations. In small groups, students tried to determine what the function of each backchannel was, and answers were ultimately shared with the whole class. (15 minutes)

D. The teacher then gave each group a list of functional categories (i.e., those based in the research) and then asked them to put each backchannel they heard in the conversation in the functional category they believed to be most appropriate. Afterwards, all answers were shared and discussed. (15 minutes)

E. Students were asked to consider/add supplemental backchannel forms which they believed to be appropriate to each functional category on the list. Students' answers were shared and discussed with the entire class, and feedback was given by the teacher. (10 minutes)

F. In small groups – the teacher gave students a sheet of backchannel forms and asked them to organise these forms into the functional categories they deemed to be most appropriate. Students' answers were shared and discussed with the entire class, with input also provided from the teacher. (20 minutes)

Week 4 (1 Lesson: 90 minutes)

1. The teacher briefly reviewed the previous lessons' contents. (5-10 minutes)

2. During the next set of activities, students had more opportunities to gage the appropriateness of various backchannel responses to specific comments – see outline below. (10 minutes)

A. Activity 1: Half of the students received cards with comments on them, while the other half received cards with backchannel responses on them. Students were required to find the students whose comment/backchannel response best corresponds with their card. (10 minutes)

B. Activity 2: Students were given a sheet with several comments and several backchannel responses on it. Students' goal in this activity was to match the comments with the most appropriate response. Students' submitted their answers to the teacher the following class, and the teacher provided them with feedback at the beginning of the next class. (homework)

3. Fourth viewing(s): This viewing focused on the frequency by which listeners send backchannels. Upon watching the video clip, students were asked to make observations about the actors' backchannel frequency.

Subsequently, with help from the teacher, students systematically calculated the number of listener backchannels per interlocutor word. Findings were shared and discussed with the entire class. (15 minutes)

4. Fifth viewing(s): This viewing focused on discourse contexts favouring backchannels in English. Before watching the video clip again, learners were asked to consider whether any patterns exist as to where the backchannels were sent – students were able to examine the transcription for any patterns as to where backchannels are sent. (15 minutes)

5. All answers to the previous activity were shared and discussed. Subsequently, the teacher demonstrated to the students the places in the video recorded conversations where backchannels frequently occur. These discourse contexts include grammatical completion points, pauses, points where pauses and grammatical completion occur simultaneously, and points where the primary speaker signals to the listener that they would like a backchannel such as by means of a nonverbal gesture or through the phrase *ya know*. (15-30 minutes)

Week 5 (1 Lesson: 90 minutes)

1. The teacher briefly reviewed the previous lessons' contents and gave feedback to the homework the students submitted. (10 minutes)

2. A. The teacher gave the students a written sample of an authentic conversation between a Japanese person and a native speaker of English. The backchannel expressions in the conversation were omitted, and students were required to add their own backchannel expressions at the frequency and discourse contexts they believe to be most appropriate. Students' answers were shared and discussed with the entire class, and feedback was provided by the teacher. (20 minutes)

B. For additional practice, the teacher gave students a similar task sheet as the one described directly above to do as homework (feedback provided at the start of Week 7).

3. The teacher put the students into pairs and asked them to mimic the activity above, but this time they were to do it verbally. That is, each member of the pair read a pre-prepared passage out loud to their partner. Their partner was required to add in backchannel expressions at the frequency and discourse contexts they believe to be most appropriate. The

teacher moved around the class and offered feedback as the need arose. (30 minutes)

At the midpoint of this lesson, the focus of this lesson was shifted to the forms and functions of backchannels. First, a series of short video recorded intercultural conversations in which the Japanese participant's backchannel behaviour was unconventional by American standards was shown. After watching each one, the students were asked various questions, which included the following: How was the Japanese person's listening behaviour? Was there anything wrong with the Japanese person's listening behaviour? If so, what was wrong? Do Japanese often do that? Are Americans and or other native English speakers different in this regard? How do you think the Japanese person's conversational partner perceived their listening behaviour? How could the Japanese person improve this in the future? After each discussion, the teacher demonstrated more efficient strategies (when necessary) to help students better deal with these types of conversational situations. To this end, the following steps were undertaken over the next two classes:

4. A. The teacher showed a video portraying a Japanese sending continuer type backchannels when they did not understand. (5 minutes)

B. Discussion (questions as shown above). (10 minutes)

C. The teacher showed a brief video clip of a Japanese person successfully conveying that they did not understand the gist of what their interlocutor was saying in English. Students were subsequently asked to read the transcribed conversation, practise it with support and ultimately role-play it with no aids. (15 minutes)

5. To assist in preventing communication breakdown (and to supplement the instruction in (4) directly above and (1), (2) and (3) in Week 6 below), the teacher gave students sheets which contain conversational management techniques and repair strategies. Besides having a list of things to say in various situations, these sheets contained specific tasks to help students understand each strategy that the teacher has chosen for instruction. The students were asked to read these sheets and do the tasks for homework over the following two weeks (corrections and feedback were provided at the beginning of Week 7). These tasks were taken from the book *Function in English* written by Blundell, Higgens and Middlemiss (1982).

Week 6 (1 Lesson: 90 minutes)

1. A. The teacher showed a video of a Japanese person sending continuer type backchannels when they did not agree with what their partner is saying. (5 minutes)

B. Discussion (questions as shown above). (10 minutes)

C. The teacher showed a brief video clip of a Japanese person successfully (and politely) conveying that they disagreed with what their partner was saying. Students, subsequently, were able to read the transcribed conversation, practise it with support and ultimately role-play it with no aids. (15 minutes)

2. A. The teacher showed two brief videos. First, a video of a Japanese person not sending enough backchannels was shown. Subsequently, a video of a Japanese person sending especially frequent backchannels (many of which occur while their partner was speaking) was shown. (5 minutes)

B. Discussion (questions as shown above). (10 minutes)

C. The teacher showed a brief video clip of a Japanese sending backchannels at the appropriate discourse contexts as shown in Lesson 4 (Step 4). (5 minutes)

D. After briefly reviewing the main discourse contexts that Americans send backchannels, the teacher showed a brief video clip of a Japanese person politely interrupting their partner. Students were subsequently able to read the transcribed conversation, practise it with support and ultimately role-play it with no aids. (10 minutes)

3. The teacher showed a video of a Japanese person sending backchannels as a way to avoid speaking (i.e., avoid taking a speaking turn). (5 minutes)

B. Discussion (questions as shown above). (10 minutes)

C. The teacher showed a brief video clip of a Japanese person taking the initiative to take the speaking turn. Students were subsequently able to read the transcribed conversation, practise it with support and ultimately role-play it with no aids. (15 minutes)

Week 7 (1 Lesson: 90 minutes)

1. The teacher briefly reviewed the previous lessons' contents and went over homework sheets given in Weeks 5 and 6. (20 minutes)

2. Similar to Lesson 1 (Step 2), the class was put into pairs, and the teacher chose half of the pairs and put them face-to-face at the front of the classroom and then instructed one student in each pair to talk about the chosen topic until told to stop. The teacher instructed the second student to listen to the speaker and react naturally but to not overtake the speaker. The rest of the class acted as observers focusing on one of the pairs and to pay attention to the way the second student listens. After the conversation was finished, the observer provided the listener with feedback regarding their listening performance. This activity was repeated until all the students had a chance to speak, listen, observe and be observed. (30 minutes)

3. The remaining part of the instruction directed at listening behaviour (in this lesson and next) involved the use of video cameras. Students were put into pairs (which they changed several times during this activity – i.e. after each conversation and analysis) and each pair was given a video camera to record brief conversations of them and their partner conversing in English. Subsequently, students re-played the conversation and analysed theirs and their partner's listening behaviour. The teacher walked around the classroom watching the recorded conversations and offered feedback as necessary. (40 minutes)

Week 8 (1 Lesson: 90 minutes)

1. The activity using video cameras, which is described directly above, was repeated for most of the class. (75 minutes)

2. Lastly, the teacher reviewed explicitly what was taught during the previous eight lessons. Students were given a chance to make comments and ask the teacher any final questions. (15 minutes)

Implicit Instruction

Week 1 (1 Lesson: 90 minutes)

1. The first lesson in this group was conducted in the same way as the first lesson for the group receiving Explicit instruction. The main difference here was that the teacher was much less involved, allowing students to make and discuss discoveries on their own. The class began by students considering the general qualities of good and bad conversationalists as follows:

Plenary – Students brainstormed what qualities make a good conversationalist and what qualities make a bad conversationalist. (15 minutes)

2. Plenary – Students were shown brief video clips of dyadic conversations between two Americans conversing in English. The teacher asked students to consider and discuss some of the individual differences in conversational style of the participants in the conversations. (15 minutes)

3. Plenary – the students were shown brief video clips of intercultural dyadic conversations between American and Japanese people conversing in English. Students were asked to consider and discuss any noticeable differences in conversational styles between the NESs and the Japanese conversational participants. (15 minutes)

4. The focus of instruction shifted to listening behaviour as follows:

Plenary – Students were asked to brainstorm what characteristics make a good listener and what characteristics make a bad listener. (15 minutes)

5. Plenary – The videos clips shown in Steps 2 and 3 were replayed, and, this time, learners were asked to consider and discuss differences in listening behaviour and the implications of how some of these differences might affect intercultural communication. (15 minutes)

6. The students watched the intercultural video clips one or two more times. To raise awareness of backchannels in English, students were provided with a scaffolding sheet in which they were required to mark the backchannel forms they hear. With minimal input from the teacher, the

students discussed the possible functions and perceptions of these listener responses. (15 minutes)

Homework: The teacher asked the students to watch an English language movie of their choice and observe tendencies regarding the communication style and listening behaviour of the people acting in the movie. The students' observations from the movie were shared and discussed the next time the members of the class met in Week 4.

Week 2 (2 Lessons: 90 minutes total)

(1) The students took part in an English conversation with a native speaker of English for 45 minutes. The register of the conversation was casual, and conversational prompts were provided to help stimulate authentic conversation. (45 minutes)

(2) This lesson followed the same format as (1). (45 minutes)

Week 3 (2 Lessons: 90 minutes total)

Following the description provided for Week 2, each student in this group conversed with a native speaker of English for 45 minutes on two separate occasions during the week.

Week 4 (1 Lesson: 90 minutes)

1. First, students were asked to report and discuss their observations regarding the movie homework assignment outlined in Lesson 2. (20-30 minutes).

2. Next, the Japanese students were asked to share their experience and observations conversing with the native speakers of English in Weeks 2 and 3. After sharing their general feelings regarding the conversations, the teacher instructed them to consider some of the differences in conversational style and listening behaviour between them and their partners. The teacher helped facilitate the conversation when necessary; however, the direction and ideas driving the conversation were always left up to the students to negotiate. (30-45 minutes)

3. The students were reminded that they would be conversing with a native speaker of English for the next three class periods. Students were asked to

consider some goals (i.e., what they hope to learn or achieve from this experience). Subsequently, students were asked to share their goals with each other. (15-30 minutes)

Week 5 (2 Lessons: 90 minutes total)

As in Weeks 2 and 3, each student conversed with a native speaker of English for 45 minutes on two separate occasions during the week.

Week 6 (2 Lessons: 90 minutes total)

Week 6 followed the same procedure as Weeks 2, 3 and 5.

Week 7 (2 Lessons: 90 minutes total)

Week 7 followed the same procedure as lessons 2, 3, 5 and 6.

Week 8 (1 Lesson: 90 minutes)

1. The teacher had the students discuss their experience conversing with the native speakers of English in lessons 5, 6 and 7. This was intended to build off the earlier discussion in Week 4, which involved consideration of some of the differences in conversational style and listening behaviour they had from their partners, and some of the goals they had set for the latter conversations. Again, the impetus driving the conversation was left to the students as the teacher's sole role was to facilitate the conversation. (60 minutes)

2. Each student met individually with the teacher. The student was asked to summarise their experience and describe what they thought they might have learnt from the previous eight lessons. Students were also given a chance to ask the teacher questions. (30 minutes)

Control Group

The control group in this study did not receive any instruction regarding backchannel behaviour. As explained in Section 3.3, Step 2, members of the Control group were not members of the Oral Communication 3 class or any other class involving spoken English at the time of the study. Members of the Control group were enrolled in other classes at the time of this study consisting of Physical Education, Law, History, Basic Writing, Essay Writing, Academic Writing and Seminar class.

APPENDIX F

Willingness to Communicate Scale

DIRECTIONS: Below are twenty situations in which a person might choose to communicate or not to communicate in English. Presume that the person in each situation does not speak Japanese but can speak English. Also, presume you have *completely free choice*. Indicate the percentage of times you would choose *to communicate* in each type of situation. Indicate in the space at the left what percent of the time you would choose to communicate.

0 = never, 100 = always

_____ 1. *Talk with a service station attendant.
_____ 2. *Talk with a physician.
_____ 3. Present a talk to a group of strangers.
_____ 4. Talk with an acquaintance while standing in line.
_____ 5. *Talk with a salesperson in a store.
_____ 6. Talk in a large meeting of friends.
_____ 7. *Talk with a police officer.
_____ 8. Talk in a small group of strangers.
_____ 9. Talk with a friend while standing in line.
_____ 10. *Talk with a waiter/waitress in a restaurant.
_____ 11. Talk in a large meeting of acquaintances.
_____ 12. Talk with a stranger while standing in line.
_____ 13 *Talk with a secretary.
_____ 14. Present a talk to a group of friends.
_____ 15. Talk in a small group of acquaintances.
_____ 16. *Talk with a garbage collector.
_____ 17. Talk in a large meeting of strangers.
_____ 18. *Talk with a spouse (or girl/boy friend).
_____ 19. Talk in a small group of friends.
_____ 20. Present a talk to a group of acquaintances.

N.B. JEFLs were provided with Japanese explanations. Further, the asterisk (*) marking the filler items above, as well as the scoring table below, were not included on the questionnaires the JEFLs completed.

SCORING: The WTC permits computation of one total score and seven subscores. The subscores relate to willingness to communicate in each of four common communication contexts and with three types of audiences. To compute your scores, merely add your scores for each item and divide by the number indicated below.

Subscore Desired	Scoring Formula
Group discussion	Add scores for Items 8, 15, and 19; then divide by 3.
Meetings	Add scores for Items 6, 11, and 17; then divide by 3.
Interpersonal conversations	Add scores for Items 4, 9, and 12; then divide by 3.
Public speaking	Add scores for Items 3, 14, and 20; then divide by 3.
Stranger	Add scores for Items 3, 8, 12, and 17; then divide by 4.
Acquaintance	Add scores for Items 4, 11, 15, and 20; then divide by 4.
Friend	Add scores for Items 6, 9, 14, and 19; then divide by 4.

To compute the total WTC scores, add the subscores for stranger, acquaintance, and friend. Then divide by 3.

Appendix F1:

(N.B. Due to space limitations, the pseudonyms below have been abbreviated.)

Group A's Raw Scores Relating to 20 Items of WTC Scale

GROUP A	Mic	Hi	Ar	Ha	Miy	Sa	Ch	Ay	Ta	Ka
WTC Q1	30	20	3	33	30	13	5	15	20	23
WTC Q2	55	30	4	43	46	23	50	28	30	25
WTC Q3	0	0	1	10	5	0	0	5	0	2
WTC Q4	65	60	46	63	48	44	35	40	40	38
WTC Q5	45	60	31	39	46	13	11	19	20	15
WTC Q6	60	40	33	48	55	31	11	46	40	35
WTC Q7	40	50	10	43	46	23	50	15	30	25
WTC Q8	20	70	10	10	22	10	0	23	0	2
WTC Q9	80	70	62	71	74	79	60	62	65	50
WTC Q10	25	60	15	40	28	13	6	15	30	22
WTC Q11	30	20	10	36	32	34	8	14	20	21
WTC Q12	50	50	24	49	40	12	7	24	15	29
WTC Q13	25	40	15	33	42	23	5	16	30	22
WTC Q14	45	10	32	51	62	45	38	39	40	38
WTC Q15	60	50	10	62	20	30	20	24	30	30
WTC Q16	20	10	0	15	10	13	5	8	20	21
WTC Q17	10	40	0	6	10	2	0	4	0	1
WTC Q18	100	80	72	88	96	85	66	80	70	65
WTC Q19	80	80	65	83	92	70	55	73	70	75
WTC Q20	30	30	5	54	46	28	71	10	25	18

Appendix F2:
Group B's Raw Scores Relating to 20 Items of WTC Scale

GROUP B	Ri	Sh	May	Me	Mad	Sa	Ke	Mi	Ta	Ko
WTC Q1	15	20	15	25	50	35	11	30	20	26
WTC Q2	28	24	15	35	50	45	15	40	30	50
WTC Q3	1	12	0	18	25	20	2	20	10	45
WTC Q4	48	40	34	49	60	58	36	50	53	45
WTC Q5	19	35	15	25	40	30	13	30	20	40
WTC Q6	40	40	22	49	60	60	39	68	58	51
WTC Q7	30	28	12	30	45	45	22	45	34	50
WTC Q8	15	9	10	30	40	20	4	25	12	38
WTC Q9	75	75	61	76	80	89	61	80	85	73
WTC Q10	20	18	15	25	55	35	12	30	35	40
WTC Q11	20	15	25	25	55	45	15	40	38	51
WTC Q12	27	32	10	31	40	30	20	23	36	35
WTC Q13	20	15	15	36	50	40	11	30	29	32
WTC Q14	50	50	44	46	70	69	39	68	63	61
WTC Q15	43	20	29	27	60	45	28	60	45	50
WTC Q16	2	8	12	15	40	4	6	20	9	10
WTC Q17	1	5	7	20	30	16	1	20	9	23
WTC Q18	90	80	73	83	90	93	75	80	90	83
WTC Q19	75	72	60	75	80	80	60	80	80	73
WTC Q20	45	32	20	39	50	40	31	50	50	51

Appendix F3:
Group Z's Raw Scores Relating to 20 Items of WTC Scale

GROUP Z	Ya	Mik	Ak	Yi	To	Yo	Mis	Yu	Aka	Hi
WTC Q1	50	25	30	26	41	35	44	10	35	20
WTC Q2	50	35	40	36	51	35	45	21	36	30
WTC Q3	30	15	15	16	31	25	10	2	21	20
WTC Q4	60	70	60	50	61	45	57	36	61	60
WTC Q5	50	30	25	26	41	35	40	15	30	20
WTC Q6	60	70	60	56	45	48	74	58	72	70
WTC Q7	50	34	40	36	35	32	45	32	37	30
WTC Q8	30	14	25	16	35	24	15	9	25	30
WTC Q9	85	84	85	76	81	75	85	71	84	90
WTC Q10	50	35	30	30	41	38	40	18	35	20
WTC Q11	60	35	30	46	31	38	47	23	52	50
WTC Q12	47	35	35	33	41	24	20	16	29	30
WTC Q13	50	35	40	26	40	35	42	21	30	20
WTC Q14	75	70	70	66	41	69	69	57	70	70
WTC Q15	60	60	60	66	45	43	50	33	57	50
WTC Q16	25	25	25	16	35	21	31	10	21	10
WTC Q17	27	10	30	16	40	20	10	8	15	20
WTC Q18	90	94	90	86	85	80	90	75	91	90
WTC Q19	90	84	80	76	76	72	80	71	80	80
WTC Q20	55	58	55	40	51	40	46	26	49	40

APPENDIX G

Inventory of Conversational Satisfaction for NES Interlocutors

Your Name:				Partner's name:
Key: 1 = Yes		7 = No		Date:

Please score the sentences below based on how often you thought they generally occurred in the conversation. Based on the key shown above, circle the number that best corresponds to your opinion.

1. S/he let me know that I was communicating effectively..1 2 3 4 5 6 7

2. The feelings that my partner expressed by means of listening feedback during the conversation seemed authentic (i.e., they conveyed what they were truly feeling and were not just agreeing and/or pretending to understand to keep the conversation going smoothly)..1 2 3 4 5 6 7

3. S/he showed me that s/he understood what I said...1 2 3 4 5 6 7

4. S/he showed me that s/he listened attentively to what I said...1 2 3 4 5 6 7

5. S/he expressed a lot of interest in what I had to say...1 2 3 4 5 6 7

6. The conversation went smoothly...1 2 3 4 5 6 7

7. S/he encouraged me to continue talking...1 2 3 4 5 6 7

8. S/he seemed impatient...1 2 3 4 5 6 7

9. S/he seemed cold and unfriendly...1 2 3 4 5 6 7

10. S/he was polite...1 2 3 4 5 6 7

11. S/he appeared warm and friendly...1 2 3 4 5 6 7

12. S/he was impolite...1 2 3 4 5 6 7

13. S/he appeared interested and concerned...1 2 3 4 5 6 7

14. S/he interrupted me...1 2 3 4 5 6 7

15. My conversation partner seemed to want to avoid speaking...1 2 3 4 5 6 7

16. Please include any other comments and/or observations regarding the Japanese participant's behaviour in the conversations. (Feel free to add any comments you have regarding Japanese people's listening behaviour in general.)

_____
_____
_____
_____

APPENDIX H

Inventory of Conversational Satisfaction for JEFLs

Inventory of conversational satisfaction （対話による満足度調査アンケート）

Key: 1 = Yes （最もそう思う）7 = No （全くそう思わない） Name（名前）:
Date（記入日）:

1. S/he let me know that I was communicating effectively..1 2 3 4 5 6 7
（私との会話を全体的に理解してくれているようだった）
2. I felt I was able to present myself fairly during the conversation............................1 2 3 4 5 6 7
（私は、自分の気持ちを会話の中できちんと言えたと思う）
3. S/he showed me that s/he understood what I said……...1 2 3 4 5 6 7
（相手は、私の話した内容を理解してくれていた）
4. S/he showed me that s/he listened attentively to what I said.....................................1 2 3 4 5 6 7
（相手は、私の話に注意深く耳を傾けてくれていた）
5. S/he expressed a lot of interest in what I had to say..1 2 3 4 5 6 7
（相手は、私の話す内容にとても興味がある様子だった）
6. The conversation went smoothly...1 2 3 4 5 6 7
（この対話はスムーズに進んだ）
7. S/he encouraged me to continue talking...1 2 3 4 5 6 7
（相手は、私が話を続けやすいようにサポートしてくれた）
8. S/he seemed impatient..1 2 3 4 5 6 7
（相手は、いらいらしている様子だった）
9. S/he seemed cold and unfriendly..1 2 3 4 5 6 7
（相手は、冷たい反応で、不親切だった）
10. S/he was polite...1 2 3 4 5 6 7
（相手は、丁寧な対応だった）
11. S/he appeared warm and friendly..1 2 3 4 5 6 7
（相手は、あたたかく、親切な反応だった）
12. S/he was impolite..1 2 3 4 5 6 7
（相手は、失礼な態度だった）
13. S/he appeared interested and concerned..1 2 3 4 5 6 7
（相手は、私の話に興味と関心を示してくれた）
14. S/he interrupted me...1 2 3 4 5 6 7
（相手は、私の話の邪魔や妨害、さえぎりをした）
15. My conversation partner seemed to want to avoid speaking...................................1 2 3 4 5 6 7
(彼ら自身が絶対話さなくていいように、他の人に話し続けてほしいと思っているという印象を与えている）
16. Please include any other comments and/or observations regarding the participant's behaviour in the conversations. （上記に無いコメントや意見、感想などがあれば書いてください）

_____
_____
_____

APPENDIX I

Inventory of Conversational Satisfaction for NES Observers

Date: _____   Name: _____
Key: 1 = Yes   7 = No

Please score the sentences below based on how often you thought they generally occurred in the conversation. Based on the key shown above, circle the number that best corresponds to your opinion.

1. The Japanese person let his/her partner know that the partner was communicating effectively.
....1 2 3 4 5 6 7

2. The Japanese person showed his/her partner that they understood what their partner said.
....1 2 3 4 5 6 7

3. The Japanese person showed that they were listening attentively to what their partner said.
....1 2 3 4 5 6 7

4. The Japanese participant expressed a lot of interest in what their partner had to say.
....1 2 3 4 5 6 7

5. The conversation went smoothly...1 2 3 4 5 6 7

6. The Japanese encouraged his/her partner to continue talking.....................1 2 3 4 5 6 7

7. The feelings that the Japanese person expressed by means of listening feedback seemed *authentic* (i.e., they conveyed what they were truly feeling and not just agreeing and/or pretending to understand for the sake of harmony and/or to keep the conversation going smoothly................................1 2 3 4 5 6 7

8. The Japanese person seemed impatient..1 2 3 4 5 6 7

9. The Japanese person seemed cold and unfriendly..1 2 3 4 5 6 7

10. The Japanese person was polite..1 2 3 4 5 6 7

11. The Japanese person appeared warm and friendly.....................................1 2 3 4 5 6 7

12. The Japanese person was impolite..1 2 3 4 5 6 7

13. The Japanese person appeared interested and concerned...........................1 2 3 4 5 6 7

14. The Japanese person interrupted their partner at times..............................1 2 3 4 5 6 7

15. The Japanese person seemed to want to avoid speaking............................1 2 3 4 5 6 7

16. When the Japanese person did not understand something, they were able to clearly convey this to their conversational partner with their listening feedback..1 2 3 4 5 6 7

17. The Japanese person's listening behaviour seemed inadequate in some ways.... 1 2 3 4 5 6 7
If you answered "yes" (i.e., 1, 2 or 3) to question 17, please explain how and/or why you think their listening behaviour seemed inadequate.
_____
_____
_____
_____

18. Any other comments and/or observations regarding the Japanese participant's behaviour in the conversation.
_____
_____
_____
_____

APPENDIX J

List of Potential Backchannel Functions

Which of the following corresponds to the utterance or action in the conversation?
1. Wanting the speaker to **continue** talking 話を続けて欲しいと思っている
2. Indicating **understanding** of content 内容を理解している
3. Indicating **agreement** 賛成している
4. Showing **empathy** and **support** to the speaker's evaluative statement 話し手の考えに共感し、その気持ちや考えを支持したい気持ちを表しています
5. Showing a **strong emotional response**: For example, this includes expressions such as "That's Great!" and "Excellent", and laughs which are more emphatic and louder than usual. 強く、もしくは大きく感情表現をしています（笑う、驚く、大きな動作をする、大きな声を出すなど
6. As a **minor addition** (such as to add a word in completing the utterance the speaker has just made and/or to correct something the speaker has just uttered) 　小さな情報を加えています
7. Asking for **clarification** もっと明確にしてほしいと思っています
8. Indicating **non-understanding** 内容を理解してない
9. Indicating **disagreement** or **dissatisfaction** 反対したり、不満に思ったりしている
10. **Other** その他

APPENDIX K

Data Record Sheet to Locate Instances of Miscommunication

Data record sheet

1. Wanting the speaker to continue = **CONT**
2. Indicating understanding of content = **UND**
3. Indicating agreement = **AGR**
4. Showing empathy and support to the speaker's evaluative statement = **EAS**
5. Showing a strong emotional response = **SER**
6. As a minor addition = **MA**
7. Asking for clarification = **CLAR**
8. Indicating non-understanding = **NONU**
9. Indicating disagreement or dissatisfaction = **DOD**
10. Other = **OTH**
11. Indicating boredom and/or disinterest in the conversation = **BODI**
12. Indicating impatience and a desire for the speaker to finish quickly = **IMP**
13. Giving the impression that their response was insincere = **INSI**
14. Giving the impression of not understanding but pretending to = **PRET**
15. Giving the impression that they want to keep the other person speaking strictly to avoid speaking themselves = **AVSP**

(N.B. More than one function is possible. It is also possible for the interviewee to be unsure, which would be demonstrated below with a question mark.)

Time								
JEFL BC Intentions								
NES BC Perceptions								
Analysis (notes)								
Time								
JEFL BI								
NES Perceptions								
Analysis (notes)								
Time								
JEFL BI								
NES Perceptions								
Analysis (notes)								

APPENDIX L

Sample Transcription

Transcription Conventions

➢ Listener responses are shown in italics below the primary speaker's talk at the point they occurred in the talk.

➢ To protect the identity of the participants, pseudonyms are used in the speaker labels on the left side of each transcribed line.

➢ To not confuse readers with the colons that are used for a different purpose described below, the speaker labels will be followed by a semi colon.

➢ To further preserve anonymity, pseudographs (i.e., notations in parentheses) will be used in instances where participants' private information such as name, address and/or telephone number has been uttered in the conversation.

➢ Numbers in parentheses indicate elapsed time in hundredths of seconds of pauses occurring in the conversations. Parentheses with a dot (.) indicate a micropause and/or hesitation under .5 seconds. Pauses are timed using transcription software in this study (Praat Version 5.0.18).

➢ The equal sign "=" indicates *latching* - i.e., no interval between the end of a prior piece of talk and the start of the next piece of talk.

➢ The beginnings of simultaneous speech utterances are marked by placing a left square bracket at each of the points of overlap, and placing the overlapping talk directly beneath the talk it overlaps.

➢ Right square brackets indicate the point at which two simultaneous utterances end.

Metatranscription will be shown as follows:

- Empty parentheses ( ) indicate that part of the transcription which is unintelligible.

- Words between parentheses indicate the transcribers' conjecture at the words or utterances in the conversation that they are not completely certain of.

- Words between double parentheses may indicate comments and/or features of the audio materials other than actual verbalisation.

- L stands for laughter.

Other than apostrophes, which are used to show contraction between words, punctuation symbols in these transcriptions are not used as regular English punctuation markers indicating grammatical category. While other, non-regular, grammatical functions are shown by symbols such as slashes and double slashes, other punctuation symbols such as question marks and colons are used to indicate prosodic features in these transcriptions.

Nonverbal behaviour is shown by the symbols indicated below.
- h stands for audible breathing.
- ^ stands for vertical head movement (head nod).
- > stands for horizontal head movement (head shake).
- S stands for smile.
- " indicates that eyebrows are raised.
- G indicates body or hand gestures.

In cases where nonverbal behaviour occurs concurrently with speech, symbols are placed directly above the speech it co-occurs with (instances where two types of nonverbal behaviour occur simultaneously are shown by underlining them both). Nonverbal behaviour that is continuous and occurs for a period longer than 2 seconds will be noted by signalling the beginning and the end of the behaviour in parentheses where it occurs in the conversation.

N.B. The parentheses containing the symbols below are solely used for separation purposes to make them easily identifiable in the specific examples below. Parentheses will not be used in this manner in the transcriptions as they have other specific functions, which have been outlined above.

- A slash (/) marks the grammatical completion point of an internal clause boundary (i.e., a clause which is continuative).

- Two slashes side by side (//) mark the grammatical completion point of a final clause boundary (i.e., a clause which terminative).

N.B. A final clause boundary is one that makes complete sense (i.e., fully meaningful) and could end the utterance there. In contrast, an internal clause is one in which the meaning is not complete, and there is a requirement for the utterance to go on in order for the meaning to be complete.

- A question mark (?) at the end of a word and/or utterance indicates a clear rising vocal pitch or intonation (i.e., one that is clearly heard, and is shown to rise by at least 600 Hz using Praat software).

- An inverted question mark (¿) at the end of a word and/or utterance indicates a clear falling pitch or intonation (i.e., one that is clearly heard and is shown to fall by at least 600 Hz using Praat software).

- A colon (:) as in the word "ye:s" indicates the stretching of the sound it follows (i.e., only marked in cases where the stretching was extended greater than .5 seconds).

- A hyphen at the end of an uncompleted word indicates the disfluency of a truncated word. For instance, if the word "bird" were truncated, it may be transcribed as "bir-".

- A part of a word and/or phrase containing CAPITAL letters indicates that it has been said with increased volume and/or more emphatically than the rest of the phrase (i.e., only marked when the highest point of the stressed part of speech was 10 decibels greater than the lowest part of the surrounding speech).

- The underscore sign (_) indicates that the talk it precedes is low in volume.

➤ (~) indicates that the talk which follows is consistent with the person's regular voice and tone. This symbol is to be used after low volume talk to indicate the point in which the volume rises back to normal. When a pause occurs after the low volume talk and the talk that follows returns to normal, this symbol will not be shown.

Conversation 19 (Post-test 2)

1. Andrea;   is it a is a type of money// (.)

          ^   G
2. Chieko;   yeah (.) and ( ) (.) _ (nantake) (.)

          G   G   ^   S ^ ^
3. Andrea;   a (.) rubber bands like a like this// (.) looks like this// =   = [ok (yeah yeah yeah)]

                                                  ^ ^ ^ G S
                                            = yeah yeah yeah = [(   )]

4. Chieko;   so (1.30) so (.65) she said (.90) maybe (.51) _ (she, said) (.) me maybe (1.22)

                ((G begins))
5. Chieko;   i saw¿ (.) i saw every day/ that [(brown)] money// (2.12) (um) (.)

                                ^ ^
                           [(yeah)]

                ((G ends))
6. Chieko;   maybe i'm crazy// [Lh   ] Lh =

                            >   ^   S   ^
                                [(yeah yeah)]

               G   ((G begins))
7. Andrea;   = that's how i feel// (.51) like people will come up with (.) (uu) (.)

                                ^

8. Andrea;   like (.) ten thousand dollars// (.)   (.) (   ) =   (.)

                                            G
                              mmm   = ten thousand

                          ((G ends))
9. Andrea;   hyaku man en (.88) about (.73) _ (wait here) (.)   (.)

                                          ^
                              ten (.) (a soka)

```
                          ^
10. Chieko;    ten [thousand]              (.) hyaku man en (.)

                              ^   ^
               [(       )] mm mhm
```

```
11. Andrea;    hyaku man en i think (.99) i think right? (.93) no no no (.65)
                                                         ^
```

```
12. Chieko;    no ju man en =              (.)

                                ^
                                = yeah ju man en
```

```
                     ^  ((G begins))  ^
13. Andrea;    no hyaku no hyaku man =      = hyaku man en. (1.27)

                                     = mm =
```

```
14. Andrea;    wait// =      [ Lh ] i'm confused// (.54) _ ( ) (1.07) (hyaku   ) (1.41)

                     = Lh  [ Lh ]
```

```
15. Chieko;    hey [teachers name] Lh (.)
```

```
                         ^   ^             G
16. Andrea;    [ ah ] hyaku man en =       (.) ten thousand dollars about (.)
                                                                    ^
               [(  )]           = hyaku man men
```

```
               G
17. Andrea;    it's about hyaku man en// =       (.) and they (.) and it's (.)
                                             ^
                                             = _ (mm)
```

```
                     >  >                ((G begins))
18. Andrea;    you cannot use credit cards// (.59) [you] can only use cash// (.)
                                                                    ^
                                                   [(m )]
```

```
19. Andrea;    (   ) so like real money paper money. (.)    = and so they ha:nd it/ to me// (.)
                                                                                       ^ S
                                           _ (mm) =
```

```
                              S
20. Andrea;  and i'm like (.) [(ooo oh my god)]//    = like h (.) to me i look at that money//
                              G                        ^                              ^
                              [(ooo    Lh   )]  Lh  =
```

```
21. Andrea;  and i say [like] (.) kay (.) this money in this hand i could buy a car// (.)
                                                      ^
                       [(L )]                                                     Lh =
```

```
22. Andrea;  = and i'm like (.50) car (.) [(my)] oh my (.) [(gosh)]// (.) (  ) (.)
                                          [(Lh)]          [(Lh)]
```

```
                  >              ((G ends))
23. Andrea;  cuz i mean i don't have th[at much mon]ey// (.)       = like definitely =
                                      [ ( _Lh ) ]           yeah =
```

```
                         G
24. Chieko;  = maybe i think (.) (  ) i want to (.) i want to (1.54)
```

```
                                  G
25. Andrea;  (you're like [i don't know]// _ (    ) (.)      [(    )] (.) [(    )] (  ) (.51)
                          G
                         [  (Lh)  ]                    _(Lh) [(    )]   [(    )]
```

```
             ((G begins))                                  ((G ends))
26. Andrea;  aaa (.) but it makes me very nervous/ (.62) [(to to)] handle that much money// aaa (.53)
                                                                                                ^
                                                        [(mm)]
```

```
                         G
27. Chieko;  so (.57) if (.) if you (.) mistake/ (.) very (.) very =     = big (.) problem// (.65)
                          ^       ^                                 G"
                                                                 = (A) =
```

```
                                    ((G begins))
28. Andrea;  [(aa aa a)] big problem// so at the end of the day (.)
             [(       )]                                          _ (mm) =
```

```
29. Andrea;  = if if i make a mistake/ i have to count my money?// (.)         (.)
                                      ^
                                                                           mm
```

```
30. Andrea;  and (.) say i made a mistake/ of a hundred dollars/ (.65) then (.)
                                                                  ^
```

```
                                       S
31. Andrea;   that one hundred dollars/ i have to pay//        (1.19)          that's why/ it's very like (.57)
                                           ((surprised expression))
```

```
32. Andrea;   ok (.) [you be very]  careful// and you count everything//
                     [(          )]
```

```
              ((G ends))
33. Andrea;   [like one two three four five] =
              _ [(                        )]
```

```
34. Chieko;   = that's very nervous job// =
```

```
                    ^  ^  S  ^
35. Andrea;   = yeah it makes me very nervous// =          (.) but you get (.)
                                                      ^
                                              = _ (yeah)
```

```
              ((G begins))              ((G ends))
36. Andrea;   you make lots of money// (.65) [ big ] pay check// like your salary is very big// (.77)
                                                                                          ^ ^
                                             [mm]
```

```
37. Andrea;   but if you make a mistake/ (.85) then (.)
                                        ^
```

```
                      G
38. Chieko;   [you should] pay// (.)         = (own) (.54)
                      S                 ^
              [ sometimes ]          yeah =
```

```
                      ^      ^
39. Andrea;   yeah your own money// so it's kind of (.59) one year i made a mistake of (1.07)
```

```
40. Andrea;   sixty five dollars// (.)         (.) which is abo:ut (.) nana (.) sen en// =         (.)
                                                _ (sixty five)                                = _ (nn )
```

```
                      G                          G    S
41. Andrea;   and so i had to pay that back// i was like [(ooo ooo ooo)]
                                                                  S
                                                         [ (ooooooooo) ]   Lh =
```

```
                  >    >    S
42. Andrea;   = i was so not happy// =
```

43. Chieko;   = (   ) (.) _ (just a little big money) =

```
                      ^  ^  ^              " G
```
44. Andrea;   = yeah kind of a lot// (.) but my friend (.79) made a mistake// o:f (.)

```
                                           ^
```
45. Andrea;   one hundred (and) eighty dollars// (.99) so: (.)   (.)

```
                                            _ (ichi man)
```

46. Andrea;   yeah ichi ma:n (1.22) kyuu

APPENDIX M

Individual Backchannel Frequencies of Cross-sectional Data

Related to the findings presented in Section 4.2, the table below is included to show how the individual observations of the data set are dispersed around the mean ($\bar{x}$). Thus, the table below shows the number of interlocutor (IL) words between backchannels (BCs) for each participant in both cultural groups. N.B. The names of the NESs are provided because each NES interlocutor participated in multiple conversations, whereas each JEFL participated in only one conversation.

NES Key: Betty = BE, Jason = JA, JE = Jerry

JEFLs		NESs	
BC/IL word $\bar{x} = 6.46$ (SD = 1.36)	Number of Occurrences	BC/IL word $\bar{x} = 7.38$ (SD = 2.12)	Number of Occurrences
4.42	1	4.72	1 BE
4.72	1	4.77	1 BE
4.97	1	4.81	1 JA
5.05	1	5.07	1 BE
5.07	2	5.55	1 BE
5.10	1	5.80	1 BE
5.41	1	6.00	2 BE, BE
5.59	1	6.08	1 BE
5.63	1	6.13	1 BE
5.69	1	6.42	1 BE
5.94	1	6.50	1 BE
6.00	2	6.67	1 BE
6.22	1	6.75	1 BE
6.40	1	6.83	1 JA
6.66	1	7.00	3 JE, BE, BE
6.70	3	7.14	1 BE

6.77	1	7.25	1 BE
6.91	1	7.29	1 BE
7.24	1	7.40	1 BE
7.28	1	7.50	1 BE
7.84	1	9.33	1 JA
7.87	1	10.27	1 JE
8.14	1	10.75	1 BE
8.88	1	10.90	1 BE
9.00	1	11.00	2 JE, BE
9.92	1	12.50	1 BE
Total	30	Total	30

APPENDIX N

Spearman rho Correlation Analyses of Cross-sectional Data

Key for Terms: BCs = Backchannels, SSBs = Simultaneous Speech Backchannels (not including laughter), EXBCs = Extended Backchannels, MINBCs = Minimal Backchannels, WORDS = Number of Words

Correlations between the JEFLs' frequencies of each conversational feature (shown on the left) and the NES observers' ratings on each item of the conversational satisfaction questionnaire (shown on the right) are shown as follows: * = $p<.05$, ** = $p<.01$

Spearman's rho		ITEM01	ITEM02	ITEM03	ITEM04	ITEM05	ITEM06
BCs	Correlation Coefficient	-.326	-.398(*)	-.260	-.283	-.415(*)	-.530(**)
	Sig. (2-tailed)	.078	.029	.166	.130	.023	.003
	N	30	30	30	30	30	30
SSBs	Correlation Coefficient	-.615(**)	-.575(**)	-.439(*)	-.678(**)	-.554(**)	-.682(**)
	Sig. (2-tailed)	.001	.001	.015	.001	.001	.001
	N	30	30	30	30	30	30
EXBCs	Correlation Coefficient	-.498(**)	-.468(**)	-.340	-.523(**)	-.364(*)	-.466(**)
	Sig. (2-tailed)	.005	.009	.066	.003	.048	.009
	N	30	30	30	30	30	30
MINBCs	Correlation Coefficient	-.206	-.284	-.178	-.153	-.315	-.342
	Sig. (2-tailed)	.275	.129	.346	.419	.090	.064
	N	30	30	30	30	30	30
WORDS	Correlation Coefficient	-.366(*)	-.383(*)	-.233	-.345	-.179	-.167
	Sig. (2-tailed)	.047	.037	.216	.062	.344	.378
	N	30	30	30	30	30	30

Spearman's rho		ITEM07	ITEM08	ITEM09	ITEM10	ITEM11	ITEM12
BCs	Correlation Coefficient	-.253	.352	.328	-.220	-.277	.341
	Sig. (2-tailed)	.177	.056	.077	.243	.139	.065
	N	30	30	30	30	30	30
SSBs	Correlation Coefficient	-.489(**)	.375(*)	.250	-.343	-.498(**)	.449(*)
	Sig. (2-tailed)	.006	.041	.183	.064	.005	.013
	N	30	30	30	30	30	30
EXBCs	Correlation Coefficient	-.341	.240	.324	-.334	-.605(**)	.325
	Sig. (2-tailed)	.065	.202	.081	.071	.001	.080
	N	30	30	30	30	30	30
MINBCs	Correlation Coefficient	-.185	.307	.215	-.169	-.081	.311
	Sig. (2-tailed)	.329	.099	.255	.373	.669	.095
	N	30	30	30	30	30	30
WORDS	Correlation Coefficient	-.477(**)	-.068	.283	-.136	-.278	.146
	Sig. (2-tailed)	.008	.720	.130	.472	.137	.441
	N	30	30	30	30	30	30

Assessing Pragmatic Competence in the Japanese EFL Context

Spearman's rho		ITEM13	ITEM14	ITEM15	ITEM16	ITEM17
BCs	Correlation Coefficient	-.290	-.265	.185	-.173	.306
	Sig. (2-tailed)	.121	.157	.329	.360	.100
	N	30	30	30	30	30
SSBs	Correlation Coefficient	-.607(**)	-.250	.400(*)	-.460(*)	.526(**)
	Sig. (2-tailed)	.001	.183	.028	.011	.003
	N	30	30	30	30	30
EXBCs	Correlation Coefficient	-.493(**)	-.169	.468(**)	-.416(*)	.561(**)
	Sig. (2-tailed)	.006	.372	.009	.022	.001
	N	30	30	30	30	30
MINBCs	Correlation Coefficient	-.098	-.174	.041	-.050	.187
	Sig. (2-tailed)	.607	.357	.829	.792	.323
	N	30	30	30	30	30
WORDS	Correlation Coefficient	-.343	-.153	.591(**)	-.473(**)	.268
	Sig. (2-tailed)	.064	.419	.001	.008	.152
	N	30	30	30	30	30

Key explaining significant findings above:

BCs
- Item 2: As the number of JEFL backchannels increased, the more the NES observers believed the JEFLs to be showing understanding ($p<.029$).
- Item 5: As the number of JEFL backchannels increased, the more the NES observers felt the conversation went smoothly ($p<.023$).
- Item 6: As the number of JEFL backchannels increased, the more the NES observers believed them to be encouraging their interlocutor to continue speaking ($p<.003$).

SSBCs
- Item 1: As the number of JEFL non-laughter SSBs increased, the more the NES observers felt the JEFLs were letting their partner know they were communicating effectively ($p<.001$).

- Item 2: As the number of JEFL non-laughter SSBs increased, the more the NES observers felt the JEFLs were showing that they understood their partner ($p<.001$).
- Item 3: As the number of JEFL non-laughter SSBs increased, the more the NES observers felt the JEFLs were listening attentively to what their partner said ($p<.015$).
- Item 4: As the number of JEFL non-laughter SSBs increased, the more the NES observers felt the JEFLs expressed a lot of interest in what their partner had to say ($p<.001$).
- Item 5: As the number of JEFL non-laughter SSBs increased, the more the NES observers felt the conversation went smoothly ($p<.001$).
- Item 6: As the number of JEFL non-laughter SSBs increased, the more the NES observers believed the JEFLs to be encouraging their interlocutor to continue speaking ($p<.001$).
- Item 7: As the number of JEFL non-laughter SSBs increased, the more the NES observers believed the JEFLs to be expressing themselves in an authentic and sincere manner ($p<.006$).
- Item 8: As the number of JEFL non-laughter SSBs increased, the less the NES observers felt the JEFLs to be impatient ($p<.041$).
- Item 11: As the number of JEFL non-laughter SSBs increased, the more the NES observers felt the JEFLs to be warm and friendly ($p<.005$).
- Item 12: As the number of JEFL non-laughter SSBs increased, the less the NES observers believed the JEFLs to be impolite ($p<.013$).
- Item 13: As the number of JEFL non-laughter SSBs increased, the more the NES observers believed the JEFLs to be interested and concerned ($p<.001$).
- Item 15: As the number of JEFL non-laughter SSBs increased, the less the NES observers believed the JEFLs wanted to avoid speaking ($p<.028$).
- Item 16: As the number of JEFL non-laughter SSBs increased, the more the NES observers believed the JEFLs were able to express that they did not understand ($p<.011$).
- Item 17: As the number of JEFL non-laughter SSBs increased, the less the NES observers believed the JEFLs' listening behaviour to be inadequate ($p<.003$).

EXBCs
- Item 1: As the number of JEFL extended responses increased, the more the NES observers felt the JEFLs were letting their partner know they were communicating effectively ($p<.005$).
- Item 2: As the number of JEFL extended responses increased, the more the NES observers felt the JEFLs were showing that they understood their partner ($p<.009$).
- Item 4: As the number of JEFL extended responses increased, the more the NES observers felt the JEFLs expressed a lot of interest in what their partner had to say ($p<.003$).
- Item 5: As the number of JEFL extended responses increased, the more the NES observers felt the conversation went smoothly ($p<.048$).
- Item 6: As the number of JEFL extended responses increased, the more the NES observers believed the JEFLs to be encouraging their interlocutor to continue speaking ($p<.009$).
- Item 11: As the number of JEFL extended responses increased, the more the NES observers felt the JEFLs to be warm and friendly ($p<.001$).
- Item 13: As the number of JEFL extended responses increased, the more the NES observers believed the JEFLs to be interested and concerned ($p<.006$).
- Item 15: As the number of JEFL extended responses increased, the less the NES observers believed the JEFLs wanted to avoid speaking ($p<.009$).
- Item 16: As the number of JEFL extended responses increased, the more the NES observers believed the JEFLs were able to express that they did not understand ($p<.022$).
- Item 17: As the number of JEFL extended responses increased, the less the NES observers believed the JEFLs' listening behaviour to be inadequate ($p<.001$).

MINBCs
No significant findings were observed.

WORDS
- Item 1: As the number of JEFL words increased, the more the NES observers felt the JEFLs were letting their partner know they were communicating effectively ($p<.047$).
- Item 2: As the number of JEFL words increased, the more the NES observers felt the JEFLs were showing that they understood their partner ($p<.037$).
- Item 7: As the number of JEFL words increased, the more the NES observers believed the JEFLs to be expressing themselves in an authentic and sincere manner ($p<.008$).
- Item 15: As the number of JEFL words increased, the less the NES observers believed the JEFLs wanted to avoid speaking ($p<.001$).
- Item 16: As the number of JEFL words increased, the more the NES observers believed the JEFLs were able to express that they did not understand ($p<.008$).

APPENDIX O

Correlation Analyses Involving JEFL Scores and Performance

Key explaining dependent variables in order presented below: Total Words, Frequency (number of backchannels per interlocutor word), Number of Questions, MinBack (percentage of backchannels constituted by minimal backchannels), ExtBack (percentage of backchannels constituted by extended backchannels), BCPauses (percentage of pauses in which backchannels occur), BCCB (percentage of overall clausal boundaries attracting backchannels), FinalBCs (percentage of clause final boundaries attracting backchannels), BCGestures (percentage of gestures eliciting backchannels), SSBs (simultaneous speech backchannels), NLSSBs (non-laughter simultaneous speech backchannels), LsSSBs (laughter simultaneous speech backchannels), NONU (number of non-understanding situations), UNCONV (percentage of non-understanding situations constituted by unconventional backchannels), MinimalRep (percentage of non-understanding situations constituted by minimal backchannel as repair strategies), FullTotal (percentage of non-understanding situations constituted by Full-turn repair strategies) and CRSNONU (percentage of non-understanding situations constituted by conversational repair strategies).

Pre-test

	Extraversion	L2WTC	TOEIC
pre_TotalWords	.02	.14	.50 **
pre_Frequency	-.01	.26	.15
pre_Questions	.10	.42 *	.47 **
pre_MinBack	-.05	-.29	-.45 *
pre_ExtBack	.29	.44 *	.51 **
pre_BCPauses	-.15	-.22	-.16
pre_BCCB	-.04	-.04	-.16
pre_FinalBCS	-.11	-.05	-.25
pre_BCGestures	-.07	-.16	.10
pre_SSBs	.15	.02	.26
pre_NLSSBs	.20	.17	.42 *
pre_LsSBBs	-.03	-.27	-.13
pre_NONU	.11	-.22	-.44 *
pre_UNCONV	-.16	-.23	-.42 *
pre_MinimalRep	.16	.23	.14
pre_FullTotal	.17	.38	.19
pre_CRSNONU	.45 *	.00	-.14

† p < .10, * p < .05, ** p < .01

Post-test 1

	Extraversion	L2WTC	TOEIC
post1_TotalWords	.34 †	.27	.43 *
post1_Frequency	-.31 †	-.16	.11
post1_Questions	-.08	-.11	.19
post1_MinBack	-.12	.15	.11
post1_ExtBack	.04	-.20	-.16
post1_BCPauses	.00	-.03	.14
post1_BCCB	.05	-.07	-.25
post1_FinalBCS	-.03	.04	.13
post1_BCGestures	.33 †	-.04	-.23
post1_SSBs	.41 *	.32 †	.41 *
post1_NLSSBs	.27	.27	.34 †
post1_LsSBBs	.37 *	.32 †	.37 *
post1_NONU	-.15	-.15	-.25
post1_UNCONV	.07	.26	-.03
post1_MinimalRep	-.07	-.26	.03
post1_FullTotal	-.14	-.05	-.11
post1_CRSNONU	.03	-.08	-.13

† p < .10, * p < .05, ** p < .01

Post-test 2

	Extraversion	L2WTC	TOEIC
post2_TotalWords	.19	.14	-.06
post2_Frequency	.01	.12	.21
post2_Questions	-.11	-.04	.22
post2_MinBack	.09	.35 †	.09
post2_ExtBack	-.12	-.23	.10
post2_BCPauses	.05	.04	-.21
post2_BCCB	.02	-.11	-.18
post2_FinalBCS	-.22	.07	-.28
post2_BCGestures	.07	-.17	-.29
post2_SSBs	.30	.22	.19
post2_NLSSBs	.23	.37 *	.30
post2_LsSSBs	.31 †	.05	-.01
post2_NONU	.07	-.17	-.32 †
post2_UNCONV	.07	.31 †	.07
post2_MinimlRep	-.05	-.35 †	-.15
post2_FullTotal	.04	.00	-.16
post2_CRSNONU	.26	-.02	-.22

† p < .10, * p < .05, ** p < .01

APPENDIX P

Development of Successful/Non-Successful JEFLs

Key: (1) Observations: A. Frequency = difference in number of interlocutor words between backchannels (from the Pre-test to Post-test 2), B. Variability = difference in percentage of backchannels constituted by extended backchannels, C. DCs = difference in percentage of clause final boundaries attracting BCs and D. SSBs = difference in percentage of backchannels constituted by non-laughter SSBs. (2) Involvement: A. WTC = difference in WTC scores, B. Words = difference in number of words and C. Questions = difference in number of questions asked. (3) Repair ability: A. BCs at NONU = difference in percentage of non-understanding situations constituted by unconventional BCs and B. CRS at NONU = difference in percentage of non-understanding situations constituted by full-turn conversational repair strategies. (4) ICC: difference in the overall scores (as associated with positive perceptions) of NES observer on the ICC questionnaire.

Successful

Improvement Categories	Explicit (TOEIC score)	
	Chieko (445)	Takanori (504)
(1) Observations		
A. Frequency	2.22	.48
B. Variability	29	31
C. DCs	-15	4
D. SSBs	-17	-7
(2) Involvement		
A. WTC	13	19
B. Words	-15	-8
C. Questions	same	1
(3) Repair Ability		
A. BCs at NONU	100	50
B. CRS at NONU	100	50
(4) ICC	16	11

Non- successful

Improvement Categories	Implicit (TOEIC score)			
	Shio (630)	Madora (500)	Sachi (475)	Keiko (560)
(1) Observations				
A. Frequency	.1	-.2	2.72	-.2
B. Variability	-3	3	14	same
C. DCs	-11	-25	12	5
D. SSBs	6	-5	2	2
(2) Involvement				
A. WTC	1	-5	2	1
B. Words	29	-84	-13	29
C. Questions	same	-2	same	same
(3) Repair Ability				
A. BCs at NONU	17	same	-7	same
B. CRS at NONU	same	same	same	same
(4) ICC	2	-1	2	1

APPENDIX Q

Development of Higher/Lower Proficiency JEFLs

Key: (see Appendix P)

Improvement Categories	Explicit (TOEIC score)		Implicit (TOEIC score)	
	Michiko (700)	Ayuka (360)	Rika (685)	Mika (390)
(1) Observations				
A. Frequency	6.14	2.14	2.32	4.22
B. Variability	10	8	6	9
C. DCs	31	-14	-25	-26
D. SSBs	-2	1	21	12
(2) Involvement				
A. WTC	5	8	20	4
B. Words	-30	50	50	59
C. Questions	0	2	1	-1
(3) Repair Ability				
A. BCs at NONU	-60	-12	-34	-25
B. CRS at NONU	67	13	33	0
(4) ICC	7	2	2	5

APPENDIX R

NES Interlocutors' Mean Ratings of JEFLs

Explicit

Items on the Questionnaire Scale ranges from 1 (strongly agree) to 7 (strongly disagree).	Pre $\bar{x}$	Post 1 $\bar{x}$	Post 2 $\bar{x}$
1. S/he let me know that I was communicating effectively.	1.9	1.6	2.1
2. The feelings that my partner expressed by means of listening feedback during the conversation seemed authentic.	1.6	2.4	2.2
3. S/he showed me that s/he understood what I said (for NESs only).	1.35	1.8	2.5
4. S/he showed me that s/he listened attentively to what I said.	1.6	1.2	1.4
5. S/he expressed a lot of interest in what I had to say.	1.5	1.2	1.3
6. The conversation went smoothly.	1.85	1.8	2.2
7. S/he encouraged me to continue talking.	2.1	1.3	2.2
8. S/he seemed impatient.	6.8	6.9	6.7
9. S/he seemed cold and unfriendly.	6.9	6.9	6.9
10. S/he was polite.	1.1	1	1.1
11. S/he appeared warm and friendly.	1.8	1.1	1.4
12. S/he was impolite.	6.9	7	6.9
13. S/he appeared interested and concerned.	1.7	1.3	2
14. S/he interrupted me.	6.6	7	6.4
15. My conversation partner seemed to want to avoid speaking.	5.9	6.7	6.3

Implicit

Items on the Questionnaire Scale ranges from 1 (strongly agree) to 7 (strongly disagree).	Pre $\bar{x}$	Post 1 $\bar{x}$	Post 2 $\bar{x}$
1. S/he let me know that I was communicating effectively.	1.35	2	1.7
2. S/he showed me that s/he understood what I said (for NESs only).	1.45	2	2.1
3. The feelings that my partner expressed by means of listening feedback during the conversation seemed authentic.	1.6	2.5	2.9
4. S/he showed me that s/he listened attentively to what I said.	1.2	1.4	1.6
5. S/he expressed a lot of interest in what I had to say.	1.3	1.6	2.2
6. The conversation went smoothly.	1.5	1.9	2.4
7. S/he encouraged me to continue talking.	1	1.5	2.3
8. S/he seemed impatient.	6.7	6.7	6.6
9. S/he seemed cold and unfriendly.	6.7	7	6.4
10. S/he was polite.	1.1	1	1.2
11. S/he appeared warm and friendly.	1.9	1.2	2.2
12. S/he was impolite.	6.9	7	6.9
13. S/he appeared interested and concerned.	1.3	1.5	2
14. S/he interrupted me.	6.5	6.9	6.7
15. My conversation partner seemed to want to avoid speaking.	6.7	6.5	6.3

Control

Items on the Questionnaire Scale ranges from 1 (strongly agree) to 7 (strongly disagree).	Pre $\bar{x}$	Post 1 $\bar{x}$	Post 2 $\bar{x}$
1. S/he let me know that I was communicating effectively.	1.8	1.5	2.1
2. The feelings that my partner expressed by means of listening feedback during the conversation seemed authentic.	2.4	1.9	3
3. S/he showed me that s/he understood what I said (for NESs only).	1.55	1.4	2.4
4. S/he showed me that s/he listened attentively to what I said.	1.1	1.3	2
5. S/he expressed a lot of interest in what I had to say.	1.3	1.4	1.8
6. The conversation went smoothly.	1.4	1.5	2.3
7. S/he encouraged me to continue talking.	1.2	1.7	2.3
8. S/he seemed impatient.	6.7	6.8	6.2
9. S/he seemed cold and unfriendly.	6.9	6	6.3
10. S/he was polite.	1.1	1.1	1.4
11. S/he appeared warm and friendly.	1.6	1.5	2.5
12. S/he was impolite.	7	6.9	6.8
13. S/he appeared interested and concerned.	1.2	1.5	1.8
14. S/he interrupted me.	6.5	6.7	6
15. My conversation partner seemed to want to avoid speaking.	7	6.8	5.8

APPENDIX S

The Six Research Questions (RQs) of this Study

(N.B. See Section 2.10 for details describing the rationale and development of these RQs.)

RQ 1: How do participants from each culture, Japanese and American, use backchannels differently in terms of frequency, variability, use in different discourse contexts, and use during their interlocutor's primary speaking turn at talk (i.e., creating simultaneous speech)?

RQ 2: Will the differences in backchannel behaviour across cultures affect communication and/or lead to miscommunication, and if so, how will this occur?

RQ 3: Will instructional treatment help facilitate the JEFL learners' conversational skills according to the backchannel assessment criteria outlined in Section 2.9?

RQ 4: If so, will explicit treatments be more effective than implicit ones (a) in the short term and (b) in the long term?

RQ 5: What are some of the common characteristics pertaining to the JEFL learners that exhibited competent backchannel behaviour and/or improvement in this area compared to those that did not?

RQ 6: Do student L2 proficiency levels, according to the TOEIC, correlate to their levels and gains in listening behaviour?

BIBLIOGRAPHY

Agawa, T. (2002). Differences in backchannel behaviour in cross language/cross cultural communication. Paper presented at AILA 2002, Singapore, 13th World Congress of Applied Linguistics (16-21 December).

Akasu, K. & Asao, K. (1993). Sociolinguistic factors influencing communication in Japan and the United States. In W. Gudykunst (Ed.), *In Communication in Japan and the United States* (pp. 88-121). Albany: New York State University Press.

Allwood, J. (1976). Linguistic communication as action and cooperation. *Gothenburg Monographs in Linguistics,* 2(1). Göteborg: Göteborg University, Department of Linguistics.

—. (1985). Tvarkulturell kommunikation. In J. Allwood (Ed.), *Tvarkulturell kommunikation, Papers in Anthropological Linguistics, Volume 12* (pp. 9-61). Göteborg: Göteborg University Press.

Apltekin, C. & Apltekin, M. (1984). The question of culture: EFL teaching in non-EFL speaking countries. *ELT Journal,* 38(1), 14-20.

Alymursy, A. & Wilson, J. (2001). Towards a definition of Egyptian complimenting. *Multilingua - Journal of Cross-Cultural and Interlanguage Communication,* 20(1), 133-154.

Ammon, U. (2003). Global English and the non-native speaker: Overcoming disadvantage. In H. Tonkin & T. Reagan (Eds.), *Language in the 21st century* (pp. 23-34). Amsterdam: John Benjamins.

Anderson, F. (1993). The enigma of the college classroom: Nails that don't stick up. In P. Wadden (Ed.), *A Handbook for Teaching English at Japanese Colleges and Universities* (pp. 101-110). New York: Oxford University Press.

Anderson, J. R. (1983). *The Architecture of Cognition.* Cambridge, MA: Harvard University Press.

Anderson, J. R. & Lebriere, C. (1998). *The Atomic Components of Thought.* Mahwah, NJ: Erlbaum.

Arima, M. (1989). Japanese culture versus schizophrenic interpretation. *Text,* 9(1), 351-365.

Armour, W. (2001). This guy is Japanese stuck in a white man's body: A discussion of meaning making, identity slippage, and cross-cultural adaptation. *Journal of Multilingual and Multicultural Development,* 22(1), 1-18.

—. (2004). Becoming a Japanese language learner, user, and teacher: Revelations from life history research. *Journal of Language, Identity, and Education,* 3(1), 101-125.

Asker, B. (1998). Student reticence and oral testing: A Hong Kong study of willingness to communicate. *Communication Research Reports,* 15(2), 162-169.

Aston, G. U. (1986). Trouble-shooting in interaction with learners: The more the merrier? *Applied Linguistics,* 7(1), 128-143.

Auer, P. (1996). On the prosody and syntax of turn-continuations. In E. Couper-Kuhlen & M. Selting (Eds.), *Prosody in Conversation* (pp. 57-100). Cambridge: Cambridge University Press.

Bardovi-Harlig, K. (1996). Pragmatics and language teaching: Bringing pragmatics and pedagogy together. In L. F. Bouton (Ed.), *Pragmatics and Language Learning* (pp. 21-39). Urbana-Champaign: University of Illinois.

—. (2001). Evaluating the empirical evidence: Grounds for instruction in pragmatics?. In K. R. Rose & G. Kasper (Eds.), *Pragmatics in Language Teaching* (pp. 11-32). Cambridge: Cambridge University Press.

Barnlund, D. (1974). The public self and the private self in Japan and the United States. In G. Condon & M. Sato (Eds.), *Intercultural Encounters with Japan* (pp. 27-96). Tokyo: Simul Press.

Barnlund, D. & Araki, S. (1985). Intercultural encounters: The management of compliments by Japanese and Americans. *Journal of Cross-Cultural Psychology,* 16(1), 9-26.

Beamer, L. (1992). Learning intercultural communication competence. *The Business Communication,* 29(1), 285-303.

Beattie, G. W. (1983). *Talk. An Analysis of Speech and Non-Verbal Behaviour in Conversation.* Milton Keynes: Open University Press.

Beebe, L. & Takahashi, T. (1989). Do you have a bag? Social status and patterned variation in second language acquisition. In S. Gass, C. Madden, D. Preston & L. Selinker (Eds.), *Variation in Second Language Acquisition, Volume 1: Discourse and Pragmatics* (pp. 103-125). Philadelphia: Multilingua Matters.

Beebe, L., Takahashi, T. & R. Uliss-Weltz (1990). Pragmatic transfer in ESL refusals. In Scarcella, R. (Ed.), *Developing Communicative Competence in a Second Language* (pp. 55-74). Rowley: Newbury House.

Befu, H. (1980a). A critique of the group model of Japanese society. *Social Analysis,* 5/6, 29-48.

—. (1980b). The group model of Japanese society and it's alternative. *Rice University Studies,* 66(1), 169-187.

Benzhi Magazine (2008). *EFL vs. ESL What is the difference?* [online] Available from: http://www.benzhi.com/content/view/22/1/ (Date viewed 22 January 2009).

Bhaskaran, N. (1997). ESL/EFL Dichotomy today: Language politics and pragmatics. *TESOL Quarterly,* 31(1), 9-38.

Billmyer, K. (1990). "I really like your lifestyle": ESL learners learning how to compliment. *Working Papers in Educational Linguistics,* 6(1), 31-48.

Bjørge, A. K. (2009). Conflict or cooperation: The use of backchannelling in ELF negotiations. *English for Specific Purposes,* 10(1), 1-13.

Blanche, P. (1987). The case for a pedagogy of pragmatics in foreign or second language teaching. *RELC Journal,* 18(1), 46-71.

Blommaert, J. (1998). Different approaches to intercultural communication: A critical survey. Plenary Lecture, Lerner und Arbeten in einer international vernetzen und multikulturellen Gesellschaft, Expertentagung Universität Bremen, Institut für Projektmanagement und Witschafsinformatik (IPMI), 27-28 February 1998.

Blundell, J., Higgens, J. & Middlemiss, N. (1982). *Function in English.* Oxford: Oxford University Press.

Books, M. (1995). *Communication styles of Japanese and Americans: Six key styles explored.* Cincinnati, Ohio: The Union Institute.

Bouton, L. (1994). Conversational implicature in a second language: Learnt slowly when not deliberately taught. *Journal of Pragmatics,* 22(1), 157-167.

Boxer, D. (1993). Complaints as positive strategies: What the learner needs to know. *TESOL Quarterly,* 27(1), 277-299.

Brady, P. T. (1968). A statistical analysis of on-off patterns in 16 conversations. *Bell System Technical Journal,* 47(1), 73-91.

Bredella, L. (1999). Zielsetzungen interkulturellen Fremdsprachenunterrichts. In L. Bredella & W. Delanoy (Eds.), *Interkultureller Fremdsprachenunterricht. Aus der Reihe Giessener Beiträge zur Fremdsprachendidaktik* (pp. 85-120). Tübingen: Narr.

Bredella, L. & Delanoy, W. (1999). *Interkultureller Fremdsprachenunterricht.* Tübingen: Narr.

Breiner-Sanders, K. E., Lowe, P., Miles, J. & Swender, E. (2000). ACTFL proficiency guidelines-speaking (Revised 1999). *Foreign Language Annals,* 33(1), 13-18.

Brinton, L. J. (1996). *Pragmatic markers in English. Grammaticalization and Discourse Function.* New York: Mouton de Gruyter.

Brown, D. D. (1998). Academic protocol and targeted rhetoric. *Literacy Across Cultures,* 2(1). 1-16.

Brown, J. (2001). *Using Surveys in Language Programs.* Cambridge: Cambridge University Press.

Brown, P. (1980). How and why women are more polite. Some evidence from a Mayan Community. In S. McConnell-Ginet, R. Borker & N. Furman (Eds.), *Women and Language in Literature and Society* (pp. 111-135). New York: Praeger.

Brown, P. & Levinson, S. C. (1978). Universals in language usage: Politeness phenomena. In E. N. Goody (Ed.), *Question and Politeness* (pp. 56-311). Cambridge: Cambridge University Press.

Brown, P. & Levinson, S. (1987). *Politeness: Some Universals in Language Usage.* Cambridge: Cambridge University Press.

Brozyna, B. (2007). The teachability of interactional discourse signals in the classroom environment. Unpublished Master's Dissertation, University of Reading, Reading.

Brumfit, C. (1980). *Problems and Principles in Language Teaching.* Oxford: Pergamon Press.

Brunner, L. (1979). Smiles can be backchannels. *Journal of Personality and Social Psychology,* 37(1), 728-734.

Burden, P. (2004). The teacher as facilitator: Reducing anxiety in the EFL university classroom. *JALT Hokkaido Journal,* 8(1), 3-18.

Burroughs, N. F., Marie, V. & McCroskey, J. C. (2003). Relationships of self-perceived communication competence and communication apprehension with willingness to communicate: A comparison with first and second languages in Micronesia. *Communication Research Reports,* 20(1), 230-239.

Byalstock, E. (1993). Symbolic representation and attentional control in pragmatic competence. In G. Kasper & S. Blum-Kulka (Eds.), *Interlanguage Pragmatics* (pp. 43-57). Oxford: Oxford University Press.

Bygate, M. (1988). Units of oral expression and language learning in small group interaction. *Applied Linguistics,* 9(1), 59-82.

Byram, M. (1997). *Teaching and Assessing Intercultural Communicative Competence.* Clevedon: Multilingual Matters.

Caine, N. A. (2005). EFL examination washback in Japan: Investigating the effects of oral assessment on teaching and learning. Unpublished Master's Dissertation, University of Manchester, Manchester.

Caine, T. M. (2008). Do you speak global?: The spread of English and the global implications for English language teaching. *Canadian Journal for New Scholars in Education,* 1(1), 1-11.

Caligiuri, W. R. & Di Santo, V. (2001). Global competence: What is it, and can it be developed through global assignments? *Human Resource*

Planning, 24(1), 27-35.
Canale, M. & Swain, M. (1980). Theoretical bases of communicative approaches to second language teaching and testing, *Applied Linguistics,* 1(1), 1-47.
Capper, S. (2000). Nonverbal communication and the second language learner: Some pedagogical considerations. *The Language Teacher,* 24(5), 19-23.
Carter, R. & McCarthy, M. (1995). Talking, creating: Interactional language, creativity, and context. *Applied Linguistics,* 25(1), 62-88.
—. (1997). *Exploring Spoken English.* Cambridge: Cambridge University Press.
—. (2004). Grammar and the spoken language. *Applied Linguistics,* 16(1), 141-158.
Chapman, D. & Hartley, B. (2000). Close encounters of the unhomely kind: Negotiating identity and Japan literacy. *Japanese Studies,* 20(1), 269-279.
Churchill, L. (1978). *Questioning Strategies in Socio-linguistics.* Rowley, MA: Newbury House.
Clancy, P. M. (1986). The acquisition of communicative style in Japanese. In B. Schieffelin & E. Ochs (Eds.), *In Language Socialization Across Cultures* (pp. 213-250). Cambridge: Cambridge University Press.
—. (1990). Acquiring communicative style in Japanese. In R. Scarcella (Ed.), *Developing Communicative Competence in a Second Language* (pp. 27-44). Rowley: Newbury House.
—. (1982). Written and spoken style in Japanese narratives. In D. Tannen (Ed.), *Conversational Style: Analyzing Talk Among Friends* (pp. 55-76). Norwood: Ablex.
Clancy, P. M., Thompson, S. A., Suzuki, R. & Tao, H. (1996). The conversational use of reactive tokens in English, Japanese, and Mandarin. *Journal of Pragmatics,* 26(1), 355-387.
Clarke, G. (2000). Why Taro can't speak English. *The Japan Times,* 30 January, p. 19.
Clegg, F. (1982). *Simple Statistics: A Course Book for the Social Sciences.* Cambridge: Cambridge University Press.
Clément, R., Baker, S. C. & MacIntyre, P. D. (2003). Willingness to communicate in a second language: The effect of context, norms, and vitality. *Journal of Language and Social Psychology,* 22(1), 190-209.
Clyne, M. (1994). *Inter-cultural Communication at Work: Cultural Values in Discourse.* Cambridge: Cambridge University Press.
Collier, M. J. (1989). Cultural and intercultural communication competence: Current approaches and directions for future research.

International Journal of Intercultural Relations, 13(1), 287-302.
Collier, M. J. & Thomas, M. (1988). Cultural identity: An interpretive perspective. In Y. Y. Kim & W. Gudykunst (Eds.), *Theories in Intercultural Communication* (pp. 287-302). Beverly Hills, CA: Sage.
Conlan, C. J. (1996). Politeness, paradigms of family and the Japanese ESL speaker. *Language Science,* 18(1), 729-42.
Cook, M. (2010). Offshore outsourcing teacher inservice education: The long-term effects of a four-month pedagogical program on Japanese teachers of English. *TESL Canada Journal,* 28(1), 60-76.
—. (2011). Improve teacher training at home. *The Japan Times,* 16 January, p. 14.
Costa, P. T. & McCrae, R. R. (1992). *Revised NEO Personality Inventory (NEO-PI-R) and NEO Five-Factor Inventory (NEO-FFI) professional manual.* Odessa, Florida: Psychological Assessment Resources.
Craig, D. & Pitts, M. (1990). The dynamics of dominance in tutorial discussions. *Linguistics,* 28(1), 125-138.
Crawford, W. (2003). Back-channel transfer in cross-cultural second language conversation: Do native Japanese transfer more than native English speakers? *Journal of Kitakyushu National College of Technology,* 36(1), 155-163.
Crichton, N. J. (1998). Statistical considerations in design and analysis. In B. Reo & C. Webb (Eds.), *Research and Development in Clinical Nursing Practice.* London.
Cross, J. (2002). 'Noticing' in SLA: Is it a valid concept? *TESL-EJ,* 6(3). [online] Available from: http://www.cc.kyoto-su.ac.jp/information/tesl-ej23/a2.html (Date viewed 14 March 2008).
Cupach, W. & Imahori, T. T. (1993). Identity management theory: Communication competence in intercultural episodes and relationships. In R. L. Wiseman & J. Koester (Eds.), *Intercultural Communication Competence* (pp. 112-131). Newbury Park, CA: Sage.
Cushner, K. & Brislin, R. W. (1996). *Intercultural Interaction: A Practical Guide* (2nd ed.). Thousand Oaks, CA: Sage.
Cutrone, P. (2001). Learner attitudes towards EFL teachers in an English conversation school in Japan. *The Language Teacher,* 25(12), 21-24.
—. (2002). Speaking English with a Japanese mind: A case study examining backchannels in conversations between Japanese-British dyads. Unpublished Master's Dissertation, University of Leicester, Leicester.
—. (2003). A look at language anxiety and how it affects Japanese EFL learners when performing oral tasks. *The Journal of Nagasaki University of Foreign Studies,* 5(1),61-72.

—. (2005). A case study examining backchannels in conversations between Japanese-British dyads. *Multilingua - Journal of Cross-Cultural and Interlanguage Communication,* 24(1), 237-274.

—. (2009). Overcoming Japanese EFL learners' fear of speaking. *University of Reading's Language Studies Working Papers,* 1(1), 55-63.

—. (2010). The backchannel norms of native English speakers: A target for Japanese L2 English learners. *University of Reading Language Studies Working Papers,* 2(1), 28-37.

D'Andrea, M., Daniels, J. & Heck, R. (1991). Evaluating the impact of multicultural counseling training. *Journal of Counseling and Development,* 70(1), 143-150.

Day, M. (1996). *Aimai no ronri: The logic of ambiguity and indirectness in Japanese.* Berkeley, CA: University of California.

Deese, J. (1980). Pauses, prosody, and the demands of production in language. In H. W. Dechert & M. Raupach (Eds.), *Temporal Variables in Speech: Studies in Honour of Frieda Goldman-Eisler* (pp. 69-84). The Hague: Mouton Publishers.

DeKeyser, R. (1995). Learning second language grammar rules: An experiment with a miniature linguistic system. *Studies in Second Language Acquisition,* 17(1), 379-410.

Dewaele, J. & Furnham, A. (2000). Personality and speech production: A pilot study of second language learners. *Personality and Individual Differences,* 28(1), 355-365.

Dittman, A. & Llewellyn, L. (1968). Relationship between vocalization and head nods as listener responses. *Journal of Personality and Social Psychology,* 9(1), 79-84.

Dittman, A. T. (1972). Developmental factors in conversational behavior. *Journal of Communication,* 22(1), 404-23.

Doi, T. (1981). *The Anatomy of Dependence: The Key Analysis of Japanese Behavior.* English trans. John Bester (2nd edition). Tokyo: Kodansha.

—. (1986). *The Anatomy of Conformity: The Individual Versus Society.* Tokyo: Kodansha.

—. (1996). The Japanese psyche: myth and reality. In C. Strozier & M. Flynn (Eds.), *Trauma and Self* (pp. 197-203). London: Rowman and Littlefield.

Donahoe, R. (1998). *Japanese Culture and Communication.* Lanham, Maryland: University Press of America.

Dörnyei, Z. & Thurrell, S. (1992). *Conversation and Dialogues in Action.* Hemel Hempstead: Prentice Hall.

—. (1994). Teaching conversation skills intensively: Course content and rationale. *ELT Journal,* 48(1), 40-49.
Drummond, K. & Hopper, R. (1993a). Backchannels revisited: Acknowledgement tokens and speakership incipiency. *Research on Language and Social Interaction,* 26(1), 157-177.
—. (1993b). Some uses of 'yeah'. *Research on Language and Social Interaction,* 26(1), 203-212.
Duncan, S. (1974). On the structure of speaker-auditor interaction during speaking turns. *Language in Society,* 2(1), 161-180.
Duncan, S. & Fiske, D. (1977). *Face to Face Interaction: Research, Methods, and Theory.* Hillsdale: Erlbaum.
Earley, P. C. & Ang, S. (2003). *Cultural Intelligence: Individual Interactions Across Cultures.* Stanford, CA.: Stanford Business Books.
Edelsky, C. (1981). Who's got the floor? *Language in Society,* 10(1), 383-421.
Eelen, G. (1999). Politeness and ideology: A critical review. *Pragmatics,* 9(1), 163-174.
—. (2001). *A Critique of Politeness Theories.* Manchester: St. Jerome.
Eggins, S. & Slade, D. (1997). *Analyzing Casual Conversation,* London: Cassell.
Ehrman, M., Leaver, B. & Oxford, R. (2003). A brief overview of individual differences in second language learning. *System,* 31(1), 313-330.
Ellis, N. C. (2005). At the interface: Dynamic interactions of explicit and implicit language knowledge. *Studies in Second Language Acquisition,* 27(1), 305-352.
—. (2006a). Language acquisition as rational contingency learning. *Applied Linguistics,* 27(1), 1-24.
—. (2006b). Selective attention and transfer phenomena in L2 acquisition: Contingency, cue competition, salience, interference, overshadowing, blocking, and perceptual learning. *Applied Linguistics,* 27(1), 164-194.
—. (2008). Usage-based and form-focused SLA: The implicit and explicit learning of constructions. In A. Tyler, Y. Kim & M. Takada (Eds.), *Language in the Context of Use: Discourse and Cognitive Approaches to Language* (pp. 93-120). Berlin: Mouton de Gruyter.
Ellis, R. (1984). Can syntax be taught? A study of the effects of formal instruction on the acquisition of WH questions by children. *Applied Linguistics,* 5(1), 138-155.
—. (1991). Communicative competence and the Japanese learner. *JALT Journal,* 13(1), 103-127.
—. (1994). *The Study of Second Language Acquisition.* Oxford: Oxford

University Press.
—. (2002). Does form-focused instruction affect the acquisition of implicit knowledge? *Studies in Second Language Acquisition,* 24(1), 223-236.
—. (2008). *The Study of Second Language Acquisition (2nd edition).* Oxford: Oxford University Press.
Ervin-Tripp, S. (1979). Children's verbal turn-taking. In E. Ochs & B. B. Shiefflelin (Eds.), *Developmental Pragmatics* (pp. 391-421). New York: Academic Press.
ETS (2000). TOEIC report on test-takers worldwide 1997-98. *Educational Testing Service.* [online] Available from: http://www.toeic.cl/images/toeicreporttesttakers.pdf (Date viewed 12 July 2007).
—. (2006). The TOEIC test: Report on test takers worldwide 2005. *Educational Testing Service.* [online] Available from: http://www.ea.toeic.eu/fileadmin/free_resources/Europe%20website/3548-TOEIC_TTRep.pdf (Date viewed 6 May 2008).
—. (2007). TOEFL test and score data summary for TOEFL internet-based test: September 2005-December 2006 test data. *Educational Testing Service.* [online] Available from: http://www.ets.org/Media/Research/pdf/TOEFL-SUM-0506-iBT.pdf (Date viewed 11 April 2009).
—. (2008). TOEFL test and score data summary for internet-based and paper-based tests: January-December 2007 test data. *Educational Testing Service.* [online] Available from: http://www.ets.org/Media/Research/pdf/71943_web.pdf (Date viewed 8 December 2009).
—. (2009). TOEFL test and score data summary for internet-based and paper-based tests: January-December 2007 test data. *Educational Testing Service.* [online] Available from: http://www.ets.org/Media/Tests/TOEFL/pdf/test_score_data_summary_2008.pdf (Date viewed 24 January 2010).
Evans, V. (2009). *How Words Mean: Lexical Concepts, Cognitive Models, and Meaning Construction.* Oxford: Oxford University Press.
Eysenck, H. (1992). *A Hundred Years of Personality Research, from Heymans to Modern Times.* Houten: Bohn, Staeu Van Loghum.
Farooq, M. U. (2005). A model for motivating Japanese EFL learners through real-life questioning strategies. *The Journal of Nagoya Gakkugei University,* 1(1), 27-42.
Farr, F. (2003). Engaged listenership in spoken academic discourse: The case for student-tutor meetings. *Journal of English for Academis Purposes,* 2(1), 67-85.

Felix-Brasdefer, J. C. (2008). *Politeness in Mexico and the United States: A Contrastive Study of the Realization and Perception of Refusals.* Amsterdam: John Benjamins.

Fewell, N. (2010). Language learning strategies and English language proficiency: An investigation of Japanese EFL university students. *TESOL Journal,* 2(1), 159-174.

Fillmore, C. (1979). On fluency. In C. Fillmore, D. Kempler & W. Wang (Eds.), *Individual Differences in Language Ability and Language Behavior* (pp. 85-102). New York: Academic Press.

Fliegel, D. (1987). Immigrant professionals must speak American. *The Boston Globe,* 16 June, p. 2.

Folse, K. S. (2006). *The Art of Teaching Speaking: Research and Pedagogy for the ESL/EFL Classroom.* Ann Arbor: University of Michigan Press.

Foster, P., Tonkyn, A. & Wigglesworth, G. (2000). Measuring spoken language: A unit for all reasons. *Applied Linguistics,* 21(1), 354-375.

Fraser, B. & Nolen, W. (1981). The association of deference with linguistic form. *International Journal of the Sociology of Language,* 27(1), 93-109.

Fries, C. (1952). *The Structure of English.* New York: Harcourt Brace.

Fuji, Y. (2008). 'You must have a wealth of stories': Cross-linguistic differences between addressee support behaviour in Australian and Japanese. *Multilingua - Journal of Cross-Cultural and Interlanguage Communication,* 27(1), 325-370.

Fujimoto, D. T. (2007). Listener responses in interaction: A case for abandoning the term, backchannel. *Journal of Osaka Jogakuin College,* 37(1), 35-54.

Fujita, M. (2002). *Second Language English Attrition of Japanese Bilingual Children.* Tokyo: Temple University Japan.

Fukushima, S. & Iwata, Y. (1985). Politeness in English. *JALT Journal,* 7(1), 1-14.

Fukuya, Y. & Clark, M. (2001). A comparison of input enhancement and explicit instruction of mitigators. In L. F. Bouton (Ed.), *Pragmatics and Language Learning, Monograph Series* (pp. 111-130). Urbana-Champaign, IL: University of Illinois.

Fukuya, Y., Reeve, M., Gisi, J. & Christianson, M. (1998). Does focus on form work for sociopragmatics? Paper presented at 12th International Conference on Pragmatics and Language (March 15-17). Urbana-Champaign: University of Illinois.

Ferguson, N. (1977). Simultaneous speech, interruptions, and dominance. *British Journal of Social and Clinical Psychology,* 16(1), 295-302.

Gardner, R. & MacIntyre, P. (1993). A student's contributions to second language learning. Part II: Affective Variables. *Language Teaching,* 26(1), 1-11.

Garman, M. (1990). *Psycholinguistics.* Cambridge: Cambridge University Press.

Gass, S. & Neu, J. (2006). *Speech Acts Across Cultures: Challenges to Communication in a Second Language.* Hawthorne. New York: Walter de Gruyter.

Gates, S. (1995). Exploiting washback from standardized tests. In J. D. Brown & S. O. Yamashita (Eds.), *Language Testing in Japan* (pp. 101-106). Tokyo: Japan Association for Language Teaching.

Gersten, M. C. (1990). Intercultural competence and expatriates. *The International Journal of Human Resource Management,* 3(1), 341-362.

Gick, M. L., & Holyoak, K. J. (1983). Schema induction and analogical transfer. *Cognitive Psychology,* 15(1), 1-38.

Gilewicz, M. & Thonus, T. (2003). Close vertical transcription in writing center training and research. *Writing Center Journal,* 24(1), 40-55.

Gilks, K. (2009-2010). Is the Brown and Levinson (1987) model of politeness as useful and influential as originally claimed? An assessment of the revised Brown and Levinson (1987) model. *INNERVATE,* 2 (1), 94-102.

Goffman, E. (1967). *Interaction Ritual: Essays on Face-to-face Behavior.* New York: Pantheon Books.

Goldschneider, J. M. & DeKeyser, R. M. (2001). Explaining the "natural order of L2 morpheme acquisition" in English: A meta-analysis of multiple determinants. *Language Learning,* 51(1), 1-50.

Goodwin, C. (1981). *Conversational Organization: Interaction Between Speakers and Hearers.* New York: Academic Press.

Gosling, S. D., Rentfrow, P. J. & Swann, W. B. (2003). A very brief measure of the big-five personality domains. *Journal of Research in Personality,* 37(1), 504-528.

Graham, J. (1990). An exploratory study of the process of marketing negotiations using a cross-cultural perspective. In R. Scarcella (Ed.), *Developing Communicative Competence in a Second Language* (pp. 239-270). Rowley: Newbury House.

Gravetter, F. J. & Wallnau, L. B. (2008). *Statistics for the Behavioral Sciences (8th edition).* Belmont, CA: Wadsworth, Cengage Learning.

Greer, D. (2000). The eyes of Hito: A Japanese cultural monitor of behavior in the communicative classroom. *JALT Journal,* 22(1), 183-195.

Grice, H. P. (1967). Logic in conversation. Paper presented at the William

James Lectures, Harvard University, Cambridge, MA.
—. (1975). Logic and conversation. In P. Cole & J. Morgan (Eds.), *Syntax and Semantics 3: Speech Acts* (pp. 41-58). New York: Academic Press.
—. (1989). *Studies in the Way of Words*. Cambridge: Harvard University Press.
Gu, Y. (1990). Politeness phenomena in modern Chinese. *Journal of Pragmatics,* 14(2), 237-257.
Gudykunst, W., Gao, B., Schmidt, K. L., Nishida, T., Bond, M., Leung, K., Wang, G. & Barraclough, R. A. (1992). The influence of individualism-collectivism, self-monitoring, and predicted-outcome value on communication in ingroup and outgroup relationships. *Journal of Cross-Cultural Psychology,* 23(1), 196-213.
Gudykunst, W. & Nishida, T. (1993). Interpersonal and intergroup communication in Japan and the United States. In W. Gudykunst (Ed.), *Communication in Japan and the United States* (pp. 149-214). Albany, NY: State of New York Press.
—. (2001). Anxiety, uncertainty, and perceived effectiveness of communication across relationships and cultures. *International Journal of Intercultural Relations,* 25(1), 55-71.
Gudykunst, W. B., Nishida, T. & Chua, T. (1986). Uncertainty reduction in Japanese-North American dyads. *Communication Research Reports,* 3(1), 39-46.
Gudykunst, W. B., Yang, S. & Nishida, T. (1985). A cross-cultural test of uncertainty reduction theory: Comparisons of acquaintances, friends, and dating relationships in Japan, Korea, and the United States. *Human Communication Research,* 11(3), 407-455.
Guest, M. (2006). Culture research in foreign language teaching: Dichotomizing, stereotyping and exoticizing cultural realities. *Zeitschrift für Interkulturellen Fremdsprachenunterricht,* 11(3), 1-19.
Guilherme, M. (2000). Intercultural competence. In M. Byram (Ed.), *Encyclopaedia of Language Teaching and Learning* (pp. 297-300). London: Routledge.
Haga, Y. (1998). *Nihongo no Shakaishinrin*. Tokyo: Ningen no Kagakusha.
Hall, E. (1974). *Handbook for Proxemic Research*. Washington: Society for the Anthropology of Visual Communication.
Hall, E. T. (1981). *Beyond Culture*. Garden City: Anchor Books.
Hammer, M. R., Bennett, M. J. & Wiseman, R. L. (2003). Measuring intercultural sensitivity: The intercultural development inventory. *International Journal of Intercultural Development,* 27(1), 421-443.
Hammer, M. R., Nishida, H. & Wiseman, R. L. (1996). The influence of situational prototypes on dimensions of intercultural communication

competence. *Journal of Cross-Cultural Psychology,* 27(3), 267-282.
Hamnett, M. P. & Brislin, R. W. (1980). *Research in Culture Learning: Language and Conceptual Studies.* Honolulu, HI: The University of Hawaii Press.
Harrington, N. G. (1995). The effects of college students' alcohol resistance strategies. *Health Communication,* 7(4), 371-391.
Hashimoto, Y. (2002). Motivation and willingness to communicate as predictors of reported L2 use: The Japanese ESL context. *Second Language Studies,* 20(2), 29-70.
Haslett, B. (1989). Communication and language acquisition within a cultural context. In S. Ting-Toomey & K. Felipe (Eds.), *Language, Communication and Culture: Current Directions.* Newbury Park: Sage Publications.
Hattori, T. (1987). A study of nonverbal intercultural communication between Japanese and Americans focusing on the use of the eyes. *JALT Journal,* 8(1), 109-118.
Haugh, M. (2003). Japanese and non-Japanese perceptions of Japanese communication. *New Zealand Journal of Asian Studies,* 5(1), 156-177.
—. (2004). Revisiting the conceptualisation of politeness in English and Japanese. *Multilingua - Journal of Cross-Cultural and Interlanguage Communication,* 23(1), 85-109.
Hayashi, R. (1988). Simultaneous talk - from the perspective of floor management of English and Japanese speakers. *World Englishes,* 7(3), 269-288.
Hayashi, T. & Hayashi, R. (1991). Backchannel or main channel: A cognitive approach based on floor and speech acts. *Pragmatics and Language Learning,* 2(1), 119-138.
Hecht, M. (1978). The conceptualization and measurement of interpersonal communication satisfaction. *Human Communication Research,* 4(3), 253-264.
Hecht, M. L., Jackson, R. L. & Ribeau, S. A. (2003). *African American Communication.* New Jersey: Lawrence Earlbaum Associates.
Heffernan, N. (2005). Leadership in EFL: Time for a change. *Asian EFL Journal,* 7(1), 183-196.
Heffernan, N., & Jones, J. (2005). *Top-Notch students: Study Skills for Japanese University Students.* Tokyo: Macmillan Language House.
Heinz, B. (2003). Backchannel responses as strategic responses in bilingual speakers' conversations. *Journal of Pragmatics,* 35(1), 1113-1142.
Helgesen, M. (1987). False beginners: Activating language for accuracy and fluency. *The Language Teacher,* 11(14), 23-29.

—. (1993). Dismantling a wall of silence: The "English conversation" class. In P. Wadden (Ed.), *A Handbook for Teaching English at Japanese Colleges and Universities.* (pp. 37-49). New York: Oxford University Press.

Helgesen, M., Brown, S. & Mandeville, T. (2007). *English Firsthand.* Tokyo: Pearson Longman.

Hess, L. J. & Johnston, J. R. (1988). Acquisition of back channel listener responses to adequate messages. *Discourse Processes,* 11(3), 319-335.

Hidasi, J. (2004). The impact of culture on second language acquisition. Paper presented at the Comparative Pragmatics Association 2nd Conference, Tokyo (3 April). [online] Available from: http://www.childresearch.net/RESOURCE/RESEARCH/2006/exfile/HIDASI.pdf (Date viewed 10 June 2009).

High, A. C. & Caplan, S. E. (2009). Social anxiety and computer-mediated communication during initial interactions: Implications for the hyperpersonal perspective. *Computers in Human Behavior,* 25(2), 475-482.

Hill, B., Ide, S., Ikuta, S., Kawasaki, A. & Ogino, T. (1986). Universals of linguistic politeness: Quantitative evidence from Japanese and American English for specific purposes. *Journal of Pragmatics,* 10, 347-371.

Hill, T. (1990). Sociolinguistic aspects of communicative competence and the Japanese learner. *Dokkyo University Studies in English,* 36(1), 69-104.

Hofstede, G. (1991). *Cultures and Organizations.* Berkshire: McGraw-Hill Book Company Europe.

Holliday, A., Hyde, M. & Kullman, J. (2004). *Inter-cultural Communication.* New York: Routledge.

Horiguchu, J. (1988). Komyunikeshon ni okeru kikite no gengo kodo [Listener's verbal acts in communication]. *Nihongo Kyoiku,* 64(1), 13-26.

Horn, L. (2004). Implicature. In L. Horn & G. Ward (Eds.), *The Handbook of Pragmatics* (pp. 3-28). Oxford: Blackwell.

Horwitz, E., Horwitz, M. & Cope, J. (1991). Foreign language classroom anxiety. In E. Horwitz & D. Young (Eds.), *Language Anxiety from Theory and Research to classroom implications* (pp. 27-37). Hemel Hempstead: Prentice Hall International.

House, J. & Kasper, G. (1981). Zur rolle der kogni-tion in kommunikationskursen. *Die Neueren Sprachen,* 80(1), 42-55.

House, J. (1996). Developing pragmatic fluency in English as a foreign language. *Studies in Second Language Acquisition,* 18(1), 225-252.

—. (2002). Developing pragmatic competence in lingua franca English. In K. Knapp & C. Meierkord (Eds.), *Lingua Franca Communication* (pp. 245-267). Frankfurt am Main: Peter Lang.

Hughes, H. J. (1999). Cultivating the walled garden: English in Japan. *English Studies,* 80(6), 556-568.

Hymes, D. H. (1971). *On Communicative Competence.* Philadelphia: University of Pennsylvania Press.

Ida, H. (2004). Current issues in teacher training. *The Language Teacher,* 28(5), 13-17.

Ide, S. (1989). Formal forms and discernment: Two neglected aspects of universals of linguistic politeness. *Multilingua - Journal of Cross-Cultural and Interlanguage Communication,* 8(1), 223-248.

Ide, S., Hill, B., Carnes, Y., Ogino, T. & Kawasaki, A. (1992). The concept of politeness: an empirical study of American English and Japanese. I. In R. Watts, S. Ide & K. Ehlich (Eds.), *Politeness in Language. Studies in its History, Theory and Practice* (pp. 281-297). Berlin: Mouton de Gruyter.

Ike, M. (1995). A historical review of English in Japan (1600-1880). *World Englishes,* 14(1), 3-11.

Ike, S. (2010). Backchannel: A feature of Japanese English. In A. M. Stoke (Ed.), *JALT 2009 Conference Proceedings* (pp. 205-215). Tokyo: JALT.

Ikegami, Y. (1989). Introduction: Special Issue on Discourse Analysis in Japan. *Text,* 9(3), 263-273.

Imai, M. (1981). *16 Ways to Avoid Saying No: An Invitation to Experience Japanese Management from Inside.* Tokyo: The Nihon Keizai Shimbun.

Ishida, M. (2002). *Zenkoku Genshoku Eigokyoin Anketo Chosa Kekka [Questionnaire Results Answered by Japanese Teachers of English all over Japan].* Tokyo: Tokyo Education Research Group.

Ito, A. (2007). Functions of backchannels in Japanese casual conversations: Comparing single backchannels and repeated backchannels. Unpublished Master's Dissertation, Kobe College, Kobe.

Iwai, T. (2007). Becoming a good conversationalist: Pragmatic development of JFL learners. In D. R. Yoshimi & H. Wang (Eds.), *Selected Papers from Pragmatics in the CJK Classroom: The State of the Art.* [online] Available from: http://nflrc.hawaii.edu/CJKProceedings/iwai/iwai.pdf (Date viewed 26 January 2009).

Iwata, Y. (1999). Toward bridging the communication gap: Cross-cultural variation in Japanese-American business communication. Unpublished

PhD Thesis, University of Mississippi, Mississippi.

James, D. & Clarke, S. (1993). Women, men, and interruptions: A critical review. In D. Tannen (Ed.), *Gender and Conversational Interaction* (pp. 231-280). New York: Oxford University Press.

Janney, R., & Arndt, H. (1993). Universality and relativity in cross-cultural politeness research: a historical perspective. *Multilingua - Journal of Cross-Cultural and Interlanguage Communication,* 12(1), 13-50.

Jefferson, G. (1973). A case of precision timing in ordinary conversation: Overlapped tag-positioned address terms in closing sequences. *Semiotica,* 9(1), 47-96.

—. (2002). Is "no" an acknowledgment token? Comparing American and British uses of (+)/(-) tokens. *Journal of Pragmatics,* 34(10-11), 1345-1383.

Jenkins, J. (1998). Which pronunciation norms and models for English as an International Language? *ELT Journal,* 52(2), 119-126.

—. (1999). Pronunciation in teacher education for English as an international language. *Speak Out!* 24(1),45-48.

—. (2000). *The Phonology of English as an International Language.* Oxford: Oxford University Press.

—. (2003). *World Englishes.* London: Routlege.

Johnson, J. P., Lenartowicz, T. & Apud, S. (2006). Cross-cultural competence in international business: Toward a definition and a model. *Journal of International Business Studies,* 37(4), 525-543.

Johnstone, B. (2000). *Qualitative Methods in Sociolinguistics.* New York: Oxford University Press.

Kachru, B. (1998). English as an Asian language. *Links and Letters,* 5(1), 89-108.

Kagawa, H. (1997). *The Inscrutable Japanese.* Tokyo: Kodansha.

Kaplan, R. B. (1966). Cultural thought patterns in inter-cultural education. *Language Learning,* 16(1/2), 1-20.

Kasper, G. & Rose, K. R. (2003). *Pragmatic Development in a Second Language.* Oxford: Wiley-Blackwell.

Keenan, E. O. (1974). The universality of conversational postulates. In R. W. Fasold & R. W. Shuy (Eds.), *Studies in Linguistic Variation* (pp. 255-268). Washington, D.C.: Georgetown University Press.

Keenan, E. O. (1976). On the universality of conversational implicatures. *Language in Society,* 5(1), 67-80.

Keesing, R. (1974). Theories of Culture. *Annual Review of Anthropology,* 3(1), 73-97.

Kelley, C. & Meyers, J. (1999). The cross-cultural adaptability inventory.

In S. M. Fowler & M. G. Mumford (Eds.), *Intercultural Sourcebook: Cross-Cultural Training Methods, Volume 2* (pp. 53-60). Yarmouth, ME: Intercultural Press.

Kendon, A. (1967). Some functions of gaze-direction in social interaction. *Acta Psychologica,* 26(1), 22-63.

—. (1977). Some functions of gaze-direction in two-person conversation. In A. Kendon (Ed.), *Studies in the Behavior of Social Interaction* (pp. 13-51). Bloomington: Indiana University Press.

Kenna, P. & Lacy, S. (1994). *Business Japan: A Practical Guide to Understanding Japanese Business Culture*. Lincolnwood: Passport Books.

Kitao, K. & Kitao, S. K. (1982). College reading textbooks do not meet needs. *The Daily Yomiuri*, 16 September, p. 7.

—. (1989). *Intercultural Communication Between Japan and the US*. Tokyo: Eichosha Shinsha.

—. (1995). *English Teaching: Theory, Research, and Practice*. Tokyo: Eichosha.

Knapp, K., & Knapp-Potthoff, A. (1987). Instead of an introduction: Conceptual issues in analyzing intercultural communication. In K. Knapp, E. Werner & A. Knapp-Potthoff (Eds.), *Intercultural Communication. Studies in Anthropological Linguistics 1* (pp. 1-13). Berlin: Mouton de Gruyter.

Knight, D. (2009). A multi-modal approach to the analysis of backchannel behaviour. Unpublished PhD Thesis, University of Nottingham, Nottingham.

Kobayashi, H. (1995). On backchannel performance in an intercultural conversation in English: Between Japanese and a native Speaker of English. *Language Labratory,* 32(1), 151-166.

Koike, I. & Tanaka, H. (1995). English in foreign language education policy in Japan: Toward the twenty-first century. *World Englishes,* 14(1), 13-25.

Koiso, H., Horiuchi, Y., Tutiya, S., Ichikawa, A. & Den, Y. (1998). An analysis of turn-taking and backchannels based on prosodic and syntactic features in Japanese map task dialogs. *Language and Speech.* 41(3), 295-323.

Koyama, W. (1992). *Japan: A Handbook in Intercultural Communication*. Sydney: Macquarie University.

Kramsch, C. (1993). *Context and Culture in Language Teaching*. Oxford: Oxford University Press.

—. (1998). *Language and Culture*. Oxford: Oxford University Press.

Krashen, S. (1982). *Principles and Practice in Second Language*

Acquisition. Oxford: Pergamon.
Kroeber, A. L. & Kluckhohn, C. (1952). *Culture: A Critical Review of Concepts and Definitions*. Cambridge, MA: Peabody Museum.
Kubota, M. (1995). Teachability of conversational implicature to Japanese EFL learners. *IRLT (Institute for Research in Language Learning)*, 9(1), 35-67.
Kubota, R (1998). Ideologies of English in Japan. *World Englishes*, 17(3), 295-306.
—. (1999). Japanese culture constructed by discourses: Implications for applied linguistics research and ELT. *TESOL Quarterly,* 33(1), 9-35.
Kupka, B., Everett, A. & Wildermuth, S. (2007). The rainbow model of intercultural communication competence: A review and extension of existing research. *Intercultural Communication Studies,* 16(2), 18-36.
Kwahn, C. H. (2002). How to fix Japan's English language deficit. *Asia Times Online*. 27 June. [online] Available from: http://www.atimes.com/japan-econ/DF27h01.html (Date viewed 19 March 2008).
Lakoff, R. (1973). The logic of politeness; or, minding your p's and q's. In T. C. Corum, C. Smith-Stark & A. Weiser (Eds.), *Papers from the Ninth Regional Meeting of the Chicago Linguistic Society, April 13-15* (pp. 292-305). Chicago: Chicago Linguistic Society.
—. (1989). The limits of politeness: Therapeutic and courtroom discourse. *Multilingua - Journal of Cross-Cultural and Interlanguage Communication*, 8(1), 101-129.
Lebra, T. (1976). *Japanese Patterns of Behavior*. Honolulu: The University of Hawaii Press.
Lee, H. (1999). Discourse marker use in native and non-native speakers. In C. L. Moder & A. Martinovic-Zic (Eds.), *Discourse Across Languages and Cultures* (pp. 117-128). Philadelphia: John Benjamins.
Lee-Wong, S. M. (2002). Contextualising intercultural communication and sociopragmatic choices. *Multilingua - Journal of Cross-Cultural and Interlanguage Communication,* 21, 79-99.
Leech, G. (1983). *Principles of Pragmatics*. London: Longman.
Leki, I. (1991). Twenty-five years of contrastive rhetoric: text analysis and writing pedagogies. *TESOL Quarterly,* 25(1), 123-143.
Levinson, S. (1983). *Pragmatics*. Cambridge: Cambridge University Press.
—. (2000). *Presumptive Meanings: The Theory of Generalized Conversational Implicature*. Cambridge: MIT Press.
Liddicoat, A. J., & Crozet, C. (2001). Acquiring French interactional norms through instruction. In K. R. Rose & G. Kasper (Eds.),

Pragmatics in Language Teaching (pp. 125-144). Cambridge, UK: Cambridge University Press.
Lindemann, S. (2006). What the other half gives: The interlocutor's role in non-native speaker performance. In R. Hughes (Ed.), *Spoken English, TESOL, and Applied Linguistics: Challenges for Theory and Practice* (pp. 23-49). Houndmills, Basingstoke: Palgrave MacMillan.
LoCastro, V. (1987). Aizuchi: A Japanese conversational routine. In L. Smith (Ed.), *Discourse Across Cultures: Strategies in World Englishes* (pp. 101-113). London: Prentice Hall.
—. (1997). Politeness and pragmatic competence in foreign language education. *Language Teaching Research,* 1(3), 239-267.
—. (1999). A Sociocultural functional analysis of fragmentation in Japanese. *Multiligua: Journal of Cross-Cultural and Interlanguage Communication,* 18(4), 369-389.
Loveday, L. (1982). *The Sociolinguistics of Learning and Using a Non-native Language.* Oxford: Permagon.
Lyster, R. (1994). The effect of functional-analytic teaching on aspects of French immersion students' sociolinguistic competence. *Applied Linguistics,* 15(1), 263-287.
MacIntyre, P. D., Babin, P. A. & Clément, R. (1999). Willingness to communicate: Antecedents and consequences. *Communication Quarterly,* 17(1), 215-229.
MacIntyre, P. D., Baker, S., Clément, R. & Donovan, L. A. (2002). Sex and age effects on willingness to communicate, anxiety, perceived competence and L2 motivation among junior high school French immersion students. *Lanuage Learning,* 52(3), 537-564.
MacIntyre, P. D. & Charos, C. (1996). Personality, attitudes, and affect as predictors of second language communication. *Journal of Language and Social Psychology,* 15(1), 3-26.
MacIntyre, P. D., Clément, R. & Donovan, L. A. (2002). Willingness to communicate in the L2 among French immersion students. Paper presented at the Second Language Research Forum, Toronto (3-6 October). [online] Available from: http://www.faculty/uccb.ns.ca/pmacintyre/research_pages_otherfiles/slrf2002.pdf (Date viewed 10 December 2007).
MacIntyre, P. D., Clément, R., Dörnyei, Z. & Noels, K. A. (1998). Conceptualizing willingness to communicate in a L2: A situational model of L2 confidence and affiliation. *The Modern Language Journal,* 82(4), 545-562.
MacWhinney, B. (1987). Applying the competition model to bilingualism. *Applied Psycholinguistics,* 8(4), 315-327.

—. (2001). The competition model: The input, the context, and the brain. In P. Robinson (Ed.), *Cognition and Second Language Instruction* (pp. 69-90). New York: Cambridge University Press.

Maeshiba, N., Yoshinaga, N., Kasper G. & Ross, S. (1996). Transfer and proficiency in interlanguage apologizing. In S. M. Gass & J. Neu (Eds.), *Speech Acts Across Cultures* (pp. 155-187). Berlin: Mouton.

Makino, S. (2002). Uchi and soto as cultural and linguistic metaphors. In R. Donahue (Ed.), *Exploring Japaneseness on Japanese Enactments of Culture and Consciousness* (pp. 29-64). Westport, CT: Ablex Publishing.

Mao, L. (1992). Invitational discourse and Chinese identity. *Journal of Asian Pacific Communication,* 31(1), 70-96.

—. (1994). Beyond politeness theory: "Face" revisited and renewed. *Journal of Pragmatics,* 21(5), 451-486.

Markel, N. (1975). Coverbal behavior associated with conversation turns. In A. Kendon, R. Harris & M. R. Key (Eds.), *Organization of Behavior in Face-to-Face Interaction* (pp. 189-197). The Hague: Mouton.

Martin, D. (2003). *Talk a Lot.* Okegawa City: EFL Press.

Matsuda, A. (2009). Desirable but not necessary? The place of World Englishes and English as an international language in English teacher preparation programs in Japan. In F. Sharifian (Ed.), *English as an International Language: Perspectives and Pedagogical Issues* (pp. 169-189). Clevedon, UK: Multilingual Matters.

Matsumoto, K. (1994). English instruction problems in Japanese schools and higher education. *Journal of Asian Pacific Communication,* 5(4), 209-214.

Matsumoto, M. & Boye Lafayette, D. (2000). *Japanese Nuance in Plain English.* Tokyo: Kodansha.

Matsumoto, Y. (1988). Reexamination of the universality of face: Politeness phenomena in Japanese. *Journal of Pragmatics,* 12(4), 403-426.

—. (1989). Politeness and conversational universals: Observations from Japanese. *Multilingua - Journal of Cross-Cultural and Interlanguage Communication*, 8(2/3), 207-221.

—. (1993). Linguistic politeness and cultural style: Observations. In P. M. Clancy (Ed.), *Japanese and Korean Linguistics, Volume 2,* (pp. 55-67). Stanford, CA: Stanford University.

Matsuoka, R. (2004). Willingness to communicate among Japanese college students. Proceedings of the 9th Conference of Pan-Pacific Association of Applied Linguistics, Namseoul University, Korea (19-20 August), 165-176. [online] Available from:

http://www.paaljapan.org/resources/proceedings/PAAL9/pdfs/matsuoka.pdf (Date viewed 7 July 2008).
—. (2005). Willingness to communicate in English among Japanese college students. Proceedings of the 10th Conference of Pan-Pacific Association of Applied Linguistics, Edinburgh University, Scotland (2-4 August), 151-159. [online] Available from: http://www.paaljapan.org/resources/proceedings/PAAL10/pdfs/matsuoka.pdf (Date viewed 30 January 2009).
Matsuoka, R. & Evans, D. R. (2005). Willingness to communicate in the second language. *Journal of National College of Nursing,* 4(1), 3-12.
Matsuura, H., Chiba, R., & Hilderbrandt, P. (2001). Beliefs about learning and teaching communicative English in Japan. *JALT Journal,* 23(1), 69-89.
Maynard, S. K. (1986). On back-channel behavior in Japanese and English casual conversation. *Linguistics,* 24(6), 1079-1108.
—. (1987). Interactional functions of a noverbal sign: Head movement in Japanese dyadic conversations. *Journal of Pragmatics,* 11(1), 589-606.
—. (1989). *Japanese Conversation: Self-Contextualization Through Structure and Interactional Management, Volume 35.* Norwood: Ablex.
—. (1990). Conversation management in contrast: Listener responses in Japanese and American English. *Journal of Pragmatics,* 14(1), 397-412.
—. (1997). Analyzing interactional management in native/non-native English conversation: A case of listener response. *IRAL,* 35(1), 37-60.
McCarthy, M. (2002). Good listenership made plain: British and American non-minimal response tokens in everyday conversation. In R. Reppen, S. M. Fitzmaurice & D. Biber (Eds.), *Using Corpora to Explore Linguistic Variation* (pp. 49-72). Philadelphia: John Benjamins.
—. (2003). Talking back: "Small" interactional response tokens in everyday conversation. *Research on Language and Social Interaction,* 36(1), 33-63.
McCarthy, M. & O'Keeffe, A. (2004). Research in the teaching of speaking. *Annual Review of Applied Linguistics,* 24(1), 26-43.
McClure, W. (2000). *Using Japanese. A Guide to Contemporary Usage.* Cambridge: Cambridge University Press.
McConnell, D. (1996). Education for global integration in Japan: A case study of the JET program. *Human Organization,* 55(4), 446-457.
McCornack, S. A. (1992). Information manipulation theory. *Communication Monographs,* 59(1), 1-16.
McCroskey, J. C. (1984). Self-report measurement. In J. A. Dally & J. C.

McCroskey (Eds.), *Avoiding Communication: Shyness, Reticence, and Communication* (pp. 81-94). Beverly Hills, CA: Sage.
—. (1992). Reliability and validity of willingness to communicate scale. *Communication Quarterly,* 40(1), 16-25.
McCroskey, J. C. & Richmond, V. P. (1987). Willingness to communicate. In J. C. McCroskey & J. A. Daly (Eds.), *Personality and Interpersonal Communication* (pp. 129-156). Newbury Park, CA: Sage.
—. (1990). Willingness to communicate: Differing cultural perspectives. *Southern Communication Journal,* 56(1), 72-77.
McMahon, R. (2005). *Travel Abroad Project.* Tokyo: Nan'Un-Do.
McVeigh, B. J. (2001). Higher education, apathy and post-meritocracy. *The Language Teacher,* 25(10), 29-32.
Miller, L. (1988). Listening behavior in conversations between Japanese and Americans. In J. Blommaert & J. Verschueren (Eds.), *Intercultural and International Communication* (pp. 111-130). Amsterdam: John Benjamins.
Mills, S. (2003). *Gender and Politeness.* Cambridge: Cambridge University Press.
Miyazaki, S. (2010). Learners' performance and awareness of Japanese listening behavior in JFL and JSL environments. *Sophia Junior College Faculty Journal,* 30(1), 23-34.
Mizutani, N. (1982). The listener's responses in Japanese conversation. *Sociolinguistics News-letter,* 13(1), 33-38.
—. (1983). Aizuchi to ootoo. In O. Mizutani (Ed.), *Hanashi Kotoba no Hyoogen [Courses on Japanese Expressions], Volume 3* (pp. 37-44). Tokyo: Chikuma Shoboo.
Moeran, B. (1996). The orient strikes back: Advertising and imagining Japan. *Theory, Culture & Society,* 13(3), 77-112.
Monbusho [The Ministry of Education, Science, Sports, and Culture]. (1989). *Koutougakko Gakushu Shi-Douyouryo Kaisetsu: Gaikokugohen [A Commentary on High School Education Guidelines: Foreign Languages].* Tokyo: Kyoikushuppan.
—. (1999a). *Koutougakko Gakushu Shi-Douyouryo Kaisetsu: Gaikokugohen [A Commentary on High School Education Guidelines: Foreign Languages].* Tokyo: Tokyoshoseki.
—. (1999b). *Koutougakko Gakushu Shi-Douyouryo Kaisetsu: Gaikokugohen [A Commentary on High School Education Guidelines: Foreign Languages].* Tokyo: Kaitakusha.
Morita, A. & Ishihara, S. (1989). *"No" To Ieru Nihon [The Japan That Can Say "No"].* Tokyo: Kobunsha.
Mura, S. S. (1983). Licensing violations: Legitimate violations of Grice's

conversational principle. In R. Craig & K. Tracy (Eds.), *Conversational Coherence*. Beverly Hills, CA: Sage.

Murray, S. O. (1985). Towards a model of members' methods for recognising interruptions. *Language in Society,* 14(1), 31-41.

—. (1987). Power and solidarity in "interruption": A critique of the Santa Barbara school conception and its application by Orcutt and Harvey (1985). *Symbolic Interaction,* 10(1), 101-110.

—. (1988). The sound of simultaneous speech, the meaning of interruption: A rejoinder. *Journal of Pragmatics,* 12(1), 115-116.

Nakai, F. (1999). Japanese communication features: a survey. Paper presented at the 12th World Congress of Applied Linguistics, Waseda University, Tokyo, World Congress of Applied Linguistics (3 August).

Nakane, C. (1970). *Japanese Society*. Tokyo: Charles E. Tuttle.

Neulliep, J. W. (2003). *Intercultural Communication: A Contextual Approach (2nd edition)*. Boston, MA: Houghton, Miffling.

Nevara, J. (2003). Teaching English in Japan to Chinese students. *Asian EFL Journal,* 5(3). [online] Available from: http://www.asian-efl-journal.com/sept_03_sub1.php (Date viewed 20 October 2008).

Nikolova, D. (2008). English teaching in elementary schools in Japan: A review of a current government survey. *Asian EFL Journal,* 10(1). [online] Available from: http://www.asian-efl-journal.com/March_08_dn.php (Date viewed 13 November 2009).

Nishiyama, K. (1993). *Japanese negotiators: Are they deceptive or misunderstood?* Paper presented at the 23rd annual convention of the Communication Association of Japan., Tama city, Tokyo (17-19 June).

Nishiyama, S. E. (1995). Speaking English with a Japanese mind. *World Englishes,* 14(1), 27-36.

Nittono, M. (1999). Strategic discourse-based hedges in Japanese: Their forms and functions in conversational interaction. Paper presented at the 12th World Congress of Applied Linguistics, Waseda University, Tokyo, World Congress of Applied Linguistics (2 August).

Numrich, C. (2005). *Tuning in: Listening and Speaking in the Real World*. New York: Pearson Longman.

Nunn, R. (2000). Intercultural communication & Grice's principle. *Asia EFL Journal,* 5(1). [online] Available from: http://www.asian-efl-journal.com/march03.sub3.php (Date viewed 14 August 2008).

Obana, Y. & Tomoda, T. (1994). The sociological significance of 'politeness' in English and Japanese languages - report from a pilot study. *Japanese Studies Bulletin,* 14(1), 37-49.

Ochs, E. (1979). Transcription as theory. In E. Ochs & B. Schiefflelin (Eds.), *Developmental Pragmatics* (pp. 43–72). New York: Academic

Press.
Ohira, K. (1998). Have you changed? Pragmatic transfer of backchannel behaviour by Japanese bilingual speakers. Unpublished PhD Thesis, University of Illinois, Urbana-Champaign.
Okabe, R. (1983). Cultural assumptions of East and West. In W. Gudykunst (Ed.), *Intercultural Communication Theory. Current Perspectives* (pp. 21-44). London: Sage.
O'Keeffe, A. & Farr, F. (2003). Using language corpora in initial teacher education: Pedagogical issues and practical applications. *TESOL Quarterly,* 37(3), 389-418.
O'Keeffe, A. (2004). 'Like the wise virgins and all that jazz': Using a corpus to examine vague categorisation and shared knowledge. *Language and Computers,* 52(1), 1-20.
O'Keeffe, A., McCarthy, M. & Carter, R. (2007). *From Corpus to Classroom: Language Use and Language Teaching.* Cambridge: Cambridge University Press.
O'Keeffe, A. & Adolphs, S. (2008). Response tokens in British and Irish discourse: Corpus, context and variational pragmatics. In A. Barron & K. Schneider (Eds.), *Variational Pragmatics* (pp. 69-98). Amsterdam: John Benjamins.
O'Keeffe, A., Clancy, B. & Adolphs, S. (2011). *Introducing Pragmatics in Use.* Routledge: London.
Okushi, Y. (1990). Misunderstood efforts and missed opportunities: An examination of EFL in Japan. *Penn Working Papers in Educational Linguistics,* 6(2), 65-75.
Olshtain, E., & Cohen, A. (1990). The learning of complex speech act behavior. *TESL Canada Journal,* 7(1), 45-65.
Orestrom, B. (1983). *Turn-Taking in English Conversation.* Lund: Lund University Press.
Ortega, L. (2003). Syntactic complexity measures and their relationship to L2 proficiency: A research synthesis of college-level L2 writing. *Applied Linguistics,* 24(4), 492-518.
Oshio, A., Abe, S. & Cutrone, P. (2011). Reliability and validity of a Japanese version of the ten item personality inventory (TIPI-J). Poster presentation at the 2nd Biennial Conference of the Association for Research in Personality. Riverside, California, USA (17 June).
Oshio, A., Abe, S. & Cutrone, P. (2012). Development, reliability, and validity of the Japanese version of the ten item personality inventory (TIPI-J). *Japanese Journal of Personality Psychology,* 21(1), 40-52.
Peaty, D. (1987). False Beginners: Who they are and what to do with them. *The Language Teacher,* 11(14), 4-5.

Planken, B. (2005). Managing rapport in lingua franca sales negotiations: A comparison of professional and aspiring negotiators. *English for Specific Purposes,* 24(4), 381-400.

Punyanunt-Carter, N. M. (2008). Father-daughter relationships: Examining family communication patterns and interpersonal communication satisfaction. *Communication Research Reports,* 25(1), 23-33.

Quinlisk, C. (2004). Communicator status and expectations in intercultural communication: Implications for language learning in a multicultural community. *Communication Research Reports,* 21(1), 84-91.

Quirk, R., Greenbaum, S., Leech, G. & Svartvik, J. (1985). *A Comprehensive Grammar of the English Language.* London: Longman.

Reesor, M. (2002). The bear and the honeycomb: A history of Japanese English language policy. *NUCB JLCC (Nagoya University of Commerce and Business Journal of Language, Culture and Communication),* 4(1), 41-52.

Reischauer, E. O. (1988). *The Japanese Today: Change and Continuity.* Cambridge, MA: The Belknap Press of Harvard University Press.

Riggenbach, H. (1991). Toward an understanding of fluency: A microanalysis of nonnative speaker conversations. *Discourse Processes,* 14(4), 423-441.

—. (1998). Evaluating learner interactional skills: Conversation at the micro level. In R. Young & A. Weiyun He (Eds.), *Talking and Testing: Discourse Approaches to the Assessment of Oral Proficiency, Volume 14* (pp. 53-67). Philadelphia: John Benjamins.

Rios-Ellis, B., Bellamy, L. & Shojic, J. (2000). An examination of specific types of ijime within Japanese Schools. *School Psychology International,* 21(3), 227-241.

Ritzer, G. (1992). *Sociological Theory.* New York: McGraw-Hill.

Robinson, M. (1992). Introspective methodology in interlanguage pragmatics research. In G. Kasper (Ed.), *Pragmatics of Japanese as native and target language, Volume 3,* (pp. 29-84). Honolulu: University of Hawaii.

Roger, A. (2008). Teaching the speaking skill to Japanese students part 1: Construct & practice. *The Journal of Kanda University of International Studies,* 20(1), 1-26.

Rose, K. R. (1992). Method and scope in cross cultural speech act research: A contrastive study of requests in Japanese and English. Unpublished PhD Thesis, University of Illinois, Urbana-Champaign.

—. (1994). Pragmatic consciousness-raising in an EFL context. In L. F. Bouton & Y. Kachru (Eds.), *Pragmatics and Language Learning, Volume 5.* Urbana-Champaign: University of Illinois.

—. (2005). On the effects of instruction in second language pragmatics. *System,* 33(3), 385-399.
Rose, K. R. & Ng, K. C. (2001). Inductive and deductive teaching of compliments and compliment responses. In K. R. Rose & G. Kasper (Eds.), *Pragmatics in Language Teaching* (pp. 145-170). Cambridge: Cambridge University Press.
Ross, S. (1998). Divergent frame interpretations in oral proficiency interview interaction. In R. Young & A. Weiyun He (Eds.), *Talking and Testing: Discourse Approaches to the Assessment of Oral Proficiency* (pp. 333-353). Philadelphia: John Benjamins.
Rowntree, D. (1981). *Statistics Without Tears: A Primer for Non Mathematicians* Harmondsworth: Penguin.
—. (2000). *Statistics Without Tears: A Primer for Non Mathematicians (2nd edition).* London: Penguin.
Ruben, B. D. (1976). Assessing communication competency for intercultural adaptation. *Group & Organization Studies,* 1(1), 334-354.
Sacks, H. E., Schegloff, E. & Jefferson, G. (1974). A simple systematics in the organization of turn-taking for conversation. *Language,* 50(1), 696-735.
Safont, M. P. (2003). Instructional effects on the use of request acts modification devices by EFL learners. In A. Martínez-Flor, E. Usó Juan & A. Fernández Guerra (Eds.), *Pragmatic Competence and Foreign Language* (pp. 211-232). Castello'n, Spain: Servei de Publicacions de la Universitat Jaume I.
Said, E. (1978). *Orientalism.* New York: Pantheon Books.
Saito, M. (1994). Functions of backchannels across cultures. *Journal of Senzoku-Gakuen College,* 23(1), 37-45.
Sakui, K. (2004). Wearing two pairs of shoes: Language teaching in Japan. *ELT J,* 58(2), 155-163.
Salazar, P. C. (2003). Pragmatic instruction in the EFL context. In A. Martínez-Flor, E. Usó Juan & A. Fernández Guerra (Eds.), *Pragmatic Competence and Foreign Language Teaching* (pp. 233-246). Castello'n, Spain: Servei de Publicacions de la Universitat Jaume I.
Sapir, E. (1929). The status of linguistics as a science. *Language,* 5(1), 207-214.
Sardegna, V. G. & Molle, D. (2010). Videoconferencing with strangers: Teaching Japanese EFL students verbal backchannel signals and reactive expressions. *Intercultural Pragmatics,* 7(2), 279-310.
Sasagawa, Y. (1996). Ibunka no kanten kara mita Nihongo no aimaisei - zainichi gaikokujin ryuugakusei choosa yori [Ambiguity in Japanese communication - from the foreign students' viewpoint]. *Nihongo*

Kyoiku, 89(1), 52-63.
Sasajima, S. (2000). Turn-taking in a Japanese EFL classroom: What kind of backchannels work in a discussion activity? *Bulletin of Saitama Medical School Premedical Course,* 8(1), 51-57.
Sasaki, A. (2006). A pilot study on back-channels in an English Interview test: Their effect on a Japanese student's utterances and anxiety level. *The Journal of Kansai English Language Education Society,* 29(1), 45-60.
Sato, C. (1990). Ethnic styles in classroom discourse. In R. C. Scarcella, S. D. Krashen & E. S. Anderson (Eds.), *Developing Communicative Competence in a Second Language* (pp. 107-119). Rowley, Mass: Newbury House.
Sato, S. & Okamoto, S. (1999). Reexamination of Japanese "cooperative" communication style. In J. Verschueren (Ed.), *Pragmatics in 1998. Selected Papers from the Sixth International Pragmatics Conference, Volume 2* (pp. 518-527). Antwerp: International Pragmatics Association.
Sato, Y. (2008). Oral communication problems and strategies of Japanese university EFL learners. Unpublished PhD Thesis, University of Reading, Reading.
Schegloff, E. (1982). Discourse as an interactional achievement: Some uses of "UH-HUH" and other things that come between sentences. In D. Tannen (Ed.), *Georgetown University Roundtable on Language and Linguistics, Analyzing Discourse: Text and Talk* (pp. 71-93). Washington: Georgetown University Press.
Schenkein, J. (1972). Towards the analysis of natural conversation in the sense of heheh. *Semiotica,* 6(1), 344-377.
Schmidt, R. (1983). Interaction, accultration, and the acquisition of communicative competence: A case study of an adult. In N. Wolfson & E. Judd (Eds.), *Sociolinguistics and language acquisition* (pp. 137-174). Rowley: Newbury House.
—. (1993). Consciousness, learning and interlanguage pragmatics. In G. Kasper & S. Blum-Kulka (Eds.), *Interlanguage Pragmatics* (pp. 21-42). Oxford: Oxford University Press.
—. (1990). The role of consciousness in second language learning. *Applied Linguistics,* 11(2), 129-158.
Schmidt, R. & Frota, S. N. (1986). Developing basic conversational ability in a second language: A case study of an adult learner of Portuguese. In R. R. Day (Ed.), *Talking to Learn: Conversation in Second Language Acquisition* (pp. 237-326). Rowley, MA: Newbury House.
Scollon, R. & Scollon, S. (1995). *Intercultural Communication: A Discourse Approach.* Oxford: Blackwell.

—. (2001). *Intercultural Communication: A Discourse Approach (2nd edition)*. Malden, MA: Blackwell

Seidlhofer, B. (2003). A concept of international English and related issues: From 'real English' to 'realistic English'. In Council of Europe (Ed.), *Language Policy Division*. Strasbourg: Council of Europe. [online] Available from: http://www.coe.int/t/dg4/linguistic/source/seidlhoferen.pdf (Date viewed 13 March 2009).

Seidlhofer, B. (2004). Research perspectives on teaching English as a lingua franca. *Annual Review of Applied Linguistic,* 24(1), 209-239.

Shaw, R. (2007). Meaning in context: The role of context and language in narratives of disclosure of sibling sexual assault. Unpublished PhD, Union Institute & University, Cincinnati, OH.

Shinmura, I. E. (1991). *Koojien (4th edition)*. Tokyo: Iwanami Shoten.

Silverstein, M. (1976). Shifters, linguistic categories, and cultural desccription. In K. Basso & H. A. Selby (Eds.), *Meaning and Anthropology* (pp. 11-56). Albuquerque: University of New Mexico Press.

Simic, M. & Tanaka, T. (2008). Language context III the willingness to communicate research works: A review. *The Journal of Humanities and Social Science, Okayama University Graduate School,* 26(1), 71-88.

Simmel, G. (1990). *The Philosophy of Money (2nd edition)*. Translation of German original (1900) by T. Bottomore & D. Frisby. London: Routledge.

Spees, H. (1994). A cross-cultural study of indirectness. *Issues in Applied Linguistics,* 5(2), 231-253.

Spelman-Miller, K. (2000). Writing on-line: Temporal features of first and second language written text production. Unpublished PhD Thesis, University of Reading, Reading.

Spencer-Oatey, H. (2000). *Culturally Speaking*. London: Continuum.

Spitzberg, B. H. (2000). A model of intercultural communication competence. In L. Samovar & R. Porter (Eds.), *Intercultural Communication: A Reader, 2nd edition* (pp. 7-24). Belmont, CA: Wadsworth Publishing.

Spitzberg, B. H., & Cupach, W. (1984). *Interpersonal Communication Competence*. Beverly Hills, CA: Sage.

Stubbe, M. (1998). Are you listening? Cultural influences on the use of supportive verbal feedback in conversation. *Journal of Pragmatics,* 29(3), 257-289.

Sugimoto, Y. (1997). *An Introduction to Japanese Society*. Cambridge:

Cambridge University Press.

Suzuki, A. (2010). Introducing diversity into ELT: Student teacher responses. *ELT Journal,* 64(3), 1-9.

Swan, M. (2005). Legislation by hypothesis: The case of task-based instruction. *Applied Linguistics,* 26(3), 376-401.

Swan, M. & Smith, B. (2001). *Learner English: A Teacher's Guide to Interference and Other Problems (2nd edition).* Cambridge University Press: Cambridge.

Szatrowski, P. (1993). *Nihongo no Danwa no Kouzou Bunseki: Kanyu no Sutorateji no kousatsu [The Analysis of Structures in Japanese Conversations: The Observations on Strategy of Persuasions].* Tokyo: Kuroshio Shuppan.

Tajima, K. (2001). Pragmatic use of aizuchi in Japanese discourse: a comparison with English backchannels. *The Academic Reports, the Faculty of Engineering, Tokyo Institute of Polytechnics,* 24(2), 54-60.

Tajino, A. (2002). Transportation process models: A systemic approach to problematic team-teaching situations. *Prospect,* 17(3), 29-44.

Takahashi, M. (2005). The efficacy of grammar instruction in EFL classes in Japan. Unpublished PhD Thesis, Kobe Shoin Graduate School of Letters, Kobe.

Takahashi, S. (1996). Pragmatic transferability. *Studies in Second Language Acquisition,* 18(1), 189-223.

—. (2001). The role of input enhancement in developing pragmatic competence. In K. R. Rose & G. Kasper (Eds.), *Pragmatics in Language Teaching* (pp. 171-199). Cambridge: Cambridge University Press.

Takahashi, T. & Beebe, L. (1987). The development of pragmatic competence by Japanese learners of English. *JALT Journal,* 8(1), 131-155.

Takanashi, Y. (2004). TEFL and communication styles in Japanese culture. *Language, Culture and Curriculum,* 17(1), 1-14.

Takimoto, M. (2009). The effects of input-based tasks on the development of learners' pragmatic proficiency. *Applied Linguistics,* 30(1), 1-25.

Tanaka, N. (1988). Politeness: Some problems for Japanese speakers of English. *JALT Journal,* 9(1), 81-102.

Tao, H. & Thompson, S. A. (1991). English backchannels in Mandarin conversations: A case study of superstratum pragmatic 'interference'. *Journal of Pragmatics,* 16(1), 209-223.

Tateyama, Y. (2001). Explicit and implicit teaching of pragmatic routines: Japanese sumimasen. In K. R. Rose & G. Kasper (Eds.), *Pragmatics in Language Teaching* (pp. 200-222). Cambridge: Cambridge University

Press.
Tateyama, Y., Kasper, G., Mui, L. P., Tay, H. & Thananart, O. (1997). Explicit and implicit teaching of pragmatic routines. In L. Bouton (Ed.), *Pragmatics and Language Learning, Volume 8* (pp. 163-177). Urbana-Champaign: University of Illinois.
Terrell, T., Gomez, E. & Mariscal, J. (1980). Can acquisition take place in the classroom? In R. Andersen (Ed.), *Research in Second Language Acquisition: Selected Papers of the Los Angeles Second Language Acquisition Research Forum* (pp. 155-161). Rowley, MA: Newbury House.
The Japan Times (1983). Japanese mannerism is a key point in IBM case. *The Japan Times,* 23 January, p. 2.
Thompson, I. (1987). 'Japanese Speakers' in learner English. In M. Swan & B. Smith (Eds.), *Learner English.* Cambridge: Cambridge University Press.
Thonus, T. (2002). Tutor and student assessments of academic writing tutorials: What is "success"?. *Assessing Writing,* 8(2), 110-134.
—. (2005). Backchannels as a pragmatic resource for learners of English. Paper presented at the 16th International Conference on Pragmatics and Language Learning, Bloomington, IN (15 April).
—. (2007). Listener responses as a pragmatic source for learners of English. *CATESOL Journal,* 19(1), 132-145.
Toolan, M. (1996). *Total Speech: An Integrational Linguistic Approach to Language.* Durham NC: Duke University Press.
Torghabeh, R. (2007). EIL, variations and the native speaker's model. *Asia EFL Journal,* 9(4). [online] Available from: http://www.asian-efl-journal.com/Dec_2007_rt.php (Date viewed 3 December 2010).
Tottie, G. (1991). Conversational style in British and American English: The case of backchannels. In K. Aijmer & B. Altenberg (Eds.), *English Corpus Linguistics: Studies in Honour of Jan Svartvik* (pp. 254–271). London: Longman.
Townsend, J. & Danling, F. (1998). Quiet students across cultures contexts. *English Education,* 31(1), 4-25.
Triandis, H. C. (1989). The self and social behavior in differing cultural contexts. *Psychological Review,* 96(1), 506-520.
—. (1995). The self and social behaviour in differing cultural contexts. In N. R. Goldberger & J. B. Veroff (Eds.), *The Culture and Psychology Reader* (pp. 326-365). New York: New York University Press.
Truscott, J. (1998). Noticing in second language acquisition: A critical review. *Second Language Research,* 14(2), 103-135.
Tsuchiya, K. (2010). Culture-sensitive taxonomy of response tokens:

Moving from listenership to speakership. Unpublished PhD Thesis, University of Nottingham, Nottingham.
Tucker, M. F. (1999). Self-awareness and development using the overseas assignment inventory. In S. M. Fowler & M. G. Mumford (Eds.), *Intercultural Sourcebook: Cross-Cultural Training Method, Volume 2* (pp. 45-52). Yarmouth, ME: Intercultural Press.
Uematsu, S. (2000). The use of back channels between native and non-native speakers in English and Japanese. *Intercultural Communication Studies,* 10(2), 85-98.
Ueno, J. (2004). Gender differences in Japanese conversation. *International Association for Intercultural Communication Studies,* 13(1), 92-107.
Ulijn, J. M. & Strother, J. (1995). *Communicating in Business and Technology.* Frankfurt am Main: Peter Lang.
Vygotsky, L. (1962). *Thought and Language.* Cambridge: The M.I.T. Press.
Walsh, M. (2007). *English as an international language. Japan: Accents in the curriculum. Working Papers of the Center of English Language Studies, University of Birmingham.* [online] Available from: http://www.cels.bham.ac.uk/resources/sociolinguistics.shtml (Date viewed 4 December 2010).
Wannaruk, A. (1997). Back-channel behaviour in Thai and American casual telephone conversation. *Suranaree J. Sci. Technol.,* 4(3), 168-174.
Ward, N. (2004). Pragmatic functions of prosodic features in non-lexical utterances. *Speech Prosody,* 4(1), 325-328.
—. (2006). Non-lexical conversational sounds in American English. *Pragmatics & Cognition,* 14(1), 113-184.
Ward, N., Escalante, R., Yaffa, A. & Solorio, T. (2007). Learn to show you're listening. *Computer Assisted Language Learning.* [online] Available from: http://www.cs.utep.edu/nigel/papers/call.pdf (Date viewed 30 October 2008).
Ward, N. & Tsukahara, W. (2000). Prosodic features which cue back-channel responses in English and Japanese. *Journal of Pragmatics,* 32(8), 1177-1207.
Wardhaugh, R. (1986). *An Introduction to Sociolinguistics.* Oxford: Blackwell.
Watts, R., Ide, S. & Ehlich, K. (1992). *Politeness in Language. Studies in its History, Theory and Practice.* Berlin: Mouton de Gruyter.
Wen, W. P. & Clément, R. (2003). A Chinese conceptualisation of willingness to communicate in ESL. *Language, Culture and Curriculum,* 16(1), 18 - 38.

White, L. (1991). Adverb placement in second language acquisition: some effects of positive and negative evidence in the classroom. *Second Language Research,* 7(1), 133-161.

White, S. (1989). Backchannels across cultures: A study of Americans and Japanese. *Language in Society,* 18(1), 59-76.

Widdowson, H. G. (1989). Knowledge of language and ability for use. *Applied Linguistics,* 10(2), 128-137.

—. (1994). The ownership of English. *TESOL Quarterly,* 28(2), 377-389.

—. (1997). EIL, ESL, EFL: Global issues and local interests. *World Englishes,* 16(1), 135-146.

Wildner-Bassett, M. E. (1984). *Improving Pragmatic Aspects of Learners' Interlanguage: A Comparison of Methodological Approaches for Teaching Gambits to Advanced Adult Learners of English in Industry.* Tübingen: Gunter Narr Verlag.

—. (1994). Intercultural pragmatics and proficiency: 'Polite' noises for cultural awareness. *International Review of Applied Linguistics in Language Teaching,* 32(1), 3-17.

Wilson, M. (1998). The guessing culture of Japan: Gain or pain. In R. Donahue (Ed.), *Japanese Culture and Communication: Critical Cultural Analysis* (pp. 215-218). Lanham, MD: University Press of America.

Wiseman, R. L. (2002). Intercultural communication competence. In W. B. Gudykunst & B. Mody (Eds.), *Handbook of International and Intercultural Communication,* 2nd edition (pp. 207-224). Thousand Oaks, CA: Sage.

Wishnoff, J. (2000). Hedging your bets: L2 learners' acquisition of pragmatic devices in academic writing and computer-mediated discourse. *Second Language Studies, Working Papers of the Department of Second Language Studies, University of Hawaii* 19(1), 119-157.

Wolf, J. P. (2008a). Backchannels, appraisal psychology, and second language fluency. *Journal of Tourism Studies,* 19(1), 123-136.

—. (2008b). The effects of backchannels on fluency in L2 oral task production. *System,* 36(2), 279-294.

Wolfson, N. (1983). An empirically based analysis of complimenting in American English. In N. Wolfson & E. Judd (Eds.), *Sociolinguistics and Language Acquisition* (pp. 82-95). Rowley: Newbury House.

—. (1989). *Perspectives: Sociolinguistics and TESOL.* Rowley: Newbury House.

Yamada, H. (1992). *American and Japanese Business Discourse: A Comparison of International Styles.* Norwood: Ablex.

—. (1997). *Different Games, Different Rules: Why Americans and Japanese Misunderstand Each Other*. New York: Oxford University Press.

Yamaguchi, C. (2002). Towards international English in EFL classrooms in Japan. *The Internet TESOL Journal*, 8(1). [online] Available from: http://iteslj.org/Articles/Yamaguchi-Language.html (Date viewed 27 August 2009).

Yano, Y. (2001). World Englishes in 2000 and beyond. *World Englishes*, 20(2), 119-131.

Yashima, T. (2002). Willingness to communicate in a second language: The Japanese EFL context. *The Modern Language Journal*, 86(1), 54-66.

Yashima, T., Zenuck-Nishide, L. & Shimizu, K. (2004). The influence of attitudes and affect on willingness to communicate and second language communication. *Language Learning*, 54(1), 119-152.

Yngve, V. (1970). On getting a word in edgewise. *Chicago Linguistic Society*, 6(1), 567-578.

Yoshimi, D. R. (2001). Explicit instruction and JFL learners use of interactional discourse markers. In K. R. Rose & G. Kasper (Eds.), *Pragmatics in Language Teaching* (pp. 223-244). Cambridge: Cambridge University Press.

INDEX

Abe, 95, 262, 333
acculturation, 92, 155
ACTFL, 91, 94, 312
active listening, 51, 56, 82
adaptive control of thought, 61
Adolphs, 36, 37, 40, 41, 240, 244, 246, 250, 333
Agawa, 52, 310
aizuchi, 34, 56, 59, 60, 143, 144, 145, 221, 222, 223, 338
Akasu, 29, 310
Allwood, 21, 22, 310
alpha level, 227
Alymursy, 16, 310
American Council on the Teaching of Foreign Languages, 91, → ACTFL
American English, 48, 54, 59, 78, 79, 80, 92, 149, 153, 253, 254, 323, 324, 330, 339, 340, 341
Ammon, 3, 310
anaphoric, 117
Anderson, F., 4, 8, 61, 310
Anderson, J., 61, 310
Anderson, S., 336
Ang, 25, 317
Apltekin, 160, 310
Applied Linguistics, 22, 310, 311, 313, 314, 317, 319, 328, 329, 330, 332, 333, 336, 337, 338, 341
Apud, 25, 325
Araki, 30, 311
Arima, 29, 310
Armour, 28, 310
Arndt, 16, 325
Asao, 29, 310
assessment criteria, 87, 161, 169, 225, 247, 309

assumption of independence, 125
Aston, 55, 159, 311
Auer, 58, 311
avoiding confrontations, 14, 159
Babin, 10, 328
backchannel output hypothesis, 251
Baker, 10, 314, 328
Bardovi-Harlig, 63, 71, 311
Barnlund, 5, 6, 14, 30, 311
Beebe, 5, 7, 8, 311, 338
Befu, 15, 311
Bellamy, 15, 334
Bennett, 84, 321
Big-Five, 94
Billmyer, 65, 66, 71, 312
Bjørge, 40, 41, 82, 312
Blanche, 31, 54, 312
Blommaert, 12, 312, 331
Books, 29
Bouton, 65, 66, 71, 311, 312, 319, 334, 339
Boxer, 48, 151, 312
Boyè Lafayette, 6, 14, 29, 31
Brady, 243, 312
Bredella, 23, 312
Breiner-Sanders, 91, 94, 312
Brinton, 41, 312
Brislin, 11, 84, 315, 322
British English, 49, 149, 230
Brown, D., 32, 312
Brown, J., 105, 313
Brown, P., 17, 18, 20, 21, 244, 245, 313
Brown, S., 4, 323
Brozyna, 62, 74, 75, 313
Brumfit, 160, 313
Brunner, 36, 37, 313
Burden, 9, 313
Burroughs, 10, 313

Byram, 23, 313, 321
Caine, 11, 78, 313
Caligiuri, 25, 313
CALL, 73, 91, 99
Canale, 22, 314
CANCODE, 240
Caplan, 85, 323
Carter, 1, 75, 77, 81, 117, 250, 314, 333, 334
casual register, 155, 157
Chapman, 28, 314
characterisation of linguistic units, 109, 113
Charos, 9, 10, 328
Chiba, 150, 330
Chua, 22, 321
Churchill, 27, 314
Clancy, 5, 14, 16, 20, 29, 38, 47, 49, 57, 58, 148, 244, 246, 314, 329, 333
clarification repetitions, 41, 111, 229
clarifications, 44, 112, 135, 186, 190, → CLARS
Clark, 3, 69, 71, 319
CLARS, 135, 136, 186, 190, 194
Clément, 10, 12, 252, 314, 328, 340
Clyne, 244, 314
Cohen, 63, 66, 333
collaborative feedback, 52
collectivism, 11
communication apprehension, 119
communication breakdown, 23, 84, 120, 150, 166, 232, 269
communicative competence, 7, 8, 11, 22, 23, 84, 222, 246, 248, 323, 336
comprehensible input, 248
Confucianism, 12, 15
Conlan, 160, 315
context-specific, 151, 154
continuer, 42, 43, 44, 55, 74, 84, 106, 120, 122, 142, 143, 144, 158, 163, 171, 269, 270
conversational analysis, 120, 242, 243, 251, 255, 257, 259

conversational implicature, 65, 69, 71, 327
conversational micro-skills, 78, 83, 84, 97, 109, 120, 123, 150, 231, 247
conversational register, 93, 155, 169
conversational repair strategies, 36, 79, 83, 106, 120, 121, 164, 165, 166, 167, 168, 169, 216, 218, 221, 227, 232, 301, 303
conversational routine, 328
conversational satisfaction questionnaire, 93, 125, 126, 129, 130, 155, 156, 157, 158, 169, 207, 295
Cook, 249, 315
cooperative overlaps, 51
cooperative principle, 2, 15, 26, → CP
Cope, 9, 323
Costa, 94, 315
CP, 26, 27, 55
Crawford, 47, 52, 53, 315
Cross-Cultural Adaptability Inventory, 84
cross-cultural communication, 122, 141, 241
cross-sectional, 6, 89, 109, 114, 124, 128, 129, 131, 148, 159, 170, 233, 240, 244
Crozet, 64, 70, 327
culturalism, 12
Culture General Assimilator, 84
Cupach, 23, 315, 337
Cushner, 84, 315
Cutrone, 1, 9, 28, 31, 36, 37, 39, 40, 43, 46, 47, 48, 49, 50, 54, 55, 77, 78, 80, 81, 82, 83, 84, 85, 86, 95, 102, 103, 108, 110, 111, 127, 148, 149, 150, 151, 152, 153, 154, 156, 157, 159, 160, 171, 229, 233, 243, 244, 248, 253, 254, 255, 257, 259, 262, 315, 333
D'Andrea, 84, 316
Daniels, 84, 316

Danling, 9, 339
Day, 29
DCTs, 5, 7, 63, 64, 67, 70, 234 →
  discourse completion tests
Deese, 108, 316
DeKeyser, 61, 66, 316, 320
Delanoy, 23, 312
descriptive statistics, 124
Dewaele, 8, 316
Di Santo, 25, 313
disagreement situations, 215
discernment, 18, 19, 324
discourse completion tests, 5
discourse contexts, 34, 38, 48, 49, 80, 83, 85, 86, 108, 109, 112, 113, 115, 117, 129, 136, 152, 153, 170, 172, 197, 202, 206, 268, 270, 309
discourse markers, 23, 41, 71, 75, 79, 84, 342
discourse theory, 120
Dittman, 35, 51, 316
Doi, 21, 29, 31, 316
Donahue, 29, 329, 341
Donovan, 10, 328
Dörnyei, 84, 120, 121, 252, 316, 328
Drummond, 243, 317
Duncan, 36, 80, 153, 239, 317
dyad, 25, 93, 103, 106
dyadic conversations, 46, 53, 61, 80, 81, 92, 101, 105, 145, 170, 240, 272, 330
dysfluency, 47, 116, 117
Earley, 25, 317
Edelsky, 38, 317
Edwards, 85
Eelen, 17, 18, 317
EFL curriculum, 150
EFL pedagogy in Japan, 89
Eggins, 77, 317
Ehlich, 16, 324, 340
Ehrman, 8, 317
eikaiwa, 248
EIL, 78, 247, 250, 339, 341
ELF, 78, 82, 312

elicited data, 5
ellipsis, 39, 114
Ellis, N., 61, 62, 235, 236, 317
Ellis, R., 3, 5, 7, 8, 11, 63, 64, 70, 72, 78, 317, 318
English as an International Language, 78, 325, 329, → EIL
English as Lingua Franca, 78, 82, → ELF
entrance examination, 2, 11, 249
Ervin-Tripp, 51, 243, 318
essentialism, 12, → culturalism
ETS, 3, 4, 318
evaluation anxiety, 156
Evans, 10, 12, 118, 318, 330
Everett, 25, 327
expansion techniques, 84, 120, 150
expectancy principle, 24, 85, 103
explicit approach, 61, 66, 70
explicit instruction, 62, 65, 66, 67, 68, 69, 232, 234, 251
explicit knowledge, 61, 62, 70, 234
extended listener responses, 40
extended responses, 86, 110, 111, 112, 134, 151, 156, 184, 189, 191, 193, 195, 224, 225, 226, 299
extraversion, 8, 87, 94, 95, 96, 97, 126, 131, 161, 164, 167, 169, 170, 225
Eysenck, 8, 318
face theory, 20
face-threatening act, 19, → FTA
face-to-face interaction, 10, 35, 243
false beginner, 4
Farooq, 3, 4, 318
Farr, 160, 246, 250, 318, 333
feedback continuum, 40, 82
Fewell, 8, 319
FFI, 63, 236, 238, 246, 315
Fillmore, 108, 232, 319
final clause boundaries, 86, 114, 117, 118, 136, 152, 202, 225, 226, 229
first-order politeness, 16, → politeness one

Fiske, 80, 153, 239, 317
FLA, 8, 9, 33
FLCAS, 9
Fliegel, 32, 319
foreign language anxiety, → FLA
foreign language classroom, 156
Foreign Language Classroom Anxiety Scale, 9, → FLCAS
form-focused-instruction, 63, → FFI
formulaic chunks, 231, 232, 237
Foster, 108, 114, 116, 117, 319
fragments, 116, 117
Fraser, 17, 319
Fries, 35, 319
FTA, 19, 20, 31, 55, 59, 60, 244
Fujita, 11, 319
Fukushima, 5, 319
Fukuya, 69, 71, 319
functional difference, 143
Furnham, 8, 316
Gardner, 9, 320
Garman, 47, 113, 127, 320
Gates, 2, 320
George Simmel, 26
Gertsen, 25
gesticulation, 80, 153, 239
Gick, 66, 320
Gilewicz, 74, 320
Gilks, 245, 320
giri, 15
globalisation, 1, 3
Goffman, 18, 320
Goldschneider, 61, 320
Gosling, 94, 320
Graham, 5, 320
grammar translation, 248
grammatical completion points, 49, 80, 113, 114, 268, 287
grammatical particles, 58
Gravetter, 125, 320
Greer, 8, 320
Grice, 2, 18, 26, 27, 28, 30, 32, 33, 55, 149, 159, 244, 320, 331, 332
Gricean theory, 27
group dynamics, 15, 26, 75, 240, 249

group harmony, 14
Gu, 19
Gudykunst, 22, 25, 29, 310, 315, 321, 333, 341
Guest, 57, 321
Guilherme, 25, 321
Hall, 35, 57, 316, 321, 323, 328
halo effect, 100, 101
Hammer, 25, 84, 321
Hamnett, 11, 322
Harrington, 103, 322
Hartley, 28, 314
Hashimoto, 9, 10, 322
Haslett, 11, 21, 322
Hattori, 36, 37, 322
Haugh, 17, 29, 30, 322
having the floor, 38
Hayashi, 35, 38, 49, 50, 80, 153, 322
Hecht, 25, 50, 85, 103, 104, 121, 125, 126, 129, 138, 155, 157, 169, 232, 322
Heck, 84, 316
Heffernan, 8, 248, 322
Heinz, 55, 56, 243, 322
Helgesen, 3, 4, 9, 322, 323
Hess, 51, 72, 323
Hidasi, 4, 323
Hilderbrandt, 150, 330
Hill, B., 17, 18, 323, 324
Hill, T., 5, 28, 29, 31, 323
hito no me, 16
Hofstede, 11, 14, 57, 323
holistic approach, 151
Holliday, 12, 13, 323
Holyoak, 66, 320
honne, 15
Hopper, 317
horizontal head movement, 37, 286
Horn, 27, 323
Horwitz, 9, 323
House, 66, 68, 70, 71, 82, 311, 314, 320, 322, 323, 336, 339, 341
Hughes, 2, 3, 4, 248, 324, 328
Hyde, 12, 13, 323
Hyme, 22

ICC, 2, 22, 23, 24, 25, 26, 78, 81, 84, 103, 109, 121, 123, 168, 169, 171, 222, 225, 232, 233, 247, 303, 304, 305, → intercultural communicative competence
Ida, 248, 324
Ide, 16, 17, 323, 324
IDs, 8, 9
iijime, 15
Ike, 2, 47, 324
Ikegami, 29, 324
illustration-interaction-induction, 75
Imai, 30, 324
implicit instruction, 66, 68, 69, 98, 220
implicit knowledge, 61
implicit learning, 62, 236
IMT, 30
independent topical noun phrase satellite units, 117
indexical creativity, 59, 60
indexical presupposition, 59
indexicality, 59
individual learner differences, 8, → IDs
individualism vs. collectivisim, 57
individualistic, 14, 154, 158, 237
individuality, 15
inferential statistics, 124, 125
information manipulation theory, 30, → IMT
input hypothesis, 61
interactive discourse, 115, 116
intercultural communication, 1, 2, 3, 4, 21, 22, 23, 29, 246, 257, 272, 311, 312, 314, 315, 321, 322, 326, 327, 332, 333, 334, 336, 337, 340, 341, → IC
intercultural communicative competence, 2, 22, 313
intercultural conversations, 46, 80, 158, 243, 269
Intercultural Development Inventory, 84
interface position, 236
interlocutor familiarity, 249

internal clause boundaries, 113, 114, 136, 152, 287
internationalisation, 247
Interpersonal Communication Satisfaction Inventory, 85, 103, 121, 169
intrinsically motivated, 96
irregular sentences, 118
Ishida, 54, 248, 324
isolated content words, 40, 111, 134, 135, 151, 184, 185, 189, 190, 193, 194
Iwai, 23, 84, 120, 324
Iwata, 5, 29, 319, 324
Jackson, 25, 322
Janney, 16, 325
Japanese communicative style, 15, 55, 159
Japanese EFL classroom, 78, 336
Japanese EFL context, 2, 342
Japanese Ministry of Education, Culture, Sports, Science and Technology, 10, → MEXT
Jefferson, 37, 38, 83, 108, 243, 325, 335
Jenkins, 78, 325
Johnson, 25, 325
Johnston, 51, 72, 323
Johnstone, 54, 85, 107, 127, 325
Jones, 8, 322
joshi, 58
Kachru, 247, 325, 334
Kaplan, 32, 325
Kasper, 52, 71, 311, 313, 323, 325, 327, 329, 334, 335, 338, 339, 342
Keenan, 27, 325
Keesing, 11, 325
Kelley, 84, 325
Kendon, 35, 80, 153, 239, 326, 329
Kenna, 6, 29, 31, 56, 326
Kitao, 2, 3, 29, 326
Kluckholm, 11
Knapp, 22, 324, 326
Knapp-Potthoff, 22, 326
Knight, 250, 326

Kobayashi, 41, 326
kohai, 21
Koike, 248, 326
Koyama, 13, 16, 326
Kramsch, 23, 160, 326
Krashen, 61, 326, 336
Kroeber, 11, 327
Kubota, 57, 69, 71, 248, 327
Kullman, 12, 13, 323
Kupka, 25, 327
Kwahn, 3, 327
Lacy, 6, 29, 31, 56, 326
Lakoff, 17, 21, 26, 327
language transfer, 1
laughter, 36, 37, 40, 119, 133, 137, 138, 152, 154, 155, 163, 204, 205, 206, 207, 225, 226, 286, 295, 297, 298, 301, 303
LCIE, 240
Leaver, 8, 317
Lebra, 14, 15, 20, 50, 148, 153, 327
Lee, 41
Leech, 26, 327, 334
Lee-Wong, 16, 327
Leki, 32, 327
Lenartowicz, 25, 325
Levinson, 18, 19, 20, 26, 27, 244, 245, 313, 320, 327
Liddicoat, 64, 70, 327
Likert-scale, 103, 104
Lindemann, 77, 328
lingua franca, 78, 247, 250, 324, 334, 337
listener responses, 23, 35, 36, 37, 41, 72, 74, 76, 77, 83, 84, 87, 88, 92, 97, 98, 99, 100, 106, 121, 130, 145, 151, 236, 237, 240, 273, 316, 323
listenership, 35, 53, 82, 88, 152, 156, 159, 161, 249, 318, 330, 340
listener-talk, 50, 56
Llewellyn, 35, 316
LoCastro, 5, 55, 56, 58, 64, 93, 160, 328
Logic and Conversation, 26

longitudinal, 52, 66, 71, 74, 89, 109, 120, 123, 124, 125, 160, 171, 172, 228, 233, 237, 240, 241, 242
Loveday, 5, 6, 29, 31, 328
low-context vs. high-context, 57
Lyster, 65, 72, 328
MacIntyre, 9, 10, 252, 314, 320, 328
Maeshiba, 7, 329
Makino, 57, 329
Mandeville, 4, 323
Mao, 19, 329
Marie, 10, 313
Markel, 38, 39, 108, 329
Martin, 4, 329
Matsumoto, K., 3, 4, 329
Matsumoto, M., 6, 29, 31, 329
Matsumoto, Y., 14, 16, 19, 20, 244, 329
Matsuoka, 10, 12, 329, 330
Matsuura, 150, 330
Maynard, 34, 36, 37, 38, 39, 42, 43, 44, 46, 47, 48, 49, 50, 52, 56, 57, 58, 80, 81, 102, 107, 108, 110, 111, 148, 152, 171, 330
McCarthy, 1, 28, 35, 48, 75, 77, 81, 82, 84, 111, 117, 151, 250, 314, 330, 333
McClure, 29, 330
McCornack, 31, 330
McCrae, 94, 315
McCroskey, 9, 10, 28, 84, 94, 102, 119, 167, 313, 330, 331
Meiji Era, 2, → *Meiji* Restoration
Meiji Restoration, 2, 247
metacognitive, 66
metalinguistic, 66, 75, 246
metapragmatic, 56, 66, 67, 69, 98, 234
MEXT, 10
micro-level analysis, 122, 129, 224
Mills, 17, 18, 127, 158, 240, 242, 331
minimal backchannel, 164

minimal responses, 40, 48, 55, 82, 86, 110, 111, 134, 135, 151, 156, 184, 189, 191, 193, 195, 226
miscommunication, 2, 22, 33, 34, 53, 54, 56, 57, 76, 87, 88, 106, 158, 160, 171, 243, 309
misunderstanding, 1, 30, 43, 44, 54, 120, 128, 242, 243
Mizutani, 50, 52, 54, 148, 153, 331
Moeran, 13, 331
Molle, 76, 250, 335
Monbusho, 10, 331
morpheme acquisition, 62, 320
morphophonological regularity, 62
motivation, 4, 8, 9, 10, 23, 24, 33, 85, 231, 328
Multicultural Awareness-Knowledge-Skills Survey, 84
multi-word backchannel phrases, 134, 184
Mura, 27, 331
Myers, 84
naturally occurring data, 5, 29
negative face, 19, 20, 244
negative perceptions, 34, 53, 56, 57, 76, 87, 88, 171, 233, 241, 244
NEO Personality Inventory, Revised, 94, → NEO-PI-R
NEO-PI-R, 94, 315
NES model, 247, 248
Neuliep, 25
Nevara, 160, 332
Ng, 67, 70, 71, 335
Nikolova, 3, 332
Nishida, 22, 25, 29, 321
Nishiyama, K., 31, 332
Nishiyama, S., 30, 332
NMMC, 250
Nolen, 17, 319
NON CLARS, 135, 136, 186, 190, 194
non-clarification repetitions, 41, 111
non-clarifications, 135, 190
non-interface position, 61

non-laughter SSBs, 119, 137, 154, 155, 163, 206, 225, 226, 297, 298, 303
non-lexical, 37, 40, 41, 340
non-parametric, 124, 125, 126
non-primary speakers, 35, 42, 45, 81, 83
non-understanding, 42, 45, 46, 106, 143, 163, 164, 165, 166, 167, 168, 169, 215, 216, 217, 218, 225, 226, 232, 283, 284, 301, 303
NONUs, 215, 216, 217, 218, 219
nonverbal backchannels, 39, 40, 52, 76, 110, 111, 133, 148, 152, 191, 243
nonverbal communication, 29, 36, 46
nonverbal cues, 36, 37
nonverbal gesture, 113, 137, 153, 199, 200, 201, 268
non-word vocalisations, 37, 40, 41, 82, 86, 111, 134, 135, 184, 185, 189, 193
noticing hypothesis, 63, 67, 230, 235, 236, 238, 245
noticing the gap, 75, 230
Nottingham Multi-Modal Corpus, 250, → NMMC
null hypothesis, 124
Nunn, 27, 332
O'Dowd, 23
O'Keeffe, 1, 22, 35, 36, 37, 40, 76, 81, 240, 244, 246, 250, 330, 333
Obana, 17, 332
observer's paradox, 107, 123, 140
Ochs, 107, 314, 318
Okabe, 29, 333
Okamoto, 30, 336
Okushi, 3, 77, 333
Olshtain, 63, 66, 333
omoiyari, 15
OPI, 251
oral proficiency interview, 251, → OPI
Ortega, 71, 333

Oshio, 95, 262, 333
Overseas Assignment Inventory, 84
Oxford, 8, 317
Paired Sample T-test, 124
parametric, 124, 125, 126
Pearson Product-Moment Correlation Coefficient, 124, 126, → PPMCC
Peaty, 4, 333
Pecchioni, 85
pedagogical interventions, 64, 66, 87, 98, 237, 238, 241
peer-mentoring, 102
Penman, 27
perceptions across cultures, 129, 157
perceptual salience, 62
personality dimensions, 94
Planken, 82, 334
politeness one, 16
politeness two, 16
positive face, 19, 244
post-conversation interview responses, 151
post-conversation interviews, 123, 153, 156, 158
post-structuralism, 127
PPMCC, 124, 126, 131, 134, 161, 225
Praat software, 108, 285, 287
pragmalinguistic, 8, 63, 67, 71, 235
pragmatic competence, 7, 82, 313, 324, 328, 338
pragmatic development, 35, 63, 87
pragmatic failure, 1, 26
pragmatic norms, 246
pragmatic routines, 68, 71, 232, 338, 339
pragmatic transfer, 7, 52
preserving harmony, 29, 32, 144, 159
primary speaker, 6, 34, 35, 36, 37, 38, 39, 40, 41, 42, 43, 44, 45, 46, 47, 50, 55, 58, 73, 76, 80, 82, 108, 110, 113, 114, 115, 116, 119, 120, 135, 136, 137, 142, 151, 153, 160, 161, 165, 171, 186, 198, 199, 200, 201, 202, 206, 230, 268, 285
primary speakership, 39, 79, 83, 119
primary speaking turn, 36, 42, 46, 83, 86, 148, 149, 165, 309
prosodic features of conversation, 239
pseudonyms, 90, 256, 258, 260, 263, 277, 285
Punyanunt-Carter, 85
Q-Q plot graphs, 126
qualitative, 69, 108, 123, 127, 172, 215, 219, 222, 325
quantitative, 17, 69, 123, 124, 127, 172, 215, 323
Quinlisk, 24, 334
Quirk, 115, 118, 334
Reesor, 3, 11, 334
reigi tadashi, 17
Reischauer, 4, 334
reliability, 7, 41, 90, 94, 102, 103, 109, 127, 243, 333
Rentfrow, 94, 320
repetition-as-backchannel, 75
repetitions, 41, 45, 47, 111, 116, 117, 135, 136, 154, 166, 186, 190, 194
repetitive listener responses, 48, 152
research questions, 35, 85, 90, 129, 309, → RQs
retrospective interviews, 31, 93, 127
rhythmic synchrony, 56
Ribeau, 25, 322
Richmond, 9, 331
Riggenbach, 23, 84, 108, 120, 334
Rios-Ellis, 15, 334
Robinson, M., 7, 31, 164, 329, 334
Roger, 3, 334
Rose, 30, 52, 63, 64, 66, 67, 70, 71, 72, 234, 242, 311, 325, 327, 334, 335, 338, 342
Ross, 28, 84, 329, 335
rote learning, 3, 248

RQs, 85, 86, 87, 88, 120, 123, 129,147, 160, 161, 169, 170, 172, 228, 234, 237, 309
Ruben, 24, 335
Sacks, 37, 38, 83, 108, 335
Safont, 64, 335
Said, 57, 335
Sakui, 11, 335
Salazar, 64, 335
Sapir, 58, 335
Sapir-Whorf hypothesis, 58
Sardegna, 76, 250, 335
Sasagawa, 29, 335
Sasajima, 73, 336
Sasaki, 251, 336
sasshi no bunka, 57
sassuru, 57
Sato, 28, 29, 30, 84, 149, 311, 336
Schegloff, 37, 38, 42, 55, 83, 108, 142, 151, 335, 336
Schenkein, 36, 37, 336
Schmidt, 7, 52, 63, 66, 67, 72, 74, 75, 230, 235, 236, 238, 245, 321, 336
Scollon, 5, 11, 22, 242, 336
second-order politeness, 16, → politeness two
Seidlhofer, 78, 337
self-adaptors, 80, 153, 239
self-confidence, 8, 9, 10, 33
self-report, 119, 235
semantic complexity, 62
senpai, 21
Shapiro-Wilk normality test, 126
Shaw, 243, 337
Shimizu, 10, 342
Shinmura, 17, 337
shitashigena, 17
Shojic, 15, 334
shuudan shugi, 29
silence, 6, 28, 38, 106, 156, 165, 323
Silverstein, 59, 337
Simic, 12, 337
simultaneous speech, 34, 49, 85, 86, 109, 118, 129, 137, 154, 162, 163, 171, 172, 204, 285, 301, 309, 332
simultaneous talk, 38, 80, → simultaeous speech
situational ellipsis, 115
Slade, 77, 317
sociolinguistic, 4, 5, 7, 22, 69, 75, 76, 92, 328
sociolinguistic competence, 4, 5, 7, 22
sociopragmatic, 63, 67, 70, 327
solo speaking, 38
speaker-talk, 50, 56
Spearman Rank Correlation Coefficient test, 124, → Spearman rho
Spearman rho, 124, 126, 130, 134, 137, 149, 295
speech acts, 6, 7, 20, 29, 30, 48, 63, 322, 33, 334
Spees, 30, 337
Spencer-Oatey, 82, 337
Spitzberg, 23, 24, 25, 85, 103, 337
SPSS, 124
SS, 49, 50, 53, 118, → simultaneous speech
SSB Laughter, 154
statistical analysis, 109, 312
Statistical Package for the Social Sciences, 124, → SPSS
STEP, 3
Strother, 82, 340
Stubbe, 28, 40, 48, 51, 82, 84, 111, 151, 152, 337
subculture, 13
suggestopedia, 68
Sugimoto, 13, 337
sumimasen, 68, 338
Suzuki, 79, 230, 314, 338
Swain, 22, 314
Swan, 77, 238, 338, 339
Swann, 94, 320
syllabus design, 77
synchronized dance, 56
synonymy, 117
syntactic category, 62

tabula rasa, 61
tabula repleta, 61
tag questions, 49, 58, 118
Tajima, 59, 60, 245, 338
Tajino, 248, 338
Takahashi, M., 3, 338
Takahashi, S., 7, 67, 70, 232, 338
Takahashi, T., 5, 7, 8, 30, 311, 338
Takanashi, 3, 338
Takimoto, 62, 69, 234, 236, 338
Tanaka, H., 248, 326
Tanaka, N., 5, 338
Tanaka, T., 12, 337
Tao, 37, 51, 314, 338
tatemae, 15
Tateyama, 68, 70, 71, 338, 339
TCU, 38
teachability, 63, 66, 69, 70, 73, 75, 79, 241, 313
teacher training programmes, 230
teacher-fronted, 67, 68
teinei(na), 17
Ten Item Personality Inventory, 94, 262, → TIPI
the private self, 15, 16, 32, 311
the public self, 15, 16, 19, 32
theory of politeness, 18, 20, 244
Thompson, S., 37
Thonus, 36, 41, 72, 74, 77, 88, 154, 230, 247, 250, 320, 339
Thurrell, 84, 120, 121, 316
TIPI, 94, 95, 262, 263, 333
TOEFL, 3, 318
TOEFL iBT, 4
TOEIC, 3, 88, 91, 92, 94, 95, 96, 97, 122, 126, 131, 134, 138, 143, 161, 162, 163, 164, 167, 168, 169, 225, 226, 227, 303, 304, 305, 309, 318
Tomoda, 17, 332
Tonkyn, 108, 114, 116, 117, 319
Toolan, 128
Torghabeh, 78, 339
Tottie, 39, 40, 107, 110, 159, 339
Townsend, 9, 339

transcription, 107, 108, 266, 268, 285, 286, 320
transition-relevant place, 38, → TRP
triad, 26
Triandis, 16, 32, 339
triangulation, 90
TRP, 38, 83
Truscott, 235, 246, 339
Tsuchiya, 53, 339
Tsukuhara, 39, 73
Tucker, 84, 340
turn-transitional, 39
turn-constructional unit, 38, → TCU
turns at talk, 37, 39, 108
turn-taking, 23, 37, 38, 42, 50, 68, 72, 73, 83, 243, 318, 326, 335
Uematsu, 40, 43, 45, 340
Ulijn, 82, 340
Uliss-Weltz, 5, 7, 311
unconventional backchannels, 143, 163, 164, 165, 168, 169, 215, 216, 227, 232, 301
understanding of content, 42, 43, 45, 283, 284
unwillingness to communicate, 33, 55, 82, 150, 231
validity, 7, 69, 75, 90, 95, 102, 103, 119, 127, 243, 331, 333
variability, 15, 34, 40, 48, 53, 55, 79, 85, 86, 109, 110, 111, 112, 129, 132, 135, 146, 151, 153, 162, 167, 168, 169, 170, 171, 172, 175, 181, 184, 186, 187, 191, 195, 221, 224, 228, 231, 241, 249, 250, 309
vertical head movement, 37, 48, 286
video conferencing, 76, 250
Vienna-Oxford International Corpus of English, 250, → VOICE
VOICE, 250
Vygotskian, 58
Vygotsky, 11, 339, 340
wa, 14, 15, 21, 29, 55, 58, 61, 152, 166

wakimae, 17, 21
Wallnau, 125, 320
Walsh, 247, 248, 340
Wannaruk, 247, 340
Ward, 39, 41, 73, 74, 80, 153, 229, 239, 323, 340
Wardhaugh, 58, 340
washback effect, 2
Watts, 16, 324, 340
Wen, 12, 340
Westernisation, 247
White, L., 250, 341
White, S., 14, 37, 38, 40, 46, 47, 49, 50, 52, 56, 57, 80, 85, 86, 93, 102, 148, 152, 155, 156, 157, 159, 233, 341
Widdowson, 78, 84, 341
Wigglesworth, 108, 114, 116, 117, 319
Wilcoxon Signed Rank test, 124, 126, 208
Wildermuth, 25, 327
Wildner-Bassett, 67, 68, 71, 341
William Adams, 2
willingness to communicate, 2, 8, 82, 276, 311, 313, 322, 328, 331, 337, 340, 342 → WTC

Wilson, 16, 57, 310, 341
Wiseman, 24, 25, 84, 315, 321, 341
Wishnoff, 65, 66, 341
Wolf, 251, 341
Wolfson, 5, 336, 341
word output, 149, 162, 179, 180, 231
WTC, 8, 9, 10, 12, 33, 78, 80, 82, 83, 87, 94, 95, 96, 97, 102, 109, 119, 121, 123, 125, 126, 131, 134, 150, 167, 168, 169, 175, 176, 177, 178, 179, 221, 225, 230, 231, 233, 247, 252, 276, 277, 278, 303, 304, 305
Yamada, 15, 28, 29, 50, 54, 56, 57, 58, 341
Yamaguchi, 78, 342
Yang, 22, 321
Yano, 3, 342
Yashima, 3, 10, 28, 33, 83, 84, 102, 342
Yngve, 6, 35, 342
Yoshimi, 65, 70, 324, 342
Zenuk-Nishide, 10